THE KIRĀTĀRJUNĪYAM OF BHĀRAVI

CANTOS I-III

Text with Mallinātha's Commentary, Prose Order of the Ślokas, Notes, Translation into English and Hindi

M.R. KALE

MOTILAL BANARSIDASS PUBLISHERS
PRIVATE LIMITED • DELHI

8th Reprint: Delhi, 2019
Fourth Revised and Enlarged Edition: 1966

ISBN: 978-81-208-0571-2 (Cloth)
ISBN: 978-81-208-0573-9 (Paper)

MOTILAL BANARSIDASS

41 U.A. Bungalow Road, Jawahar Nagar, Delhi 110 007
1 B, J S Compound, Kennedy Bridge, Nana Chowk, Mumbai 400 007
203 Royapettah High Road, Mylapore, Chennai 600 004
No. 49, 8th F Main, 3rd Block Jayanagar, Bengaluru 560 011
9, Panchanan Ghosh Lane, 1st Floor, Kolkata 700 009
Ashok Rajpath, Patna 800 004
Chowk, Varanasi 221 001

Printed in India

by RP Jain at NAB Printing Unit,
A-44, Naraina Industrial Area, Phase I, New Delhi–110028
nd published by JP Jain for Motilal Banarsidass Publishers (P) Ltd,
41 U.A. Bungalow Road, Jawahar Nagar, Delhi-110007

PREFACE TO THE FOURTH EDITION

This edition of KIRĀTĀRJUNIYA annotated by my father late Mr. M. R. Kale, B.A. is revised and enlarged by addition of Hindi translation of prose order and English translation in 3rd edition. This Hindi matter is supplied by Prof. Jaipal Vidyalankar, of Hans Raj College Delhi, to whom my thanks are due. The arrangement of printing Sanskrit Text, followed by prose order etc. in Sanskrit Hindi and English is hoped to be of more convenience to students studying with Hindi medium. I also thank M/s. Motilal Banarsidass of Delhi for publishing this edition.

V. M. Kale
Feb. 1966

25 B Goodwill Building,
MAHIM,
Bombay—16

INTRODUCTION

I. THE POEM.

The Kirātārjuniya is a Mahākāvya and is named after its chief incident, *viz.* the fight between Śiva under the guise of a Kirāta or Mountaineer and Arjuna. A Mahākāvya is a metrical composition which ought to be divided into cantos, not less than eight and more than thirty in number, and not containing less than thirty and more than two hundred ślokas in each.* It may be concerned with the life of a single hero as the Śiśupālavadha or the present poem, or may have for its theme a whole race of kings, as the Raghuvamśa. If there be one hero he must be either a celestial character or a Kshatriya of high descent and possessed of the qualities of the Dhīrodāttā Nāyaka and if more than one, they must be of the same race.× Every canto must have a uniform metre which must be changed at its end. There may, however, be occasionally a canto composed in a variety of metres as the 5th of the present poem or the 4th of the Śiśupālavadha. At the end of each canto the

---

* अष्टसर्गान्न तु न्यूनं त्रिंशत्सर्गाच्च नाधिकम्। नात्यन्तविस्तरः सर्गस्त्रिंशतो वा न चोनता। द्विशतश्लोकानाधिकं कार्यमेतत्पद्यस्य लक्षणम्॥ Iśānasamhita. (Sometime, however, this rule is departed from. The Haravijaya published in the Kāvya Mālā series has as many as 50 cantos).

×A hero of sublime qualities (धीरोदात्त) is one who possesses great mental strength, is grave, patient, free from boasting and of firm resolve, with his spirit controlled by modesty. महासत्त्वोऽतिगम्भीरः क्षमावानविकत्थनः। स्थिरो निगूढाहंकारो धीरोदात्तो दृढव्रतः॥ Daśarupaka.

सर्गबन्धो महाकाव्यं तत्रैको नायकः सुरः। सद्वंशः क्षत्रियो वापि धीरोदात्तगुणान्वितः॥ एकवंशभवा भूपाः कुलजा बहवोऽपि वा। Sah. Dar.

subject matter of the succeeding one should be indicated. The principal sentiment may be Śṛingāra (the Erotic), or Vīra the (Heroic) or Śānta (the Tranquil).

A Mahākāvya must, as well, contain descriptions of great cities, oceans, mountains, seasons, the rise of the sun and the moon, sportings with ladies in gardens and water, drinkings, separations and unions of lovers &c. The style should be highly sentimental and embellished with figures of speech &c. Nothing that violates the dignity of poetry, such as unmeaning talk &c. should find place in a Mahākāvya.

The Kirātārjuniya has, for its theme, the journey of Arjuna to the mountain Indrakila, part of the Himālayas, for the propitiation of the gods Indra and Śiva and the final obtainment of divine weapons, Pāśupata and others, from the gods. The hero is Arjuna, the 3rd son of Pāndu and an incarnation of Nara, one of the two famous sages, Nara and Nārāyana. To magnify his greatness, Śiva is represented as coming in the garb of a Kirāta and fighting with him on terms of equality. The heroic is the chief sentiment in the poem, the sentiment of love &c. being subsidiary to it. Descriptions of mountains, rivers, seasons, sunrise and sunset, sportings of women &c. are found in their proper places in the poem.

The word श्री which is auspicious, being a name of the goddess of fortune, is used at the begin of the poem and in the concluding stanza of each canto.

1. PREVIOUS HISTORY.

The Kauravas and the Pandavas both belonged to the lunar race, which was divided into two principal branches, the Yādavas and the Pauravas. Bharata (after whom the race was called Bhārata) was a descendent of Puru. Ninth in descent from him (according to the Vishnu P.) was Kuru and fourteenth from Kuru came Śāntanu. Bhīshma was his eldest son by his first wife Gangā. By Satyavatī he had two other sons, Chitrāngada who was killed by a Gandharva of the same name in a battle, and Vichitravīrya who also died childless leaving two widows, named Ambikā and Ambālikā. Dhṛtarāshtra and Pāndu were the Kshetraja sons of Vichitravīrya. The sons of Dhritarāshtra and of Pāndu were both the descendants of Kuru and were designated by the patronymic Kaurava, which, however, came to be generally applied to the former after the great war.

Pāndu, who had retired into solitude, leaving Dhṛitarāshtra king of the Kuru country, died while his sons were yet children. The Princes were then brought to Dhritarāshtra and presented to him as his nephews. He took charge of them, treated them with great kindness and had them educated along with his own sons. When the proper time came, Dhritarāshtra nominated Yudhishthira as heir-apparent to the kingdom of Hastinapura in preference to his own eldest son, Duryodhana. This embittered the jealousy which had long existed between the Kauravas and the Pāndavas and which, as circumstances arose, ripened into down-right hatred on the part of the former. The result was that Duryodhana succeeded in inducing his father to send the Pāndavas to Vāranāvata where a plot was laid to burn them in their dwelling-house which was secretly made of lac and other combustibles. The Pāndavas, however, knew the plot in time and secretly escaped. The house was burnt as previously arranged, and it was believed that they had perished there with their mother.

The Pāndavas then lived in forests disguised as Brāhmanas, and it was in the disguise of a Brāhmana that Arjuna won the princess Draupadi, who afterwards became the common wife of the five Pāndavas. Their existence was made known after this incident, and they were called back to Hastināpura by Dhritarāshtra who divided the kingdom among his sons and then asking them to live at Indraprastha on the Yamuna their capital. There Yudhisthira after conquering the four quarters, performed the Rājasūya sacrifice. Dharma was also praised for his good rule and wisdom. This excited still more the enmity of the Kauravas. They induced their father to call the Pāndavas to Hastinapura and insidiously prevailed upon Dharma to gamble. His opponent was Śakuni who was not only a skilful player but also a dexterous cheat, Dharma lost his all in the gambling—his wealth, his kingdom, his brothers with himself, and his wife. Draupadi was then brought into the assembly by the order of Duryodhana and openly insulted by Duśśāsana, who pulled her by the hair and tried to divest her of her raiment. Duryodhana also insulted her by showing his thigh to her and asking her to sit on it. This exhausted the patience of Bhima and his anger rising to its highest pitch, he most solemnly vowed to drink the blood of Duśśāsana and smash the thigh of Duryodhana. Alarmed at the report of this dreadful vow and some evil omens manifesting themselves just at the time, Dhritarāshtra interfered, restored their freedom and the lost property to the Pāndavas and asked them to go back pleased. Thus baffled in his plan to ruin the Pāndavas Duryodhana held consultation with Śakuni, Karna and others, and invited Dharma again to play the game on one condition, that the losing party should pass twelve years in a forest and live *incognito* during the thirteenth. If discovered another period of thirteen years should be similarly passed. Dharma was again the loser and retired with his brothers and wife into exile. Here begins the story of the poem.

2. THE PRINCIPAL PERSONS.

The principal persons (with their short lives as far as the story is concerned) with whom we are immediately concerned are Yudhishthira, Bhīma, Arjuṇa, Draupadi and Duryodhana.

YUDHISHTHIRA.

Yudhishthira, the eldest of the five Pāndavas, was the son of Dharma, the god of justice, who called for that reason Dharma or Dharmarāja. As he hated no one he came to be called Ajātaśatru. He is represented as a man of calm, passionless judgment, strict veracity, unswerving rectitude and rigid justice. Although trained along with the other princes in the science of war by the military preceptor Drona, he did not much distinguish himself as a warrior. He was so virtuous and loved by the people that when the time came for naming the Yuvarāja (Heir-apparent) Dhritarāshtra had to select him in preference to his own son, Duryodhana. The Kauravas then began to hate the Pāndavas openly, and Duryodhana succeeded by his expostulations with his father in sending them into exile in which they won Draupadī at her Svayamvara. After their return Yudhishthira got established at Indraprastha and ruled his subjects with great justice protecting them as his own children. While there Yudhishthira's power grew and he performed the Rājasūya sacrifice. The dignity and supremacy thus gained by the Pāndavas excited again the jealousy of Duryodhana, and as the easiest means of depriving them of their wealth and power he invited Yudhishthira to the well known gambling match.

BHĪMA.

Bhīma (the fierce one), the second of the Pāndu princes, was the son of Vāyu (the god of wind). Possessed of vast size and gigantic strength, he was wrathful in temper, rather coarse in taste and manners and a great eater, so that he was called Vrikodara or 'Wolf-belly'. Half of the food of the family was allotted to him while the other half was used by the four brothers and their mother. He was jovial and jocular when in good humour, but abusive, turbulent and brutal when his anger was roused. The weapon used by him was Gadā or a kind of club, in the use of which he was trained by Drona but specially by Balrāma. He was also taught the use of other weapons and missiles by Dronāchārya. His great strength early excited the enmity of Duryodhana, who gave him poisoned food to eat, and when in a trance threw him into the Ganges; on sinking to the nether world he was taken to the Śesha who gave him Amṛita to drink and sent him back to Hastināpura, blessed and restored to health and vigour. When the princes were examined after their military training was complete, Bhīma and Duryodhana engaged each other with clubs, but the mimic duel soon turned into a fierce personal conflict could only be stopped by Drona's forcible interference. When Draupadi was openly insulted in the assembly he almost went mad with rage and even put his hand to his club to smash the hand of Dharma with which he threw the dice, but was checked by Arjuna. We need not refer to his numerous exploits here.

ARJUNA.

Arjuna (the white one), the third Pāndava prince, was also, like his two elder brothers, of divine paternity, his father being the mighty Indra. Hence he was called Aindri. A warrior of the first rank, he was noble-minded, generous, upright and handsome and the most eminent and the most amiable of all the five brothers. He was taught the science of archery by the family preceptor Drona and was his most favourite disciple. By his marksmanship and strength of arm he won Draupadi at her Svayamvara. He obtained from Agani, whom he promised to assist in consuming the Khāndava forest, the bow Gāndiva, for fighting with Indra. He had several appelations, such as Pārtha, Jishnu, Dhananjaya, Kirītin, &c. When Dharma, at the advice of Vyāsa, asked him to go to the mountain Himālaya to practise penance to propitiate the gods, and to obtain from them celestial weapons to be used in the contemplated war against the Kauravas, he readily obeyed, willingly undertaking all the hardships of a life of penance.

DRAUPADĪ.

Draupadī was the daughter of Drupada, king of the Pānchalas and wife of the five Pāndavas. She is one of the five Pativratās whose names are uttered in the morning as auspicious even to this day. When in the gambling match, which Yudhishthira played with the Kauravas, he lost everything else, he staked Draupadī and lost her also. She thus became a slave of Duryodhana who called her to come and sweep his rooms. She was dragged by the hair by Duśśāsana to the assembly at the gambling hall. She then asked the men there if she was really won by the Kauravas. No body replied to her and Duśśāsana insult ed her—in what manner is known to all. She bore all that without a word of murmur against Dharma.

DURYODHANA.

Duryodhana (Lit. hard to fight with) was the eldest son of king Dṛitarāshtra and the chief of the Kaurava princes. Upon the death of Pāndu, Dhritarashtra took his five sons to his palace and had them educated along with his sons. Quarrels and jealousies soon sprang up between the cousins and Duryodhana took a special dislike (which afterwards ripened into deep hatred) to Bhīma on account of his enormous strength and skill in wielding the Gadā. When Dhritarāshtra proposed to appoint Yudhishthira heir-apparent, he remonstrated with his father and got the Pāndavas exiled. When the Pāndavas returned from exile and were established at Indraprastha, Yudhishthira performed the Rājasuya sacrifice. This excited Duryodhana's enmity still further and after deliberating with his friends, Karna and others, he proposed to invite Dharma to a gambling match as the easiest means of depriving the Pāndavas of their kingdom and wealth. The result of this was that Dharma lost every thing and returned to a forest.

In the Kirātārjuniya he is represented as the very type of an excellent king, well versed in state policy, winning the love of all, offending none—even his menials, promptly taking measures to defeat the object of secret plotters and ruling his kingdom with perfect justice and paternal care.

3. THE STORY.

The story as told in the Mahābhārata is a simple one. After their return to the Dwaita forest the Pāndavas sat, one evening, talking over their misfortunes. Draupadi smarting under the insults offered to her and pained at heart to see her husbands fallen from their former greatness was the first to speak. She asked Dharma how his own fall from his exalted position, the miserable condition to which his mighty brothers were reduced, and above all the insults offered to her, the daughter of a mighty king and the wife of renowned heroes, could not cause pain to his mind or induce him to shake off his apathy, and urged him to display his valour and regain his lost kingdom. She also condemned his policy of forbearance as unworthy of a Kshatriya and added that fortune would not smile on one who had no self-respect. Yudhishthira replied to his wife saying that he would do nothing in hot haste but adhere to his policy of righteousness and patience as that alone would ensure success. Bhīma, however, was incensed at this and spoke at great length in support of Draupadi's speech. He was for speedy and energetic action on the part of his brother. His chief points was that kingdom and glory could not be won by meekness and resignation. Yudhishthira, his coolness of temper unshaken, said that he (Bhīma) was justified in making his remarks, but gently pointed out to him that the enemy's party was too strong to be overpowered by them and how any hasty action on their part would ruin their cause. Convinced by his brother's words Bhīma grew moody and stood silent. While the two brothers were thus talking, the great sage Vyāsa suddenly made his appearance. Received with due reverence by the Pāndavas, the sage told Yudhishthira that he knew what his fears were and that he hastened to him to set them at rest. He then initiated him into the mysteries of a *mantra*, which being duly imparted to A.juna would enable him to propitiate Indra and Śiva by religious austerities and to obtain such miraculous weapons from them as would make him invincible in battle and ensure final victory to the Pāndavas. He also asked the Pāndavas to live in some other forest and vanished from view just there. The Pāndavas accordingly then repaired to the Kāmyaka forest. While there Dharma called Arjuna to him one day and speaking in affectionate terms in private explained to him the invincibility of Bhishma and Drona, and the impossibility of getting victory without divine help. He then imparted to him the secret Vidyā obtained from the sage Vyāsa and asked him to go to the Indrakila mountain in the Himālayas to practise very severe penance in propitiation of Indra. In obedience to the will of Dharma Arjuna set out equipped with his usual weapons. The Brāhmanas conferred blessings upon him to the effect that he would soon gain his object. Draupadi also wished him speedy success and to fire his spirits reminded him of the words 'a *Gau*, a *Gau*,' uttered by Duśśāsana. By the power of the *Mantra*, Arjuna flew to the *Indrakila* mountain as swift as thought. As soon as he reached his destination he met an old Brāhman who was no other than Indra himself in that guise. The latter tried to dissuade Arjuna from engaging in penances. Pleased to see that nothing could shake Arjuna's determination, Indra revealed himself and advised him to practise austerities to propitiate Śiva for winning the celestial weapons he sought. Arjuna then devoted himself to the severest asceticism. This filled the great Rishis with so great a fear that they went to Śiva and prayed him to make Arjuna desist from his austerities. The great God told them that they need entertain no fear on account of Arjuna, as he knew the object of Arjuna's asceticism which he would fulfil that very day. When the Rishis had departed Śiva assumed the stalwart form of a Kirāta (wild hunter) armed with a bow and arrows. Accompanied by Umā and some attendants—all disguised as Kirātas, he went to the forest where Arjuna was practising penance. As he drew near Arjuna, he saw a demon named Mūka in the form of a boar rushing at the ascetic, Instantly Arjuna strung his bow and shot an arrow at the boar. The very moment an arrow from the Kirāta's bow struck the brute. Pierced by two arrows simultaneously the Rākshasa assuming his real form gave up his life. Now ensued a hot dispute between the Kirāta and Arjuna as to the claim to the animal. Arjuna reproached the mountaineer for having acted in violation of the usage of chase in shooting the boar aimed at by him. The Kirāta, on the other hand, declared that he it was who had aimed at the boar first and that it was his arrow that had slain the beast. High words soon led to blows. A terrible fight followed in which each poured on the other showers of poisonous-serpent-like arrows. To Arjuna's great amazement, the Kirāta stood quite invulnerable, till at last all his arrows were exhausted. The hero then took up his great bow and struck thunderbolt—like blows at the Kirāta. Even the bow was snatched away by the mountaineer. Arjuna's great sword, too, hurled with all his might at the head of the Kirāta broke to pieces. Even a shower of trees and stones proved of no avail. At last nothing was left to Arjuna but to strike his adversary with fists as powerful as thunderbolt. These were no more effectual than his weapons and Arjuna caught in the terrible grip of Śiva's arms fell senseless to the ground. He soon recovered and as he rose to his feet, he saw the very garland he had offered to the clay-image of Shiva now adorning the head of the Kirāta. Arjuna at once recognised the Great God and falling at his feet besought forgiveness for his late audacity. Śiva who had now resumed his own form, cheerfully embraced the saintly hero and spoke in very high terms of the courage and prowess he had displayed in the recent encounter. He then imparted to Arjuna what he most desired—the knowledge of the Pāshupata weapons, and bidding him visit Heaven, vanished in the sky. After this there appeared on the mountain all the gods, Varuna, Kubera, Indra and others, and bestowed upon Arjuna their respective weapons. The gods then departed and Arjuna was taken in Indra's aerial car to Heaven, where Indra showed to him all the glories of the abode of the gods, and giving him many celestial weapons sent him back to join his brothers and wife who had come to the *Gandhamādana* to receive him.

This story in the *Māhābhārata* is followed in the main by the poet. The changes introduced by the poet are changes in the details, not affecting the main thread of the story, indeed, but transforming the simple tale of the epic into a poem of a very high order. The new elements that characterise the poems are all of Bhāravi's introduction and it is these that mark it out as a Mahākāvya. We shall now proceed to note some of these changes.

The poet, knowing that he has to describe the fortunes of a royal family ousted out from their rightful share of the kingdom, introduces in the first and the second cantos an animated discussion of the various policies of statecraft.

The poet, again, never forgets that he treats of human beings. Thus he makes all his characters act and speak like human beings actuated by the motives and passions that prompt human action. In fact the poet invests with remarkable power the whole poem with human interest. The supernatural that is so predominant in the original story is made subsidiary to the human. Yudhishthira seeks to know, by employing spies, the policy and actions of Duryodhana, the usurper. The rough Bhīma of the Mahābharata is turned into a statesman, seeing far into the future when the prospects of the Pāndavas would brighten. He argues that Duryodhana was incapable of continuing the wise policy he had adopted, that disaffection and disunion in his own party were sure to be created by his overbearing and insolent conduct. Bhima is quite confident of the support of many friends to the righteous cause of the Pāndavas. He however, forgets that there was but small hope for their cause as long as Duryodhana had such invincible heroes as Bhishma, Drona and Karna to fight on his side. To this fact Vyāsa draws his attention, and advises Arjuna to seek by penances the celestial missiles, which alone would enable him to overcome his enemies. Vyāsa accordingly teaches Arjuna the *Mantra* for propitiating Indra. In the original story Vyasa first imparts the knowledge of the *Mantra* to Yudhishthira who again teaches it to Arjuna. According to the epic, Arjuna flies to the Indrakila as swift as thought, through the power of the *Mantra*. But in the poem the supernatural agency disappears and Arjuna is guided by a Yaksha at the command of the sage to the mountain. Then are introduced in the poem magnificient descriptions of the mountain sceneries of the Himalaya, the Gandhamādana and the Indrakila, of the seasons, of dawn and of the rise of the moon. Then the picture of Arjuna, engaged in penances in the wild forest, shows the poet's descriptive powers at their highest. The contrast that is here drawn between Arjuna the proud and valient hero and Arjuna the stern and self-controlled saint is as powerful as it is picturesque. Not less beautiful is the description of the influence of Arjuna's penances on the animate and inanimate Nature. It is in this part of the poem that we see Bhāravi winging his highest poetical flights.

The present poem departs from the original as to the means employed by Indra to tempt Arjuna to break his vow. In the story in the epic, Arjuna, as soon as he reaches the Indrakila, meets Indra in the guise of an ascetic who, after a vain attempt to dissuade the hero, reveals himself and advises him to propitiate Śiva. In the present poem however Indra, informed by the guardians of the Indrakila forest, first sends, as is usual with him, celestial nymphs to lure him from his penances. Nearly four cantos are devoted to a description of the *Apsarases*, their sportive movements and amorous devices for enticing the saintly hero. The unshaken determination of the self-controlled anchorite baffles all the wiles of the nymphs, who have to retire thoroughly discomfited. Then comes Indra himself in the guise of an old ascetic to accomplish by exhortation what the nymphs could not with all their charms. All the convincing arguments brought forward by the sage to impress on the mind of the hero the ideal of renunciation, the mutability of worldy objects, the vanity of the human desire and the wisdom of a life of true virtue leading to salvation—fail to move him from his purpose. The god then discloses himself and advises him to practise austerities to propitiate Śiva, who alone could bestow on him the celestial weapons he sought.

In the *Mahābharata*, Śiva comes to meet Arjuna disguised as a Kirāta accompanied by Umā and some of his attendant goblins, all disguised as Kirātas. And the fight from the first to the last goes on between Śiva and Arjuna. In the poem, however, Śiva enconnters Arjuna with a host of armed Kirātas. Arjuna scatters the followers of Śiva and meets him in single combat. The armed followers are purposely introduced by the poet to show to advantage the prowess of Arjuna who could withstand successfully even the followers of Śiva. The spirited description of the fight is one of the best in the poem and shows that the poet was a master in describing vigorous action. The account of the fight in the Mahābhārata appears quite tame by the side of that in the present poem. Lastly, the manner in which the combat is brought to a close in the poem is quite different from that in the epic. According to the epic, Arjuna is thrown senseless by the terrible grasp of Śiva's embrace, and recovering recognises the God by the garland on the Kirāta's head, the same that had been placed by himself on the head of the clay-image of Śiva. The poem tells us that during the wrestling combat between Śiva and Arjuna, the former springs into the air, and Arjuna, to bring him down, leaps up and holds him by the feet. His feet being touched by his faithful worshipper, the Great God already pleased at Arjuna's supreme courage and valour is quite overcome. Lovingly pressing the hero to his bosom, Śiva reveals himself, and bestows on him the whole science of arms as well as his own Pāśupata weapon, with which Arjuna was to win back but his kingdom. The story is also given in the Śiva Purāna, it seems to be an adaptation of the Kirā, interpolated into it.

II. THE POET.

Of the personal history of Bhāravi absolutely nothing is known to us.* He himself did not think it necessary to tell us anything about his family, his native place, his predecessors or contemporaries or even his Guru, as Bhavabhuti or Bāna Bhatta has done. In determining the age in which Bhāravi

* There is an anecdote told about the poet in connection with Sl. I. 22, for which see end of the Intro.

lived and flourished two inscriptions which have been discovered afford some clue. One of them, an inscription of 634 A. D. mentions the name of Bhāravi along with that of Kālidāsa.* From this inscription we only learn that Bhāravi was, by the middle of the seventh century, acknowledged as a great poet —even to the extent of being mentioned in the same breath with Kālidāsa. The other inscription—The Gummareddipur plate inscription, says that one king, Durvinīta, (दुर्विनीत), wrote a commentary on the canto XV. of the Kirātārjuniya. This inscription is assigned to the early part of the 6th century.+ From this inscription one fact is clear that by the end of the fifth century, Bhāravi had attained such celebrity as a poet that a royal scholar thought it worth his while to write a commentary on a portion of the work. Now it rarely happens that the merits of a poet or any author, however great, are recognised in a few years; least of all would this happen to a poet like Bhāravi whose style and subject-matter of composition are such as would scarcely commend themselves to the taste of ordinary scholars or critics. It must have been more than one century before Bhāravi could become

---

* येनायोजि न वेश्म स्थिरमर्थविधौ विवेकिना जिनवेश्म ।
स विजयतां रविकीर्तिः कविताश्रितकालिदासभारविकीर्तिः ॥

\+ Indian Antiquary Vol XLII p. 204, as quoted by Prof. Apte in his introduction to Svapnavāsavadattam, p. 31.

"Prof. Max Muller in his 'India, what can it teach us' mentions one Avinīta who wrote a commentary of the Kirātārjuniyam up to the 14th canto, and is said to have lived about 470 A. D. On the strength of this remark it may be held that the poem Kirātārjuniyam must have been composed at least half a century before the time of Avinīta to have attained sufficient celebrity to require a commentator for its exposition. It seems probable, therefore, that Bhāravī might have lived in the last decade of the 4th century or at any rate, at the beginning of the 5th century A. D." Prof. Goswami. Intro. to canto II.

a standard of comparison in the world of letters and take his rank by the side of Kālidāsa, and half a century at least must have elapsed before he could acquire such fame that a reigning king deemed it an honour to write a commentary on a portion of his work. Basing our calculation on the facts now available and the principle mentioned above we conclude that Bhāravi lived and flourished by or before the end of the fourth century.

Bhāravi was certainly not the contemporary of Kālidasa. Tradition does not place them in the same age, nor is there any positive evidence pointing to their being contemporaries. Even making allowance for the individual style of each, Bhāravi, it would seem, lived in an age of artificial poetry, in which the use of alliteration, fanciful use of words, strange conceits, ingenious turns of expression, the various बंधs such as the गोमूत्रिकाबंध, सर्वतोभद्रबंध &c. were indulged in by the poets.

About the home of Bhāravi—the place where he was born, brought up, and flourished nothing can be determined. The late Prof. R. R. Bhāgwat Shastri on the strength of Bhāravi's reference to "the huge violent waves of the ocean which beat in vain against the sides of the Sahya Mountain's* concluded that Bhāravi belonged to Southern India. Probably Bhāravi lived and flourished in Southern India. For we think that the telling simile which describes vividly the scene at the Sahya Mountain is some, if not a conclusive, proof that Bhāravi was a poet from Southern India. Again his description of the mountain Himālaya is rather fanciful and he does not describe the intervening places when sending his hero to Indrakila, as Kālidāsa has done in the Meghadūta.

---

* उरसि शूलभृतः प्रहिता मुहुः प्रतिहतिं ययुरर्जुनमुष्टयः ।
भृशरया इव सह्यमहीभृतः पृथुनि रोधसि सिन्धुमहोर्मयः ॥

Canto XVIII.5.

He does not, therefore, seem to be a Northern poet or to have travelled in Northern India.

Bhāravi is, doubtless, one of the great poets that have shed lustre on the literary history of this country. Only one poem of his, "Kirātārjuniya" has come down to us. This *kāvya* has obtained a place among the five great kāvyas (पञ्चमहाकाव्य) रघुवंश, कुमारसम्भव, किरातार्जुनीय, शिशुपालवध, and नैषध. "Kirātārjuniya", as Mr. R. C. Dutt remarks "is one of the most vigorous and spirited poems in the Sanskrit language." In this poem Bhāravi shows himself a master-hand at depicting the heroic sentiment (वीररस). His descriptions of natural scenery, though inferior to those of Kālidāsa and Bhavabhūti in beauty and grandeur, are vivid and impressive. He also displays great skill in portraying the characters of the principal personages that figure in the poem. Draupadi, a true Kshatriya princess, admonishing her husband with all the spirited eloquence of a proud woman smarting under the disgrace and hardships of her family, Yudhishtira of unruffled serenity and quiet dignity trying to moderate the impatient ardour of Bhima with words of calm, farsighted wisdom, Duryodhana, of firm purpose, skilled in the art of government, striving his utmost to win the hearts of his subjects by adopting a policy of sagacious statesmanship, Bhīma of fiery temper, strong, haughty, and bold trying to stir up his elder brother to energetic action against the enemy, Arjuna, a peerless warrior, undergoing rigid austerities with all the self-control of a perfect Muni—all these are delineated with the skill and sureness of touch of a successful painter of human nature. Bhāravi seems to be thoroughly acquainted with works on politics. The political disquisitions in the first three cantos are worthy of a great master of statecraft. Bhāravi's style lacks the grace, sweetness and lucidity of Kālidāsa, but it has strength and vigour. Sometimes his style grows obscure and difficult to understand. His sacrifices perspecuity to ingenious turns of expression. Hence

Mallinātha has composed his style to a cocoanut,* which has to be broken before one can get at the sweet kernel within. It was once a prevalent opinion among Pandits that Bhāravi's chief merit lay in the profundity of thought (अर्थगौरवं)×. This is to a certain extent true. General truths clothed in a vigorous language are interpersed in his poem. Pithy sayings such as "हितं मनोहारि च दुर्लभं वचः ; सहसा विदधीत न क्रियां &c; वसन्ति हि प्रेम्णि गुणा न वस्तुषु &c. have passed into familar quotation and are in the mouth of every Sanskrit scholar. Regarding Bhāravi's merits as a poet Mr. R. C. Dutt's judgment will, we think, be accepted by every Scholar. In his Civilization in Ancient India, observes that competent critic and scholar—"In the richness of a creative fancy, in true tenderness and pathos, and even in the sweetness and melody of verse, Kālidāsa is incomparably a greater poet. But nevertheless Bhāravi boasts of a vigour of thought and of language, a spirited and lofty eloquence in expression, which Kālidāsa seldom equals."

In Sanskrit Literature the name of Bhāravi is inseparably associated with that of Māgha, as the name of Thackeray is with that of Dickens in the history of English Literature. Māgha, says the tradition, was put on his mettle to write his poem "Śiśupalavadha" after reading Bhāravi's "Kirātārjuniya" as Dickens was spurred on to write his Masterpiece "David Copperfield" after reading Thackeray's "Vanity Fair." It is said that the name Māgha was assumed by the poet to indicate that when Māgha (a month in the cold season) comes Bhāravi (the sun) loses his splendour. Most of the Pandits of the old school hold that Māgha has

---

* नारिकेलफलसंमितं वचो भारवेः ।

× उपमा कालिदासस्य भारवेरर्थगौरवं ।
नैषधे पदलालित्यं माघे सन्ति त्रयो गुणाः ।

eclipsed Bhāravi in the art of writing a महाकाव्य* Māgha's poetry, however, is more artificial, his conceits more farfetched and his manner more digressive than those of his great rival. Besides Māgha wrote his poem in imitation of Bhāravi's Kirātārjuniya. There are many points of resemblance in the general plan and details between the two poems. But as this is not meant to be a general introduction to the whole poem, nor exhaustive either, we refrain from giving them here. A writer in the Vividha Jnāna Vistar (a monthly magazine in Marāthi) has pointed out all these points of similarity; (Vol. XXIII-9); and those curious to know them may refer to that.

The Anecdote above referred to as given by
Mr. Pāngārkar, B.A.

Bhāravi was ground by poverty and being ever emersed in poetic life, was often troubled by the furious remarks of his wife. She once reproached him for his dulness in as much as he did not stir himself about money, and the poet, graded by necessity and the constant reproaches of his wife, did set out to try his fortune to seek royal support. When he had gone few miles, he saw a beautiful tank. Fatigued by the labours of the journey, he stopped there and wrote the verse (सहसा विदधीत न क्रियाम् &c.) on a lotus leaf. The king, who happened to be on the very spot as he had left his palace for hunt, was so much delighted with it that he ordered the poet to see him in his palace at a particular time and then galloped off. The poet, mean-looking and dressed in rage, found no admittance to the royal presence and had in despair to go back.

The King, however, had the verse painted in gold in his private chamber. A year silently passed when the king set out with his chosen few to hunt, declaring that he would

* तावद्भा भारवेर्भाति यावन् माघस्य नोदयः ।
उदिते च पुनर्माघे भारवेर्भा रवेरिव ॥

return after a week. Second night, however, his camp not being far off he rode alone to his private chamber and to his extreme wonder and rage, found the queen lying with another person on his bed ! Suddenly he drew out his sword and was about to strike both dead, when the verse in golden letters attracted his attention. His rage abated and he resolved to awaken both and tell them of their heinous offence and then to pass the sentence of capital punishment on them. But what was his surprise when, on awakening them, he was told that the youth was no other than his son, who, being stolen away by a nurse from his cradle, was discovered that very evening ! The king, immediately in tears, thanked God that he had not rashly murdered his wife and his only son, the sole heir to his throne. Need it be told that the king out of gratefulness for the author of the verse that saved his empire, soon discovered him and conferring the title of Poet Laureate on him, saw him in opulent circumstances ! !

There is another version of the anecdote but it is not given here as not being of any great use to the students.

In preparing this edition of the first three cantos of the Kirāt., I have used the editions of the Kāvya by the Nirnaya-sagar press, by Mr. Pāngārkara (Canto I-X) and by Prof. Goswami of Calcutta (Cantos I, II) and acknowledge the help derived from these, especially that from the last mentioned one is solving some points of grammar. I have also to thank my friend Mr. L. S. Bhāndāre B. A. who made some additions in the 3rd and 4th parts of the Introduction. I am aware of the imperfections to be found in the book; these will be removed in the 2nd ed. if called for.

GIRGAON, BOMBAY. } M. R. KĀLE.

महाकवि श्रीभारविप्रणीतम्

किरातार्जुनीयम्[1]

'घण्टा'-'विवृति'-सहितम्

प्रथमः सर्गः

॥ श्री विश्वेश्वरो जयति ॥

(कोलाचलश्रीमल्लिनाथसूरिकृतो घण्टापथः)

अर्धाङ्गीकृतदाम्पत्यमपि गाढानुरागि यत् ।
पितृभ्यां जगतस्तस्मै कस्मैचिन्महसे नमः ॥

आलम्बे जगदालम्बे हेरम्बचरणाम्बुजे ।
शुष्यन्ति यद्रजःस्पर्शात्सद्यः प्रत्यूहवार्धयः ॥

तद्दिव्यमव्ययं धाम सारस्वतमुपास्महे ।
यत्प्रकाशात्प्रलीयन्ते मोहान्धतमसश्छटाः ॥

वाणीं काणभुजीमजीगणदवासासीच्च वैयासकी-
मन्तस्तन्त्रमरंस्त पन्नगगवीगुम्फेषु चाजागरीत् ।
वाचामाकलयद्रहस्यमखिलं यश्चाक्षपादस्फुरां
लोकेऽभूद्यदुपज्ञमेव विदुषां सौजन्य-जन्यं यशः ॥

मल्लिनाथकविः सोऽयं मन्दात्माऽनुजिघृक्षया ।
तत्किरातार्जुनीयाख्यं काव्यं व्याख्यातुमिच्छति ॥

१—किरातः—वनेचरो म्लेच्छजातिविशेषः अत्र तु किरातवेषधारी शिवः, अर्जुनश्च तृतीयः पाण्डवः । किरातश्च अर्जुनश्च किरातार्जुनौ (द्वन्द्वः समासः), किरातार्जुनौ अधिकृत्य कृतं काव्यं किरातार्जुनीयम् "अधिकृत्य कृते ग्रन्थे" इत्यनुवर्तमाने "शिशुक्रन्दयमसभद्वन्द्वेन्द्रजननादिभ्यश्छः" इति छ प्रत्ययः, "आयनेयी......" इति छस्य ईय्, किरातार्जुनीयमित्यन्वर्था संज्ञा ॥

नारिकेलफलसंमितं वचो भारवेः सपदि तद्विभज्यते ।
स्वादयन्तु रसगर्भनिर्भरं सारमस्य रसिका यथेप्सितम् ।[1]
नानानिबन्धविषमैकपदैर्नितान्तं साशङ्कचङ्क्रमणखिन्नधियामशङ्कम् ।
कर्तुं प्रवेशमिह भारविकाव्यबन्धे घण्टापथं कमपि नूतनमातनिष्ये ।।
इहान्वयमुखेनैव सर्वं व्याख्यायते मया ।
नामूलं लिख्यते किञ्चिन्नानपेक्षितमुच्यते ।।

अथ तत्रभवान्भारविनामा कविः—

'काव्यं यशसेऽर्थकृते व्यवहारविदे शिवेतरक्षतये ।
सद्यः परनिर्वृतये कान्तासंमिततयोपदेशयुजे ।।'

—इत्याद्यालङ्कारिकवचनप्रामाण्यात्काव्यस्यानेकश्रेयः साधनताम्, 'काव्यालापांश्च वर्जयेत्' इति निषेधशास्त्रस्याऽसत्काव्यविषयतां च पश्यन्किरातार्जुनीयाख्यं महाकाव्यं चिकीर्षुश्चिकीर्षितार्थाऽविघ्नपरिसमाप्ति-सम्प्रदायाविच्छेद-लक्षणफलसाधनत्वात्, 'आशीर्नमस्क्रिया वस्तुनिर्देशो वाऽपि तन्मुखम्' इत्याद्याशीर्वादाद्यन्यतमस्य प्रबन्धमुखलक्षणत्वाच्च वनेचरस्य युधिष्ठिरप्राप्तिरूपं वस्तु निर्दिशन्कथामुपक्षिपति—

श्रियः कुरूणामधिपस्य पालनीं प्रजासु वृत्तिं यमयुङ्क्त वेदितुम् ।
स वर्णिलिङ्गी विदितः समाययौ युधिष्ठिरं द्वैतवने वनेचरः ।।१।।

अन्वयः—कुरूणाम्, अधिपस्य, श्रियः, पालनीं, प्रजासु, वृत्तिं, वेदितुं, यम्, अयुङ्क्त, वर्णिलिङ्गी, सः, वनेचरः, विदितः (सन्), द्वैतवने, युधिष्ठिरं समाययौ ।

घण्टापथः—**श्रिय इति ।** आदितः श्रीशब्दप्रयोगाद्वर्णगणादिशुद्धिर्नात्रातीवोपयुज्यते । तदुक्तम्—

'देवतावाचकाः शब्दा ये च भद्रादिवाचकाः ।
ते सर्वे नैव निन्द्याः स्युर्लिपितो गणतोऽपि वा ।।' इति ।।

कुरूणां निवासः कुरवो जनपदाः । 'तस्य निवासः' इत्यण्प्रत्ययः । 'जनपदे लुप्' । तेषाम् [कुरूणां] अधिपस्य [=स्वामिनः] सम्बन्धिनीम् । शेषे षष्ठी । श्रियः=राजलक्ष्म्याः । 'कर्तृकर्मणोः कृति' इति कर्मणि षष्ठी । पाल्यतेऽनयेति

पालनी, ताम् [पालनीं]=प्रतिष्ठापिकामित्यर्थः। प्रजारागमूलत्वात्सम्पद इति भावः। 'करणाधिकरणयोश्च' इति करणे ल्युट्। 'टिड्ढाणञ्'–इत्यादिना ङीप्। प्रजासु=जनेषु विषये। 'प्रजा स्यात्सन्ततौ जने' इत्यमरः। वृत्तिं=व्यवहारं। वेदितुं=ज्ञातुं। यं=वनेचरम्। अयुङ्क्त=नियुक्तवान्। वर्णः=प्रशस्तिरस्यास्तीति वर्णी=ब्रह्मचारी

तदुक्तम्—'स्मरणं कीर्तनं केलिः प्रेक्षणं गुह्यभाषणम्।
सङ्कल्पोऽध्यवसायश्च क्रियानिर्वृत्तिरेव च॥
एतन्मैथुनमष्टाङ्गं प्रवदन्ति मनीषिणः।
विपरीतं ब्रह्मचर्यमेतदेवाष्टलक्षणम्॥'

एतदष्टविधमैथुनाऽभावः प्रशस्तिः। 'वर्णाद्ब्रह्मचारिणि' इतीनिप्रत्ययः। तस्य लिङ्गं=चिह्नमस्यास्तीति–वर्णिलिङ्गी=ब्रह्मचारिवेषवानित्यर्थः। सः=नियुक्तः। वने चरतीति वनेचरः=किरातः। 'भेदाः किरातशबरपुलिन्दा म्लेच्छजातयः' इत्यमरः। 'चरेष्टः' इति टप्रत्ययः। 'तत्पुरुषे कृति बहुलम्' इत्यलुक्। विदितं=वेदनम्–अस्यास्तीति विदितः=परवृत्तान्तज्ञानवानित्यर्थः। ('अर्श आदिभ्योऽच्' इत्यच्प्रत्ययः। अथवा=विदितवृत्तान्तो विदितः) उभयत्रापि 'पीता गावः' 'भुक्ता ब्राह्मणाः' विभक्ता भ्रातरः' इत्यादिवत्साधुत्वम्। न तु कर्तरि क्तः। सकर्मकेभ्यस्तस्य विधानाऽभावात्। अत एव भाष्यकारः–'अकारो मत्वर्थीयः। विभक्तमेषामस्तीति विभक्ताः, पीतमेषामस्तीति 'पीताः' इति सर्वत्र। अथवोत्तरपदलोपोऽत्र द्रष्टव्यः–विभक्ताः, पीता इति'। अत्र लोपशब्दार्थमाह कैयटः–'गम्यार्थस्याप्रयोग एव लोपोऽभिमतः। 'विभक्ता भ्रातरः' इत्यत्र च धनस्य यद्विभक्तत्वं तद्भ्रातृषूपचरितम्। 'पीतोदका गावः' इत्यत्राप्युदकस्य पीतत्वं गोष्वारोप्यते' इति। तद्वदत्रापि वृत्तिगतं विदितत्वं वेदितरि वनेचरे उपचर्यते। एतेन 'वनाय पीतप्रतिबद्धवत्साम्' पातुं न प्रथमं व्यवस्यति जलं युष्मास्वपीतेषु या' एवमादयो व्याख्याताः। अथवा विदितः=विदितवान्। सकर्मकादप्यविवक्षिते कर्मणि कर्तरि क्तः। यथा 'आशितः कर्ता' इत्यादौ।

यथाऽऽहुः—

'धातोरर्थान्तरे वृत्तेर्धात्वर्थेनोपसङ्ग्रहात्
प्रसिद्धेरविवक्षातः कर्मणोऽकर्मिका क्रिया'॥ इति॥

द्वैतवने=द्वैताख्ये तपोवने। यद्वा—द्वेइते गते यस्मात्तद्द्वीतम्। तच्च तद्वनञ्च तस्मिन्। शोकमोहादिवर्जिते इत्यर्थः। युधि=रणे स्थिरं युधिष्ठिरं=धर्मराजम्। 'हलदन्तात्सप्तम्याः संज्ञायाम्' इत्यलुक्। 'गवियुधिभ्यां स्थिरः' इति षत्वम्। समाययौ=सम्प्राप्तवान्। अत्र 'वने वनेचरः' इति द्वयोः स्वरव्यञ्जनसमुदाययोरेकदैवावृत्त्या वृत्त्यनुप्रासो नामाङ्कलारः। अस्मिन्सर्गे वंशस्थवृत्तम्। तल्लक्षणम्—'जतौ तु वंशस्थमुदीरितं जरौ' इति ॥ १ ॥

अन्वयार्थः—(**कुरूणामधिपस्य**) कुरुजनपद के स्वामी के (**श्रियः**) राज्य-लक्ष्मी के (**पालनीम्**) रक्षक (**प्रजासु**) प्रजाओं में (**वृत्तिम्**) व्यवहार को (**वेदितुम्**) जानने के लिए (**यम्**) जिसको **अयुङ्क्त** नियुक्त किया था (**वर्णिलिङ्गी**) ब्रह्मचारी वेष वाला (**सः**) वह (**वनेचरः**) किरात (**विदितः**) ज्ञात है जिसको ऐसा (**द्वैतवने**) द्वैतनामक तपोवन में (**युधिष्ठिरम्**) युधिष्ठिर को (**समाययौ**) प्राप्त हुआ। १

कुरु जनपद के स्वामी दुर्योधन के, प्रजाओं के प्रति व्यवहार को, जिस व्यवहार पर उसकी राज्य-लक्ष्मी संरक्षित थी, जानने के लिए जिस किरात को नियुक्त किया था वह ब्रह्मचारी-वेषधारी किरात शत्रु के वृत्तान्त को जान कर द्वैतवन में युधिष्ठिर के पास आया।

Sl. 1. The forester, whom Yudhishṭhira had appointed to know (ascertain) the behaviour of the lord of the Kurus towards his subjects, on which depended the stability of (or, the safeguard of) his royalty, came, in the disguise of a religious student, to him (who was) in the Dvaita forest, after having gathered the (desired) information.

किराताजुर्नीयम्—किरातश्चाजुर्नश्च किराताजुर्नौ तावधिकृत्य कृतं काव्यम्।
The aff. छ (ईय) is added to the words शिशुक्रन्द &c. and to a Dwandwa (as here किरा०नौ) in the sense of 'a composition on that' by (शिशुक्रन्द—यमसभ—द्वन्द्वेन्द्रजननादिभ्यश्छः।) Păn. IV. 3. 87, 88, so शिशुक्रन्दीय, यमसभीय &c., विक्रमोर्वशीय &c. The present poem is concerned with Kirăta or Śiva disguised as such and Arjuna, and so is named किराताजुर्नीयम्.

The modes of introducing literary composition, sanctioned by writers on poetics are three, *viz.* आशीर्नमस्क्रिया &c. (see Malli's introduction) *i. e.* the author may pronounce a blessing on his readers, or address a salutation to his favourite deity or refer to the subject matter. Adopting the third of these modes Bhàravi opens his poem by ferring to the subject matter at once.

He, however, has not neglected the usual *Maṅgala.* By using the word श्री (expressive of the goddess of wealth and therefore of all blessings) as the firstword of the poem he has performed it. The group (गण) ज is also auspicious on account of the presence of the word श्री. In this respect compare the word वृद्धि (which indicates prosperity) used by Panîni at the beginning of his work—(वृद्धिरादैच). Not only this but following the words of Patañjali, (see Malli. on the last sl.) he uses the word लक्ष्मी in the concluding stanza of each canto also. In this he is followed by Mágha who in his Sis. uses the word in the last sl. of each canto.

N. B. In writing out the notes the words are taken in the order of the prose construction.

Sl. कुरूणाम्—Of the Kuru country. The names of countries are used in the plural in Sans. as they are named after the people inhabiting them. The word कुरु is derived from कुरु by adding the aff. अण् (अ) which is dropped when the word so derived refers to a country. See Malli; निवास means one's own residence (and not the residence of one's ancestors; see Sid. Kau. on Pán. IV. 3. 90). The Kurus formed a tribe of ancient Aryans (for they are mentioned in the Aitareya Bráhmaṇa VII. 14) who crossed the north-west boundary of India and formed a strong kingdom round Delhi, see Dutt's A. H. of C. Vol. 1 pp. 120-21, 149. Kuru also was the name of one of the kings of the lunar race, the son of Samvaraṇa and Tapatî, daughter of the sun and the common ancestor of both Dhṛtaráshṭra and Pāṇḍu.

अधिपस्य—अधिपातीति अधिपः, fr. अधिका+अ (क) added by आतश्चोपसर्गे Pán. III, 1. 136. The then reigning monarch of the Kurus, Duryodhana. (See Introduction). श्रियः पालनीं—The means of protecting or safe-guarding; on which depended the safety of श्री which was the object of the Cau. verb. पालय् takes the Gen. case beausec of the कृत् aff. ल्युट् in पालन. The *fem.* aff. ई is added to पालन because the aff. ल्युट has an indicatory ट. See Malli. *Cf.* सदानुरक्तप्रकृतिः प्रजापालनतत्परः । विनीतात्मा हि नृपतिर्भूयसीं श्रियमश्नुते ।। Kăm I. 24; see also III. 39.

प्रजासु वृत्ति—His conduct towards, his treatment of. Or we may take the two words as one प्रजानां सुवृत्ति the loyal conduct of his subjects towards him (to see how far they were attached to him.)

वेदितुम्—क्रियार्थायां क्रियायां तुमुन् Yuddhishṭhira employed the Kirāta that he (the Kiráta) should know &c. Hence it is not necessary that the subject of the inf. should be the subject of the finite verb.

वनेचरः—Upapada Tat., there being *aluk* of the Loc. term. by the rule तत्पुरुषे &c.; see com. The word चर is formed by adding the *Krt*. aff. ट (अ) to चर्. And in a Tat. when a कृत् प्रत्यय is added the case ending of the उपपद may sometimes be retained, sometimes dropped, sometimes optionally retained and at others something not provided for in the rule may take place, by the बाहुलक प्रमाण. It is thus explaind—क्वचित्प्रवृत्तिः क्वचिदप्रवृत्तिः क्वचिद्विभाषा क्वचिदन्यदेव । विधेर्विधानं बहुधा समीक्ष्य चतुर्विधं बाहुलकं वदन्ति ।।

वर्णिलिङ्गी—In the disguise of, wearing the marks of, a religious student. Malli translates वर्ण by प्रशस्ति to which he assigns a special meaning, that of moral excellence due to abstinence from the eight kinds of carnal pleasures. The aff, *matub* इन् is added to वर्ण in the sense of a Brahmachārin.

विदितः—Full of knowledge, having gathered the necessary

information. But विदित does not mean this; it simply means 'what is known; while the context requires that it should be in the active voice.—'One who knew. To obviate the difficulty, Malli. adds the मत्वर्थीय अच *i. e.* अ (विदित+अ). The question is fully discussed in the com. which see.

द्वैतवने—See Malli.; the forest in which there was the absence of शोक or affliction and मोह or infatuation, aberation. वने—mark the alliteration. युधिष्ठिर—There is an *aluk* of the Loc. when the noun ends in a consonant or अ and the whole is a name.

The mention of वनेचर here foreshadows the coming of Śiva in that disguise in the penance-forest of Arjuna.

कृतप्रणामस्य महीं महीभुजे जितां सपत्नेन निवेदयिष्यतः ।
न विव्यथे तस्य मनो न हि प्रियं प्रवक्तुमिच्छन्ति मृषा हितैषिणः ॥२॥

अन्वयः—कृतप्रणामस्य सपत्नेन जितां महीं महीभुजे निवेदयिष्यतः तस्य मनः न विव्यथे । हि हितैषिणः मृषा प्रियं प्रवक्तुं न इच्छन्ति ॥ २ ॥

कृतप्रणामस्येति ॥ [कृतः प्रणामो येन स कृतप्रणामः, तस्य] कृतप्रणामस्य तत्कालोचितत्वात्कृतनमस्कारस्य सपत्नेन रिपुणा दुर्योधनेन ॥ "रिपौ वैरिसपत्नारिद्विषद्द्वेषणदुर्हृदः" इत्यमरः ॥ जितां स्वायत्तीकृतां महीं [पृथ्वीं, महीं भुनक्तीति महीभुक्, तस्मै] महीभुजे युधिष्ठिराय ॥ क्रियाग्रहणात्संप्रदानत्वम् ॥ निवेदयिष्यतो ज्ञापयिष्यतः ॥ "लृटः सद्वा" इति शतृप्रत्ययः । तस्य वनेचरस्य मनो न विव्यथे । कथममीगप्रियं राज्ञे विज्ञापयामीति मनसि न चचालेत्यर्थः ॥ "व्यथ् भयचलनयोः" इति धातोर्लिट् ॥ उक्तमर्थमर्थान्तरन्यासेन समर्थयते—न हीति ॥ हि यस्मात् । हितमिच्छन्तीति हितैषिणः स्वामिहितार्थिनः पुरुषा मृषा मिथ्याभूतं प्रियं [मधुरं वचः] प्रवक्तुं [जल्पितुं] नेच्छन्ति । अन्यथा कार्यविघातकतया स्वामिद्रोहिणः स्युरिति भावः ॥ "अमौढ्यमान्द्यममृषाभाषित्वमभ्यूहकत्वं चेति चारगणाः" इति नीतिवाक्यामृते ॥

अन्वयार्थः—(**कृतप्रणामस्य**) किया है प्रणाम जिसने ऐसे (**तस्य**) उस किरात का (**मनः**) मन (**सपत्नेन**) शत्रु द्वारा (**जिताम्**) जीती हुई (**महीम्**) पृथ्वी

को (महीभुजे) राजा के लिए (निवेदयिष्यतः) जताते हुए (न विव्यथे) पीड़ित नहीं हुआ (हि) क्योंकि (हितैषिणः) हितैषी लोग (मृषा) असत्य (प्रियम्) प्रिय को (प्रवक्तुं) कहना (न इच्छन्ति) नहीं चाहते हैं। २

प्रणाम करके शत्रु दुर्योधन द्वारा विजित पृथ्वी के सत्य वृत्तान्त को उसने युधिष्ठर से कहा, और ऐसा करते हुए उसे कोई दुःख नहीं हुआ। क्योंकि हित चाहने वाले व्यक्ति झूठी प्रिय लगने वाली बात नहीं करते।

2. His mind experienced no pain as he was going to relate to the lord of the earth, after having respectfully saluted him, how the world was won over by his rival (Duryodhana): for, true well-wishers do not wish to utter an agreeable falsehood (lit. to make a falsely agreeable statement).

Sl. 2. सपत्नः:—समाने वस्तुनि पतति इति सपत्नः one who tries to seize the same thing; hence a rival; fr. समान irregularly changed to स (निपातनात्) + पत् + न. Probably this must have meant originally 'the son of a सपत्नी (properly सापत्न) and then an enemy or a rival (*Cf. Vik.* IV.) in general. The com. on Amara derives it as सपत्नीव lit. one like a co-wife; the final ई being changed to अ irregularly as indicated by the Sūtra व्यन्सपत्ने.

जितां—*i. e.* नयजितां won over by his good policy. See sl. 7. महीभुजे—महीं भुङ्क्ते भुनक्ति पालयति इति वा महीभुक् तस्मै; fr. भुज् + क्विप् (°). मही मही—alliteration. निवेदयिष्यतः—Fut. p. of विद् with नि, Cau; who was going to relate or communicate. मृषा—False हितैषिणः—fr. हितं + इष् + इन्। सुप्यजातौ णिनिस्ताच्छील्ये। न हि प्रियं &c.—We have such propositions and pithy sayings (*cf.* हितं मनोहारि in sl. 4.) interspersed throughout the poem. *Cf.* स इदानीं स्निग्धो जनो यः पृष्टः परुषमपि हितं वदति। Veṇ. II. The qualifications of a spy (see Malli. अमौढ्य &c.) are— 'His being intelligent, active, a speaker of truth and one able to draw right inference from circumstantial evidence.

तथापि प्रियार्हे राज्ञि कटुनिष्ठुरोक्तिर्न युक्तेत्याशङ्क्य स्वाम्यनुज्ञया न दुष्यतीत्याशयेनाह—

द्विषां विघाताय विधातुमिच्छतो रहस्यनुज्ञामधिगम्य भूभृतः ।
स सौष्ठवौदार्यविशेषशालिनीं विनिश्चितार्थामिति वाचमाददे ॥३॥

अन्वयः—द्विषां विघाताय विधातुम् इच्छतः भूभृतः अनुज्ञाम् अधिगम्य सः रहसि सौष्ठवौदार्यविशेषशालिनीं विनिश्चितार्थाम् इति वाचम् आददे ॥ ३ ॥

द्विषामिति ॥ रहस्येकान्ते स वनेचरो द्विषां शत्रूणाम् ॥ कर्मणि षष्ठी ॥ विघाताय । द्विषो विहन्तुमित्यर्थः ॥ "तुमर्थाच्च भाववचनात्" इति चतुर्थी । "भाववचनाच्च" इति तुमर्थे घञ्प्रत्ययः । अत्र तादर्थ्ये चतुर्थ्यामपि न दोषः । तथापि प्रयोगवैचित्र्यविशेषस्याप्यलङ्कारत्वादेवं व्याचक्षते, विधातुं व्यापारं कर्तुमिच्छतः ॥ "समानकर्तृकेषु तुमुन् ॥" द्विषो विहन्तुमुद्युञ्जानस्येत्यर्थः ॥ अतएव [भुवं बिभर्त्तीति भूभृत् तस्य] भूभृतोयुधिष्ठिरस्यानुज्ञामधिगम्य प्राप्य । सुष्ठु भावः सौष्ठवं शब्दसामर्थ्यम् ॥ सुष्ठुशब्दादव्ययादुद्गात्रादित्वादञ्प्रत्ययः ॥ उदारस्य भाव औदार्यमर्थसम्पत्तिः ॥ तयोर्द्वन्द्वः सौष्ठवौदार्ये ॥ [अत्रौदार्यशब्दस्याजाद्यदन्तत्वेऽपि "लक्षणहेत्वोः क्रियायाः" इत्यत्राल्पस्वरस्यापि हेतुशब्दस्य पूर्वनिपातंकुर्वता सूत्रकृतैव पूर्वनिपातशास्त्रस्यानित्यत्वज्ञापनान्न पूर्वनिपातः । उक्तं च काशिकायाम्—"अयमेव लक्षणहेत्वोरिति निर्देशः पूर्वनिपातव्यभिचारचिह्नम्" इति ।] त एव विशेषः । तेन शालते शोभत इति सौष्ठवौदार्यविशेषशालिनी ताम् ॥ ताच्छील्ये णिनिः ॥ विनिश्चितार्था विशेषतः प्रमाणतो निर्णीतार्थामिति वक्ष्यमाणरूपां वाचमाददे स्वीकृतवान् । उवाचेत्यर्थः ॥

अन्वयार्थः—(**द्विषाम्**) शत्रुओं के (**विघाताय**) विनाश के लिए (**विधातुम्**) उपाय को [करना] (**इच्छतः**) चाहते हुए (**भूभृतः**) राजा की (**अनुज्ञाम्**) अनुमति को (**अधिगम्य**) पाकर (**रहसि**) एकान्त में (**सः**) वह वनेचर (**सौष्ठव**) शब्द-सामर्थ्य (**औदार्य**) [एवं] अर्थ सम्पत्ति (**विशेष**) [रूप] वैशिष्ठ्य से (**शालिनीम्**) सुशोभित (**विनिश्चितार्थाम्**) प्रमाण से निर्णीत है अर्थ जिसका ऐसी (**वाचम्**) वाणी को (**आददे**) बोला ।

३

दुर्योधन आदि शत्रुओं के विनाश के लिए उद्यम करना चाहते हुए युधिष्ठिर

की अनुमति पा कर, एकान्त में उस किरात ने, समर्थ शब्दों एवं गम्भीर अर्थ से सुशोभित तथा प्रमाणों से निश्चित अर्थ वाली बात कही।

3. Having obtained the permission of the king (Dharma) who was desirous of adopting measures for the destruction of his foes, he made, in private, the following speech, which was brilliant with peculiarly graceful and highly significant expressions and the import whereof was well-checked (clear and definite).

Sl. 3. विधाताय—Malli. says the Dat. may also be explained by the rule तादर्थ्ये चतुर्थी वाच्या; but it is preferable to support it by तुमर्थाच्चा &c. because it is a special rule and its application gives variety and beauty to the composition. विधातुं—To take measures or devise schemes for. भूभृत्—भुवं बिभर्ति इति; Upapadasamāsa; fr. भृ+क्विप् तुक् (त् final) च. रहसि—goes with वाचमादद़े.

सौष्ठवौ०—सुष्ठु इत्यस्य भाव: fr. सुष्ठु *indec.*+अञ्. सौष्ठव elegance; gracefulness; capability of words to yield a good sense (Malli.) By प्राणभृज्जातिवयोवचनोद्गात्रादिभ्योऽञ्। Pān. V. 1 129, अञ् is added to प्राणभृज्जाति (as आश्वं, औष्ट्रम्), to express age (वयोवचन, as कौमारं) and to the words of the उद्गातृ group of which सुष्ठु is one (as औद्गात्रम्, सौष्ठवं &c.); see Malli. औदार्यं—उदारस्य भावः depth of meaning, richness of expression; *cf.* यत्प्रौढित्वमुदारता च वचसां यच्चार्थतो गौरवम् &c. Māl. Mād. I. 7. or औदार्य may mean that by which some noble quality, sense or sentiment is brought out; *cf.* उत्कर्षवान्गुणः कश्चिद्यस्मिन्नुक्ते प्रतीयते। तदुदाराह्वयं तेन सनाथा काव्यपद्धतिः॥ Dandin, K. D. विशेष०शालिनी—brilliant or graceful with the excellence of words elegant and prolific in sense, or its elegance and depth of meaning; or सौष्ठवोदार्ये एव विशेषस्तेन शालते—by its distinguishing mark *viz.* सौ०। By the rule अजाद्यदन्तं (a word with an initial vowel and ending in अ should precede in a Dwa. consisting of two members), सौष्ठ० should have been औदार्यसौष्ठवे but Malli. justifies the Comp., as it is, by saying that the rules about the precedence of words in a Dwa. are not meant to be absolute as can be inferred from the Sūtra लक्षणहेत्वोः &c. where Pān. himself puts लक्षण first against the rule अल्पाच्तरं by which हेतु should have preceded. See Malli. Similarly Pán. has violated the rule अजाद्य० in समुद्राभ्राद् घः Pán. IV. 4. 118.

विनिश्चितार्थां—The meaning of which was definite (and not equivocal or of doubtful import), exact in sense.

In the last two lines the poet perhaps tells us what the language of a good poetic composition ought to be like. Its chief features must be style and sense.

प्रथमं तावदप्रियनिवेदकमात्मानं प्रत्यक्षोभं याचते—

क्रियासु युक्तैर्नृप ! चारचक्षुषो न वञ्चनीयाः प्रभवोऽनुजीविभिः ।
अतोऽर्हसि क्षन्तुमसाधु साधु वा हितं मनोहारि च दुर्लभं वचः ॥ ४ ॥

अन्वयः— [हे] नृप, क्रियासु युक्तैः अनुजीविभिः चारचक्षुषः प्रभवः न वञ्चनीयाः । अतः असाधु साधु वा [मदुक्तं] क्षन्तुं अर्हसि हितं मनोहारि च वचः दुर्लभम् ॥ ४ ॥

क्रियास्विति ॥ हे नृप । क्रियासु कृत्यवस्तुषु युक्तैर्नियुक्तैरनुजीविभिर्भृत्यैः । चरादिभिरित्यर्थः । चरन्तीति चराः ॥ पचाद्यच् ॥ त एव चाराः ॥ चरेः पचाद्यजन्तात्प्रज्ञादित्वादण्प्रत्ययः ॥ त एव चक्षुर्येषां ते चारचक्षुषः "स्वपरमण्डल-कार्याकार्य विलोकने चाराश्चक्षूंषि क्षितिपतीनाम्" इति नीतिवाक्यामृते । तदुक्तम्—"गावः पश्यति गन्धेन वेदैः पश्यन्ति पण्डिताः । चारैः पश्यन्ति राजानश्चक्षुर्भ्यामितरे जनाः" इति ॥ प्रभवो निग्रहानुग्रहसमर्थाः स्वामिनो न वञ्चनीया न प्रतारणीयाः सत्यमेव वक्तव्या इत्यर्थः । चारापचारे चक्षुरचारवद्राज्ञां पदे पदे निपात इति भावः । अतोऽप्रतार्यत्वाद्धेतोः । असाध्वप्रियं साधु प्रियं वा । मदुक्तमिति शेषः । वाशब्दोऽप्यर्थे । क्षन्तुं सोढुमर्हसि । कुतः । हितं पथ्यं मनोहारि प्रियं च वचो दुर्लभम् । अतो मद्वचोऽपि हितत्वादप्रियमपि क्षन्तव्यमित्यर्थः ॥

अन्वयार्थः—(**नृप**) हे राजन् (**क्रियासु**) कार्यों में (**युक्तैः**) नियुक्त (**अनुजीविभिः**) सेवकों के द्वारा (**चारचक्षुषः**) गुप्तचर ही हैं आँखें जिनकी ऐसे (**प्रभवः**) स्वामी (**न वञ्चनीयाः**) ठगे नहीं जाने चाहिएं । (**अतः**) इसलिए (**असाधु**)अप्रिय (**साधु वा**)अथवा अप्रिय [बात को](**क्षन्तुम्**)सहने के (**अर्हसि**)

तुम योग्य हो। क्योंकि (हितम्) हितकारी (मनोहारि च वचः) और प्रियवाणी सुलभम् दुर्लभ होती है।

गुप्तचर ही राजाओं की आँख होते हैं। कार्य में नियुक्त इन सेवकों को अपने मालिक को धोखा नहीं देना चाहिए। अतः हे राजन्! मैं जो भी अच्छा या बुरा कहूँ आप उसे सहन करें; क्योंकि मनमोहक और साथ-ही-साथ हित करने वाली बात दुर्लभ होती है।

4. Sire, kings (masters), who see through spies, should never be misled (misinformed) by their servants entrusted with (respective) duties. It, therefore, behoves you to pardon me for what agreeable or disagreeable things I shall have to say : a speech which is (at once) beneficial and pleasing is rare (lit. not easy to have).

Sl. 4. क्रिया :—duties, particular business assigned to each. चारचक्षुषः—seeing through the spies, *i. e.* who have entirely to rely and act on the information supplied by the spies. प्रभवः—For the propriety of the word see com.; if a king acts on wrong information he may do injustice or may be led into danger. अर्हसि—mark the use of अर्ह्; you will please; kindly. असाधु &c. —*Cf.* अप्रियस्य च पथ्यस्य वक्ता श्रोता च दुर्लभः। Rāmā Araṇya. XXXVII 2.

तर्हि तूष्णींभाव एव वरमित्याशङ्क्याह—

स किंसखा साधु न शास्ति योऽधिपं हितान्न यः संशृणुते स किंप्रभुः।
सदाऽनुकूलेषु हि कुर्वते रतिं नृपेष्वमात्येषु च सर्वसम्पदः ॥५॥

अन्वयः—यः अधिप साधु न शास्ति स किंसखा? यः हितात् न संशृणुते स किंप्रभुः? नृपेषु अमात्येषु च सदाअनुकूलेषु हि सत्सु सर्वसम्पदः रतिं कुर्वते ॥ ५ ॥

स इति ॥ यः सखामात्यादि[अधिपातीत्यधिपः तं]अधिपं स्वामिनं साधु हितं न शास्ति नोपदिशति ॥ "ब्रुविशासि—" इत्यादिना शासेर्दुहादिपाठाद्द्विकर्मकत्वम् ॥ सहितानुपदेष्टा। कुत्सितः सखा किंसखा। दुर्मन्त्रीत्यर्थः ॥ "किमः क्षेपे" इति समासान्तप्रतिषेधः। तथा यः प्रभुर्निग्रहानुग्रहसमर्थः स्वामी हितादाप्तजनाद्धितोपदेष्टुः

सकाशात् ।। "आख्यातोपयोगे" इत्यपादानत्वात्पञ्चमी ।। न संशृणुते न शृणोति । हितमिति शेषः ।। "समो गम्यृच्छि"–इत्यादिना सम्पूर्वाच्छृणोतेरकर्मकत्वादात्मनेपदमकर्मकत्वं वैवक्षिकम् ।। स हितमश्रोता प्रभुः किंप्रभुः कुत्सितस्वामी ।। पूर्ववत्समासः ।। सर्वथा सचिवेन वक्तव्यं श्रोतव्यं च स्वामिना । एवं च राजमन्त्रिणोरैकमत्यं स्यादित्यर्थः ।। ऐकमत्यस्य फलमाह—सदेति ।। हि यस्मान्नृपेषु स्वामिषु । अमा सह भवा अमात्यास्तेषु [अमात्येषु मंत्रिषु] च ।। "अव्ययात्त्यप्" ।। अनुकूलेषु परस्परानुरक्तेषु सत्सु सर्वाश्च ताः सम्पदः सदा सर्वसम्पदः विविधैश्वर्या रतिमनुरागं कुर्वते कुर्वन्ति । न जातु जहतीत्यर्थः । अतो मया वक्तव्यं त्वया च श्रोतव्यमिति भावः ।। अत्रैवं राजमन्त्रिणोर्हितानुपदेशतदश्रवणनिन्दासामर्थ्यसिद्धेरैकमत्यलक्षणकारणस्य निर्दिष्टस्य सर्वसम्पत्तिसिद्धिरूपकार्येण समर्थनात्कार्येण कारणसमर्थनरूपोऽर्थान्तरन्यासोऽलङ्कारः । तदुक्तम्—"सामान्यविशेषकार्यकारणभावाभ्यां निर्दिष्टकृतसमर्थनमर्थान्तरन्यासः" इति ।।

अन्वयार्थः—(**यः**) जो (**अधिपम्**) राजा को (**हितम्**) हितकारी (**न शास्ति**) उपदेश नहीं देता है (**सः**) वह (**किं सखा**) कुत्सित मित्र है। और (**यः**) जो (**हितात्**) हितकारी से (**न संशृणुते**) नहीं सुनता है (**सः**) वह (**किं प्रभुः**) निन्दनीय स्वामी है । (**हि**) क्योंकि (**नृपेषु**) राजाओं (**अमात्येषु च**) और मन्त्रियों के (**अनुकूलेषु**) परस्पर अनुरक्त रहने पर (**सर्वसंपदः**) सभी सम्पदायें (**सदा**) सर्वदा (**रतिं कुर्वते**) अनुराग को करती हैं।

निन्दनीय है वह मित्र जो स्वामी को हितकर बात नहीं कहता; और जो हितकारी की बात नहीं सुनता वह स्वामी भी गर्हित है । वास्तव में राजाओं एवं मन्त्रियों के एक-दूसरे के अनुकूल रहने पर ही सब प्रकार का वैभव सदैव बना रहता है ।

5. He is a bad (undesirable) friend (counsellor) who does not give proper advice to his master; and he is a bad master who does not listen to the advice of his well-wisher: for, prosperity of every kind delights to live there where kings and their ministers are always mutually well-disposed (act in perfect accord or union.)

Sl. 5. **साधु—What is proper or to the benefit of; here used** as a noun being the direct object of शास् . किंसखा— see com. The word किम् when it implies censure or blame is compounded and the Comp. does not take the augment अ by राजाहः सखिभ्यष्टच् । In other senses there is no compound; as को राजा पृच्छ्याम् । This may also be taken separately—स किं सखा is he a friend (a well-wisher)? no. संशृणुते —The root श्रु is used here in transitively and is preceded by the preposition सम् so it takes the Atm.; see com. किंप्रभुः—may also be similarly explained. सदा irregularly derived fr. सर्व with the aff. दा; also सर्वदा.

अमात्य—Fr. अमा (अमान्तिकसहार्थयोः) +त्य which is added to अमा, इह, and adverbs in तस् and त्र, by the Värt. अमेहक्वतसित्रेभ्य एव so इहत्य, ततस्त्य, तत्रत्य &c. अनुकूलेषु—Prādi. Tat.; properly अनुगतः कूलं moving alongside the same bank; hence acting in concert or union with.

संप्रति स्वाहंकारं परिहरति—

निसर्गदुर्बोधमबोधविक्लवाः क्व भूपतीनां चरितं क्व जन्तवः ।

तवानुभावोऽयमवेदि यन्मया निगूढतत्त्वं नयवर्त्म विद्विषाम् ॥ ६ ॥

अन्वयः—निसर्गदुर्बोधं भूपतीनां चरितं क्व अबोधविक्लवा (मादृशाः) जन्तवः क्व । [तथापि] यत् मया विद्विषां निगूढतत्त्वं नयवर्त्म अवेदि अयं तव अनुभावः ॥ ६ ॥

निसर्गेति ॥ [निसर्गाद् दुर्बोधनं] निसर्गदुर्बोधं स्वभावदुर्ग्रहम् ॥ "ईषद्॰ :—" इत्यादिना खल्प्रत्ययः ॥ [भुवः पतयः भूपतयः] भूपतीनां चरितं [व्यवहारः]क्व ? [अबोधेन विक्लवाः] अबोधविक्लवा अज्ञानोपहता जन्तवः । मादृशाः । पामरजना इत्यर्थः । क्व । नोभयं संघटत इत्यर्थः । तथापि [निश्चयेन गूढं तत्त्वं यस्य तत्] निगूढतत्त्वं संवृतयाथार्थ्यं विद्विषां [शत्रूणां] नयवर्त्म[नयस्य वर्त्म] षाड्गुण्यप्रयोगः "सन्धिविग्रहयानानि संस्थाप्यासनमेव च । द्वैधीभावश्च विज्ञेयाः षड्गुणा नीतिवेदिनाम्"इत्यादिरूपो यन्मयावेदि । ज्ञातमिति यावत् ॥ विदेः कर्मणि लुङ् ॥ अयम् । इदं वेदनमित्यर्थः ॥ विधेयप्राधान्यात्पुलिङ्गनिर्देशः ॥ तवानुभावः सामर्थ्यम् ॥ अनुगतोभावोऽनुभावः । [राज्ञां प्रकृष्टो भाव] इति घञन्तेन प्रादिसमासः । न तूपसृष्टाद्घञ्प्रत्ययः । "श्रिणीभुवोऽनुपसर्गे" इत्यनुपसर्गाद्भवतेर्धातोर्घञ्विधानात् । अतएव

काशिकायाम्—"कथं प्रभावो राज्ञां प्रकृष्टो भाव इति ादिसमासः" इति ॥ दोषपरिहारी सम्यग्ज्ञात्वैव विज्ञापयामि न तु वृथा कर्णकठोरं प्रलपामीत्याशयः ॥

अन्वयार्थः—(निसर्गदुर्बोधम्) स्वभाव से ही दुर्बोध (भूपतीनाम्) राजाओं का (चरितं क्व) आचरण कहाँ ? और (अबोधविक्लवाः) अज्ञान से आहत (जन्तवः क्व) [मुझ जैसे] प्राणी कहाँ ? तो भी (निगूढतत्त्वम्) छिपा हुआ है यथार्थ जिसका ऐसा (विद्विषाम्) शत्रुओं का (नयवर्त्म) नीति-मार्ग (यन्मयाऽवेदि) जो मैंने जान लिया (अयम्) यह (तवानुभावः) तुम्हारा [ही] प्रभाव है ।

कहाँ स्वभाव से ही दुर्बोध राजाओं का व्यवहार और कहाँ मुझ जैसे अज्ञानी प्राणी ! फिर भी जो मैंने शत्रुओं का अत्यन्त गुप्त नीति-मार्ग जान लिया है, यह आप के ही प्रभाव के कारण है । ६

6. How naturally difficult to penetrate is the policy (lit. doings, actions) of kings and how (unequal to the task) are insignificant persons like myself incapacitated by ignorance ! (Still) it is by Your Majesty's greatness that the line of action (policy) of the enemies, very intricate as to its real nature, was comprehended by me.

Sl. 6. निसर्ग०—difficult to grasp from its very nature (for diplomacy requires that all plans should be kept secret). क्व—क्व—*Kva* when repeated in coordinate sentences indicates great disparity or incongruity; *cf.* क्व सूर्यप्रभवो वंशः क्व चाल्पविषया मतिः, Rag. I. 2. क्व वयं क्व परोक्षमन्मथो मृगशावैः सममेधितो जनः । Śak. II. 18. तपः क्व वत्से क्व च तावकं वपुः । Kum. V. 4. &c.

अबोधविक्लवाः—न बोधः अबोधः ignorance *i. e.* inability to understand the policy or to penetrate the secret doings of others; तेन विक्लवाः—Properly helpless; hence overcome with ; fr. क्लु with वि 1 A. to go and aff. अ (अच्) Or नास्ति बोधो येषां ते अबोधाः, अबोधाश्च ते विक्लवाश्च; Karma. विद्विषा—great or inveterate foes. निगूढ०—निगूढं profoundly secret तत्वं real nature यस्य तत् तस्य भावस्तत्वं the real truth. नयवर्त्म—the course of the policy of, the schemes formulated by. अवेदि—Aor. 3rd sing. pass. of विद्

अनुभाव:—royal power or power due to a king's peculiar dignity. This must be taken as a प्रादिसमास and not a word derived fr. भू with अनु; for the aff. घञ् (अ) cannot be added to भू when preceded by a preposition. See Malli. With a prep. अप् or अच will have to be added, Remark—The modesty of the speaker shows that he is not a man of pretension. He would report the true state of things.

संप्रति यद्वक्तव्यं तदाह—

विशङ्कमानो भवतः पराभवं नृपासनस्थोः अपि वनाधिवासिनः ।
दुरोदरच्छद्मजितां समीहते नयेन जेतु जगतीं सुयोधनः ॥ ७ ॥

अन्वयः—सुयोधनः नृपासनस्थोऽपि वनाधिवासिनः भवतः पराभवं विशङ्कमानः दुरोदरच्छद्मजितां जगतीं नयेन जेतुं समीहते ॥ ७ ॥

विशङ्कमान इति ॥ सुखेन युध्यते स सुयोधनः ॥ "भाषायां शासियुधिदृशिधृषिमृषिभ्यो युज्वाच्यः ॥ [नृपस्य, आसनं नृपासनं, तस्मिन् तिष्ठतीति] नृपासनस्थः । सिंहासनस्थोऽपि । वनमधिवसतीति [तस्मात्] वनाधिवासिनो वनस्थात् । राज्यभ्रष्टादपीत्यर्थः । भवतस्त्वत्तः पराभवं पराजयं विशङ्कमान उत्प्रेक्षमाणः सन् । दुष्टमुदरमस्येति दुरोदरं द्यूतम् ॥ पृषोदरादित्वात्साधु ॥ "दुरोदरो द्यूतकारे पणे द्यूते दुरोदरम्" इत्यमरः ॥ "तस्य छद्मना मिषेण जितां लब्धां दुर्नयाजितां जगतीं महीम् ॥ जगती विष्टपे मह्यां वास्तुच्छन्दोविशेषयोः" इति वैजयन्ती ॥ नयेन नीत्या जेतुं वशीकर्तुं समीहते व्याप्रियते । न तूदास्ते इत्यर्थः । बलवत्स्वामिकमविशुद्धागमं च धनं भुञ्जानस्य कुतो मनसःसमाधिरिति भावः ॥ अत्र "दुरोदरच्छद्मजिताम्" इति विशेषणद्वारेण पदार्थं प्रति हेतुत्वेनोपन्यासद्वितीयकाव्यलिङ्गमलङ्कारः । तदुक्तम्—"हेतोर्वाक्यपदार्थत्वे काव्यलिङ्गमुदाहृतम्" इति ॥

अन्वयार्थः—(**सुयोधनः**) दुर्योधन (**नृपासनस्थोऽपि**) सिंहासन पर बैठा हुआ भी (**वनाधिवासिनः**) वन में रहने वाले (**भवतः**) आप से (**पराभवम्**) पराजय की (**विशङ्कमानः**) शङ्का करता हुआ (**दुरोदर**) जूए के (**छद्म**) बहाने से (**जिताम्**) जीती हुई (**जगतीम्**) पृथ्वी को (**नयेन**) नीति से (**जेतुम्**) जीतना (**समीहते**) चाहता है ।

राज्य-भ्रष्ट आप से, सिंहासन पर बैठा हुआ भी वह दुर्योधन डरता है ।

अतः द्यूत-छल से जीते हुए राज्य को अब नीति पूर्वक जीतना चाहता है ।

7. Though occupying the throne Suyodhana, apprehensive of defeat from Your Majesty (now) living in a forest, wishes to win over by (conciliatory) policy the world (already) gained by the dishonest means (lit. under the pretext) of gambling.

Sl. 7. सुयोधनः—See Malli. who quotes the Vārt on Pān. III. 3. 128. The roots शास्, युध् &c. take the aff. युच् (अन) in the sense of the aff, खल् (see Malli. further on sl. 22.) *i. e.* ease or difficulty. नृपासन० वनाधि०—Mark the contrast. Being in actual possession of the throne he has no reason to fear you. But he has a guilty conscience and feels his position insecure as long as he has not secured the affection of the people.

दुरोदर—Malli. takes this as a comp. of the पृषो० class. But in his com. on Rag. IX. 7. he explains it as दुर् दुष्टमासमन्तादुदरं यस्य । as a regular comp.; दुरोदरमेव छद्म; or दुरोदरस्य छद्म तेन जिता— See Mah. Bhăr. Sab. P. Dyūtaparva and Ch. 76.

नयेन—By judicious conduct and wise statesmanship. The policy pursued is described in the following Ślokas.

"नयेन जेतुं जगतीं समीहते" इत्युक्तम् । तत्प्रकारमाह—

तथापि जिह्मः स भवज्जिगीषया तनोति शुभ्रं गुणसम्पदा यशः ।

समुन्नयन्भूतिमनार्यसङ्गमाद्वरं विरोधोऽपि समं महात्मभिः ॥ ८ ॥

अन्वयः—तथा जिह्मःअपि स भवज्जिगीषया गुणसम्पदा शुभ्रं यशः तनोति । भूतिं समुन्नयन् महात्मभिः समं विरोधःअपि अनार्यसङ्गमात् वरम् ॥८॥

तथापीति ॥ तथापि साशङ्कोऽपि । जिह्मो वक्रः । वञ्चक इति यावत् । स दुर्योधनो (भवन्तं जेतुमिच्छा भवज्जिगीषा, तया) भवज्जिगीषया । गुणैर्भवन्तमाक्रमितुमिच्छयेत्यर्थः ॥ "हेतौ" इति तृतीया ॥ (गुणानांसम्पत् तया) गुणसम्पदा दानदाक्षिण्यादिगुणगरिम्णा । करणेन । शुभं यशस्तनोति । स खलो गुणलोभनीयां त्वत्सम्पदमात्मसात्कर्तुं त्वत्तोऽपि गुणवत्तामात्मनः प्रकटयतीत्यर्थः ॥ नन्वेवं गुणिनः सतोऽपि सज्जनविरोधो महानस्त्यस्य दोष इत्याशङ्क्य सोऽपि सत्संसर्गाऽलाभे नीचसङ्गमाद्वरमुत्कर्षावहत्वादित्याह—**समिति**॥ तथाहि ।

भूतिं [ऐश्वर्यं] समुन्नयन्नुत्कर्षमापादयन् ॥ "लटः शतृशानचौ—" इत्यादिना शतृप्रत्ययः । पुनर्लड्ग्रहणसामर्थ्यात्प्रथमासामानाधिकरण्यम् ॥ महात्मभिः [सज्जनैः] समम् । सहेत्यर्थः । "साकं सत्रा समं सह" इत्यमरः ॥ [न आर्याः अनार्याः, अनार्याणां सङ्गमः, तस्माद्] अनार्यसङ्गमाद्दुर्जनसंसर्गात् ॥ "पञ्चमी विभक्ते" इति पञ्चमी ॥ विरोधोऽपि वरं मनाक्प्रियः ॥ "देवाद्वृते वरः श्रेष्ठे त्रिषु क्लीबं मनाक्प्रिये" इत्यमरः । अत्र मैत्र्यपेक्षया मनाक्प्रियत्वं विरोधस्य "भूतिं समुन्नयन्" इत्यस्य पूर्ववाक्यान्वये समाप्तस्य वाक्यार्थस्य पुनरादानात्समाप्तपुनरात्ताख्यानदोषापत्तिः । तदुक्तं काव्यप्रकाशे—"समाप्तपुनरादानात्समाप्तपुनरात्तकम्" इति । न च वाक्यान्तरमेतत् । येनोक्तदोषपरिहारः स्यात् ॥ अर्थान्तरन्यासोऽलङ्कारः । स च भूतिसमुन्नयनस्य पदार्थविशेषणद्वारा विरोधवत्त्वं प्रति हेतुत्वाभिधानरूपकाव्यलिङ्गानुप्राणित इति ॥

अन्वयार्थः—(**तथापि**) वैसा [आशङ्कित] भी (**जिह्मः**) धूर्त (**सः**) वह (**भवज्जिगीषया**) आपको जीतने की इच्छा से, (**गुणसंपदा**) [दान-दाक्षिण्यादि] गुण-सम्पत्ति से (**शुभ्रं यशः**) [अपना] धवल यश (**तनोति**) फैला रहा है। (**भूतिं समुन्नयन्**) उत्कर्ष को करता हुआ (**महात्मभिः समम्**) महापुरुषों के साथ (**विरोधोऽपि**) विरोध भी (**अनार्यसंगमात्**) दुर्जन के संसर्ग से (**वरम्**) श्रेष्ठ है।

कुटिल होता हुआ भी वह दुर्योधन गुणों में आप को जीतना चाहता है। अतः विनम्र व्यवहार करता है, खूब दान-दक्षिणा देता है और इससे उसका धवल यश चारों ओर फैल रहा है। सचमुच दुर्जन की मैत्री से तो, उत्कर्ष को बढ़ाता हुआ महापुरुषों का विरोध भी अच्छा है।

8. Though so deceitful, (lit. crooked) he (now), with a view to excel you, gives rise to spotless fame by (the display of) the wealth of noble virtues (such as munificence, affability, &c.): even enmity with the magnanimous, tending as it does to bring about one's elevation (prosperity), is to preferred to friendship (lit. companionship) with the pusillanimous.

Sl. 8. तथापि—See Malli.; or it may be better taken as स तथा (in that manner *i.e.* so wicked as to deprive you of your kingdom by illicit means) जिह्मः अपि जिह्मः—जहाति सन्मार्गं हीयते वा fr. हा 3. P. to abandon; +म (Uṇādi मन् by I. 141. ह being changed to जिह and आ dropped). 'जिह्मस्तु कुटिले मन्दे' इति हैमः। morally crooked, deceitful. जिगीषया—जेतुमिच्छा जिगीषा desi. noun in आ fr. जि; with the desire to outshine or surpass you (in virtue or dutiful conduct). गुणसम्पदा—गुणानां सम्पत्त्या; by the greatness or pre-eminence arising from the practice of such virtues as दान giving gifts or rewarding servic edone, दाक्षिण्य or courteous conduct &c; see also Kăm. I. 21, 22.

समुन्नयन्—Bringing about, contributing to; an instance of a pre. p. agreeing with a nuon in the Nom. (विरोध here). See Malli. The whole Sūtra is लटः शतृशानचावप्रथमासमानाधिकरणे। Păn. III. 2. 124. *i. e.* the terminations अत् and आन are added to form pre. participles to Par. and Atm. roots respectively provided the participles so formed do not agree with a noun in the Nomi. But समुन्नयन् agrees with a noun in the Nom. (प्रथमान्तपद). To support the use of शतृ here Malli. following Kăśikă, says the mention of *Lat* again in the Sūtra allows sometimes the use of these participles with the Nom. also. भूति—excellence, greatness (due to one's elevation or edification). महात्मभिः—magnanimous or high-souled persons *i. e.* persons who do not know what hatred is, who possess all the characteristics of an *Ārya*; *cf.* कुलं शीलं दया दानं धर्मः सत्यं कृतज्ञता। अद्रोह इति येष्वेतत्तानार्यान्संप्रचक्षते ॥ Bharata, as quoted by Jag. in his com, on the Măl. Măd. Another description of an Ārya is कर्तव्यमाचरन्कार्यमकर्तव्यमनाचरन्। तिष्ठति प्रकृताचारे स तु आर्य इति स्मृतः ॥ Vasishṭha.

अनार्य—One who is not an Ārya; (see above); a wicked person. The word आर्य is derived fr. ऋ+ण्यत् (अर्यते अर्तुं योग्यो वा) According to Max Muller the word आर्य originally meant the cultivator of land, leading a peaceful, honest life. Such an occupation was looked upon as noble and so the word आर्य also came to signify 'noble'. He thinks the root ऋ to be the same as the A. S. root *ear* 'to plough' from which the word earth is derived. The term Anărya was applied in Vedic times to the original inhabitants of India who were called by the Aryas Dasyus or Dăsas. सख्य— means here friendship. वरं मनाक् प्रिय: desirable a little; slightly better *i. e.* to be preferred though not desirable. It is an *adj.* to विरोध. According to Amara. it is always *neu.* in this sense. According to others it is an indeclinable.

Malli. detects in the 2nd half of this sl. the fault of composition called समाप्त० or the resumption of what is concluded. Here the idea of भूतं समुन्नयन् is already expressed by the previous sentence तनोति शुभ्रं &c. while भूतिं समुन्नयन् must again be taken in connection with the previous sentence; see com.

Cf. for a similar idea वरं पण्डितशत्रुश्च न मूर्खो हितकारकः । वानरेण हतो राजा विप्राश्चौरेण रक्षिताः ।।

ननु "कातर्यं केवला नीतिः" इत्याशङ्क्य नीतियुक्तं पौरुषमस्येत्याह—

कृतारिषड्वर्गजयेन मानवीमगम्यरूपां पदवीं प्रपित्सुना ।

विभज्य नक्तंदिवमस्ततन्द्रिणा वितन्यते तेन नयेन पौरुषम् ।। ९ ।।

अन्वयः—कृतारिषड्वर्गजयेन अगम्यरूपां मानवीं पदवीं प्रपित्सुना अस्ततन्द्रिणा तेन पौरुषं नक्तंदिवं विभज्य नयेन वितन्यते ।। ९ ।।

कृतेति ।। षण्णां वर्गः समूहः षड्वर्गः । अरीणामन्तःशत्रूणां कामक्रोधादीनां षड्वर्गोऽरिषड्वर्गः ।। शिवभागवतवत्समासः तस्य जयः कृतो येन तथोक्तेन । विनीतेनेत्यर्थः । विनीताधिकारं प्रजापालनमिति भावः । (अगम्यंरूपं यस्या सा, तां) अगम्यरूपां पुरुषमात्रदुष्प्राप्याम् । मनोरिमां मानवीम् । मनूपदिष्टसदाचारक्षुण्णमित्यर्थः । पदवीं प्रजापालनपद्धतिं (प्रपत्तुमिच्छति प्रपित्सति, प्रपित्सतीति प्रपित्सुः, तेनप्रपित्सुना प्रतिपत्तुमिच्छुना ।। प्रपद्यतेः सन्नन्तादुप्रत्ययः । "सनि मीमा—" इत्यादिनेसादेशः । "अत्र लोपोऽभ्यासस्य" इत्यभ्यासलोपः ।। अस्ता तन्द्रिरालस्यं यस्य तेनास्ततन्द्रिणा । अनलसेनेत्यर्थः ।। तदिः सौत्रो धातुः । तस्मात् "तङ्क्र्यादयश्च" इत्यौणादिकः किन्प्रत्ययः । "कृदिकारादक्तिनः" इति वा ङीष् । "वन्दीघटीतरीतन्द्रीति ङीषन्तोऽपि" इति क्षीरस्वामी । तथा रामायणप्रयोगः—"निस्तन्द्रिरप्रमत्तश्च स्वदोषे परदोषवित्"

इति ॥ तेन दुर्योधनेन । पुरुषस्य कर्म पौरुषं पुरुषकारः । उद्योग इति यावत् ॥ युवादित्वादणप्रत्ययः ॥ "पौरुषं पुरुषस्योक्तं भावे कर्मणि तेजसि" इति विश्वः ॥ नक्तं च दिवा च नक्तंदिवम् । अहोरात्रमित्यर्थः ॥ "अचतुर—" इत्यादिना सप्तम्यर्थवृत्त्योरव्यययोर्द्वन्द्वनिपातेऽच्समासान्तः ॥ विभज्यास्यां वेलायामिदं कार्यमकार्यमिति विभागं कृत्वा नयेन नीत्या वितन्यते विस्तार्यते ॥

अन्वयार्थः—(**कृतारिषड्वर्गजयेन**) किया है काम-क्रोधादि छः अन्तः शत्रुओं का जय जिसने ऐसे (**अगम्यरूपाम्**) पुरुष मात्र के लिए दुष्प्राप्य (**मानवीम्**) मनु की (**पदवीम्**) [प्रजापालन] पद्धति को (**प्रपित्सुना**) पाने के इच्छुक, (**अस्ततन्द्रिणा**) समाप्त हो गया है आलस्य जिसका ऐसे, (**तेन**) उस दुर्योधन के द्वारा (**पौरुषम्**) पुरुषार्थ, (**नक्तं दिवं विभज्य**) दिन और रात का विभाग करके (**नयेन**) नीतिपूर्वक, (**वितन्यते**) विस्तृत किया जाता है।

काम-क्रोधादि आभ्यन्तर छह शत्रुओं का विजेता, सामान्य मनुष्य के लिए दुष्प्राप्य मनु द्वारा निर्दिष्ट प्रजापालन की पद्धति को चाहने वाला तथा आलस्य-रहित वह दुर्योधन, अपने सभी कृत्यों को समय के विभागानुसार नीतिपूर्वक करता है। ९

9. By him ambitious to reach the line of conduct laid down by Manu (for kings to follow), the nature of which is not within the reach (of ordinary men), and therefore with the six (spiritual) enemies quelled, and all lethargy cast aside, is displayed strong action with due regard to policy, the days and nights being properly apportioned to the discharge of different duties.

Sl. 9. Malli.'s introduction to this sl. कातर्यं & c. is from Rag. XVII. 47. कृतारि०—For dissolution of the comp. see com. अरिष०—The collection of the six spiritual enemies of mankind. The comp. अरिष०, remarks Malli., must be explained like शिवभागवतम्. In the present comp. the numeral षष् properly qualifies अरि and should have gone with it, the comp. being षडरयः and then तेषां वर्गः । The word वर्ग is related to अरि and has, yet, been compounded with षष्. This is ungrammatical. But Malli. thinks that it must be defended by citing a parallel instance, which is शिवभागवत. It means शिवस्य भागवतं which again means भगवत इदम्. Now the word भगवत् from which भागवत is derived with the aff. अण् is an *adj.* and as such it should quality शिव rather than take the aff. अण् itself and yet the comp. occurs in language.—जयेन—विनीतेन says. Malli. ; *cf.* आत्मानं प्रथमं राजा विनयेनोपपादयेत्। कामः क्रोधस्तथा लोभो हर्षो मानो मदस्तथा। षड्वर्गमुत्सृजेदेनमस्मिंस्त्यक्ते सुखी नृपः॥ नयस्य सिद्धौ विनयः पुरःसरः Kăm, Nit. I. 23; 55, 64.

अगम्य॰—Not easy to be attained by every man *i. e.* to be attained by men of exceptional merits and self-control. मानवीं पदवीं—the path or line of conduct marked out for kings by Manu. मानवीं fr. मनु+अण् (इदमर्थे)+ई; of Manu, hence laid down by Manu. पद्यते अनया इति पदविः fr. पद+अवि (Uṇădi.) by पद्यतिभ्यामविः; also पदवी see note on तन्द्रि next sloka. प्रपित्सु—Desi. noun in उ fr. पद with प्र, wishing to attain to.

अस्ततन्द्रिणा—with all lethargy or inactivity entirely shaken off. Malli. derives the word तन्द्रि fr. the सौत्र root तद् with the Unădi aff. क्रिन्,and says the form तन्द्रा also is available by the rule कृदिकारादक्तिनः 'all *fem.* bases, provided they are formed with a K*r*t. aff. or a terminal vowel, excepting the इ of क्तिन् take the *fem.* ई optionally. The Sid. Kau. also endorses this view saying तदिः सौत्रो धातुः। तन्द्रिमेद्दि बाहुलकाद्गुणः। But Bhănuji Dikshit finds faults with this (for which see his com. on Amara) and derives it as तत्पूर्वाद्द्रातेः (the root रा) स्पृहिगृहि (III. 2. 158) इत्यादिना तन्द्रा इति निपात्यते (irregularly formed). तन्द्रायाः करणम्। तत्करोति (Văr̥t. on III. 1. 26) इति णयन्ताद् अच्च इः (Uṇădi IV. 139) तन्द्रिः कृतिकारादिति ङीष् वा। नक्तंदिवं—Dwandwa see com. The indeclinables नक्तं and दिवा are always used in the sense of the Loc; and the Dwandwas नक्तंदिवं, रात्रिदिवं &c. are also used in the sense of the Loc. But there are such instances as व्यस्तरात्रिन्दिवस्य (Kum. II.

8.) and the Bhāshyakāra has used दोषा and दिवा as Acc. in दोषा-मन्यमह:; दिवामन्याराात्रि:. On the strength of such usage it can be held that नक्तं and दिवा (in the present case) may as well be used in the sense of the Nom. or Acc. and so the poet may have used नक्तंदिवं as Acc. to विभज्य; see Malli. on Kum. referred to above. विभज्य—separating into parts *i. e.* having assigned different parts of night and day to the performance of different duties. See note on षष्ठे भागे Vik. II. 1.

नयेन—with proper regard to policy. वितन्यते—is continuously put forth. Fired by the ambition to reach the high level marked out by Manu for an ideal king Duryodhana has been discharging his royal duties at stated times without ever being remiss in them asserting his royal position at the same time.

From Sls. 10-22 is described the general policy pursued by Duryodhana. He has won the affections of all—

संप्रति भृत्याद्यनुरागमाह—

सखीनिव प्रीतियुजोऽनुजीविनः समानमानान्सुहृदश्च बन्धुभिः ।
स सन्ततं दर्शयते गतस्मयः कृताधिपत्यामिव साधु बन्धुताम् ॥१०॥

अन्वयः—गतस्मयः सः अनुजीविनः प्रीतियुजः सखीनिव सुहृदः बन्धुभिः समानमानान् इव बन्धुतां कृताधिपत्यामिव साधु सन्ततं दर्शयते ॥ १० ॥

सखीनिति ॥ [गतःस्मयो यस्य सः] गतस्मयो निरहङ्कारोऽतएव स दुर्योधनः सन्ततमनारतं साधु सम्यक् । अकपटमित्यर्थः । अनुजीविनो भृत्यान् । [प्रीतिं युञ्जन्ति तान्] प्रीतियुजः स्निग्धान्सखीनिव मित्राणीव । दर्शयते । लोकस्येति शेषः ॥ "हेतुमति च" इति णिच् "णिचश्च" इत्यात्मनेपदम् ॥ शोभनं हृदयं येषां तान्सुहृदो मित्राणि च ॥ "सुहृद्दुर्हृदौ मित्रामित्रयोः" इति निपातः ॥ बन्धुभिर्भ्रात्रादिभिः [समानः मानः येषां ते, तान्] समानमानांस्तुल्यसत्कारान्दर्शयते । बन्धूनां समूहो बन्धुता ताम् ॥ "ग्रामजनबन्धुसहायेभ्यस्तल्" कृतमाधिपत्यं स्वाम्यं यस्यास्तां कृताधिपत्यामिव दर्शयते । बन्धूनधिपतीनिव दर्शयत इत्यर्थः । यथा भृत्यादिषु सख्यादिबुद्धिर्जायते लोकस्य तथा तान्सम्भावयतीत्यर्थः ॥ अनुजीव्यादीनाम् "कर्तुरीप्सिततमं कर्म" इति कर्मत्वम् ।

पूर्वं त्वस्मिन्नेव पदान्वये वाक्यार्थमित्थं वर्णयन्ति । स राजानुजीव्यादीन्सख्यादीनिव दर्शयते । सख्यादय इव ते तु तं पश्यन्ति । सख्यादिभावेन पश्यतस्तांस्तथा दर्शयते । स्वयमेव छन्दानुवर्तितया स्वदर्शनं तेभ्यः प्रयच्छतीत्यर्थः । अत्रापि स्वस्येप्सितकर्मत्वम् । "अणिचि कर्तुरनुजीव्यादेरभिवादिदृशोरात्मनेपदमुपसंख्यानम्" इति पाक्षिकं कर्मत्वम् । एवं चात्राण्यन्तकर्मणो राज्ञोऽण्यन्ते कर्तृत्वेऽपि "आरोह्यते हस्ती स्वयमेव" इत्यादिवदश्रूयमाणकर्मान्तराभावान्नायं णेरणादिसूत्रस्य विषय इति मत्वा "णिचश्च" इत्यात्मनेपदं प्रतिपेदिरे । भाष्ये तु णेरणादिसूत्रविषयत्वमप्यस्योक्तम् । यथाह—" 'पश्यंति भृत्या राजानम्' 'दर्शयते भृत्यान्राजा' 'दर्शयते भृत्यै राजा' अत्रात्मनेपदं सिद्धं भवति" इति । अत्राह कैयटः—ननु कर्मान्तरसद्भावादत्रात्मनेपदेन संभाव्यम् । उच्यते । अस्मादेवोदाहरणाद्भाष्यकारस्यायमेवाभिप्राय ऊह्यते । अण्यन्तावस्थायां ये कर्तृकर्मणी तद्व्यतिरिक्तकर्मान्तरसद्भावादात्मनेपदं न भवति । यथा—"स्थलमारोहयति मनुष्यान्" इतीह त्वण्यन्तावस्थायां कर्तॄणां भृत्यानां णौ कर्मत्वमिति भवत्येवात्मनेपदमिति ।

अन्वयार्थः—(**गतस्मयः**) चला गया है अहंकार जिसका ऐसा (**सः**) वह (**संततम्**) निरन्तर (**साधु**) भलीभाँति (**अनुजीविनः**) नौकरों को (**प्रीतियुजः**) (**सखीनिव**) प्रिय मित्रों की तरह, (**सुहृदः**) मित्रों को (**बन्धुभिः समानमानान्**) बन्धुओं जैसा आदरणीय (**बन्धुताम्**) बन्धु-समुदाय को (**कृताधिपत्यामिव**) बनाया है स्वामित्व जिसका ऐसा (**दर्शयते**) [दुनियां को] दिखाता है ।

निरभिमानी वह दुर्योधन निष्कपट होकर सदा, सेवकों के साथ मित्रों जैसा मित्रों के साथ सगे-सम्बन्धियों जैसा तथा आदरणीय और सगों के प्रति, मानो उन्हें ही अधिपति बना दिया हो ऐसा, सांसारिक व्यवहार करता है ।

10. With his arrogance gone (set aside) he always shows (conducts himself towards) in a skilful manner (or with sincerity) his servants, as if they were his affectionate friends, his friends as if they commanded the respect due to relatives (*i. e.* treats them as his relatives) and his relatives as if the sovereignty were made over to them (*i. e.* makes them feel that they were the possessors of royal power).

Sl. 10. A good king, if he wishes to please all must set aside self-conceit and this he has done. मतस्मयः—गतः + स्मयः यस्य with his hauteur or vanity gone. स्मय fr. स्मि + अच्; *cf.* तस्मै स्मयावेशविवर्जिताय Rag. V. 19. प्रभवः स्मयदूषिताः Bh. प्रीतियुजः—प्रीत्या युज्यते ते प्रीतयुजः fr. युज् + क्विप् (०) तान् साधु—Well, earnestly (and not outwardly). दर्शयते—shows to the world, *i. e.* treats, गिणच्श्च (com.) means.—In the case of causal verbs also (कर्तृगे फले आत्मनेपदं) the Atm. is used when the fruit of the action accures to the agent. Here Suyodhana would reap the benefit of showing to the people his treatment of his servants as friends &c. and so the Atm. is used. अनुजीविनः &c. are the objects of the verb as they are ईप्सिततम to the agent. That which the agent desires most to attain by an action is its Karman. See com.

How does he treat his friends then, सुहृदः:—see com.—हृदय becomes हृद् when compounded with सु and दुर् in the sense of a friend and enemy respectively. समान०—with the respect due to one's brothers *i.e.* as brothers. बन्धुता—बन्धु fr. बन्ध् + उ (Uṇādi) बध्नन्ति इति बन्धवः. The aff. ता shows collection; similarly ग्रामता, जनता, सहायता. The meaning is, from his conduct towards his servants &c. the people come to believe that they are his friends and so on. The Commentators that preceded Malli. hold a different view. According to them the meaning is the king treats his servants as friends. The servants too regard him as a friend and so on; and he also acts towards them in conformity with the belief of theirs. See com. The gram. discussion introduced by Malli is not of much interest to the student. Those who wish to know it may read the following—

Having given his own interpretation Malli. cites the opinion of the Commentators anterior to him. Thus—Former Commentators while giving the same construction interpret the passage thus—The king shows *i. e.* treats his servants as if they were his friends, and so on. They too look upon (act towards) him like friends; and as they behold him in the capacity of a friend he allows them to appear like that. In other words acting according to their wishes he allows himself to be looked upon in that light. So here he *i. e.* स्वं or आत्मानं is the ईप्सितकर्म अनुजीविन: &c. were the subjects of the root दृश् in its non-causal (अणि) form and they become the objects (optionally) of the root in its causal form by the rule अभिवादि—*i. e.* —The original subjects of the roots अभिवाद् and दृश when used in the Atm. in their causal forms may be put in the objective or the instrumental case.

Now the Sūtra णेरणौ यत्कर्म णौ चेत्स कर्ताऽनाध्याने (Pān. I. 3. 67) lays down that if the object of a verb in its non- causal form becomes its subject in its causal form; and if the action implied by the verb in the causal form is the same as in the primitive form, then the verb would take Atm. but not when it means to remember anxiously (ण्यन्तादात्मनेपदं स्यादणौ या क्रिया सैव चेत् ण्यन्तेनोच्येत अणौ यत्कर्मकारकं स चेत् णौ कर्ता स्यादनाध्याने Sid. Kau.) Now here though the object of the primitive root दृश् (सखाय इव ते तं पश्यन्ति &c.) has become the subject of the the causal verb (स तान् &c.) yet the Sūtra does not wholly apply to the present case, for it is not analogous to the example आरोहयते हस्ती स्वयमेव in which there is absence of a directly mentioned object while in the present instance there is no absence of a directly mentioned object (श्रूयमाण कर्म is distinguished from a karma which is गम्यमान or उह्य to be understood or inferred). The Atm. therefore, must be explained by the rule णिचश्च.

Malli. then remarks that according to the Bhāshyakāra the present instance comes under the operation of the rule णेरणौ&c. and quotes Kaiyaṭa's opinion who says—if there be an object in the causal form different from the subject or the object of the non-causal verb then the Atm. would be barred; as in

स्थलमारोहयति मनुष्यान् (मनुष्या हस्तिनमारोहन्ति...हस्ती स्वयमेव मनुष्यानारोहयते हस्ती मनुष्यान्स्थलमारोहयति.) But here the servants, the subject of the non-causal verb become the object in the Cau. form and so the Atm. does have scope.

Next he shows that he (Dur.) is not inattentive to the securing of the triad, Dharma, Artha and Kăma.

न चायं त्रिवर्गात्प्रमाद्यतीत्याह—

असक्तमाराधयतो यथायथं विभज्य भक्त्या समपक्षपातया ।
गुणानुरागादिव सख्यमीयिवान्न बाधतेऽस्य त्रिगणः परस्परम् ॥११॥

अन्वयः—यथायथं विभज्य समपक्षपातया भक्त्या असक्तम् आराधयत अस्य त्रिगणः गुणानुरागात् सख्यम् ईयिवान् इव परस्परं न बाधते ॥ ११ ॥

असक्तमिति ॥ यथायथं यथास्वं विभज्य । असङ्कीर्णरूपं विविच्येत्यर्थः ॥ "यथास्वे यथायथम्" इति निपातनाद् द्विर्भावो नपुंसकत्वं च। "ह्रस्वो नपुंसके प्रातिपदिकस्य" इति ह्रस्वत्वम् ॥ पक्षे पातः पक्षपात आसक्तिविशेषः समस्तुल्यो यस्यां सा तया समपक्षपातया । भक्त्यानुरागविशेषेण । पूज्येष्वनुरागो भक्तिरित्युपदेशः । पूज्यश्चायं त्रिवर्गः इति भावः । असक्तमनासक्तम् । अव्यसनितयेति यावत् । आराध्रयतः सेवमानस्यास्य दुर्योधनस्य त्रयाणां धर्मार्थकामानां गणस्त्रिगणस्त्रिवर्गः ॥ "त्रिवर्गो धर्मकामार्थैश्चतुर्वर्गः समोक्षकैः" इत्यमरः ॥ गुणानुरागात्तदीयगुणेष्वनुरागात् । गुणवदाश्रयलोभादित्यर्थः । सख्यं मैत्रीम् ॥ "सख्युर्यः" इति यप्रत्ययः ॥ ईयिवानुपगतवानिवेत्युत्प्रेक्षा ॥ "उपेयिवाननाश्वाननूचानश्च" इति क्वसुप्रत्ययान्तो निपातः ॥ नात्रोपसर्गस्तन्त्रम्" इति काशिकाकार आह स्म ॥ परस्परं न बाधते । समवर्तित्वादस्य धर्मार्थकामाः परस्परानुपमर्देन वर्धन्त इत्यर्थः । उक्तं च— "धर्मार्थकामाः सममेव सेव्या यो ह्येकसक्तः स जनो जघन्यः" इति ।

अन्वयार्थः—(**यथायथम्**) यथानुरूप (**विभज्य**) विभाग करके (**समपक्षपातया**) समान पक्षपात वाली (**भक्त्या**) भक्ति से (**असक्तम्**) अनासक्त (**आराधयतः**) सेवन करते हुए (**अस्य**) इसका (**त्रिगणः**) त्रिवर्ग (**गुणानुरागात्**)

गुणों में अनुरक्ति के कारण (**इव**) मानो (**सख्यम्**) मैत्री को (**ईयिवान्**) प्राप्त हुआ-हुआ (**परस्परम्**) आपस में (**न बाधते**) संघर्ष को प्राप्त नहीं होता ।

वह दुर्योधन निष्पक्ष होकर भक्तिपूर्वक धर्मार्थकाम-रूप त्रिवर्ग का सेवन कार्यक्रमानुसार [इस समय धर्म का सेवन, उस समय अर्थ का एवं अमुक काल में काम का] निःसङ्ग भाव से करता है । इस कारण त्रिवर्ग दुर्योधन के गुणों में अनुरक्त है, और इस त्रिवर्ग का, स्वभावतः परस्पर-विरोधी होते हुए भी कभी संघर्ष नहीं होता, मानो एक-दूसरे के साथ इनकी मित्रता हो गई हो ।

11. The three objects (of human life) which he seeks to obtain with proper discrimination and with a devotion showing equal regard for all, but without being specially attached to any one of these, do not conflict with one another, in his case, as if having formed a friendly relation between themselves out of their love for his virtues.

Sl. 11. यथायथं—*Adv.* यथास्वे यथायथं (Păn. VIII. 1. 14) यथास्वमिति वीप्सायामव्ययीभावः । यः आत्मा यच्चात्मीयं तद्यथास्वं तस्मिन् यथा-शब्दस्य द्वे क्लीबत्वं च निपात्यते Sid. Kau. The word यथायथं is irregularly formed in the sense of यथास्व. What is one's proper nature or whatever is natural to one is यथास्व. In this sense is formed the *indec.* यथायथं there being the doubling of यथा and *neuter* gender. It means according to one's nature, विभज्य—dividing them according to their respective natures; with due discrimination. समपक्ष०—With equal attachment to or leaning towards each. असक्तं—न सक्तं यथा तथा without being specially attached to. आराधयतः—of him trying to secure, seeking.

त्रिगणः—The three objects of human existence, according to Hindu writers, are—Dharma or merit accruing from the performance of religious duties. This is the first object to which is subordinate, Artha or wealth the second object should be gained but in a manner not to do violence to Dharma. *Káma* or the satisfaction of desires is the third object. This should be attained in conformity with the other two; *i. e.* in a manner not contrary to religious injunctions and the proper saving of money. These three are preparatory to the fourth, *viz. Moksha.*

परस्परं न—Acc. of बाधते. This is not a compound word. By the rule कर्मव्यतीहारे सर्वनाम्नो द्वे वाच्ये। समासवच्च बहुलम्। Vărtikas on Păn. VIII. 1. 12 a pronoun is reduplicated when reciprocity or interchange of action is implied, and the word so formed is often a comp. and sometimes not. A compound is not allowed in the case of पर and अन्य as remarked by Bhaṭṭoji Dikshita (बहुलग्रहणादन्यपरयोर्न समासवत् इतरशब्दस्य तु नित्यम्). Then by the Vărtika 'असमासवद्भावे पूर्वपदस्थस्य सुपः सुर्वक्तव्य' When compounding is precluded whatever may be the case ending of the first word it is replaced by स् (सु of the Nom. sing.). So we have here first परंपरम् and then परःपरम्. Then by the rule कस्कादिषु च (Păn. VIII. 3. 48.) the Visarga is changed to स् and we have परस्परम्.

ईयिवान्—इयाय इति. The Sūtra sanctions the form उपेयिवस् (the perf. p. of इ with उप), but ईयिवस् also occurs in language, as here. Hence Vămana, the author of the Kăśik'ā, remarks—The mention of the prep. उप in the Sūtra must be regarded as immaterial. See com. न बाधते—*i. e.* does not invade or trench upon the province of the other.

In the following three Ślokas is described his mastery over the four *Upāyas* or political expedients or means of success.

अथ श्लोकत्रयेणोपायकौशल्यं दर्शयन्नादौ सामदाने दर्शयति—

निरत्ययं साम न दानवर्जितं न भूरि दानं विरहय्य सत्क्रियाम् ।
प्रवर्तते तस्य विशेषशालिनी गुणानुरोधेन विना न सत्क्रिया ॥१२॥

अन्वयः—तस्य निरत्ययं साम दानवर्जितं न प्रवर्तते सत्क्रियां विरहय्य भूरिदानं न (प्रवर्तते) गुणानुरोधेन विना विशेषशालिनी सत्क्रिया न (प्रवर्तते) ॥१२॥

निरत्ययमिति ॥ तस्य दुर्योधनस्य निरत्ययं निर्बाधम् । अमायिकमित्यर्थः ।

अन्यथा जनानां दुर्ग्रहत्वादिति भावः। साम सान्त्वम् ॥ "साम सान्त्वमुभे समे" इत्यमरः ॥ दानवर्जितं न प्रवर्तते। अन्यथा लुब्धप्रवर्तनस्य शुद्धाप्रियैर्वाक्यैर्दुष्करत्वादिति भावः। उक्तं च—"लुब्धमर्थेन गृह्णीयात्साधुमञ्जलिकर्मणा। मूर्खं छन्दानुरोधेन तत्त्वार्थेन च पण्डितम्" इति। तथा भूरि प्रभूतम्। न तु कदाचित्स्वल्पमित्यर्थः। दानं धनत्यागः ॥ सदित्यादरार्थेऽव्ययम् ॥ "आदरानादरयोः सदसती" इति निपातसंज्ञास्मरणात् ॥ तस्य क्रियां सत्क्रियां विरहय्य विहाय ॥ "ल्यपि लघुपूर्वात्" इत्ययादेशः ॥ न प्रवर्तते ॥ अनादरे दानवैफल्यादिति भावः। न चैवं सर्वत्र येनाविवेकित्वं कोशहानिश्च स्यादित्याह—प्रेति ॥ विशेषशालिन्यतिशययोगिनी सत्क्रियादरक्रिया गुणानुरोधेन गुणानुरागेण विना न प्रवर्तते ॥ "पृथग्विना—" इत्यादिना तृतीया ॥ "गुणेष्वेवादरो भूरिदानं च" इति नोक्तदोषावकाश इत्यर्थः ॥ अत्रोत्तरोत्तरस्य पूर्वपूर्वविशेषणतया स्थापनादेकावल्यलङ्कारः। तदुक्तं काव्यप्रकाशे—"स्थाप्यतेऽपोह्यते वापि यथापूर्वं परस्परम्। विशेषणतया वस्तु यत्र सैकावली द्विधा" इति ॥

अन्वयार्थः—(**तस्य**) उसकी (**निरत्ययम्**) निर्दोष=निश्छल (**साम**) साम उपाय (**दानवर्जितम्**) बिना दान के (**न प्रवर्तते**) प्रवृत्त नहीं होता। (**भूरि दानम्**) प्रभूत दान (**सत्क्रियाम्**) सत्कार को (**विरहय्य**) छोड़ कर (**न**) नहीं होता। (**विशेषशालिनी**) वैशिष्ट्य सम्पन्न करने वाली (**सत्क्रिया**) आदर-क्रिया (**गुणानुरोधेन विना न**) गुणानुराग के बिना नहीं होती।

दुर्योधन की तुष्टिकरण की नीति (साम-दाम-दण्ड-भेद में से प्रथम उपाय) निश्छल एवं दान से युक्त होती है। दूसरा उपाय अर्थात् दान सत्कार सहित दिया जाता है। वैशिष्ट्य से युक्त कराने वाला यह सत्कार, सत्कृत व्यक्ति के गुणानुराग के कारण होता है।

12. His adoption (policy) of conciliation which is unobstructed (ever successful) does not proceed without being accompanied by gifts; his munificient gifts are not made without due honour being shown; and his conferring of honour, which is marked by special distinction, does not proceed without due regard to merits.

Sl. 12. Herein is described his use of *Sámon* and *Dána*.

निरत्ययं—निर्गतः अत्ययः यस्मात् which is free from obstruction or failure ; unobstructed; successful, effective. सामन्—conciliation; adoption of pacific measures. दान०—a money gift is necessary to conciliate those who are avaricious or in need of money. भूरि—munificent, liberal. विरहय्य —*Indec.* p. of रह् ; before य अय् is retained. सत्क्रिया—सत् तस्य क्रिया Gen. Tat. सत् and असत् are indeclinable in the sense of respect and disrespect respectively. विशेष—असत् विशेषेन शालते असौ marked by special distinction or honour (excess, according to Malli.).

अथ दण्डप्रकारमाह—

वसूनि वाञ्छन्न वशी न मन्युना 'स्वधर्म इत्येव' निवृत्तकारणः ।
गुरूपदिष्टेन रिपौ सुतेऽपि वा निहन्ति दण्डेन स धर्मविप्लवम् ॥१३॥

अन्वयः—स वशी वसूनि न वाञ्छन् न च मन्युना निवृत्तकारणः (सन्) स्वधर्म इत्येव गुरूपदिष्टेन दण्डेन रिपौ सुतेऽपि वा (स्थितं) धर्मविप्लवं निहन्ति ॥१३॥

वसूनीति ॥ वशी स दुर्योधनो वसूनि धनानि वाञ्छन्न । लोभान्नेत्यर्थः "वसु तोये धने मणौ" इति वैजयन्ती ॥ निहन्तीति शेषः । तथा मन्युना कोपेन न च ॥ "मन्युर्दैन्ये क्रतौ क्रुधि" इत्यमरः ॥ "धर्मशास्त्रानुसारेण क्रोधलोभविवर्जितः" इति स्मरणादित्यर्थः । किंतु निवृत्तकारणो निवृत्तलोभादिनिमित्तः सन्स्वधर्म इत्येव । स्वस्य राज्ञः सतो ममायं धर्मो ममेदं कर्तव्यमित्यस्मादेव हेतोरित्यर्थः । "अदण्ड्यान्दण्डयन्राजा दण्ड्यांश्चैवाप्यदण्डयन् । अयशो महदाप्नोति नरकं चैव गच्छति" इति स्मरणादिति भावः । गुरूपदिष्टेन प्राड्विवाकोपदिष्टेन । "धर्मशास्त्रं पुरस्कृत्य प्राड्विवाकमते स्थितः । समाहितमतिः पश्येद्व्यवहारानानुक्रमात्" इति नारदस्मरणात् । दण्डेन दमेन । शिक्षयेत्यर्थः । रिपौ सुतेऽपि वा । स्थितमिति शेषः । एतेनास्य समदर्शित्वमुक्तम् । धर्मविप्लवं धर्मव्यतिक्रमम् । अधर्ममिति यावत् । निहन्ति निवारयति । दुष्ट एवास्य शत्रुः शिष्टः एव बन्धुः । न तु सम्बन्धनिबन्धनः पक्षपातोऽस्तीत्यर्थः ॥

अन्वयार्थः—(**वशी**) जितेन्द्रिय (**सः**) वह (**वसूनि**) धनों को (**वाञ्छन् न**) चाहता हुआ नहीं, (**मन्युना न**) न ही क्रोध से [किन्तु] (**निवृत्तकारणः**) समाप्त हो गये हैं [उपर्युक्त लोभादि] कारण जिसके ऐसा हुआ-हुआ (**स्वधर्म इत्येव**) अपना कर्तव्य है, इसी कारण से, (**गुरूपदिष्टेन**) न्यायाधीश के कहे हुए (**दण्डेन**) दण्ड से (**रिपौ**) शत्रु में (**सुतेऽपि वा**) अथवा पुत्र में (**धर्मविप्लवम्**) धर्मोल्लङ्घन (**निहन्ति**) को रोकता है।

जितेन्द्रिय वह दुर्योधन शत्रु और पुत्र का लिहाज किये बिना, अधर्म का दण्ड से दमन करता है। उसका यह दमन कर्तव्य-भावना से होता है, इसमें न किसी प्रकार का आर्थिक लाभ कारण होता है और न ही किसी के प्रति व्यक्तिगत क्रोध।

13. Neither desirous of wealth nor influenced by spite (lit. anger), but because it is his (absolute) duty to do so and from no other motive, he, who is self-controlled, checks any infringement of duty (crime), be it on the part of his son or a foe, by inflicting punishment according to the advice of the judges.

Sl. 13. In this sl. he describes Duryodhana's *Daṇḍa* or punishment of offenders.

वशी—वशोस्यास्तीति self controlled (able to resist temptations). वसूनि...न मन्युना किंतु स्वधर्म इति *i.e.* in chastising offenders it is not his object to swell his treasury by inflicting heavy fines or to satisfy private grudge by punishing those not really guilty. He does it because it is his stern duty to do so. इति is here हेतौ. इति हेतुप्रकरणप्रकाशादिसमाप्तिषु। इत्यमरः निवृत्त०—निवृत्तं कारणं यस्य सः।

गुरूप०—Guru means here व्यवहारगुरु a legal guide or judge. दण्डेन—दण्ड is derived fr. दम 4 p. to tame, to subdue, and the Uṇādi aff. ड (I. 114). It is of three kinds—वधोर्थग्रहणं चैव परिक्लेशस्तथैव च इति दंड विधानज्ञैर्दण्डोऽपि त्रिविधः स्मृतः।। रिपौ, सुते—आधारे सप्तमी धर्मविप्लव—Dharma means here secular and religious duties, any unrighteous and illegal deed. विप्लव—transgression or violation of.

संप्रति भेदकौशलं दर्शयति—

विधाय रक्षान्परितः परेतरानशङ्किताकारमुपैति शङ्कितः ।
क्रियापवर्गेष्वनुजीविसात्कृताः कृतज्ञतामस्य वदन्ति सम्पदः ॥१४॥

अन्वयः—शङ्कितः (सन्) परितः परेतरान् रक्षान् विधाय अशङ्किताकारम् उपैति । क्रियापवर्गेषु अनुजीविसात्कृताः सम्पदः अस्य कृतज्ञतां वदन्ति ॥ १४ ॥

विधायेति ॥ शङ्का सञ्जातास्य शङ्कितोऽविश्वस्तः सन्परितः सर्वत्र स्वपरमण्डले परेतरानात्मीयान् । अवञ्चकानिति यावत् । यद्वा परानितरयन्ति भेदेनात्मसात्कुर्वन्तीति परेतरान् ॥ तत्करोतीति ण्यन्तात्कर्मण्यण्प्रत्ययः ॥ रक्षन्तीति रक्षान्रक्षकान् । मन्त्रगुप्तिसमर्थानित्यर्थः ॥ "नन्दिग्रहि—" इत्यादिना पचाद्यच् ॥ विधाय कृत्वा । नियुज्येत्यर्थः अशङ्किताकारमुपैति । स्वयमविश्वस्तोऽपि विश्वस्तवदेव व्यवहरन्परमुखेनैव परान्भिनत्तीत्यर्थः । न च तान्रक्षानुपेक्षते येन तेऽपि विकुर्वीरन्नित्याह—**क्रियेति** ॥ क्रियापवर्गेषु कर्मसमाप्तिष्वनुजीविसात्कृता भृत्याधीनाः कृताः । अपरावर्तितया दत्ता इत्यर्थः ॥"देये त्रा च" इति सातिप्रत्ययः ॥ सम्पदोऽस्य राज्ञः कृतज्ञतामुपकारित्वं वदन्ति । प्रीतिदानैरेवास्य प्रकाश्यते न तु वाङ्मात्रेणेत्यर्थः । कृतज्ञे राजन्यनुजीविनोऽनुरज्यन्तेऽनुरक्ताश्च तं रक्षन्तीति भावः ॥

अन्वयार्थः—(शंकितः) अविश्वस्त [होता हुआ] **(परितः)** सर्वत्र **(परेतरान्)** आत्मीय **(रक्षान्)** रक्षकों को **(विधाय)** [नियुक्त] करके **(अशङ्किताकारमुपैति)** निःशङ्क भाव को प्राप्त करता है । **(क्रियापवर्गेषु)** कार्य-समाप्तियों पर **(अनुजीविसात्कृताः)** भृत्यों के आधीन की हुई **(संपदः)** संपत्तियाँ **(अस्य)** इसकी **(कृतज्ञताम्)** कृतज्ञता को **(वदन्ति)** कहती हैं ।

अपने एवं शत्रु-राज्य में सर्वत्र विश्वसनीय गुप्तचरों को नियुक्त करके, वस्तुतः उनके प्रति अविश्वस्त होता हुआ भी, विश्वस्त-जैसा व्यवहार करता है; और फिर कार्य की समाप्ति पर कृतज्ञता को अनुभव करता हुआ इन सेवकों को खूब पुरस्कार देता है ।

14. Having placed all round trusty guards (or, according to Malli.—having employed secret agents skilled in discord to

watch the doings of his party as well as that of the enemy) he puts on the appearance of being unsuspicious (or approaches *i. e.* deals with them with an unsuspecting air), although (inwardly) suspicious (apprehensive of treachery), while his riches fully (liberally) bestowed on his servants when their (respective) duties are performed, proclaim his gratefulness (or, appreciation of their services).

Sl. 14. शङ्कितः—तदस्य सञ्जातमिति तारकादिभ्य इतच् Suspecting treachery, apprehensive of danger from them. परेतरान् परेभ्य इतरे परेतराः those other than strangers or treacherously disposed i. e. faithful, trusted. Or परानितरयन्ति (see com.) उपपदसमासः the comp. is not a pronoun, those who win over others to their side weaning them from their masters (by भेद or sowing dissention in an enemy's party). Or परे enemies इतरे येभ्यः । ते परेतराः Bah. This also has no सर्वनामसंज्ञा. The first two ways are better, however, रक्षान्—body.guards or, persons able to observe secrecy. अशङ्किता°—न शङ्कितः अशङ्कितः तस्य आकारः अशङ्किताकारस्तमुपैति or अशङ्कितः आकारो यथा स्यात्तथा तानुपैति in a manner not to show that he suspects or distrusts them, *i. e.* although he knows that the men are trustworthy he does not repose absolute confidence in them; or with a look or air of confidence. *Cf.* अविश्वासी तथा च स्याद्यथा च व्यवहारवान् । विश्वासयेदविश्वस्तान्विश्वस्तान्नातिविश्वसेत् ॥ Kăm. Nit. V. 89, 90.

क्रियापवर्ग—क्रिया the business entrusted. अपवर्ग fr. वृज् with अप+अ (घञ्) means here the completion of, execution or accomplishment of. अपवर्गस्त्यागमोक्षयोः । क्रियावसाने साकल्ये' इति हैमः । For the meaning of त्याग or discharging *cf.* further on मुष्टेरसंभेद इवापवर्गे (XVI. 20). °सात्कृताः—given so as not to be taken back *i. e.* given as a reward. In this sense the affix त्रा or सात् may be used. The Sūtra देये त्राच must be taken along with the previous Sūtra तदधीनवचने (V. 41 54); विप्राधीनं देयं करोति विप्रत्राकरोति पक्षे

विप्रसात्करोति (Sid. Kau.) **कृतज्ञता**—appreciation of service done. **सम्पदः**—*i. e.* he rewards his servants' discharge of their duties not by praises alone but by actual money-presents.

अथोपायप्रयोगस्य फलवत्तां दर्शयति—

अनारतं तेन पदेषु लम्भिता विभज्य सम्यग्विनियोगसत्क्रियाः ।
फलन्त्युपायाः परिबृंहितायतीरुपेत्य संघर्षमिवार्थसम्पदः ॥ १५ ॥

अन्वयः—तेन पदेषु सम्यक् विभज्य विनियोगसत्क्रियाः लम्भिताः । उपायाः संघर्षम् उपेत्य इव परिबृंहितायतीः अर्थसम्पदः अनारतं फलन्ति ॥ १५ ॥

अनारतमिति ॥ तेन राज्ञा दुर्योधनेन पदेषूपायवस्तुषु ॥ "पदं व्यवसितत्राणस्थानलक्ष्माङ्घ्रिवस्तुषु" इत्यमरः ॥ सम्यगसङ्कीर्णमव्यस्तं च विभज्य विविच्य । विनियोग एव सत्क्रियानुग्रहः । सत्कार इति यावत् । यासां ता लम्भिताः । स्थानेषु सम्यक्प्रयुक्ता इत्यर्थः । उपायविशेषणं वा । उपायाः सामादयः । संघर्षं परस्परस्पर्धामुपेत्येवेत्युत्प्रेक्षा । परिबृंहितायतीः प्रचितोत्तरकालाः । स्थिरा इत्यर्थः । अर्थसम्पदोऽनारतमजस्रं फलन्ति । प्रसुवत इत्यर्थः ॥

अन्वयार्थः—(**तेन**) उसके द्वारा (**पदेषु**) उपयुक्त प्रयोग-स्थानों पर (**सम्यक्**) भलीभाँति (**विविच्य**) विवेचना करके (**विनियोग एव**) [यह समीचीन] प्रयोग ही है (**सत्क्रिया**) सत्कार जिनका, ऐसे (**लम्भिता**) प्राप्त कराये गये [प्रयोग किये गए] (**उपायाः**) साम-दामादि उपाय (**संघर्षम्**) परस्पर स्पर्धा को (**उपेत्य इव**) मानो प्राप्त करके (**परिबृंहितायतीः**) सुसमृद्ध भविष्य वाली (**अर्थसंपदः**) धन-सम्पदाओं को (**अनारतम्**) निरन्तर (**फलन्ति**) फलते हैं ।

वह दुर्योधन उपयुक्त अवसरों पर सूझ-बूझ के साथ साम-दामादि उपायों का प्रयोग करता है । यह समीचीन प्रयोग ही इन उपायों का सत्कार है । और यों सत्कारपूर्वक प्रयुक्त ये उपाय मानो आपस में होड़ लगाकर चिरस्थायी सम्पदाओं को निरन्तर उत्पन्न करते हैं ।

15. The (four) means of success being used by him in their proper spheres of action with due regards to their expediency and thus honoured by being rightly employed, ever produce

(lead to), as if emulating with one another, happy results that have a prosperous future (permanent prosperity).

Sl. 15. पदेषु—proper spheres of action, right places. सम्यक् विभज्य—having judiciously assigned; *i. e.* without mixing them up or confusion, विनियोगस०—लम्भिता qualifies उपाया:, विनियोग—proper employment. लम्भित—p. p. p. of लभ् Cau. In the Cau. form the subject of the primitive root takes the objective case by the rule गतिबुद्धिप्रत्यवसानार्थ &c. (Păn. I. 4. 52) लभ् is a गत्यर्थ root. उपाया; विनियोगसत्क्रियां लभन्ते; Cau. स उपायान् विनि० लम्भयति। Active voice, तेन उपाया: विनि० लम्भिता:। Pass, voice. Or विनियो० may qualify उपाया: directly विनियोग एव सत्क्रिया येषां ते॥ उपाया:—means of success भेदो दण्ड: साम दानमित्युपायचतुष्टयम् Amara. संघर्ष—fr. घृष् with सम्+अ (घञ्); lit. collision, friction; hence emulation, rivalry. *Cf.* नाट्याचार्ययोर्महान् ज्ञानसंघर्षो जात: Mal. I. परिबृंहिता०—परिबृंहित p. p. p. of बृह with परि 6, P. to grow or increase (all round); hence thriven or grown prosperous. आयति—future time (see *infra*, sl. 23; II. 14, 43; III, 43 &c.); having a prosperous future, hence steady, permanent, अर्थसं०—अर्थानां सम्पद:। or अर्था एव सम्पदस्ता:। अनारतं—always, continuously; अविद्यमानम् आरतं (stoppage) यस्मिन् आरत p. p. n. fr. रम with आ.

अर्थसम्पदमेवाह—

अनेकराजन्यरथाश्वसङ्कुलं तदीयमास्थाननिकेतनाजिरम्।
नयत्ययुग्मच्छदगन्धिरार्द्रतां भृशं नृपोपायनदन्तिनां मद:॥ १६॥

अन्वय:—नृपोपायनदन्तिनां अयुग्मच्छदगन्धि: मद: तदीयम् अनेकराजन्यरथाश्वसङ्कुलं आस्थाननिकेतनाजिरं भृशं आर्द्रतां नयति॥ १६॥

अनेकेति॥ अयुग्मच्छदस्य सप्तपर्णपुष्पस्य गन्ध इव गन्धो यस्यासावयुग्मच्छदगन्धि:॥ "सप्तम्युपमान–" इत्यादिना बहुव्रीहिरुत्तरपदलोपश्च। "उपमानाच्च इति समासान्त इकार:॥ नृपाणामुपायनान्युपहारभूता ये दन्तिनस्तेषां मद:॥ 'उपायनमुपग्राह्यमुपहारस्तथोपदा" इत्यमर:॥ राज्ञामपत्यानि पुमांसो राजन्या:

क्षत्रियाः ॥ "राजश्वशुराद्यत्" इति यत्प्रत्ययः राज्ञोऽपत्ये जातिग्रहणादण् ॥ रथाश्चाश्वाश्च रथाश्वम् ॥ सेनाङ्गत्वादेकवद्भावः ॥ अनेकेषां राजन्यानां रथाश्वेन सङ्कुलं व्याप्तं तदीयमास्थाननिकेतनाजिरं सभामण्डपाङ्गणम् ॥ "अङ्गणं चत्वराजिरे" इत्यमरः ॥ भृशमत्यर्थमार्द्रतां पङ्किलत्वं नयति । एतेन महासमृद्धिरस्योक्ता । अत एवोदात्तालङ्कारः । तथा चालङ्कारसूत्रम्—"समृद्धिमद्वस्तुवर्णनमुदात्तः" इति ॥

अन्वयार्थः—(**नृपोपायनदन्तिनाम्**) राजाओं के उपहारभूत हाथियों का (**अयुग्मच्छदगन्धिः**) सप्तपर्ण के पुष्प की गन्ध के समान है गन्ध जिसकी ऐसा (**मदः**) मदजल, (**अनेकराजन्यरथाश्वसंकुलम्**) अनेक राजाओं के रथ के घोड़ों से व्याप्त (**तदीयम्**) उसके (**आस्थाननिकेतनाजिरम्**) सभामण्डप के प्राङ्गण को (**आर्द्रताम्**) गीलेपन को (**नयति**) प्राप्त कराता है।

उस दुर्योधन के सभामण्डप का आँगन राजाओं के रथ के घोड़ों से खचाखच भरा रहता है। और इस आँगन में छिड़काव, उपहार रूप में प्राप्त हाथियों के सुगन्धित मदजल से होता है।

16. The rut, having the smell of (the flowers of) the *saptaparṇa* tree, of the elephants got as presents from kings, wets considerably (causes to be covered with deep mud) the courtyard of his council-hall, crowded with the chariots and horses of numerous tributary princes.

Sl. 16. In this sl. is described the happy result accomplished by his employment of the four means. ०दन्तिनां—अतिशयितौ दन्तौ अस्य दन्ती; here इन shows hugeness. अयुग्मच्छद—छाद्यते अनेन इति च्छदः । पुंसि संज्ञायाम् इति घः (अ); or छाद्यते अनेन fr. छद् Cau; the आ of छाद् is shortened by छादेर्घे द्वयुपसर्गस्य Păn VI. 4. 96. The आ of छाद् is shortened when not preceded by two Upasargas but समुपच्छादः । अयुग्माः not even, odd *i.e.* seven छदा यस्य स अयुग्मच्छदः The word युग्म when it does not mean 'a pair' is an *adj.* अयुग्मच्छदस्य पुष्पम् अयुग्मच्छदं by adding अण् (अ) which is dropped by the rule फले लुक् and the word becomes neuter अयुग्मच्छदस्य इव गन्धः यस्य । Malli.

seems here to follow the Bhăshya which says 'सप्तम्युपमानपूर्वपदस्य उत्तरपदलोपश्च वक्तव्यः' *i. e.* in a Bah. comp. the word following a सप्तम्यन्तपद or an उपमानपद disappears; so here the comp. must be dissolved as अयुग्मच्छदस्य गन्धः अयुग्मच्छदगन्धः which becomes the Upamănapada; अयु०न्ध इव गन्धः यस्य. Then गन्ध forming the latter part of अयु० is dropped. But later grammarians do not follow this verbal rigour of the Bhăshya and the comp. is dissolved as above. The final इ is added to the comp. by the rule उपमानाच्च ।

अनेक—अनेके च ते राजन्याश्च now see com. The aff. यत् is added to राजन् when जाति is meant (राज्ञो जातावेवेति वाच्यम् Vărtika). The अन् of राजन् is not dropped before यत् as it does not imply भाव or कर्मन् (ये चाभावकर्मणोः). आस्थान—आतिष्ठन्त्यस्मिन् इत्यास्थानं (अधिकरणे ल्युट्) the place where a king holds his council, तस्य निकेतनं house or building, तस्य अजिरं; अजन्त्यत्र अजिरं fr. अज् गतौ + aff. इर (किरच् Uṇădi. I. 53).

संप्रति जनपदक्षेमकरत्वमाह—

सुखेन लभ्या दधतः कृषीवलैरकृष्टपच्या इव सस्यसंपदः ।
वितन्वति क्षेममदेवमातृकाश्चिराय तस्मिन्कुरवश्चकासते ।। १७ ।।

अन्वयः—चिराय तस्मिन् क्षेमं वितन्वति (सति) अदेवमातृकाः कुरवः अकृष्टपच्या इव कृषीवलैः सुखेन लभ्याः सस्यसम्पदः दधतः सन्तः चकासते ।। १७ ।।

सुखेनेति ।। चिराय तस्मिन्दुर्योधने क्षेमं वितन्वति क्षेमंकरे सति । देवः पर्जन्य एव माता येषां ते देवमातृकाः वृष्ट्यम्बुजीविनो देशाः । ते न भवन्तीत्यदेवमातृकाः । नदीमातृका इत्यर्थः ।। "देशो नद्यम्बुवृष्ट्यम्बुसम्पन्नव्रीहिपालितः । स्यान्नदीमातृको देवमातृकश्च यथाक्रमम्" इत्यमरः ।। एतेनास्य कुल्यादिपूर्तप्रवर्तकत्वमुक्तम् । कुरूणां निवासाः कुरवो जनपदविशेषाः । कृष्टेन पच्यन्त इति । कृष्टपच्याः ।। "राजसूय—" इत्यादिना कर्मकर्तरि क्यप्प्रत्ययान्तो निपातः ।। तद्विपरीता अकृष्टपच्या इव । कृषिरेषामस्तीति कृषीवलाः । कर्षकैरित्यर्थः ।।

"रजःकृषि—" आदिना वलच्प्रत्ययः। "वले" इति दीर्घः ॥ सुखेनाक्लेशेन लभ्या लब्धुं शक्याः सस्यसम्पदो दधतो धारयन्तः ॥ "नाभ्यस्ताच्छतुः" इति नुमागमप्रतिषेधः ॥ चकासते। सर्वोत्कर्षेण वर्तन्त इत्यर्थः ॥ "अदभ्यस्तात्" इति झेरदादेशः। "जक्षित्यादयः षट्" इत्यभ्यस्तसंज्ञा ॥ सम्पन्नजनपदत्वादसन्तापकरत्वाच्च दुःसाध्योऽयमिति भावः ॥

अन्वयार्थः—(**चिराय**) चिरकाल से (**तस्मिन्**) उस दुर्योधन के (**क्षेमम्**) कल्याण को (**वितन्वति**) [सति] विस्तृत करते हुए होने पर (**अदेवमातृकाः**) केवल पर्जन्य ही नहीं हैं माता [पोषक] जिनकी ऐसे (**कुरवः**) कुरु प्रदेश, (**कृषीवलैः**) कृषकों के द्वारा (**सुखेन लभ्याः**) सुख से प्राप्त होने वाली, (**अकृष्टपच्या इव**) मानो बिना कृषि-कर्म के ही पकने वाली (**सस्य-संपदः**) धान्य-संपदाओं को (**दधतः**) धारण करते हुए (**चकासते**) दीप्त होते हैं।

वह दुर्योधन चिरकाल से लोक-कल्याण पर ध्यान दे रहा है। परिणामतः सिंचाई के समुन्नत साधनों के कारण कृषकों को इतनी सरलता से फसल प्राप्त होती है मानो बिना जुताई के ही खेत स्वयमेव पकते हों। एवं इस प्रकार की फसलों से कुरु-प्रदेश के खेत लहलहाते रहते हैं।

17. He having long attended to the well-being of his subjects, the Kuru provinces, which have not to depend on rain for fertilisation (which are well-irrigated) are smiling with their plentiful crops obtained by husbandmen with ease as though they were obtained without tillage (lit. they grew on unploughed lands).

Sl. 17. क्षेमं वितन्वति—conferring benefits upon; taking steps to promote the well being of his subjects. अदेवमातृकाः—देवमा०—lit. having rain for their fostermother *i. e.* depending upon rain water only (and not on irrigation) for the growth of crops; अदेवमातृ०—not such, *i. e.* नदीमातृक or watered by rivers, canals &c.; cf. अदेवमातृका चेति शस्यते भूर्विभूतये। Kăm. IV. 52. अकृष्टपच्याः—See Malli. कृष्टपच्य is a word irregularly derived by adding the aff. य to पच्. कृष्टे *स्वयमेव पच्यन्ते इति (those that ripen of themselves in cultivated ground) कृष्टपच्या: कर्मकर्तरि शुद्धे तु कर्मणि कृष्टपाक्या Sid. Kau. अकृष्ट०—growing or ripening without requiring the ground to be tilled. सस्यसं०—Gen. Tat. Abundance of corn of every kind or सस्यान्येव सम्पद: Karm. कृषीवल—see com; the Sūtra is रजःकृष्यासुतिपरिषदो वलच् । V. 2. 112; रजस्वल, आसुतीवल: a distiller, परिषद्वल:; before वल the preceding vowel is lengthened when the whole signifies a class (संज्ञायाम्). *Cf.* Kăm. IV. 50-52 (भूगणैर्वर्धते राष्ट्रं तद्वृद्धिनृपवृद्धये &c.).

नन्वेवं जनपदानुवर्तिन: कथमर्थलाभ इत्यत आह—

उदारकीर्तेरुदयं दयावतः प्रशान्तबाधं दिशतोऽभिरक्षया ।

स्वयं प्रदुग्धेऽस्य गुणैरुपस्नुता वसूपमानस्य वसूनि मेदिनी ॥ १८ ॥

अन्वयः—उदारकीर्तेः दयावतः अभिरक्षया प्रशान्तबाधम् उदयं दिशतः वसूपमानस्य अस्य गुणैः उपस्नुता मेदिनी वसूनि स्वयं प्रदुग्धे ॥१८॥

उदारेति ॥ उदारकीर्तेर्महायशसः ॥ "उदारो दातृमहतोः" इत्यमरः ॥ दयावतः परदुःखप्रहरणेच्छोः । अतएव प्रशान्तबाधं प्रशमितोपद्रवं यथा स्यात्तथेति क्रियाविशेषणम् । उदयविशेषणं वा ॥ "वा दान्तशान्त—" इत्यादिना शमिधातोर्ण्यन्तान्निष्ठान्तो निपातः ॥ अभिरक्षया सर्वतस्त्राणेनोदयं वृद्धिं दिशतः सम्पादयतो वसूपमानस्य कुबेरोपमस्य ॥ "वसुर्मयूखाग्निधनाधिपेषु" इति विश्वः ॥ अस्य दुर्योधनस्य गुणैर्दयादाक्षिण्यादिभिरुपस्नुता द्राविता मेदिनी वसूनि धनानि ॥ "वसु तोये धने मणौ" इति वैजयन्ती ॥ स्वयं प्रदुग्धे । अक्लेशेन दुह्यत इत्यर्थः ॥ दुहेः कर्मकर्तरि लट् । "न दुहस्नुनमां यक्चिणौ" इति यक्प्रतिषेधः ॥ यथा केनचिद्विदग्धेन नवप्रसूता रक्षिता च गौः स्वयं प्रदुग्धे इति भावः ॥ "अलंकारस्तु विशेषणमात्रसाम्यादप्रस्तुतस्य गम्यत्वे समासोक्तिः" इति सर्वस्वकारः । अत्र प्रतीयमानया गवा सह प्रकृताङ्गया मेदिन्या भेदेऽभेदलक्षणातिशयोक्तिवशादपोह्यत्वेनोक्तिरिति संक्षेपः ॥

अन्वयार्थः—(**अभिरक्षया**) सर्वत्र रक्षण से (**प्रशान्तबाधम्**) शान्त कर दी गई हैं बाधाएँ जिसमें ऐसी (**उदयम्**) उन्नति को (**दिशतः**) संपन्न करते हुए (**उदारकीर्तेः**) महायशस्वी (**दयावतः**) दयावान् (**वसूपमानस्य**) कुबेर-सदृश

(अस्य) इस दुर्योधन के (गुणैः) गुणों से (उपस्नुता) द्रवित कराई गई (मेदिनी) पृथ्वी (वसूनि) धनों को (स्वयं प्रदुग्धे) स्वयमेव दुहाती है।

उसके उपयुक्त रक्षा-साधनों के कारण चारों ओर निर्बाध उन्नति हो रही है। महायशस्वी, दयावान् एवं कुबेर-जैसे इस दुर्योधन के गुण-रूपी बछड़े से पवसाई (पेन्हाई) हुई पृथ्वी-रूपी गाय स्वयमेव धन-रूपी दूध को दुहाती है।

18. The earth wetted (or, with her inner flow induced) by the merits of that king comparable with Kubera (or Agni) yields of her own accord, treasures to him, highly renowned, merciful, and contributing, by his universal protection, to the uninterrupted prosperity (of the people) (or contributing to general prosperity), all disturbances being warded off.

Sl. 18. उदार०—उदार wide, great उदारा कीर्तिर्यस्य प्रशान्त०—प्रशान्ता बाधा यथा स्यात्तथा (Avya.)or यस्मिन् (Bah.) The former is better. अभिरक्षा०—protection all round *i. e.* of all उपस्नुता—The metaphor is taken from a cow; just as a cow's udder is made to overflow with milk by the touch of the calf so the earth was made to yield its treasures by his merits.

मेदिनी—*cf.* the Pauraṇic derivation मेदमस्त्यस्याः; मधुकैटभयोरासीन्मेदसैव परिप्लुता। तेनेयं मेदिनी नाम्ना सर्वतः परिकीर्तिता॥ प्रदुग्धे—In the कर्मकर्तृवाच्य the य (यक्) of the pass. must be added and so the form should have been प्रदुह्यते But the य is prohibited by the rule (see Malli.)—'roots दुह्, स्नु and नम do not admit it.' दुहेरनेन यक एव निषेधः। गौः पयो दुग्धे Sid. Kau. Generally in कर्मकर्तृवाच्य the verb is used intransitively; for the Obj. case becomes the Nom. and the former disappears. But दुह् and पच् are exceptions—दुहिपच्योर्बहुलं सकर्मयोरिति वाच्यम्. Vārt. on Pān. III. 1. 87.

वीरानुकूल्यमाह—

महौजसो मानधना धनार्चिता धनुर्भृतः संयति लब्धकीर्तयः।
न संहतास्तस्य न भिन्नवृत्तयः प्रियाणि वाञ्छन्त्यसुभिः समीहितुम्॥१९॥

अन्वयः—महौजसः मानधनाः धनार्चिताः संयति लब्धकीर्त्तयः न संहताः न भिन्नवृत्तयः धनुर्भृतः असुभिः तस्य प्रियाणि समीहितुं वाञ्छन्ति॥

महौजस इति ॥ **महौजसो महाबला:** । अन्यथा दुर्बलानामनुपकारित्वादिति भाव: । मान: कुलशीलाद्यभिमान एव धनं येषां ते मानधना: । अन्यथा कदाचिद्वलदर्पाद्विकुर्वीरन्निति भाव: । धनार्चिता धनैरर्चिता: सत्कृता: । अन्यथा दारिद्र्यादेनं जह्यु रिति भाव: । सयति संग्रामे लब्धकीर्तय: बहुयशस: । अन्यथा कदाचिन्मुह्येयुरिति भाव: । संहता मिथ: सङ्गता: स्वार्थनिष्ठा न भवन्तीति न संहता: ॥ नञर्थस्य नशब्दस्य सुप्सुपेति समास: ॥ भिन्नवृत्तयो मिथो विरोधात्स्वामिकार्यविघातकरा न भवन्तीति नभिन्नवृत्तय: ॥ पूर्ववत्समास: ॥ अन्यथा स्वामिकार्यविघातकतया स्वामिद्रोहिण: स्युरित्युभयत्रापि तात्पर्यार्थ: । धनुर्भृतो धानुष्का: । आयुधीयमात्रोपलक्षणमेतत् । प्राधान्याद्धनुर्ग्रहणम् । तस्य दुर्योधनस्यासुभि: प्राणै: प्रियाणि समीहितुं कर्तुं वाञ्छन्ति । आनृण्यार्थं प्राणान्दातुमिच्छन्ति । अन्यथा दोषस्मरणादिति भाव: ॥ अत्र महौजसादिपदार्थानां प्राणदानकर्तव्यतां प्रति विशेषणगत्या हेतुत्वाभिधानात्काव्यलिङ्गमलङ्कार: । लक्षणं तूक्तम्—"तथा साभिप्रायविशेषणत्वात्परिकरालङ्कार:" इति । द्वयोस्तिलतण्डुलवद्विभक्ततया स्फुरणात्संसृष्टि: ॥

अन्वयार्थ:—(**महौजस:**) महाबलशाली (**मानधना:**) मान ही है धन जिनका ऐसे (**धनार्चिता:**) धनों से सत्कृत (**संयति**) युद्ध में (**लब्धकीर्तय:**) प्राप्त किया है यश जिन्होने ऐसे (**न संहता:**) [आपस को] साँठ-गाँठ से रहित (**न भिन्नवृत्तय:**) [परस्पर] विरोधी आचरणों से रहित (**धनुर्भृत:**) धनुर्धारी, (**तस्य**) उसका (**असुभि:**) प्राणों से [भी] (**प्रियाणि**) अभीप्सितों को (**समीहितुम्**) करना (**वाञ्छन्ति**) चाहते हैं ।

अत्यन्त बलवान्, आत्मसम्मानी, अच्छा वेतन पाने वाले, युद्धों में यशस्वी साँठ-गाँठ एवं तोड़-फोड़ की प्रवृत्ति से रहित, सैनिक, अपने प्राणों की बाजी लगाकर भी उसका हित करने से नहीं चूकते ।

19. Warriors (lit. bow-wielders) mighty in spirit, regarding personal honour as their wealth and honoured with money

gifts (or by being properly paid), and distinguished in battles, wish to accomplish his objects even at the cost of their lives without combining or acting treacherously towards him.

19. महौजसः—महत् ओजः strength, vigour, energy येषां ते. This shows that they can be of real use to the king. मानधनाः—who regard the honour of their family &c., or self respect as their wealth; *i. e.* who will never stoop down to mean acts such as causing disturbance in the state and so on. But all this would be useless if they were not to get pecuniary gelp lest poverty might compel them to act meanly or desert the king. So धनार्चिताः—they were honoured by being paid according to their merit *Cf.* न नरस्य नरो दासो दासस्त्वर्थस्य भूपते। गौरवं लाघवं वापि धनाधननिबन्धनम्॥

संयति—संयत् fr. यत् to strive; or from संयम्, म being dropped by the Văr. गमादीनाम् (VI. 4. 40). and त् added by तुक् VI. 1. 71. लब्धकीर्तयः—This is necessary. They were men of tried valour. An inexperienced man, however brave he may be, may lose heart in the hour of trial. न संहताः—a comp. called सुप्सुपा. See Păn. II. 1. 4. An inflected word may be compounded with an inflected word. A comp. which does not fall under the head of any of the principal compounds falls under this general head of com ounds. न संहताः—not forming bodies or combining to plot against him; not conspiring नभि०—भिन्ना वृत्तिर्येषां ते भिन्नवृत्तयः may mean—(1) not acting in a hostile manner towards one another (Malli.); or (2) not acting treacherously towards the king. A king must not have servants who form conspiracies or act treacherously, *Cf.* राज्योपघातं कुर्वाणा ये पापा राजवल्लभाः। एकैकशः संहता वा दूष्यांस्तान्परिचक्षते। Kăm. VI. 9. धनुर्भृतः—धनुः बिभ्रतीति those holding bows; here धनु also refers to other weapons; see Malli; bow-men, warriors. असुभिः—used in the pl. अस्यन्ते इति fr. अस्—उ (उन् Uṇădi). स हि अस्तः शरीरे भवति तस्य तत्र नित्यमवस्थानम्। Nirukta.

संप्रति स्वराष्ट्रवत्परराष्ट्रवृत्तान्तमपि वेत्तीत्याह—

महीभृतां सच्चरितैश्चरैः क्रियाः स वेद निःशेषमशेषितक्रियः ।
महोदयैस्तस्य हितानुबन्धिभिः प्रतीयते धातुरिवेहितं फलैः ॥२०॥

अन्वयः—अशेषितक्रियः स सच्चरितैः चरैः महीभृतां क्रियाः निःशेषं वेद । धातुः इव तस्य ईहितं महोदयैः हितानुबन्धिभिः फलैः प्रतीयते ॥२०॥

महीभृतामिति ॥ अशेषितक्रियः समापितकृत्यः । आफलोदयकर्मेत्यर्थः । स दुर्योधनः सच्चरितैः । अवञ्चकैरित्यर्थः । चरन्तीति चरास्तैश्चरैः प्रणिधिभिः ॥ पचाद्यच् । महीभृतां क्रियाः प्रारम्भान्निःशेषं वेद वेत्ति ॥ "विदो लटो वा" इति णलादेशः ॥ स्वरहस्यं तु न कश्चिद्वेदेत्याह—महोदयैरिति ॥ धातुरिव तस्य दुर्योधनस्येहितमुद्योगो महोदयैर्महावृद्धिभिः । हितमनुबध्नन्त्यनुरुन्धन्तीति हितानुबन्धीनि तैः स्वन्तैरित्यर्थः । फलैः कार्यसिद्धिभिः प्रतीयते ज्ञायते । फलानुमेयास्तस्य प्रारम्भा इत्यर्थः ॥

अन्वयार्थः—(**अशेषितक्रियः**) समाप्त किया है कार्यों को जिसने ऐसा (**सः**) वह (**सच्चरितैः चरैः**) सच्चरित्र गुप्तचरों के द्वारा (**महीभृताम्**) [अन्य] राजाओं के (**क्रियाः**) कार्यों को (**निःशेषम्**) समग्र-रूप से (**वेद**) जानता है। (**धातुः इव**) विधाता की भाँति (**तस्य**) उसका (**ईहितम्**) उद्योग [अभीप्सित] (**महोदयैः**) महावृद्धि वाले (**हितानुबन्धिभिः**) एवं हित को करने वाले (**फलैः**) परिणामों से (**प्रतीयते**) जाना जाता है।

अपने कामों को समाप्त करके, गुप्तचरों की सहायता से अन्य राजाओं के क्रियाकलापों को वह पूर्णतः जानता है। जैसे विधाता के कार्यों का ज्ञान उनके परिणामों से होता है इसी प्रकार उसके भी कार्यों का पता प्रभूत समृद्धि एवं हितकारी परिणामों से चलता है।

20. He, who persists in his undertakings till they bear fruit (Malli); or who has left nothing to be done *i.e.* adopted

all the measures necessary for the safety of his kingdom, learns fully the doings (plans) of (other) kings through his faithful emissaries; while his own aims (plans), like those of Providence, are known from their grand results leading to (carrying in their train) general welfare.

Sl. 20. अशेषितक्रियः—शेषित p. p. p. of the Nomi, verb fr. शेषं (शेष करोति) or of शिष् Cau. अशेषिता क्रिया येन he who leaves nothing imperfectly or incompletely done *i. e.* carries to its completion what he undertakes (Malli.); or क्रिया may mean the things to be done (policy to be pursued) for the stability of his rule. सच्च०—सत् चरितं येषां doing their duty faithfully. निःशेषं निर्गतः शेषः यस्मिन्कर्मणि तद्यथा तथा. ईहितं—P. P. P. of ईह् to desire, objects wished to be accomplished, aims, plans. महोदयैः—महान् उदयो येषां येषु वा तैः leading to or fraught with great prosperity.

मित्रबलमाह—

न तेन सज्यं क्वचिदुद्यतं धनुः कृतं न वा कोपविजिह्ममाननम् ।

गुणानुरागेण शिरोभिरुह्यते नराधिपैर्माल्यमिवास्य शासनम् ॥ २१ ॥

अन्वयः—तेन क्वचित् सज्यं धनुः न उद्यतम् । आननं वा कोपविजिह्मं न कृतम् । नराधिपैः अस्य शासनं गुणानुरागेण माल्यमिव शिरोभिः उह्यते ॥२१॥

नेति ॥ तेन राज्ञा क्वचित्कुत्रापि । सह ज्यया मौर्व्या सज्यम् ॥ "मौर्वी ज्या शिञ्जिनी गुणः" इत्यमरः ॥ "तेन सहेति तुल्ययोगे" इति बहुव्रीहिः ॥ धनुर्नोद्यतं नोर्ध्वीकृतम् । आननं वा कोपविजिह्मं कोपेन कुटिलं न कृतम् । यस्य कोप एव नोदेति कुतस्तस्य युद्धप्रसक्तिरिति भावः ॥ कथं तर्ह्याज्ञां कारयति राज्ञ इत्यत्राह—गुणेति ॥ गुणेषु दयादाक्षिण्यादिष्वनुरागेण प्रेम्णा । माल्यपक्षे सूत्रानुषङ्गेण । यद्वा सौरभ्यगुणलोभेन । नराधिपैरन्यभूपालैरस्य शासनमाज्ञा । मालेव "चातुर्वर्ण्यादित्वात्स्वार्थे ष्यञ्" इति क्षीरस्वामी । शिरोभिरुह्यते धार्यते ॥ "वचिस्वपियजादीनां किति" इति यकि संप्रसारणम् ॥ अत्रोपमा स्फुटैव ॥

अन्वयार्थः---(**तेन**) उसने (**क्वचित्**) कहीं भी (**सज्यम्**) डोरी-सहित (**धनुः**) धनुष (**न उद्यतम्**) ऊपर नहीं उठाया। (**आननम् वा**) अथवा मुंह (**कोपविजिह्मम्**) क्रोध से टेढ़ा (**न कृतम्**) नहीं किया। (**नराधिपैः**) राजाओं से (**अस्य शासनम्**) इसकी आज्ञा (**गुणानुरागेण**) गुणों में अनुरक्ति के कारण [माला-पक्ष] धागे से अनुस्यूत होने के कारण (**माल्यमिव**) माला की तरह (**शिरोभिः**) शिरों से (**उह्यते**) धारण की जाती है।

न उसने कहीं धनुष ताना है, और न ही गुस्से से मुंह विकृत किया है। तो भी उसके गुणों के कारण अन्य राजा उसकी आज्ञा को ऐसे सिर पर धारण करते हैं जैसे माला पहन रहे हों।

21. Nowhere (against none) is the ready (lit. strung) bow raised by him nor is the face made wry through anger (is put on the cross look of anger): his commands are borne on their heads (respectfully obeyed) by the (feudatory) kings, out of regard for his virtues, like a garland woven in a string.

Sl. 21. सज्यं—see com.; also सहज्यं by the rule वोपसर्जनस्य Pān. VI. 3. 82. विजिह्म—see जिह्म sl. 25. आननं—fr. अन to breathe + ल्युट् (अन); the mouth also is the means of respiration. गुणानु०—when taken with माल्य means on account of its अनुरा० *i. e.* attachment, hence connection with the string holding the flowers together; or गुण fragrance, through love for its fragrance. शिरोभिरु०—शिरसा वह् means to obey respectfully (lit. with a respectful bending of the head); *cf.* अशेषनरपतिशिरः—समभ्यर्चितशासनः। Kād. p. 1. तथेति शेषामिव (प्रसाददत्तां मालामिव Malli.) भर्तुराज्ञामादाय मूर्ध्ना मदनः प्रतस्थे। Kum. III. 22. माल्यम्—इव this may also be an उत्प्रेक्षा as if it were a garland. माला एव माल्यं see com.; the *neu.* gender is by the maxim क्वचित्स्वार्थिकाः प्रकृतेर्लिङ्गवचनान्यतिवर्तन्ते।

संप्रत्यस्य धार्मिकत्वमाह—

स यौवराज्ये नवयौवनोद्धतं निधाय दुःशासनमिद्धशासनः।
मखेष्वखिन्नोऽनुमतः पुरोधसा धिनोति हव्येन हिरण्यरेतसम्॥२२॥

अन्वयः—इद्धशासनः सः नवयौवनोद्धतं दुःशासनं यौवराज्ये निधाय पुरोधसा अनुमतः अखिन्नः मखेषु हव्येन हिरण्यरेतसं धिनोति ॥२२॥

स इति ॥ इद्धशासनोऽप्रतिहताज्ञः स दुर्योधनो नवयौवनेनोद्धतं प्रगल्भम् । धुरंधरमित्यर्थः । दुःखेन शिष्यत इति दुःशासनस्तम् ॥ "भाषायां शासियुधि—" इत्यादिना खलर्थे युच्प्रत्ययः ॥ यौवराज्ये युवराजकर्मणि ॥ ब्राह्मणादित्वात्ष्यञ् ॥ निधाय नियुज्येत्यर्थः । पुरोधसा पुरोहितेनानुमतोऽनुज्ञातः । तस्मिन्याजके सतीत्यर्थः । तदुल्लङ्घने दोषस्मरणादिति भावः ॥ "निष्ठा" इति भूतार्थे क्तः । न तु "मतिबुद्धि—" इत्यादिना वर्तमानार्थे । अन्यथा "पुरोधसा" इत्यत्र "क्तस्य च वर्तमाने" इति षष्ठी स्यात् ॥ अखिन्नोऽनलसो मखेषु क्रतुषु हव्येन हविषा । हिरण्यं रेतो यस्य तं हिरण्यरेतसमनलं धिनोति प्रीणयति ॥ धिन्वेः प्रीणनार्थात् "धिन्विकृण्व्योर च" इत्यप्रत्ययः । अकारश्चान्तादेशः ॥

अन्वयार्थः—(**इद्धशासनः सः**) [प्रज्वलित है आज्ञा जिसकी ऐसा] जिसकी आज्ञा का कहीं व्याघात नहीं होता ऐसा वह (**नवयौवनोद्धतम्**) नयी जवानी के कारण ऊपर उठे हुए [चतुर एवं सर्वसमर्थ] (**दुःशासनम्**) दुःशासन को (**यौवराज्ये**) युवराज-पद पर (**निधाय**) स्थापित करके (**पुरोधसा**) पुरोहित से (**अनुमतः**) अनुज्ञात हो कर (**अखिन्नः**) निरालस्य (**मखेषु**) यज्ञों में (**हव्येन**) आहुति से (**हिरण्यरेतसम्**) अग्नि को (**धिनोति**) तृप्त करता है ।

अप्रतिहत आज्ञा वाले दुर्योधन ने युवराज-पद पर नयी जवानी के कारण कार्य-समर्थ दुःशासन को नियुक्त किया है और स्वयं पुरोहित की देख-रेख में निरन्तर यज्ञ करता रहता है ।

22. He whose rule is supreme (lit. whose orders are unresistingly obeyed) having appointed as heir-apparent Duśśásana, lofty (capable) by (the vigour of) fresh youth, propitiates unremittingly (lit. without feeling fatigued) the god of fire with oblations in sacrifices, with the approval (following the advice) of his family priest.

Sl. 22. इद्धशासनः—इद्ध (p. p. p. of इन्ध् 7 A. to kindle) lit. blazing, bright, hence difficult to be resisted, readily obeyed शासनं यस्य. द्धतं०—उद्धत p. p. of हन् with उद् lit. upborne by, in the high spirit or vigour of youth *i. e.* in budding youth and energetic. उद्धत can not be taken to mean 'haughty' here. The spy is representing Sud. as a consummate politician. To say that he has placed a haughty man at the head of affairs would be doing small credit to Suyo.'s judgement. दुःशासनः—see सुयोधनः *supra*, sl. 7. यौवराज्ये—युवा चासौ राजा च युवराजः तस्य कर्म यौवराज्यम् the duties of an heir-apparent; fr. युवराज+य (ष्यञ्) in the sense of तस्य कर्म by गुणवचनब्राह्मणादिभ्यः कर्मणि च Păn. V. 1. 124. The ब्राह्मणादि is an आकृतिगण, so words not actually mentioned in it may also be included in it.

पुरोधसा—पुरो धीयते इति पुरोधाः; fr. धा+Uṇādi. अस्. अनुमतः—with the aprroval of or having obtained the consent of (to act as the officiating priest). Here the p. p. is used in the sense of the past tense (and not in that of the present by मतिबुद्धिपूजार्थेभ्यश्च) and so it is used with the Inst. (पुरोधसा). When the p. p. has the sense of the Pres. tense it is used with the Gen. by क्तस्य च वर्तमाने (II. 3. 67). अखिन्नः—without feeling tired. मखेषु—मखन्ति देवा अत्र अनेन वा fr. मख 1 p. to go, and aff. अ (घञ्).

हव्येन—हूयन्ते देवा अनेन इति हव्यं; हू+य (यत्) by अचो यत् (III. 1. 97). Before य Guṇa substitute takes place and ओ is changed to अव् before य by वान्तो यि प्रत्यये (VI. 1. 79)—before a term, beginning with य the preceding ओ, औ are changed to अव and आव् respectively. हिरण्यरेतसं—Gold on account of its brilliance is regarded by the Aryan writers (the Naiyăyikas as product of beat and not earthy (also because the strongest heat is insufficient to calcine it) and hence it is regarded as the semen of fire. *Cf.* the Smṛti.—अग्नेरपत्यं प्रथमं सुवर्णम् ।

धिनोति—धि or धिन्व् 5. P. to delight, to please. धिन्व् and कृण्व् to kill are properly root of the भ्वादि or 1st class but as they take the augment उ instead of अ they may be looked upon as roots of the 5th class.

स चेत्तादृश उद्योगी तर्ह्यस्माभिर्निरुद्योगैर्भाव्यमित्याशङ्क्योद्योगाशां दर्शयति—

प्रलीनभूपालमपि स्थिरायति प्रशासदावारिधि मण्डलं भुवः ।
स चिन्तयत्येव भियस्त्वदेष्यतीरहो दुरन्ता बलवद्विरोधिता ॥२३॥

अन्वयः—प्रलीनभूपालं स्थिरायति भुवो मण्डलं आवारिधि प्रशासदपि सः त्वदेष्यतीः भियः चिन्तयत्येव । अहो बलवद्विरोधिता दुरन्ता ॥२३॥

प्रलीनेति ॥ स दुर्योधनः प्रलीनभूपालम् । निःसपत्नमित्यर्थः । स्थिरायति । चिरस्थायीत्यर्थः । भुवो मण्डलमावारिधिभ्य आवारिधि ॥ "आङ्मर्यादाभिविध्योः" इत्यव्ययीभावः ॥ प्रशासदाज्ञापयन्नपि ॥ "जक्षित्यादयः षट्" इत्यभ्यस्तसंज्ञा । "नाभ्यस्ताच्छतुः" इति नुमागमप्रतिषेधः ॥ त्वत्त्वत्त एष्यतीरागमिष्यतीः । आगामिनीरिति यावत् । धातूनामनेकार्थत्वादुक्तार्थसिद्धिः । अथवाङ्पूर्वः पाठः ॥ "एत्येधत्यूठ्सु" इति वृद्धिः । "लटः सद्वा" इति शतृप्रत्ययः । "उगितश्च" इति इति ङीप् । "आच्छीनद्योर्नुम्" इति विकल्पान्नुमभावः ॥ भियो भयहेतून् । विपद इत्यर्थः । चिन्तयत्यालोचयत्येव तथाहि । —अहो बलवद्विरोधिता दुरन्ता दुष्टावसाना । सार्वभौमस्यापि प्रबलैः सपत्नैः सह वैरमनर्थपर्यवसाय्येवेति तात्पर्यम् ॥ सामान्येन विशेषसमर्थनरूपोऽर्थान्तरन्यासोऽलङ्कारः ॥

अन्वयार्थः—(**प्रलीनभूपालम्**) नष्ट हो गये हैं शत्रु जिसमें ऐसे (**स्थिरायति**) चिरस्थायी (**भुवः**) पृथ्वी के (**मण्डलम्**) मण्डल को (**आवारिधि**) समुद्र-पर्यन्त (**प्रशासदपि**) शासन करता हुआ भी (**सः**) वह (**त्वदेष्यतीः**) तुमसे आने वाले (**भियः**) भय को (**चिन्तयत्येव**) सोचता ही है । **अहो** (**बलवद्विरोधिता**) अहो, बलवान् से विरोध (**दुरन्ता**) बुरे परिणाम वाला होता है ।

शत्रु-रहित अतएव चिरस्थायी भूमण्डल पर समुद्रपर्यन्त राज्य करता हुआ भी वह तुम्हारे भय के कारण निश्चिन्त नहीं है। अहो ! बलवान् से विरोध कितना अनर्थकारी होता है !

23. Although ruling the circle of the earth to the shores of the oceans, with not a rival king left threon and its future (permanency) well-secured, he does apprehend dangers (to come) from you: Oh how woeful the consequences to which enmity with the mighty leads !

Sl. 23. प्रलीन०—प्रलीनाः (have entirely vanished being subdued) भूपालाः rival kings यस्मिन् स्थिरायतिः—स्थिरा firm आयतिः future stability यस्य आयति fr. यम with आ+ति वारिधिः—वारि धीयतेऽस्मिन् । एष्यतीः—Acc. pl. of the Fut. p. *fem.* of इ going forth from you (to him) the other form is एष्यन्ती. Malli. takes it in the sense of coming and hence his remark or suggestion to read त्वदैष्यतीः, चिन्तयति—contemplates or expects (although he should have absolutely no cause for any such). —बलव०—बलवता विरोधिता A comp. सङ्सुपा. विरोधोस्यास्तीति विरोधी तस्य भावः विरोधिता. दुरन्ता—दुष्टः अन्तः यस्याः सा ।

ननु गूढाकारेङ्गितस्य तस्य भयं त्वया कथं निरधारीत्यत्राह—

कथाप्रसङ्गेन जनैरुदाहृतादनुस्मृताखण्डलसूनुविक्रमः ।

तवाभिधानाद् व्यथते नताननः सुदुःसहान्मन्त्रपदादिवोरगः ॥ २४ ॥

अन्वयः—कथाप्रसङ्गेन जनैः उदाहृतात् दुःसहात् तवाभिधानात् मन्त्रपदात् अनुस्मृताखण्डलसूनुविक्रमः उरग इव सः नताननः (सन्) व्यथते ॥२४॥

कथेति ॥ कथाप्रसङ्गेन गोष्ठीवचनेन जनैः । तत्रत्यैरित्यर्थः । अन्यत्र कथाप्रसङ्गेन विषवैद्येन ॥ "कथाप्रसङ्गो वार्तायां विषवैद्येऽपि वाच्यवत्" इति विश्वः ॥ एकवचनस्यातन्त्रत्वाज्जनविशेषणम् ॥ यद्वा कथाप्रसङ्गे इनाश्च ते जनाश्चेत्येकं पदम् । उदाहृतादुच्चारितात् तवाभिधानान्नामधेयात्स्मारकाद्धेतोः ॥ "हेत्वर्थे" पञ्चमी ॥ "आख्याह्वे अभिधानं च नामधेयं च नाम च" इत्यमरः ॥ अन्यत्र तवाभिधानात् । "नामैकदेशग्रहणे नाममात्रग्रहणम्" इति न्यायात् । तश्च वश्च तवौ तार्क्ष्यवासुकी तयोरभिधानं यस्मिन्पदे तस्मात् । अनुस्मृताखण्डलसूनुविक्रमः स्मृतार्जुनपराक्रमः सन्दुःसहादतिदुःसहान्मन्त्रपदान्मंत्रशब्दात्स्मारकाद्धेतोः । आखण्डलसूनुरिन्द्रानुजः । उपेन्द्रो विष्णुरिति यावत् । "सूनुः पुत्रेऽनुजे रवौ" इति विश्वः ॥ तस्य विः पक्षी । गरुड इत्यर्थः । तस्य क्रमः पादविक्षेपः । सोऽनुस्मृतो येन स तथोक्तः स्मृतगरुडमहिमा । उरग इव । नताननः सन् ॥ "उरगः पन्नगो भोगी" इत्यमरः ॥ व्यथते दुःखायते ॥ "पीडा बाधा व्यथा दुःखम्" इत्यमरः ॥ अत्युत्कटभयदोषादिविकारा दुर्वारा इति भावः । "सर्वतो जयमन्विच्छेत्पुत्रादिच्छेत्पराजयम्" । इति न्यायादर्जुनोत्कर्षकथनं युधिष्ठिरस्य भूषणमेवेति सर्वमवदातम् ॥

अन्वयार्थः—(**कथाप्रसङ्गेन**) वार्ता के प्रसंग से (**जनैः**) लोगों से (**उदाहृतात्**) उच्चारण किये गए (**दुःसहात्**) असह्य (**तवाभिधानात्**) तुम्हारे नाम से (**अनुस्मृताखण्डलसूनुविक्रमः**) स्मरण हो आया है इन्द्र-पुत्र [अर्जुन] का पराक्रम

जिसे ऐसा (**उरगः इव**) सर्प की तरह (**नताननः**) झुके हुए सिर वाला हुआ-हुआ (**व्यथते**) पीड़ित होता है ।

सर्प-पक्ष में—(**कथाप्रसङ्गे**) [षु] विषवैद्यों में (**इनाः**) श्रेष्ठ (**जनैः**) लोगों के द्वारा (**उदाहृतात्**) उच्चारण किये गए (**दुःसहात्**) असह्य (**तव अभिधानात्**) तार्क्ष्य और वासुकि नाम हैं जिसमें ऐसे (**मन्त्रपदात्**) मन्त्र-पद से (**अनुस्मृताखण्डलसूनुविक्रमः**) स्मरण हो आया है इन्द्र के छोटे भाई [विष्णु] के पक्षी [गरुड़] का झपट्टा जिसे ऐसे (**उरग इव**) सर्प की भाँति......।

बातचीत के प्रसंग में लोगों के मुँह से निकले हुए तुम्हारे नाम को वह सह नहीं पाता। नाम सुनते ही उसे अर्जुन का पराक्रम याद आ जाता है और फिर नतमुख हुआ वह ऐसे पीड़ित होता है जैसे सर्प-विष का इलाज करने वाले लोगों से प्रयुक्त, तार्क्ष्य एवं वासुकि पदों वाले मन्त्र से गरुड़ का झपट्टा याद आने पर साँप डरता है।

24. At the unbearable utterance of your name by people in the course of conversation, he, being at once reminded of the valour of the son of Indra (Arjuna), hangs down his face and experiencespain, as does a serpent, with its hood sunk down at the utterance of the unbearable words of the incantation (used in catching snakes) containing mention of the names of Garuda and Văsuki, being at once put in mind thereby of the tread (swoop) of Garuda (lit. Vishnu's bird).

Sl. 24. This sl. has a double application. कथाप्रसङ्गेन—(1) in the course of conversation; (2) by a curer of poisons, especially snake poison; a serpent charmer. Malli. seems to take कथा० in the first case as a Bah. comp. (कथायाः प्रसङ्गः यस्य) when engaged in conversation, qualifying जनैः and hence remarks एकवचन &c.; as if dissatisfied with this he proposes to take कथा० जनैः as one word explaining it as 'people who are experts (इनाः masters) at the time of conversation (कथाप्रसङ्गे). But this is needless trouble. We may better take कथाप्र० as a Gen. Tat. जनैः कथाप्रसङ्गेन उदाहृतात् In the second case the comp. must be taken as कथाप्रसङ्गेषु इनाः (the best of poison-curers) ते च ते जनाः। तवा०—(1) the mention of your name, (2) त stands for तार्क्ष्य

and व for Văsuki; (being initial letters). See com., (नामैकदेश &c. as भामा means सत्यभामा बल means बलराम and so on) containing mention of the names of Garuda and Văsuki (the serpent king). Mark the different meanings of अभिधान—(1) name; (2) utterance. आखण्डल०—आखण्डयति splits पर्वतान् इति; fr. खण्ड् with आ+अल (डलच् डस्य नेत्त्वम्) or वृषादिभ्यः कलच् (Uṇădi. I. 106). सूनुवि०—the valour or exploits of the son of Indra (Arjuna); (2) the swoop क्रम of the bird (वि) of the younger brother (सूनु) of Indra (Vishṇu) *i.e.* Garuḍa. Vishṇu in his dwarf incarnation was the younger brother of Indra being Aditi's younger son. उरगः—उरसा गच्छति इति, fr. उरस+गम्+डः by the Vărt. उरसोलोपश्च (III. 2. 48) स् of उरस् is dropped before the aff. ड (अ).

निगमयति—

तवाशु कर्तुं त्वयि जिह्ममुद्यते विधीयतां तत्र विधेयमुत्तरम् ।

परप्रणीतानि वचांसि चिन्वतां प्रवृत्तिसाराः खलु मादृशां गिरः ॥ २५ ॥

अन्वयः—तत् (तस्मात्) त्वयि जिह्मं कर्तुम् उद्यते तत्र (तस्मिन्) विधेयम् उत्तरम् आशु विधीयताम् । परप्रणीतानि वचांसि चिन्वतां मादृशां गिरः प्रवृत्तिसाराः खलु ॥२५॥

तदिति ॥ तत्तस्मात्कारणात्त्वयि जिह्मं कपटं कर्तुमुद्यते । त्वां जिघांसावित्यर्थः । तत्र तस्मिन्दुर्योधने विधेयं कर्तव्यमुत्तरं प्रतिक्रिया आशु विधीयतां क्रियताम् । ननु कर्तव्यमपि त्वयैवोच्यतामिति चेत्तत्राह—परेति ॥ परप्रणीतानि परोक्तानि वचांसि चिन्वतां गवेषयतां मादृशाम् । वार्ताहारिणामित्यर्थः । गिरः प्रवृत्तिसारा वार्तामात्रसाराः खलु ॥ "वार्ता प्रवृत्तिर्वृत्तान्तः" इत्यमरः ॥ वार्तामात्रवादिनो वयं न तु कर्तव्यार्थोपदेशसमर्थाः । अतस्त्वयैव निर्धार्यं कार्यमिति भावः ॥ सामान्येन विशेषसमर्थनादर्थान्तरन्यासः ॥

अन्वयार्थः—(**तत्**) उस कारण से (**त्वयि**) तुममें [तुम्हारे प्रति] (**जिह्म कर्तुम्**) कपट करने के लिए (**उद्यते तत्र**) तैय्यार उस दुर्योधन में [के प्रति] (**विधेयम्**) करणीय (**उत्तरम्**) प्रतिक्रिया को (**आशु**) शीघ्र (**विधीयताम्**)

कीजिये। (परप्रणीतानि) दूसरों से कहे हुए (वचांसि) वचनों को (चिन्वताम्) इकट्ठा करते हुए (मादृशां गिरः) मुझ जैसों की वाणियां (प्रवृत्तिसाराः खलु) निश्चय से वृत्तान्त ही है सार जिनका, ऐसी होती हैं।

इसलिए आपके प्रति कपटाचरण करने के लिए तत्पर उस दुर्योधन के प्रति आप जो करना चाहें सो तुरन्त करें। दूसरों की बातों का संग्रह करने वाले मुझ जैसे गुप्तचरों की बात का तत्त्व तो पर-उक्ति मात्र होता है।

25. Let therefore proper counter-measures by at once taken against him who is ready (or endeavouring) invidiously to do harm to you. The words of men like myself, whose business is to ascertain what the utterances of others are, have, indeed, for their essence the communication of intelligence (only).

Sl. 25. जिह्म—is a noun here; fr. हा+मन; see sl. 8. *supra* What is morally crooked, fraud, perfidy; hence doing harm wickedly or by unfair means. उद्यते—उद्यत p. p. part. of यम् with उत्, क्त being added कर्तरि. As the root यम is here used intransitively, the p. p. is used in the active voice. विधेयं—fit to be adopted; fr. विधा+यत् (कर्मणि). उत्तरं—Lit. the course to be followed next, counter measures. To connect the 2nd half with the first Malli. says—ननु कर्तव्यमपि &c. If Yudhis. were to ask him to point out the future policy he says—चिन्वतां &c.—*i. e.* I am a mere spy and not a councillor; the duty of us, spies; is simply to gather what information we can form the words of others and communicate the same to you. There our best duty ends. It is for you to see what line of policy to follow or what measures to adopt to thwart the plans of the enemy. मादृशा—अहमिव दृश्यन्ते ते मादृशः or मामिव पश्यन्ति यान ते।

इतीरयित्वा गिरमात्तसत्क्रिये गतेऽथ पत्यौ वनसंनिवासिनाम्।
प्रविश्य कृष्णासदनं महीभुजा तदाचचक्षेऽनुजसन्निधौ वचः॥ २६॥

अन्वयः—वनसन्निवासिनां पत्यौ इति गिरमीरयित्वा आत्तसत्क्रिये गते (सति)

अथ महीभुजा कृष्णासदनं प्रविश्य अनुजसन्निधौ तत् वचः आचचक्षे; अथवा सदनं प्रविश्य तत् वचः कृष्णा आचचक्षे ॥२६॥

इतीति ॥ वनसन्निवासिनां पत्यौ वनेचराधिप इति गिरमीरयित्वोक्त्वा आत्तसत्क्रिये गृहीतपारितोषिके गते सति ॥ "तुष्टिदानमेव चाराणां हि वेतनम्। ते हि तल्लोभात्स्वामिकार्येष्वतीव त्वरयन्ते।" इति नीतिवाक्यामृते ॥ अथ महीभुजा राज्ञा कृष्णासदनं द्रौपदीभवनं प्रविश्यानुजसन्निधौ तद्वनेचरोक्तं वचो वाक्यमाचचक्षे आख्यातम्। अथवा। कृष्णेति पदच्छेदः। सदनं प्रविश्यानुजसन्निधौ तद्वचः कृष्णा आचचक्षे आख्याता ॥ चक्षिङो दुहादेर्द्विकर्मकत्वादप्रधाने कर्मणि लिट् ॥

अन्वयार्थः—(वनसंनिवासिनां पत्यौ) वन में रहने वालों के अधिपति के **(इति गिरम्)** इस प्रकार की बात को **(ईरयित्वा)** कह कर **(आत्तसत्क्रिये)** प्राप्त किया है पुरस्कार [रूप] सत्कार जिसने ऐसे [उसके] **(गते)** चले जाने पर **(अथ)** उसके बाद **(महीभुजा)** राजा द्वारा **(कृष्णासदनं प्रविश्य)** द्रौपदी के कक्ष में घुस कर **(अनुजसन्निधौ)** छोटे भाइयों के सामने **(तत्)** वह **(वचः)** **(आचचक्षे)** कही गई।

उपर्युक्त समाचार देकर तथा अनुरूप पुरस्कार पाकर वह वनेचर चला गया। तदनन्तर युधिष्ठिर ने द्रौपदी के भवन में जाकर सब भाइयों के सामने बात वह समाचार कहा।

26. When the chief of the foresters, having thus said his say, had taken his departure after being duly rewarded, the monarch entered the apartment of Draupadi and repeated the speech in the presence of his younger brothers (or entered the house and recounted the speech to Draupadi in the presence of his brothers).

Sl. 25. ईरयित्वा— ईर् 10 P. A. to utter &c. प्रवृत्ति०—प्रवृत्तिः वार्ताकथनं एव सारो यासाम्। आत्त०—आत्ता (p. p. p. of दा with आ, *fem.*) सत्क्रिया येन; सत् आदरः। सदसती चादरानादरयोः इति गतिसंज्ञा। तस्य क्रिया सत्क्रिया। Gatisamāsa. कृष्णासदनं—the apartment of Krishṇā, Draupadi; or कृष्णा तद्वच आचचक्षे (pass perf.). चक्ष् governs two accusatives. अनुजानां सन्निधिस्तत्र।

निशम्य सिद्धिं द्विषतामपाकृतीस्ततस्ततस्त्या विनिगन्तुमक्षमा।
नृपस्य मन्युव्यवसायदीपिनीरुदाजहार द्रुपदात्मजा गिरः ॥ २७ ॥

अन्वयः—ततः द्रुपदात्मजा द्विषतां सिद्धिं निशम्य ततस्त्याः अपाकृती विनियन्तुम् अक्षमा (सती) नृपस्य मन्युव्यवसायदीपिनीः गिरः उदाजहार ॥२७॥

निशम्येति ॥ अथ द्रुपदात्मजा द्रौपदी द्विषतां सिद्धिं वृद्धिरूपां निशम्य ततस्तदनन्तरम् । ततो द्विषद्भ्य आगतास्ततस्त्याः ॥ "अव्ययात्त्यप्" इति यप् ॥ अपाकृतीर्विकारान्विनियन्तुं निरोद्धुमक्षमा सती नृपस्य युधिष्ठिरस्य मन्युव्यवसाययोः क्रोधोद्योगयोर्दीपिनीः संवर्धिनीर्गिरो वाक्यान्युदाजहार । जगादेत्यर्थः ॥

अन्वयार्थः—(**ततः**) उसके पश्चात् (**द्रुपदात्मजा**) द्रुपद-पुत्री (**द्विषतां**) शत्रुओं की (**सिद्धिम्**) सफलता को (**निशम्य**) सुन कर (**ततस्त्याः**) उससे आने वाले (**अपाकृती**) विकारों को (**विनियन्तुम्**) नियन्त्रित करने में (**अक्षमा**) [**सती**] असमर्थ हुई-हुई (**नृपस्य**) राजा के (**मन्युव्यवसायदीपिनीः**) क्रोध एवं उद्योग को उद्दीप्त करने वाली (**गिरः**) वाणी को (**उदाजहार**) बोली ।

दुर्योधन की इस सफलता को सुनकर क्रोधाभिभूत द्रौपदी युधिष्ठिर के क्रोध एवं उद्यम को भडकाने वाली वाणी बोली ।

27. Having heard of the success attained by the enemies, the daughter of Drupada, unable to restrain the emotions (of anger &c.) proceeding therefrom, delivered a speech capable of exciting the King's anger and stimulating action on his part.

Sl. 27. द्रुपदात्मजा—आत्मनो जायते इत्यात्मजा Upapadasamāsa; fr. जन् + अ (ड) + आ (स्त्रियां टाप्) द्रुपदस्यात्मजा द्रुप० Drupada, also called Yajnasena, was the son of Prishata and king of the country of Pāñchāla which extended, in his time, from the banks of the Charmanvatī (Chambal) up to Gaṅgdwāra on the north. The northern portion from Bhāgirathi was called Uttara—Pāñchāla (Ahichchhatra). The Southern portion, called Dakshiṇa Pāñchāla became part of the kingdom of Hāstināpura after Drupada's death. Draupadī, also called Yājnasenī, was his daughter. See Introduction. द्विषतां—द्विषत् an enemy; the aff. अत् (शतृ) forms a noun by द्विषोऽमित्रे Pān. III. 2. 131.

सिद्धिं—success attained, prosperity; fr. सिध्—ति (क्तिन्) निशम्य —having heard. Also निशाम्य according to some. Dikshit however, thinks it to be the root शम् of the 10th class, meaning to hear by the principle धातूनामनेकार्थत्वात्. ततस्त्याः—Fr. ततः—त्य (त्यप); see Malli. क्षमते इति क्षमा । क्षम् + अच् + टाप्; न क्षमा अक्षमा. on this the Vărt. says अमेहक्वतसित्रेभ्य एव see अमात्य sl. 5. अपाकृतीः—अपाकृति usually means rejection or removal. Here it means 'the emotion or outward manifestation of anger, fear &c. मन्यु०—दीपयन्तीति दीपिन्यः, ग्रहादित्वात् णिनिः that would kindle anger and stimulate action, stir up his wrath and fire his energy. व्यवसाय—fr. सो with वि and अव—अ (घञ्)

भवादृशेषु प्रमदाजनोदितं भवत्यधिक्षेप इवानुशासनम् ।
तथापिवक्तुं व्यवसाययन्ति मां निरस्तनारीसमया दुराधयः ॥ २८॥

अन्वयः—भवादृशेषु प्रमदाजनोदितम् अनुशासनम् अधिक्षेप इव भवति । तथापि निरस्तनारीसमयाः दुराधयः मां वक्तुं व्यवसाययन्ति ॥२८॥

भवादृशेष्विति ॥ भवादृशा भवद्विधाः । पण्डिता इत्यर्थः । तेषु विषये ॥ "त्यदादिषु—" इत्यादिना कञ् । "आ सर्वनाम्नः" इत्याकारादेशः ॥ प्रमदाजनोदितं स्त्रीजनोक्तम् ॥ वदेः क्तः । "वचिस्वपि—" इत्यादिना संप्रसारणम् ॥ अनुशासनं नियोगवचनमधिक्षेपस्तिरस्कार इव भवति । अतो न युक्तं वक्तुमित्यर्थः । तथापि वक्तुमनुचितत्वेऽपि निरस्तनारीसमयास्त्याजितशालीनतारूपस्त्रीसमाचाराः ॥ "समयाः शपथाचारकालसिद्धान्तसंविदः" इत्यमरः ॥ दुराधयः समयोल्लङ्घनहेतुत्वाद् दुष्टा मनोव्यथाः ॥ "पुंस्याधिर्मानसी व्यथा" इत्यमरः ॥ मां वक्तुं व्यवसाययन्ति प्रेरयन्ति । न किंचिदयुक्तं दुःखिनामिति भावः ॥

अन्वयार्थः—(**भवादृशेषु**) आप जैसों के विषय में (**प्रमदाजनोदितम्**) एक स्त्री द्वारा उक्त (**अनुशासनम**) उपदेश (**अधिक्षेप इव**) तिरस्कार की भाँति (**भवति**) होता है। (**तथापि**) तो भी (**निरस्तनारीसमयाः**) छुड़ा दिया है स्त्रियोचित आचार जिन्होंने ऐसी (**दुराधयः**) बुरी मनोव्यथाएँ (**माम्**) मुझ को (**वक्तुम्**) कहने के लिए (**व्यवसाययन्ति**) प्रेरित करती हैं।

आप-सदृश पण्डित को स्त्री उपदेश दे, यह सरासर अपमान है; फिर भी स्त्रियोचित मर्यादा का उल्लङ्घन कराने वाली यह मानसिक व्यथा मुझे मुखर बना रही है।

28. Advice given by a woman (lit. one of tne woman class) to persons like you is like an insult; still agonising mental afflictions, setting aside (making me overstep) the bounds of conduct proper for women, prompt me to speak.

Sl. 28. भवादृशेषु—भवान् इव दृश्यन्ते ते भवादृशाः Upa. Tat. तेषु See note on मादृश *supra* sl. 25. प्रमदा—प्रकृष्टो मदो यस्याः प्रमदो हर्षोऽस्त्यस्या इति वा । प्रमदा एव जनः तेन उदितम् । अनुशासनम्—Properly an order or direction as to the course to be followed, implying superiority or authority in the person from whom it proceeds. Here it means advice or counsel. अधिक्षेपः—अधिक्षिप्—अ (घञ्) reproach, an insult to or reflection on. निरस्त०—निरस्तः (p. p. p. of अस् with निर्) set aside (here as a Cau. p. making one set aside) or done away with नारीणां समयः proper conduct यैः ते । दुरा०—दुष्टा आधयः दुराधयः Prădi samăsa. आधिः—आधीयते दुःखमनेन, आधीयते प्रतीकाराय मनोऽनेन इति वा; fr. आ+धा+इ (कि) by उपसर्गे घोः किः । Păn. III. 3. 92; mental pain or anguish. व्यवसाययन्ति—Cau. of सो with वि and अव; The roots शो, छो &c. take the augment य (युक्) instead of प (पुक्) before the causal aff. णिच् (इ) by शाच्छासाह्वाव्यावेपां युक् । Păn. VII. 3. 37. The fig. of speech in the last two lines is पदार्थहेतुकं काव्यलिङ्गं as the cause of the abandon ment of नारीसमय is stated.

अखण्डमाखण्डलतुल्यधामभिश्चिरं धृता भूपतिभिः स्ववंशजैः ।
त्वयात्महस्तेन मही मदच्युता मतङ्गजेन स्रगिवाऽपवर्जिता ॥ २९ ॥

अन्वयः—आखण्डलतुल्यधामभिः स्ववंशजैः भूपतिभिः चिरम् अखण्डं धृता मही त्वया मदच्युता मतङ्गजेन स्रक् इव आत्महस्तेन अपवर्जिता ॥२९॥

अखण्डमिति ॥ आखण्डलतुल्यधामभिरिन्द्रतुल्यप्रभावैः ॥ "धाम रश्मौ गृहे देहे स्थाने जन्मप्रभावयोः" इति हैमः ॥ स्ववंशजैः भूपतिभिर्भरतादिभिश्चिरमखण्डमविच्छिन्नं धृता मही त्वया । मदं च्योततीति मदच्युत् ॥ क्विप् ॥ तेन मदस्राविणा मतङ्गजेन स्रगिवात्महस्तेन स्वकरेण । स्वचापल्येनेत्यर्थः ॥ अपवर्जिता परिहृता त्यक्ता । स्वदोषादेवायमनर्थागम इत्यर्थः ॥

अन्वयार्थः—(**आखण्डलतुल्यधामभिः**) इन्द्र सदृश तेजस्वी (**स्ववंशजैः**) अपने वंश में उत्पन्न (**भूपतिभिः**) राजाओं द्वारा (**चिरम्**) चिरकाल-पर्यन्त (**अखण्डम्**) अखण्ड-रूप से (**धृता**) धारण की गई (**मही**) पृथ्वी (**त्वया**) तुम्हारे द्वारा (**मदच्युता मतङ्गजेन**) मदस्रावी हाथी से (**स्रक् इव**) माला की भाँति (**आत्महस्तेन**) अपने हाथ से (**अपवर्जिता**) छोड़ दी गई।

इन्द्र-सरीखे तेजस्वी आपके अपने कुल के राजाओं ने चिरकाल-पर्यन्त जिस अखण्ड पृथ्वी का उपभोग किया, वह पृथ्वी आपने स्वयं अपने हाथ से ऐसे फेंक दी जैसे मदमस्त हाथी अपने पर पड़ी हुई माला को फेंक देता है।

29. The earth that was long held in possession entirely by kings born of your race, equalling Indra in prowess (lit. having valour equal to that of Indra) has been thrown away (lost) by you, with your own hands, like a garland cast away by an elephant in rut with his own trunk.

Sl. 29. आखण्डल०—आखण्डलेन तुल्यं धाम येषां तैः। For आखण्डल see *supra* sl. 24. धामन् fr. धा + मन् (मनिन्) अखण्डम्—नास्ति खण्डो यस्मिन् कर्मणि तद्यथा तथा। मतङ्गज—an elephant. Bhănuji Dikshit says मतङ्गात् ऋषेर्जातः. But it is difficult to see what he means. Probably the sage मतङ्ग was the first to tame elephants and to show their utility to the world. Perhaps this has reference to Priyamvada, the son of Chitraratha (the Gandharva King) who was cursed to be an elephant by the sage Matanga and so मतं० came to signify an elephant in general *Cf.* Raghu V. 53. मतङ्गशापादवलेपमूलादवाप्तवानस्मि मतङ्गजत्वम्। Tărānăth in his Văcha. derives the word as मतङ्गो मेघ इव जायते मतङ्गजस्य तदाकारत्वात्। स्रज्—सृज्यते इति that which is made with skill; सृज् + क्विप् (०) कर्मणि. आत्महस्तेन—with your own hand. Here she indirectly refers to gambling wherein the dice are thrown with the hand. In the case of the elephant हस्त means 'the trunk'. अपवर्जिता—P. p. p. of वृज् Cau. with अप. The Fig. is Upamă.

स्वदोषादेवायमनर्थागम इत्युक्तम् स च दोषः कुटिलेष्वकौटिल्यमेवेत्याह—

व्रजन्ति ते मूढधियः पराभवं भवन्ति ते मायाविषु ये न मायिनः।
प्रविश्य हि घ्नन्ति शठास्तथाविधानसंवृताङ्गान्निशिता इवेषवः ॥ ३० ॥

अन्वयः—ये मायाविषु मायिनः न भवन्ति ते मूढधियः पराभवं व्रजन्ति। शठाः तथाविधान् असंवृताङ्गान् निशिता इषव इव प्रविश्य घ्नन्ति ॥३०॥

व्रजन्तीति ॥ मूढधियो निर्विवेकबुद्धयस्ते पराभवं व्रजन्ति ये मायाविषु मायावत्सु विषये ॥ "अस्मायामेधा—" इत्यादिना विनिप्रत्ययः ॥ मायिनो मायावन्तः ॥ व्रीह्यादित्वादिनिप्रत्ययः ॥ न भवन्ति ॥ अत्रैवार्थान्तरं न्यस्यति–प्रविश्येति ॥ शठा अपकारिणो धूर्तास्तथाविधानकुटिलानसंवृताङ्गानवर्मितशरीरान्निशिता इषव इव प्रविश्य प्रवेशं कृत्वात्मीया भूत्वा घ्नन्ति हि। "आर्जवं कुटिलेषु न नीतिः।" इति भावः ॥

अन्वयार्थः—(**ये**) जो (**मायाविषु**) धूर्तों के विषय में (**मायिनः**) धूर्त (**न भवन्ति**) नहीं होते हैं (**ते मूढधियः**) वे मूढमति (**पराभवम्**) पराजय को (**व्रजन्ति**) प्राप्त होते हैं। (**शठाः**) धूर्त लोग (**तथाविधान्**) उस प्रकार के (**असंवृताङ्गान्**) नहीं छिपाया है स्वकीय अंगों को जिन्होंने ऐसों को (**निशिता इषव इव**) तेज बाणों की भाँति (**प्रविश्य**) प्रवेश कर के (**घ्नन्ति**) मार देते हैं।

जो कपटियों के साथ कपटाचार नहीं करता है वह निर्बुद्धि पराभव को प्राप्त होता है। ऐसे असुरक्षित अंगों वाले लोगों को धूर्त व्यक्ति, तीक्ष्ण बाणों की तरह अन्दर प्रविष्ट होकर नष्ट कर डालते हैं।

30. Those men of dull intellect who do not use fraud against those who have used fraud, meet with defeat. For artful persons, having entered into the secrets of such persons destroy them just as sharp arrows enter into (pierce) and kill those whose bodies are not protected with armour.

Sl. 30. मूढधियः—ध्यायत्यनया इति धीः fr. ध्यै + क्विप् the faculty of reasoning or judging of things rightly. मूढा धीर्येषां ते। मायाविषु—माया fr. मय् 2d cl. विश्वं मात्यस्यां or मा 3rd cl. मीमीते इति + य (उणादि) by माच्छाससिभ्यो यः। IV. 109; or मां याति। आतोनुपसर्गे कः Pān. III. 2. 3. माया एषां विद्यते मायाविनः; विन् is added optionally to words ending in अस् and to माया, मेधा and स्रज् by अस्मायामेधास्रजो विनिः so मायावत् and मायिन् also

तथाविधान्—तथा विधा प्रकारः येषां ते तथाविधास्तान्। असं०—संवृतानि concealed (by an armour) अङ्गानि येषां ते संवृताङ्गाः; न संवृताङ्गाः असं-

धृताश्चास्तान् । निशित—P. p. p. of शो to whet or sharpen; also निशात. इषु—fr. इष्+कु (उ) Uṇādi. प्रविश्य—Having entered into (1) their secrets; (2) their body; *cf.* सतः शीलोपसम्पन्नानकस्मादेव दुर्जनः । अन्तः प्रविश्य दहति शुष्कवृक्षानिवानलः ॥ Kām. Nīt. III. 17: Fig. A fusion of *Arthāntaranyāsa* and *Upamā*.

न च लक्ष्मीचाञ्चल्यादयमनर्थागमः । किंतु स्वोपेक्षादोषमूलत्वादित्याशयेनाह—

गुणानुरक्तामनुरक्तसाधनः कुलाभिमानी कुलजां नराधिपः ।
परैस्त्वदन्यः क इवापहारयेन्मनोरमामात्मवधूमिव श्रियम् ॥३१॥

अन्वयः—अनुरक्तसाधनः कुलाभिमानी त्वदन्यः कः इव नराधिपः गुणानुरक्तां कुलजां मनोरमाम् आत्मवधूम् इव श्रियं परैः अपहारयेत् ॥३१॥

गुणेति ॥ अनुरक्तसाधनोऽनुकूलसहायवान् ॥ उक्तं च कामन्दकीये—"उद्योगादनिवृत्तस्य सुसहायस्य धीमतः । छायेवानुगता तस्य नित्यं श्रीः सहचारिणी ॥" इति ॥ कुलाभिमानी क्षत्रियत्वाभिमानी कुलीनत्वाभिमानी च त्वदन्यस्त्वत्तोऽन्यः ॥ "अन्यारात्—" इत्यादिना पञ्चमी ॥ क इव ? नराधिपो गुणैः संन्ध्यादिभिः सौन्दर्यादिभिश्चानुरक्तामनुरागिणीं कुलजां कुलक्रमादागतां कुलीनां च मनोरमां श्रियमात्मवधूमिव स्वभार्यामिव ॥ "वधूर्जाया स्नुषा स्त्री च" इत्यमरः ॥ परैः शत्रुभिरन्यैश्चापहारयेत् । स्वयमेवापहारं कारयेदित्यर्थः । कलत्रापहारवल्लक्ष्म्यपहारोऽपि राज्ञा मानहानिकरत्वादनुपेक्षणीय इति भावः ॥

अन्वयार्थः—(**अनुरक्तसाधनः**) अनुकूल सहायकों से युक्त (**कुलाभिमानी**) जिसे अपने कुल का अभिमान है ऐसा (**त्वदन्यः**) तुम्हारे सिवाय (**क इव नराधिपः**) भला और कौन राजा, (**गुणानुरक्ताम्**) गुणों में अनुरक्त (**कुलजाम्**) कुलीन (**मनोरमाम्**) सुन्दर (**आत्मवधूमिव**) अपनी पत्नी की तरह (**श्रियम्**) राज्य-लक्ष्मी को (**परैः**) शत्रुओं के द्वारा (**अपहारयेत्**) स्वयं ही चुरवा देगा ?

अनुकूल सहायकों से युक्त, क्षत्रियत्व का अभिमानी, तुम्हारे सिवाय भला और कौन राजा कुलीन एवं सुन्दर पत्नी जैसी राज्य-लक्ष्मी को स्वयं ही दूसरों से चुरवा सकता है ?

31. What king other than yourself, who has all the means (friends and followers) favourable to himself, and who loves his high family, will allow his royalty to be snatched away by his enemies—royalty which has descended to him from his ancestors, and is attached to him by the proper employment of the six political expedients, and gratifying to the heart, like his own wife, beautiful, sprung from a noble family and attached to him by reason of his virtues ?

Sl 31. अनुरक्त०—अनुरक्तं साधनं an ally, a helper यस्य कुलाभिमानी—कुलस्य अभिमानः (fr. मन् with अभि+घञ्) कुलाभिमानः सोस्य विद्यते । इनि प्रत्ययः । (1) proud of his Kshatriyahood; (2) of the purity or dignity of his family. क इव who possibly or I should like to know. त्वदन्यः—may be a comp. त्वद् अन्यः त्वदन्यः or two words as Malli. has them. गुणानु० —Inst. Tat. गुणैः—(1) The six expedients to be used in foreign policy. These are सन्धिर्नो विग्रहो यानमासनं द्वैधमाश्रयः । Amara. सन्धि—forming peace or alliance, विग्रह or war; यान marching or leading an expedition (at the proper time) against; आसन or halting or waiting for a suitable opportunity; संश्रय resorting to a powerful king for help; and द्वैध or duplicity. (2) Personal merits कुलजां—कुले जायते इति । Upapadasamăsa; (1) when qualifying श्रियं, hereditary); when qualifying वधू-born in a good family. मनो०—रमयतीति रमा, fr. रम्+अच् and the *fem.* aff. आ; मनसो रमा मनोरमा ताम्. परैः अपहारयेत्—Pot. of the Cau. of हृ with अप. By the rule हृक्रोरन्यतरस्याम् । Pān. I. 4. 53; the original subj. of the roots हृ and कृ may be put in the Acc. or Inst case; so परानपहारयेत् also. The fig. is *Śleśánupraṇitá Upamá.*

अथ दशभिः कोपोद्दीपनं करोति—

भवन्तमेतर्हि मनस्विगर्हिते विवर्तमानं नरदेव वर्त्मनि ।

कथं न मन्युर्ज्वलयत्युदीरितः शमीतरुं शुष्कमिवाग्निरुच्छिखः ॥३२॥

अन्वयः—(हे) नरदेव, एतर्हि मनस्विगर्हिते वर्त्मनि विवर्तमानं भवन्तं उदीरितः मन्युः शुष्कं शमीतरुम् उच्छिखः अग्निरिव कथं न ज्वलयति ॥३२॥

भवन्तमिति ॥ हे नरदेव नरेन्द्र एतर्हीदानीम् । अस्मिन्नापत्कालेऽपीत्यर्थः ॥

"एतर्हि संप्रतीदानीमधुना सांप्रतं तथा" इत्यमरः ॥ "इदमो र्हिल्" इति र्हिल्प्रत्ययः । "एतेतौ रथोः" इत्येतादेशः ॥ आपदमेवाह—मनस्विगर्हिते शूरजनजुगुप्सिते वर्त्मनि मार्गे विवर्तमानम् । शत्रुकृतां दुर्दशामनुभवन्तं त्वामुदीरित उद्दीपितो मन्युः क्रोधः । शुष्कं नीरसम् ॥ "शुषः कः" इति निष्ठातकारस्य ककारः ॥ शमी चासौ तरुश्चेति विशेषणसमासः । तम् । शमीग्रहणं शीघ्रज्वलनस्वभावात्कृतम् । उच्छिख उद्गतज्वालः ॥ "घृणिज्वाले अपि शिखे" इत्यमरः ॥ वह्निरिव । कथं न ज्वलयति ? ज्वलयितुमुचितमित्यर्थः ॥ "मितां ह्रस्वः" इति ह्रस्वः ॥

अन्वयार्थः—(**नरदेव**) हे राजन् ! (**एतर्हि**) अब (**मनस्विगर्हिते**) मनस्वियों से निन्दित (**वर्त्मनि**) मार्ग में (**विवर्तमानम्**) चक्कर काटते हुए (**भवन्तम्**) आप को (**उदीरितः**) उद्दीप्त किया गया (**मन्युः**) क्रोध, (**शुष्कम्**) सूखे (**शमीतरुम्**) शमी वृक्ष को (**उच्छिखः**) उन्नत ज्वालाओं वाले (**अग्निरिव**) अग्नि की भाँति (**कथं न**) कैसे नहीं (**ज्वलयति**) जलाता है ?

हे नरश्रेष्ठ ! वीर पुरुषों से निन्दित पथ पर आप भटक रहे हैं । आप के क्रोध को जगाने का प्रयत्न मैंने किया है । पर समझ में नहीं आता कि सूखे शमी वृक्ष को जैसे आग जला देती है वैसे यह उद्दीप्त हुआ क्रोध आप को भस्म क्यों नहीं कर रहा ?

32. How is it, O king, that your anger, being excited, does not inflame you (fire your spirit) now rolling on a path condemned by the high-spirited, as fire with flames bursting forth does a dry S'ami tree ?

S. 32. Slokas 32-41 are meant to excite Yud.'s anger. नरदेव—नरेषु देव इव नरदेवः । Loc. Tat., a king. The word देव is purposely used. It comes fr. दिव् to shine. You have the brilliance (majesty) and strength of a god and yet &c. एतर्हि—now. Fr. इदं changed to एत and र्हिल aff.; इदं becomes एत and इत before an aff. beginning with र or थ.

मनस्विन्—प्रशस्तं मनोस्यास्तीति; विन् shows excellence; noblemind-ed, intelligent, wise. मनस्विभिः गर्हिते.

विवर्तमानं—वृत् with वि means 'to undergo change repeatedly

to revolve; hence here—moving along again and again. The word विवर्त has a philosophical meaning. It means apparent or phenomenal (स्वरूपानुपमर्दन) change (as bubbles of water) as distinguished from विकार or nominal change. विवर्त is defined as अतत्त्वतोऽन्यथा प्रथा विवर्त इत्युदाहृतः । There may be a shade of this meaning here. Dharma passed through the vicissitudes of his life without being affected by them.

उदीरितः—P. p. p. of ईर् 10th conj. with उद् ; raised or roused up, excited. उच्छिखः—उद्गता: शिखा यस्य. शिखा fr. शी 2 A.+ख by शीङः किद्ध्रस्वश्च (Uṇădi. V. 24).

अग्निः—अङ्गति गच्छति इति fr. अङ्ग् to go + नि; अङ्गेर्नलोपश्च (Uṇădi IV. 50) *cf.* Ignis (Lat.) Ogni Slavonian. शुष्क—p. p. p. of शुष् , त being changed to क. शमीतरु—Śamī is a kind of tree which was employed to kindle the sacred fire. Its susceptibility to catch fire more readily than any other tree must have been noticed by the ancient Aryans and they believed fire to lurk within it. For the Paurāṇic account comp. Mah. Bhārata—

Agni bearing the seed of Śiva felt a consuming fire spread through his body and to save himself from its effect first entered the Aśvattha and then the Śami tree. The gods found him there and made it its final abode. इत्युक्त्वा तं शमीगर्भे वह्निमालक्ष्य देवताः । तदेवायतनं चक्रुः पुण्यं सर्वक्रियास्वपि ॥ ततः प्रभृति चाप्यग्निः शमीगर्भेषु दृश्यते । उत्पादने तथोपायमभिजग्मुश्च मानवाः ॥ *cf.* शमीमिवाभ्यन्तरलीनपावकाम् । Rag. III. 9; अग्निगर्भां शमीमिव । Śak. IV. 4. It is related that Purūravas generated fire by rubbing together two branches of the Śami and Aśvattha trees. The simile is aptly chosen. Anger is in the mind and is brought out by some provocation. The fire is in the tree and is manifested by friction.

नन्वन्तःशत्रुत्वादयं क्रोधस्त्याज्य एवेत्याशङ्क्याह—

अवन्ध्यकोपस्य विहन्तुरापदां भवन्ति वश्याः स्वयमेव देहिनः ।
अमर्षशून्येन जनस्य जन्तुना न जातहार्देन न विद्विषादरः ॥३३॥

अन्वयः—अवन्ध्यकोपस्य आपदां विहन्तुः देहिनः स्वयमेव वश्याः भवन्ति ।

अमर्षशून्येन जन्तुना जातहार्देन (सता) जनस्य आदरः न विद्विषा च (सता) दरः न ॥३३॥

अवन्ध्येति ॥ अवन्ध्यः कोपो यस्य तस्यावन्ध्यकोपस्यात एवापदां विहन्तुः । निग्रहानुग्रहसमर्थस्येत्यर्थः । पुंस इति शेषः । देहिनो जन्तवः स्वयमेव वश्या वशङ्गता भवन्ति ॥ "वशं गतः" इति यत्प्रत्ययः ॥ अतस्त्वया कोपिना भवितव्यमित्यर्थः व्यतिरेके त्वनिष्टमाचष्टे—अमर्षशून्येन निःकोपेन जन्तुना ॥ कन्यया शोक इतिवत् "हेतौ" इति तृतीया ॥ हृदयस्य कर्म हार्दं स्नेहः ॥ "प्रेमा ना प्रियता हार्दं प्रेम स्नेहः" इत्यमरः ॥ युवादित्वादण् । "हृदयस्य हृल्लेखयदण्लासेषु" इति हृदादेशः ॥ जातहार्देन जातस्नेहेन सता जनस्यादरो न । विद्विषा द्विषता च सतादरो न । अमर्षहीनस्य रागद्वेषावकिंचित्करत्वादगण्यावित्यर्थः । अथवा विद्विषा सता दरो भयं न ॥ "दरोऽस्त्रियां भये श्वभ्रे" इत्यमरः ॥ एतस्मिन्नेव प्रयोगे सन्धिवशाद्द्विधा पदच्छेदः । पुंवाक्येषु न दोषः । अतः स्थाने कोपः कार्यस्त्याज्यस्त्वस्थाने कोप इति भावः ॥

अन्वयार्थः— (**अवंध्यकोपस्य**) जिसका क्रोध कभी निष्फल नहीं होता ऐसे [अतः] (**आपदाम**) आपत्तियों को (**विहन्तुः**) नष्ट करने वाले के (**देहिनः**) प्राणी (**स्वयमेव वश्या भवन्ति**) स्वयं ही वश में होते हैं । (**अमर्षशून्येन**) क्रोध से रहित (**जन्तुना**) प्राणी से (**जातहार्देन**) उत्पन्न स्नेह के कारण (**जनस्य**) व्यक्ति का (**आदरः न**) आदर नहीं होता, (**द्विषता च**) और द्वेषी होने के कारण (**दरः न**) भय नहीं होता ।

सफल क्रोध वाले व्यक्ति की आपद् नष्ट हो जाती है, सब व्यक्ति स्वयं ही उसका आधिपत्य स्वीकार कर लेते हैं । इसके विपरीत क्रोध-रहित व्यक्ति की न तो मैत्री से कुछ बनता है और न ही शत्रुता से कुछ बिगड़ता है ।

33. Men, of their own accord, submit to him whose anger does not prove futile and who is able to remove calamities (distress): (1) when a man is void of anger the spirit of resentment, (lit. on account of a man's being void of &c.) people are quite regardless as to his being friendly or inimically disposed towards them; or, (2) people have no regard for him for being friendly or no dread of him for being inimically disposed. Or, (3) people have no regard for a man devoid of anger, though a friend; they have no fear of one who is niggardly though a bitter foe

Sl. 33. अवन्ध्य०—न वन्ध्यः fruitless, futile अवन्ध्यः; now see com; वन्ध्य fr. बन्ध् +य (यत)

अमर्ष &c.— न मर्ष, fr. मृष् to bear+अ (घञ्). अमर्षः anger, spirit of resentment तेन शून्यः; ft. श्वन्+य;शुने हितं; शुनः संप्रसारणं वा च दीर्घः (गण० V. 1. 2) इति यत् Tărănāth in his Văchaspatya derives it as शून्याय प्राणिवधाय हितं रहस्यस्थानत्वात् ।

जन्तुना—जायते इति जन्तुः fr. जन्+तु (तुन्) by कमि मनि जनिगाभाया- हिभ्यश्च Unadi I. 13. The Inst. is हेतौ see com.; by reason of. जातहार्देन—जातं हार्दं यस्य तेन । हार्द fr. हृदय+अण् , see com हृदय is changed to हृत् when followed by लेख the affixes यत्, अण् and the word लास हृल्लेख; हृद्यं, हृल्लासः । विद्विषादरः—may also be separated as—षा दरः; दर fr. दृ I. P. to fear or 9 Par. to tear,+अप् by ऋदोरप् III. 3. 57.

Sloka quoted in K. P. VII. as an instance of the fault called अवाचकत्व or inexpressiveness, अत्र जन्तुपदम् अदातर्यर्थे (in the sense of one not generous) विवक्षितं तत्र च नाभिधायकम् । He argues that the word जन्तु which appears from the first line to have been used to express want of generosity fails to do that, as it means by derivation 'a man' only. For in the first line it is stated that people submit to one who is अवन्ध्यकोप and आपदां विहन्ता by removing poverty. People yield to a man who is a great hero, out of fear or to one who is munificent (दाता) out of respect. In the 2nd line अमर्षशून्य corresponds to अवन्ध्यकोप (being an opposite attribute) and जन्तु to आपदां विहन्तृ. The meaning of the 2nd line is—अवन्ध्यामर्षशून्येन भवादृशा (a man like you—Dharma) विद्विषा दरः भयं न जातहार्देन जातस्नेहेनापि जन्तुना (a poor, insignificant person) अदात्रा आदरोपि न । जनस्यापि दरादरौ न किं पुनर्वक्तव्यं देहिन इति सूचयितुं भग्नप्रक्रममपि जनपदमुपात्तम् । तत्र भयादरयोरभावकथनेन भंङ्ग्यन्तरेण वश्यत्वाभाव एवोक्तः । Năgeśabhatta. Such is the interpretation of the rhetoricians.

Mammata, however, seems to have misunderstood the point here. The speaker's object here is to rouse Dharma to action by stirring up his anger. It is not necessary to take आपदां विह-

हन्तुः separately. Besides the poet uses the word आपदां and not आपदः that it can refer to poverty only. आपदां विहननं may rather be by पौरुष than by mere money-gifts, as in the case of the Păṇḍavas themselves, and so the reference to generosity is irrelevant. If we follow Malli's interpretation, which is natural, no fault will arise.

परिभ्रमंल्लोहितचन्दनोचितः पदातिरन्तर्गिरि रेणुरूषितः ।
महारथः सत्यधनस्य मानसं दुनोति नो कच्चिदयं वृकोदरः ॥३४॥

अन्वयः—(प्राक्) लोहितचन्दनोचितः महारथः अयं वृकोदरः (संप्रति) रेणुरूषितः पदातिः अन्तर्गिरि परिभ्रमन् सत्यघनस्य (ते) मानसं नो दुनोति कच्चित् ॥३४॥

परिभ्रमन्निति ॥ लोहितचन्दनोचित उचितलोहितचन्दनः ॥ "वाहिताग्न्यादिषु" इति साधुः ॥ अभ्यस्तरक्तचन्दन इत्यर्थः ॥ "अभ्यस्तेत्युचितं न्याय्यम्" इति यादवः ॥ महारथो रथचारी । उभयत्रापि प्रागिति शेषः । अद्य तु रेणुरूषितो धूलिच्छुरितः । पद्भ्यामतति गच्छतीति पदातिः पादचारी ॥ "अज्यतिभ्यां च" इत्यनुवृत्तौ "पादे च" इत्यौणादिक इन्प्रत्ययः । "पादस्य पदाज्यातिगोपहतेषु" इति पदादेशः ॥ अन्तर्गिरि गिरिष्वन्तः ॥ विभक्त्यर्थेऽव्ययीभावः ॥ "गिरेश्च सेनकस्य" इति विकल्पात्समासान्ताभावः । परिभ्रमन्नयं वृकोदरो भीमः । सत्यघनस्येति सोल्लुण्ठवचनम् । अद्यापि त्वया सत्यमेव रक्ष्यते न तु भ्रातर इति भावः । तवेति शेषः । मानसं नो दुनोति ॥ "स्वान्तं हृन्मानसं मनः" इत्यमरः ॥ कच्चिन्न परितापयति ॥ "कच्चित्कामप्रवेदने" इत्यमरः । स्वाभिप्रायाविष्करणं कामप्रवेदनम् ॥

अन्वयार्थः— [प्राक्] पहले (**लोहितचन्दनोचितः**) रक्त चन्दनावलेप के योग्य (**महारथः**) महारथी (**अयं वृकोदरः**) यह भीम [संप्रति] अब (**रेणुरूषितः**) धूलधूसरित (**पदातिः**) पैदल (**अन्तर्गिरि**) पहाड़ों के अन्तराल में (**परिभ्रमन्**) घूमता हुआ (**सत्यधनस्य**) सत्य ही है धन जिसका ऐसे [ते] तुम्हारे (**मानसम्**) मन को (**नो दुनोति कच्चित्**) क्या नहीं संतप्त करता है ?

रक्त चन्दनावलेप का पात्र यह महारथी भीम, जो पहले रथ में बैठता था,

आज धूलिधूसरित गात से पैदल ही पर्वत-कन्दराओं में भटकता हुआ, हे सत्य-वादी ! तुम्हारे मन को कष्ट कैसे नहीं पहुँचाता ?

34. Does not this Vṛkodara, accustomed to use (apply to his body) red sandal and to move in a large chariot, but now walking about on foot in the mountain regions and besmeared with red dust, pain the mind of you who (yet) regard truth as your treasure?

Sl. 34. लोहित—लोहितं च तच्चन्दनं च लोहि० उचितं लोहितचन्दन यस्य स लोहि० तः। Also उचितलो०न्दनः। In the case of compounds of the आहिताग्न्यादि class (Pān. II. 2. 37), the first member, which is generally a par, adj. in त, may optionally come last; as आहिताग्निः or अग्न्याहितः, ऊढभार्यः or भार्योढः &c. It is an आकृतिगण *i. e.* compounds requiring a similar explanation may be included in it.

महारथः—महान् रथः यस्य। Bah. moving in a large chariot. This is contrasted with पदाति (now) Mahăratha has a special meaning also. वृकोदरः—वृकस्य इव उदरं यस्य। उपमानपूर्वपदबहु०, Having the appetite of a wolf. Or वृकनामा अग्निः उदरे यस्य। उदर is placed last by the rule गड्वादिभ्यः परा सप्तमी। Vărt. on Păn. II. 2. 35. पदातिः—पादाभ्यां पद्भ्यां वा अतति इति see Malli.; fr. पाद+अत् to go+इ. The Unădi aff. इण् is added to अज् and अत् (as आजि, आति) and also when preceded by पाद as उपपद, पाद being shortened to पद before आजि आति ग (पद्गं) and उपहत (पदोपहत).

रेणु०—रेणुभिः रूषितः। is contrasted with लोहितच० रूष् I. P. to adorn, to overlay (as with dust). अन्तर्गिरि Av. comp. The comp. has the sense of the loc. case. According to Senaka (a grammarian anterior to Păn.) an Avy. ending to गिरि optionally takes the final टच् (अ); so अन्तगिरम् also.

सत्यधनस्य—सत्यं धनं यस्य तस्य qualifies तव understood. This is meant to be sarcastic. She means—you wish to be true to your promise to your deceitful foes and disregard the honour and position of your brothers so faithful to you! मानसं—मन एव मानसं स्वार्थे अण्. The word is appropriately used here. *Mánasa* is the seat of thought. If you think over it the thought must pain your mind.

विजित्य यः प्राज्यमयच्छदुत्तरान् कुरूनकुप्यं वसु वासवोपमः ।
स वल्कवासांसि तवाधुना हरन् करोति मन्युं न कथं धनञ्जयः ॥३५॥

अन्वयः—वासवोपमः यः उत्तरान् कुरून् विजित्य प्राज्यं अकुप्यं वसु अयच्छत्, स धनंजयः अधुना तव वल्कवासांसि आहरन् (तव) मन्युं कथं न करोति ॥३५॥

विजित्येति ॥ वासव इन्द्र उपमा उपमानं यस्य स वासवोपम इन्द्रतुल्यो यो धनंजयः । उत्तरान्कुरून्मेरोरुत्तरानमानुषान्देशविशेषान्विजित्य प्राज्यं प्रभूतम् ॥ "प्रभूतं प्रचुरं प्राज्यम्" इत्यमरः ॥ कुप्यादन्यदकुप्यं हेमरूप्यात्मकम् ॥ "स्यात्कोशश्च हिरण्यं च हेमरूप्ये कृताकृते । ताभ्यां यदन्यत्तत्कुप्यम्" इत्यमरः ॥ वसु धनमयच्छद्दत्तवान् ॥ "पाघ्रा—" इत्यादिना दाणो यच्छादेशः ॥ स धनं जयतीति धनंजयोऽर्जुनः ॥ "संज्ञायां भृतृवृजि—" इत्यादिना खच्प्रत्ययः । "अरुर्द्विषत्—" इत्यादिना मुमागमः ॥ अधुनाऽस्मिन्काले ॥ "अधुना" इति निपातनात्साधु ॥ तव वल्कलवासांस्याहरन् । कथं तव मन्युं क्रोधं दुःखं वा न करोति ।

अन्वयार्थः—(**वासवोपमः**) इन्द्र-तुल्य (**यः**) जो (**उत्तरान् कुरून्**) उत्तर-कुरुओं को (**विजित्य**) जीत कर (**प्राज्यम्**) प्रभूत (**अकुप्यम्**) स्वर्ण-चाँदी रूप (**वसु अयच्छत्**) धन को देता था (**स धनंजयः**) वह अर्जुन (**अधुना**) अब (**तव**) तुम्हारे लिए (**वल्कवासांसि**) वल्कल वस्त्रों को (**आहरन्**) लाता हुआ [तव] तुम्हारे (**मन्युम्**) क्रोध को (**कथं न करोति**) कैसे नहीं बढ़ाता है ?

इन्द्र-जैसा अर्जुन, जो पहले उत्तर-कुरुओं को जीत कर तुम्हें खूब सोना-चाँदी देता था, वही अर्जुन अब तुम्हारे लिए वल्कल-वस्त्रों को लाता है । फिर भी तुम्हें गुस्सा क्यों नहीं आता ?

35. How is it that the plight of Dhanañjaya, who, comparable to Vāsava (Indra), having conquered the Northern Kurus brought ample wealth, consisting of silver and gold to you, but who has now to carry your bark garment, does not excite your anger ?

Sl. 35. वासवोपम:—उपमीयते अनया इति उपमा used here in the sense of उपमान (उपमोपमानं स्यात् Amara.) or standard of comparison. Malli. उपमा is derived from मा with उप + अङ् (करणे बाहुलकात्); or अङ् may be taken भावे; उपमा similarity or resemblance, when the comp. will be dissolved as वासवेन उपमा यस्य Vyad. Bah. A third way of taking the comp. is to treat as a नित्यसमास (अस्वपदविग्रह) वासवेन सदृश: on the authority of Amara स्युरुत्तरपादे त्वमी । निभसंकाशनीकाशप्रतीकाशोपमादय: ।

उत्तरान् कुरून्—one of the nine divisions of the world (said to be a country of eternal beatitude). These are (1) Bharata south of the Himālayas; Kimpurusha; (3) Harivarsha; (4) Ilāvrita; containing Meru; (5) Ramyak (6) Hiraṇmaya; (7) Uttarakuru-each to the north of the preceding one; (8) Bhadrāśva and (9) Ketumāla lying respectively to the east and west of Ilāvrita, the central region.

"In the Aitareya Brāhmana (VIII. 14) it is stated that the Uttarakurus lived beyond the Himalaya. "In later works, the the Mahābhārata (I. 47, 19, &c). and the Rāmāyaṇ (IV. 44, 88 &c.) the land of the Uttara Kurus has already become a mythical country. Uttara Kuru is identified with Ottorakorra of Ptolemy, and Lassen places the country somewhere east of modern Kashgar; but we would place the Uttara Kuru alluded to in the Aitareya Brāhmaṇa somewhere north of the sub-Himalayana range *i. e.* in Kāshmir." Dutt's History of Civi. in Ancient India. Vol. I. p.p. 120-1.

प्राज्यं—प्रवीयते इति fr. अज् to go,+ण्यत् (य), अज् not being changed to वी by बहुलं तणि । Vārt. on II. 4. 54. Or it may be derived fr. अञ्ज् 7 P. ; प्रकर्षेण आज्यते + क्यप् by आङ्पूर्वादञ्जे: संज्ञायामुपसंख्यानम् Vārt. on Pān. III. 1. 109. अञ्जि व्यक्तिम्रक्षणादिषु । बाहुलकाकरणे क्यप्. In the sense of म्रक्षण (besmearing or anointing) we get आज्य clarified butter; in that of manifestation

प्राज्य great (greatness of magnitude being necessary for manifestation.

अकुप्यं—The meaning of (the nega, particle) here is तदन्यत्व (see com.); wealth other than what is denominated कुप्य, silver and gold. कुप्य is irregularly derived (निपातनात्) from गुप् to protect (गुप्यते इति)+क्यप् (य), by राजसूयसूर्य—Pān. III. 1. 114; गुपेरादेः कुत्वं च संज्ञायाम् । The ग् of गुप् is changed to क् when the word so derived is a संज्ञा (name) गोप्यमन्यत्. Wealth not consisting of gold or silver was not considered precious enough to be concealed and was called कुप्य.

धनंजयः—see com. fr. धन+जि+खच् (अ). Before affixes with an indicatory ख् bases अरुष्, द्विषत् and those ending in a vowel, standing as an उपपद admit a nasal. The sūtra quoted by Malli. is—वृजिधारिसहितमिदमः । Pān. III. 2. 46. खच् is added to the roots भृ, तृ &c. with a noun as their object standing as an उपपद and the whole implying a name; विश्वं बिभर्तीति विश्वंभरः, रथन्तरं साम, पतिंवरा &c. धनंजय, युगन्धर, सर्वंसहा, अरिन्दम. The Mahābhā. thus accounts for the name—सर्वाञ्जनपदाञ्जित्वा वित्तमादाय केवलम् । मध्ये धनस्य तिष्ठामि तेनाहुर्मां धनञ्जयम् ।।

वल्कवा०—वस्यते आच्छाद्यते अनेन इति वासः । वस्+असुन् (अस) करणे कर्मणि वा. Before this aff. the अ of वस् takes वृद्धि.

> वनान्तशय्याकठिनीकृताकृती कचाचितौ विष्वगिवागजौ गजौ ।
> कथं त्वमेतौ धृतिसंयमौ यमौ विलोकयन्नुत्सहसे न बाधितुम् ।। ३६ ।।

अन्वयः—वनान्तशय्याकठिनीकृताकृती विष्वक् कचाचितौ अगजौ गजौ इव एतौ यमौ विलोकयन् त्वं धृतिसंयमौ बाधितुं कथं न उत्सहसे ।।३६।।

वनान्तेति ।। वनान्तो वनभूमिरेव शय्या तया कठिनीकृताकृती कठिनीकृतदेहौ ।। "आकारो देह आकृतिः" इति वैजयन्ती ।। विष्वक्समन्तात् ।। "समन्तस्तु परितः सर्वतो विष्वगित्यपि" इत्यमरः ।। कचाचितौ कचव्याप्तौ । विशीर्णकेशावित्यर्थः । अतएव अगजौ गिरिसंभवौ गजाविव स्थितावेतौ यमौ युग्मजातौ । माद्रीपुत्रावित्यर्थः ।। "यमो दण्डधरे ध्वाङ्क्षे संयमे यमजेऽपि च" इति

विश्वः ॥ विलोकयंस्त्वं कथं धृतिसंयमौ संतोषनियमौ ॥ "धृतिर्योगान्तरे धैर्ये धारणाध्वरतुष्टिषु" इति विश्वः ॥ बाधितुं नोत्सहसे न प्रवर्तसे ॥ "शकधृष—" इत्यादिना तुमुन् ॥ अहो ते महद्धैर्यमिति भावः ॥

अन्वयार्थः—(**वनान्तशय्याकठिनीकृताकृती**) वनभूमि रूप शय्या से कठोर हो गई है देह जिनकी ऐसे (**विष्वक्**) सब ओर (**कचाचितौ**) बालों से व्याप्त [अतः] (**अगजौ**) पहाड़ में उत्पन्न (**गजौ इव**) हाथियों की भाँति (**एतौ**) इन दोनों (**यमौ**) जुड़वाँ भाइयों को (**विलोकयन्**) देखते हुए (**त्वम्**) तुम (**धृतिसंयमौ**) संतोष एवं नियम को (**बाधितुम्**) छोड़ने के लिए (**कथं न उत्सहसे**) कैसे प्रवृत्त नहीं होते हो ?

जंगल में भूमि पर सोने से कठोर देह हो गई है, शरीर चारों ओर बालों से भर गया है, इस प्रकार जंगली हाथियों-जैसे इन नकुल और सहदेव को देखते हुए भी तुम अपने संतोष और नियम को क्यों नहीं छोड़ते हो ?

36. How is it that you are not roused to set aside your patience and self-control, looking at these twin-brothers, with their bodies hardened by sleeping on forest-grounds and covered all over with hair and therefore looking like two wild (lit. mountain-born) elephants ?

Sl. 36. वनान्त०—वनस्य अन्तः a place or spot; *cf.* अन्तः कूजन्मुखरशकुनो यत्र रम्यो वनान्तः Uttar. II. 25. आवर्तमानं वनिता वनान्तात् Rag. II. 19. शय्या—Karm. Comp. शय्या शेते अत्र इति fr. शी+य (क्यप् अधिकरणे) तया कठिनीकृता आकृतिर्ययोः । न कठिना अकठिना, अक० कठिना सम्पद्यमाना कृता कठिनीकृता. विष्वक्—fr. वि+सु+अन्च् (अन्चति) +क्विन् (०); on all sides, every where.

अगजौ—न गच्छति इति अगः; also नगः । नगोऽप्राणिष्वन्यतरस्याम् fr. न+गम्+ड (अ). अगात् जायेते तौ । Upapada Sa. गजौ—The comparison shows that Nakula and Sahadeva too were huge and well built in body. Mark the alliterations in this sl.

अथ राज्ञो दुर्दशां दर्शयितुमुपोद्घातमाह । प्रकृतार्थं वर्णयितुमर्थान्तरवर्णनमुपोद्घातः—

इमामहं वेद न तावकीं धियं विचित्ररूपाः खलु चित्तवृत्तयः ।
विचिन्तयन्त्याः भवदापदं परां रुजन्ति चेतः प्रसभं ममाधयः ॥३७॥

अन्वयः—इमां तावकीं धियम् अहं न वेद। चित्तवृत्तयः विचित्ररूपाः खलु। (किन्तु) परां भवदापदं विचिन्तयन्त्याः मम चेतः आधयः प्रसभं रुजन्ति ॥३७॥

इमामिति ॥ इमां वर्तमानाम्। तवेमां तावकीं त्वदीयाम् ॥ "तस्येदम्" इत्यण्प्रत्ययः। "तवकममकावेकवचने" इति तवकादेशः ॥ धियं त्वदापद्विषयां चित्तवृत्तिमहं न वेद न वेद्मि। परबुद्धेरप्रत्यक्षत्वादिति भावः। "विदो लटो वा" इति लटो णलादेशः। न चात्मदृष्टान्तेनापन्नत्वाद् दुःखित्वमनुमातुं शक्यते। धीरादिष्वनैकान्तिकत्वादित्याशयेनाह—चित्तवृत्तयो विचित्ररूपा धीराधीराद्यनेकप्रकाराः खलु। किंतु परामुत्कृष्टां भवदापदं विचिन्तयन्त्या भावयन्त्या मम चेतश्चित्तम्। आधयो मनोव्यथाः ॥ "उपसर्गे घोः किः" इति किप्रत्ययः ॥ प्रसभं प्रसह्य रुजन्ति भञ्जन्ति ॥ "रुजो भङ्गे" इति धातोर्लट् ॥ पश्यतामपि दुःसहा दुःखजननी त्वद्विपत्तिरनुभवितारं त्वां न विकरोतीति महच्चित्रमित्यर्थः ॥ चेत इति "रुजार्थानां भाववचनानामज्वरेः" इति षष्ठी न भवति। तत्र शेषाधिकाराच्छेषत्वस्य विवक्षितत्वादिति ॥

अन्वयार्थः—(**इमाम्**) इस (**तावकीम्**) तुम्हारी (**धियम्**) बुद्धि को (**अहम्**) मैं (**न वेद**) नहीं जानती। (**खलु**) निश्चय से (**चित्तवृत्तयः**) चित्तवृत्तियाँ (**विचित्र रूपाः**) विचित्र प्रकार की होती हैं। [किन्तु] (**पराम्**) अत्यधिक (**भवदापदम्**) आपकी आपत्ति को (**विचिन्तयन्त्याः**) सोचते हुए (**मम चेतः**) मेरे चित्त को (**आधयः**) मनोव्यथाएँ (**प्रसभम्**) हठपूर्वक (**रुजन्ति**) पीड़ित करती हैं।

हर व्यक्ति का अपना-अपना ढंग होता है। मैं तुम्हारी समझ को नहीं जानती। परन्तु आपकी इस आपत्ति को सोच-सोच कर मुझे अत्यधिक मानसिक कष्ट होता है।

37. I do not understand this disposition of your mind; the attitudes of the mind have, indeed, various forms. As I ponder over your serious misfortune, anguish deeply afflicts my mind.

Sl. 37. इमां—This *i. e.* which makes you sit contented with your present state. तावकी—तव इयं तावकीं In the sing. तवक and ममक are substituted for युष्मद् and अस्मद् respectively before the affixes अण् and खञ् (ईन); so तावक, तावकीन; मामक, मामकीन.

वेद—विद् takes the terminations of the perf. optionally in the pres. tense. धियं—धी fr. ध्यै + क्विप्. विचित्र०—विचित्रं रूपं यासां ताः। of various forms or different nature. आधयः—see I. 28. प्रसभं—adv. प्रगता सभा विचारो यस्मात्; thoughtlessly; hence forcibly. —चेतः—Fr. चित् 1. P. to know, + अस् (असुन्); चेतति अनेन इति। Acc.; on this Malli. remarks—In the case of verbs having the sense of रुज् 'to give pain' with the exception of ज्वर् cau. (and संतप् cau.) the object is put in the Gen. case when the subject is an abstract noun. (भावकर्तृकाणां). But this sutra belongs to शेषाधिकार which depends upon the will of the writer. Here there is no शेषविवक्षा and so the Acc. is used.

रुजन्ति—She means.—When I think of your present misery it causes writhing pain to my mind, while you remain quite unaffected. So the dispositions of men's minds must be various.

तदापदमेव श्लोकत्रयेणाह—

पुराऽधिरूढः शयनं महाधनं विबोध्यसे यः स्तुतिगीतिमङ्गलैः।
अदभ्रदर्भामधिशय्य स स्थलीं जहासि निद्रामशिवैः शिवारुतैः॥ ३८॥

अन्वयः—यः (त्वं) महाधनं शयनम् अधिरूढः (सन्) स्तुतिगीतिमङ्गलैः पुरा (वैतालिकैः) विबोध्यसे सः (त्वं) अदभ्रदर्भां स्थलीम् अधिशय्य अशिवैः शिवारुतैः निद्रां जहासि ॥३८॥

पुरेति॥ यस्त्वं महाधनं बहुमूल्यं श्रेष्ठम्॥ "महाधनं महामूल्ये" इति विश्वः॥ शयनं शय्यामधिरूढः सन्। स्तुतयो गीतयश्च ता एव मङ्गलानि तैः। करणभूतैः। विबोध्यसे। वैतालिकैरिति शेषः। पूर्वं बोधित इत्यर्थः॥ "पुरि लुङ् चास्मे" इति भूतार्थे लट्॥ स त्वमदभ्रदर्भां बहुकुशाम्॥ "अस्त्री कुशं कुथो दर्भः" इति। "अदभ्रं बहुलं बहु" इत्युभयत्राप्यमरः॥ स्थलीमकृत्रिमभूमिम्॥ "जानपद—" इत्यादिना कृत्रिमार्थे ङीप्॥ एतेन दुःसहस्पर्शत्वमुक्तम्॥ "अधिशीङ्स्थासां कर्म" इति कर्मत्वम्। अधिशय्य शयित्वा॥ "अयङ्यिक्ङिति"

इत्ययङादेशः ॥ अशिवैरमङ्गलैः शिवारुतैः क्रोष्टुवासितैः ॥ "शिवा हरीतकी कोष्ठा शमी नद्यमलक्युभे" इति वैजयन्ती ॥ निद्रां जहासि । अद्येति शेषः ॥

अन्वयार्थः—(**यः**) [त्वम्] जो तुम (**महाधनम्**) बहुमूल्य (**शयनम्**) पलंग पर (**अधिरूढः**) चढ़े हुए (**स्तुतिगीतिमङ्गलैः**) मांगलिक स्तुति-गानों से (**पुरा**) पहले (**बिबोध्यसे**) जगाये जाते थे, (**सः**) वह [अब तुम] (**अदभ्रदर्भाम्**) विपुल कुशों वाले (**स्थलीम्**) [बिना बनाये] स्थल पर (**अधिशय्य**) सो कर (**अशिवैः**) अमांगलिक (**शिवारुतैः**) गीदड़ियों के क्रन्दन से (**निद्राम्**) नींद को (**जहासि**) छोड़ते हो।

बहुमूल्य पलंग पर सो कर वैतालिकों द्वारा मांगलिक स्तुतिगानों से जगाये जाने वाले आप अब कुशाच्छादित ऊबड़-खाबड़ थड़े पर सोते हो, और अमांगलिक गीदड़ियों के रुदन से जगाये जाते हो।

38. You who, sleeping on a very costly couch, were formerly roused from slumber by the auspicious eulogistic songs (or eulogies and songs) of bards, now lie on the ground covered with luxuriant Kuśa grass and give up your sleep on hearing the inauspicious howlings of jackals.

Sl. 38. महाधनं— महत् धनं यस्य. Here धन is used in the peculiar sense of 'price'. अधिरूढः—रुह् being a गत्यर्थक root the p. p. is used in an active sense. ०मङ्गलैः—*i. e.* मङ्गलस्तु०भिः the auspicious songs &c. पुरा बिबोध्यसे—विबोध्यसे is pres. pass. but here it is used in the sense of the past tense. See Malli. पुराशब्दयोगे भूतानद्यतने विभाषा लुङ् ०चाल्लट् न तु स्मयोगे । Sid. Kau. With the particle पुरा not joined with स्म, the Aorist or present tense (also the Imperf.) may be used to indicate indefinite past time. You who were roused, *cf.* Bhoja—मृदुभिर्मर्दनैः पादे शीतैर्व्यंजनकैस्तथा । श्रुतौ वा मधुरैर्गीतैर्निद्रातो बोधयेन्नृपम् ॥

अदभ्र०—न दभ्रा अदभ्राः; दभ्र scanty; few; fr. दृम्भ+र; अदभ्रा दर्भा यस्याम्. स्थली—स्थल takes ई in the fem. when the sense is a spot in its natural state (unimproved by art); otherwise the fem. is स्थला. अशिवैः—The howling of a female jackal is considered inauspicious. *cf.* Bṛh. Sam. सर्वदिक्स्वरिवा दीप्ता विशेषेणा-ह्नशोभना । पुरे सैन्येपसव्या च कष्टासूर्योन्मुखी शिवा ॥ Fig. Alliteration.

पुरोपनीतं ! नृप रामणीयकं द्विजातिशेषेण यदेतदन्धसा ।

तदद्य ते वन्यफलाशिनः परं परैति कार्श्यं यशसा समं वपुः ॥३९॥

अन्वयः—(हे) नृप, यत् एतत् वपुः पुरा द्विजातिशेषेण अन्धसा रामणीयकम् उपनीतम् वन्यफलाशिनस्ते तत् वपुः अद्य यशसा समं परं कार्श्यं परैति ॥३९॥

पुरेति ॥ हे नृप, यदेतत्पुरोवर्ति वपुः पुरा द्विजातिशेषेण द्विजभुक्तावशिष्टेनान्धसान्नेन ॥ "भिस्सा स्त्री भक्तमन्धोऽन्नम्" इत्यमरः ॥ द्वे जाती येषां ते द्विजातयः ॥ तदुक्तम्—"जन्मना जायते शूद्रः संस्कारैर्द्विज उच्यते" इति ॥ "दन्तविप्राण्डजा द्विजाः" इत्यमरः ॥ रमणीयस्य भावो रामणीयकं मनोहरत्वमुपनीतं प्रापितम् ॥ नयतेर्द्विकर्मकत्वात्प्रधाने कर्मणि क्तः । "प्रधानकर्मण्याख्येये लादीनाहुर्द्विकर्मणाम्" इति वचनात् ॥ अद्य वन्यफलाशिनस्ते तव तद्वपुर्यशसा समं परमतिमात्रं कार्श्यं परैति प्राप्नोति । उभयमपि क्षीयत इत्यर्थः ॥ अत्र सहोक्तिरलङ्कारः । तदुक्तं काव्यप्रकाशे—"सा सहोक्तिः सहार्थस्य बलादेकं द्विवाचकम्" इति ॥

अन्वयार्थः—(**नृप**) हे राजन् ! (**यत् एतत् वपुः**) जो यह शरीर (**पुरा**) पहले (**द्विजातिशेषेण**) ब्राह्मणों से बचे हुए (**अन्धसा**) अन्न से (**रामणीयकमुपनीतम्**) सुन्दरता को प्राप्त कराया गया था, (**वन्यफलाशिनस्ते**) जंगली फलों को खाने वाले तुम्हारा (**तत् वपुः**) वह शरीर (**अद्य**) आज (**यशसा समम्**) यश के साथ (**परं कार्श्यम्**) अत्यन्त कृशता को (**परैति**) प्राप्त हो रहा है !

ब्राह्मणों के भोजनोपरान्त भोजन करने से सुन्दर बना हुआ यह तुम्हारा शरीर. जंगली फलों पर आश्रित रहने के कारण आज तुम्हारे यश के साथ ही क्षीण हो रहा है ।

39. That same body of ours, O king, to which formerly loveliness was imparted by food (eaten) after the Brāhmaṇas had partaken of it, now becomes greatly emaciated, along with your glory, living as you do now on wild fruits.

Sl. 39. द्विजाति॰—द्विजातिभ्यः शेषं तेन; this is equivalent to द्विजातिभुक्तात् शेषं; तेन. The term द्विजाति was applied to the three higher castes who were entitled to wear the sacred thread.

As the investiture with the sacred thread authorised a man to study the Veda it was regarded as a moral birth. The term came to be restricted afterwards generally to the Brāhmaṇa class. See Malli. and *cf.* Ms. मातुरग्रेधिजननं द्वितीयं मौञ्जिबन्धनात् । II. 169. अन्धसा—अन्धस् fr. अद् to eat, अद्यते इति; अद्+अस् (असुन् added कर्मणि) the द् being changed to ध् and न् inserted irregularly (Uṇādi IV. 206.)

रामणीयकं—Fr. रमणीय+अक (वुञ्) by योपधाद् गुरूपोत्तमाद्वुञ् । Pān. V. I 132. In the case of words consisting of three or more vowels with a penultimate य preceded by a long vowel वुञ् is added in the sense of भाव or कर्मन्. रामणीयकं being the indirect object of उपनीतं retains its case in the passive, वपुः the direct object being changed into the Nom.

वन्य०—वने भवानि वन्यानि; fr. वन+य (यत्) वन्यानि च तानि फलानि वन्यफलानि तानि अश्नातीति तस्य । कार्श्यं—कृशस्य भावः; कृश irreg. p. p. p. of कृश् Fig. सहोक्ति in the last line.

अनारतं यौ मणिपीठशायिनावरञ्जयद्राजशिरःस्रजां रजः ।
निषीदतस्तौ चरणौ वनेषु ते मृगद्विजालूनशिखेषु बर्हिषाम् ॥ ४० ॥

अन्वयः—(प्राक्) राजशिरःस्रजां रजः अनारतं मणिपीठशायिनौ यौ ते चरणौ अरञ्जयत् तौ (अद्य) मृगद्विजालूनशिखेषु बर्हिषां वनेषु निषीदतः ॥४०॥

अनारतमिति ॥ अनारतमजस्रं मणिपीठशायिनौ मणिमयपादपीठस्थायिनौ यौ चरणौ राजशिरःस्रजां नमद्भूपालमौलिस्रजां रजः परागोऽरञ्जयत्, तौ ते चरणौ मृगैर्द्विजैश्च तपस्विभिरालूनशिखेषु च्छिन्नाग्रेषु बर्हिषां कुशानाम् ॥"बर्हिः कुशहुताशयोः" इति विश्वः ॥ वनेषु निषीदतस्तिष्ठतः ॥

अन्वयार्थः— [प्राक्] पहले (**राजशिरःस्रजाम्**) राजाओं की शिरोमालाओं का (**रजः**) पराग, (**अनारतम्**) निरन्तर (**मणिपीठशायिनौ**) मणिमय पाद-पीठ पर रखे हुए (**यौ**) जिन (**ते चरणौ**) तुम्हारे पैरों को (**अरञ्जयत्**) लाल करता था, (**तौ**) वे [तुम्हारे चरण आज] (**मृगद्विजालूनशिखेषु**) पशुओं एवं तपस्वियों से काटा गया है अग्र भाग जिनका ऐसे (**बर्हिषाम्**) कुशाओं के (**वनेषु**) जंगली-स्थलों पर (**निषीदतः**) ठहरते हैं ।

मणिमय पाद-पीठ पर स्थित तुम्हारे जिन चरणों को पहले झुके हुए राजाओं की शिरोमालाओं का पराग रञ्जित करता था, वे तुम्हारे चरण-कमल आज तीक्ष्ण कुशाओं से आच्छादित वन-भूमि पर टिकते हैं ।

40. These your feet, which once resting on a stool made of (or set with) jewels, had a red hue imparted to them by the pollen dropping from the wreaths (on the heads) of tributary princes, do now rest (tread) on forest-grounds overgrown with Kuśa grass with its tops lopped off by deer or the Bráhmaṇas.

Sl. 40. अनारतं—see *supra* sl. 15. मणिपीठ०—मणीनां पीठं; or मणिमयं पीठं मणिपीठं a comp. of the (शाकपार्थिवादि class) तस्मिन् शयाते इति । राज०—राज्ञां शिरांसि तेषां स्रजः तासाम् । स्रज् fr. सृज्+क्विप् (०) सृज्यते इति । रजः—fr. रञ्ज्+असुन् (अस्) the न being dropped. अरञ्जयत्—When the meaning is to hunt deer रञ्ज् drops its न in the cau. (रजयति). मृगद्विजा०—मृगाश्च द्विजाश्च मृगद्विजास्तैः आलूनाः शिखा येषां तेषु. Properly this should qualify बर्हिषां but as the वनs are of Barhis they may be regarded as identical with them. द्विज—द्विर्जायते इति; fr. द्वि+जन+ड (अ). In the comp. मृगद्विजा० the rules about the proper position of words are not observed as they are obligatory; else मगद्विजं should have been द्विजमृग by the rule अभ्यर्हितं पूर्वं, but that would not have suited the metre.

ननु सर्वप्राणिसाधारण्यामापदि का परिदेवनेत्यत्राह—

द्विषन्निमित्ता यदियं दशा ततः समूलमुन्मूलयतीव मे मनः ।
परैरपर्यासितवीर्यसम्पदां पराभवोऽप्युत्सव एव मानिनाम् ॥ ४१ ॥

अन्वयः—यत् इयं दशा द्विषन्निमित्ता ततः मे मनः समूलम् उन्मूलयतीव । परैः अपर्यासितवीर्यसम्पदां मानिनां पराभवोऽपि उत्सव एव ॥४१॥

द्विषदिति ॥ यद्यतः कारणादियं दशावस्था । "दशा वर्ताववस्थायाम्" इति विश्वः ॥ द्विषन्तो निमित्तं यस्याः सा ॥ "द्विषोऽमित्रो" इति शतृप्रत्ययः ॥ अतो मे मनः समूलं निःशेषमुन्मूलयतीवोत्पाटयतीव । दैविकी त्वापन्न दुःखायेत्याह —परैरिति ॥ परैः शत्रुभिरपर्यासिता अपर्यावर्तिता वीर्यसंपद्येषां तेषां मानिनां

पराभवो विपदप्युत्सव एवेति ॥ वैधर्म्येणार्थान्तरन्यासः ॥ मानहानिर्दुःसहा न त्वापदिति भावः ॥

अन्वयार्थः—(**यत् इयं दशा**) क्योंकि यह अवस्था (**द्विषन्निमित्ता**) शत्रु के कारण है (**ततः**) इसलिए (**मे मनः**) मेरे मन को (**समूलम्**) जड़ सहित (**उन्मूलयतीव**) उखाड़ रही है। (**परैः**) शत्रुओं से (**अपर्यासितवीर्यसम्पदाम्**) नहीं छीना गया है पराक्रम-धन जिनका ऐसे (**मानिनाम्**) मानयुक्त व्यक्तियों की [तो] (**पराभवोऽपि**) पराजय भी (**उत्सव एव**) उत्सव ही है।

उपर्युक्त अवस्था शत्रु के कारण है अतः मन को अधिक कष्ट होता है। जो शत्रु को अपना यश नहीं दे डालते उन मानशालियों की तो पराजय भी उत्सव ही होती है।

41. Since this miserable condition is occasioned by our enemies, it tears up my heart, as it were, by the roots. To men having a high sense of self-respect, whose wealth in the form of their valour has not been snatched away by their foes, even a reverse of fortune is as good as a festival (quite welcome).

Sl. 41. द्विषन्नि—The word निमित्त is neu. and retains its gender being used in apposition with द्विषत्. अपर्यासित०—पर्यासित p. p. p. of आस् or अस् to throw, cau. with परि. वीर्यमेव सम्पत् or वीर्यस्य सम्पत् excess; now see Malli. or वीर्यं च सम्पच्च वीर्यसम्पदौ. परैः अविपर्यासिते वीर्यसम्पदौ येषाम्। वीरस्य कर्म वीर्यं Valour, heroic deeds. पराभवः—*i. e.* if due to the working of fate.

विहाय शान्तिं नृप धाम तत्पुनः प्रसीद सन्धेहि वधाय विद्विषाम्।
व्रजन्ति शत्रूनवधूय निःस्पृहाः शमेन सिद्धिं मुनयो न भूभृतः ॥ ४२ ॥

अन्वयः—(हे) नृप, शान्तिं विहाय तत् (क्षात्रं) धाम विद्विषां वधाय पुनः सन्धेहि। प्रसीद। निःस्पृहा मुनयः शत्रून् (षड्रिपून्) अवधूय शमेन सिद्धिं (मोक्षसिद्धिं) व्रजन्ति। भूभृतः (तु) शमेन सिद्धिं (राज्यसिद्धिं) न व्रजन्ति ॥४२॥

विहायेति ॥ हे नृप! शान्तिं शमं विहाय तत्प्रसिद्धं धाम तेजो विद्विषां वधाय पुनः सन्धेह्यङ्गीकुरु प्रसीद ॥ प्रार्थनायां लोट् ॥ ननु शमेन कार्यसिद्धौ किं क्रोधेनेत्यत्राह—व्रजन्तीति ॥ निःस्पृहा मुनयः शत्रून्कामादीनवधूय निर्जित्य

शमेन क्रोधवर्जनेन सिद्धिं मोक्षाख्यां व्रजन्ति । भुभृतस्तु न। कैवल्यकार्यवद्राजकार्यं न शान्तिसाध्यमित्यर्थः ॥

अन्वयार्थः–(**नृप**) हे महाराज ! (**शान्तिं विहाय**) शान्ति को छोड़ कर (**तत्**) उस प्रसिद्ध (**धाम**) [क्षात्र] तेज को (**विद्विषां वधाय**) शत्रुओं के नाश के लिए (**पुनः**) फिर से (**संधेहि**) स्वीकार कीजिये ! (**प्रसीद**) प्रसन्न होओ ! (**निःस्पृहा**) स्पृहारहित (**मुनयः**) मुनिजन (**शत्रून् अवधूय**) काम-क्रोधादि शत्रुओं को जीत कर (**शमेन**) शान्ति के द्वारा (**सिद्धिं व्रजन्ति**) [मोक्ष-रूप] सिद्धि को प्राप्त करते हैं, (**न भूभृतः**) राजा लोग नहीं ।

हे महाराज ! हम पर कृपा कीजिये । शान्ति की नीति को त्याग कर प्रसिद्ध क्षात्र तेज को धारण कीजिये । शान्ति की नीति से आभ्यंतर शत्रुओं को जीत कर मुनि-जन सिद्धि को प्राप्त किया करते हैं, राजा शान्ति से राज्य नहीं पाया करते !

42. Give up, therefore, O King, this quietude (of your mind *i. e.* policy of peace), and be pleased to resume your heroic spirit, so well known, for the destruction of your enemies sages, free from all worldly desires, having subdued their enemies (the passions attain their desired object by means of quietude, and not kings (by a disregard of their foes.)

Sl. 42. तत्—that, so well known. धामन्—दधाति धीयते वा; fr. धा + मन् (मनिन्) heroic spirit, puissance, valour. शत्रून्—शातयन्ति इति शत्रवः fr. शद् cau. + त्र (कृ न Unādi IV. 104).

अवधूय—(1) having conquered; (2) having disregarded or not minded the doings of. मुनि—मन्यते इति; fr. मन्—इ (इन) the penul. अ being changed to उ by मनेरुच्च. Unā. IV. 123. Properly one who observes the vow of silence (वाचं यमो मुनिः Amara); here sages in general.

पुरःसरा धामवतां यशोधनाः सुदुःसहं प्राप्य निकारमीदृशम् ।
भवादृशाश्चेदधिकुर्वते रतिं निराश्रया हन्त हता मनस्विता ॥ ४३ ॥

अन्वयः—धामवतां पुरःसराः यशोधनाः भवादृशाः सुदुःसहम् ईदृशं निकारं प्राप्य रतिं अधिकुर्वते चेत् हन्त मनस्विता निराश्रिता (सती) हता ॥४३॥

पुर इति ।। किं च धामवतां तेजस्विनाम् । परापकारासहिष्णूनामित्यर्थः । पुरः सरन्तीति पुरःसरा अग्रेसराः ।। "पुरोऽग्रतोऽग्रेषु सर्तेः" इति टप्रत्ययः । यशोधना भवादृशाः सुदुःसहमतिदुःसहमीदृशमुक्तप्रकारं निकारं पराभवं प्राप्य रतिं संतोषमधिकुर्वते स्वीकुर्वते चेत्तर्हि हन्त इति खेदे । मनस्विताभिमानिता निराश्रया सती हता । तेजस्विजनैकशरणत्वान्मनस्वितायां इत्यर्थः । अतः पराक्रमितव्यमिति भावः ।। यद्यप्यत्र प्रसहनस्यासङ्गतेरधिपूर्वात्करोतेः "अधेः प्रसहने" इत्यात्मनेपदं न भवति । "प्रसहनं परिभवः" इति काशिका । तथाप्यस्याः कर्त्रभिप्रायविवक्षायामेव प्रयोजकत्वात्कर्त्रभिप्राये "स्वरितञितः—" इत्यात्मनेपदं प्रसिद्धम् ।।

अन्वयार्थः – (**धामवताम्**) तेजस्वियों में (**पुरःसराः**) अग्रेसर (**यशोधनाः**) यश ही है धन जिनका ऐसे (**भवादृशाः**) आप-जैसे (**सुदुःसहम्**) अत्यन्त असह्य इस (**ईदृशम्**) प्रकार के (**निकारम्**) तिरस्कार को (**प्राप्य**) पाकर (**रतिमधिकुर्वते चेत्**) यदि सन्तोष करते हैं [तो फिर] (**हन्त**) दुःख है, (**मनस्विता**) अभिमानिता (**निराश्रिता**) [सती] निराश्रय हुई-हुई (**हता**) मर गई !

तेजस्वियों में अग्रगण्य, यशस्वी आप-जैसे व्यक्ति यदि इस प्रकार के असह्य तिरस्कार को सहन करते हैं तो हाय ! बेचारी स्वाभिमानता बिना आश्रय के कारण समाप्त हो गई ।

43. If men like you who regard glory as their wealth and who are the foremost among the high-spirited, resort to contentment, after having met with such an insult very difficult to bear, then alas ! sealed is the lot (or lost is the cause) of highmindedness, being rendered supportless.

Sl. 43. निकार—निकृष्टीकरणं; fr. कृ+अ (घञ् भावे) insult, disgrace or degradation. भवादृशाः—see *supra sl*. 28. रति—peaceful state of mind, contentment. अधिकुर्वते—The rule अधेः प्रसहने *i. e.* कृ with अधि is Atm. in the sense of overpowering does not apply here. But as the fruit of the action is intended to be reaped by the agent the Atm. is used here as कृ is P. and A. Pān. I. 3. 37. See Malli. मनस्विता—प्रशस्तं मनोस्यास्तीति मनस्वी तस्य भावः । high-mindedness, high sense of self-respect. हता—It is used here to imply futurity; हता भविष्यति. But Draupadi regards it as already हता and so the past tense is used by आशंसायां भूतवच्च । Pān. III. 3. 132. हता—For यदचेतनोपि पादैः स्पृष्टः प्रज्वलति सवितुरिनकान्तः । तत्तेजस्वी पुरुषः परकृतनिकृतिं कथं सहते ॥ Bhar. Nit.

अथ क्षमामेव निरस्तविक्रमश्चिराय पर्येषि सुखस्य साधनम् ।
विहाय लक्ष्मीपतिलक्ष्म कार्मुकं जटाधरः सञ्जुहुधीह पावकम् ॥ ४४ ॥

अन्वयः—अथ निरस्तविक्रमः (सन्) चिराय क्षमाम् एव सुखस्य साधनं पर्येषि, (तर्हि) लक्ष्मीपतिलक्ष्म कार्मुकं विहाय जटाधरः सन् इह पावकं जुहुधि ॥४४॥

कथेति ॥ अथ पक्षान्तरे । निरस्तविक्रमः सन् । चिराय चिरकालेनापि क्षमां क्षान्तिमेव ॥ "क्षितिक्षान्त्योः क्षमा" इत्यमरः ॥ सुखस्य साधनं पर्येष्यवगच्छसि, तर्हि लक्ष्मीपतिलक्ष्म राजचिह्नं कार्मुकं विहाय । धरतीति धरः । पचाद्यच् ॥ जटानां धरो जटाधरः सन्निह वने पावकं जुहुधि । पावके होमं कुर्वित्यर्थः । अधिकरणे कर्मत्वोपचारः । विरक्तस्य किं धनुषेत्यर्थः ॥ "हुझल्भ्यो हेर्धिः" ॥

अन्वयार्थः—(**अथ**) और यदि (**निरस्तविक्रमः**) समाप्त हो गया है पराक्रम जिसका ऐसे [हुए-हुए तुम] (**चिराय**) चिरकाल-पर्यन्त (**क्षमामेव**) सहनशीलता को ही (**सुखस्य साधनम्**) सुख का साधन (**पर्येषि**) समझते हो, [तो] (**लक्ष्मीपति-लक्ष्म**) राज-चिह्न (**कार्मुकम्**) धनुष को (**विहाय**) छोड़ कर (**जटाधरः सन्**) जटाधारी हुए-हुए (**इह**) यहाँ जंगल में (**पावकं जुहुधि**) यज्ञाग्नि में हवन करो

और यदि निस्तेज हुए तुम अपनी इस क्षमा की नीति को ही सुख का उपाय समझते हो तो राज-चिह्न रूप इस धनुष को छोड़ दो, जटाएँ बढ़ा लो तथा जंगल में बैठे-बैठे हवन करते रहो।

44. If, on the other hand, setting aside all idea of making vigorous efforts you deem forbearance for a long time to be the means of getting happiness, then giving up the bow, the emblem of Royalty, and wearing matted hair, be offering oblations to the sacred fire here (in this forest.)

Sl. 44. निरस्त०—निरस्तः विक्रमः येन । लक्ष्मी०—लक्ष्मीपतेः लक्ष्म। कार्मुकं—कर्मणे प्रभवतीति; fr. कर्मन्—उक (उकञ्) पावकं—पुनाति इति पावकः; fr. पू+अक (ण्वुल्). Fire is properly the अधिकरण or that into which ghee and other oblations are offered. But it is put in the objective case by the principle विवक्षावशात् कारकाणि See Malli.

अथ समयोल्लङ्घनाद्बिभेषि, तदपि न किंचिदित्याह—

न समयपरिरक्षणं क्षमं ते निकृतिपरेषु परेषु भूरिधाम्नः।
अरिषु हि विजयार्थिनः क्षितीशा विदधति सोपधि सन्धिदूषणानि ॥४५॥

अन्वयः—परेषु निकृतिपरेषु (सत्सु) भूरिधाम्नस्ते समयपरिरक्षणं न क्षमम्। (तथापि) विजयार्थिनः क्षितीशाः अरिषु सोपधि सन्धिदूषणानि विदधति ॥४५॥

नेति ॥ परेषु शत्रुषु। निकृतिः शाठ्यं परं प्रधानं येषु तेषु तथोक्तेष्वपकारतत्परेषु सत्सु भूरिधाम्नो महौजसः प्रतीकारक्षमस्य ते तव समयस्त्रयोदशसंवत्सरान्वने वत्स्यामीत्येवंरूपा संवित् ॥ "समयाः शपथाचारकालसिद्धान्तसंविदः।" इत्यमरः ॥ तस्य परिरक्षणं प्रतीक्षणं न क्षमं न युक्तम् ॥ "युक्ते क्षमं शक्ते हिते त्रिषु" इत्यमरः ॥ हि यस्माद्विजयार्थिनो विजिगीषवः क्षितीशा अरिषु विषये सोपधि सकपटं यथा तथा ॥ "कपटोऽस्त्री व्याजदम्भोपधयश्छद्मकैतवे।" इत्यमरः ॥ सन्धिदूषणानि विदधति केनचिद्व्याजेन दोषमापाद्य सन्धिं दूषयन्ति। विघटयन्तीत्यर्थः। शक्तस्य हि विजिगीषोः सर्वथा कार्यसाधनं प्रधानमन्यत्समयरक्षणादिकमशक्तस्येति भावः ॥ अर्थान्तरन्यासोऽलङ्कारः ॥ पुष्पिताग्रा वृत्तम् ॥

अन्वयार्थः—(**परेषु**) शत्रुओं के (**निकृतिपरेषु**) [सत्सु] कपट-प्रधान होने पर (**भूरिधाम्नः**) अति तेजस्वी (**ते**) तुम्हारे लिए (**समयपरिरक्षणम्**) प्रतिज्ञा की रक्षा (**न क्षमम्**) उपयुक्त नहीं है। [तथापि यदि ऐसा न करना चाहो तो भी] (**विजयार्थिनः**) विजय चाहने वाले (**क्षितीशाः**) नरपति (**अरिषु**) शत्रु-विषय में (**सोपधि**) कपटपूर्वक (**संधिदूषणानि**) संधि-दोषों को (**विदधति**) करते हैं।

शत्रु जब कपट पर उतर आया हो तो अति तेजस्वी आप के लिए प्रतिज्ञा का पालन करना उपयुक्त नहीं है। यदि यह न कर सको तो, प्रायः विजयेच्छु राजा किसी-न-किसी बहाने से संधि में दोष निकाल कर उसे तोड़ देते हैं, ऐसा ही आप भी कीजिये।

45. When your enemies are bent on doing harm to you, it is not proper for you, possessed of great might, to keep to the agreement (entered into with them): for, in respect of enemies, kings intent on victory, effect breaches of peace under some pretext (or plausible excuse).

Sl. 45. निकृति०—निकृतिः परं येषां भूरिधाम्नः—भूरि धाम यस्य तस्य having mighty prowess. This epithet is used to show to Yudh. that he has the power to punish his foes. He must only manifest it. समय—The condition or agreement made *viz.* to pass 13 years in exile. See Sabh. P. ch. 76 slokas 12-14. परिरक्षणं—its observance or fulfilment. विजयार्थिनः—विजयमर्थयन्ते इति; desiring victory. सोपधि—उपधि fraud. pretext; उपधिना सह वर्तन्ते यथा तथा । सन्धि०—सन्धेः दूषणानि breaking of.

उक्तमर्थमाशीर्वादपूर्वकमुपसंरहति—

विधिसमयनियोगाद्दीप्तिसंहारजिह्मं
शिथिलवसुमगाधे मग्नमापत्पयोधौ ।
रिपुतिमिरमुदस्योदीयमानं दिनादौ
दिनकृतमिव लक्ष्मीस्त्वां समभ्येतु भूयः ॥४६॥

अन्वयः—विधिसमयनियोगात् अगाधे आपत्पयोधौ मग्नं दीप्तिसंहार-जिह्मं शिथिलवसुं रिपुतिमिरम् उदस्य उदीयमानं त्वां दिनादौ दिनकृतमिव लक्ष्मी भूयः समभ्येतु ॥४६॥

विधीति ॥ विधिर्दैवम् ॥ "विधिर्विधाने दैवे च" इत्यमरः ॥ समयः कालः तयोर्नियोगान्नियमनाद्धेतोः । तयोर्दुरतिक्रमत्वादिति भावः । अगाधे दुस्तरे । आपत्पयोधिरिवेत्युपमितसमासः । दिनकृतमिवेति वक्ष्यमाणानुसारात्तस्मिन्नापत्पयोधौ मग्नम् । सूर्योऽपि सायं सागरे मज्जति परेद्युरुन्मज्जतीत्यागमः । दीप्तिः प्रताप आतपश्च तस्याः संहारेण जिह्ममप्रसन्नं शिथिलवसुं शिथिलधनमन्यत्र शिथिलरश्मिम् ॥ "वसुर्देवेऽग्नौ रश्मौ च वसु तोये धने मणौ" इति वैजयन्ती ॥ "शिथिलबलम्" इति पाठे तूभयत्रापि शिथिलशक्तिकमित्यर्थः ॥ रिपुस्तिमिरमिवेति रिपुतिमिरमुदस्य निरस्योदीयमानमुद्यन्तम् ॥ "ईङ गतौ" इति धातोर्दैवादिकात्कर्तरि शानच् ॥ त्वां दिनादौ दिनकृतमिव लक्ष्मीर्भूयः समभ्येतु भजतु ॥ "आशिषि लिङ्लोटौ"

इति लोट् ।। चमत्कारकारितया मङ्गलाचरणरूपतया च सर्गान्त्यश्लोके लक्ष्मीशब्द-प्रयोगः । यथाह भगवान्भाष्यकारः—"मङ्गलादीनि मङ्गलमध्यानि मङ्गलान्तानि च शास्त्राणि प्रथन्ते धीरपुरुषाण्यायुष्मत्पुरुषकाणि च भवन्त्यध्येतारश्च प्रवक्तारो भवन्ति ।। पूर्णोपमेयम् ।। मालिनी वृत्तम् । सर्गान्तत्वाद् वृत्तभेदः । यथाह दण्डी—"सर्गैरनतिविस्तीर्णैः श्रव्यवृत्तैः सुसंधिभिः । सर्वत्र भिन्नवृत्तान्तैरुपेतं लोक-रञ्जनम् ।। इति ।।

अन्वयार्थः—(**विधिसमयनियोगात्**) भाग्य और समय के फेर से (**अगाधे**) अति गहरे (**आपत्पयोधौ**) आपद्-समुद्र में (**मग्नं**) डूबे हुए, (**दीप्तिसंहारजिह्मम्**) प्रताप के नाश से अप्रसन्न, (**शिथिल वसुम्**) क्षीण हो गया है धन जिसका ऐसे, (**रिपुतिमिरमुदस्य**) अन्धकार-रूपी शत्रु को समाप्त करके (**उदीयमानम्**) उठते हुए (**त्वाम्**) तुमको (**दिनादौ**) दिन के आरम्भ में (**दिनकृतमिव**) सूर्य की भाँति (**लक्ष्मी भूयो सनम्येतु**) राज्य-लक्ष्मी फिर से प्राप्त होवे ।

सूर्य-पक्ष में—सम्पूर्ण पद्य का सूर्य-पक्ष में भी अर्थ होगा ।

(**दीप्तिः**) गरमी । (**शिथिलवसुम्**) संक्षिप्त किरणों वाले । (**रिपुतिमिरम्**) शत्रु-रूप अन्धकार को । (**उदीयमानम्**) उदित होते हुए । अन्य पदों का इस पक्ष में भी पूर्वोक्त ही अर्थ होगा ।

संध्या-समय पश्चिम-सागर में डूबे हुए, गरमी से रहित एवं संक्षिप्त किरणों वाले सूर्य को जैसे प्रातःकाल अन्धकार का नाश करके पुनः ऐश्वर्य प्राप्त होता है, उसी प्रकार भाग्य के फेर से आपत्सागर में डूबे हुए आप को भी शत्रु का नाश करके पुनः राज्य-लक्ष्मी प्राप्त होवे ।

46. May the goddess of royalty come again to you rising up (making efforts to rise) after having destroyed the darkness in the form of your enemies, you, who, owing to the irresistible direction of fate and time (or of fate and the condition imposed at the time of gambling) are now plunged into the fathomless ocean of misery, who are graceless on account of the loss of majesty, and who are deprived of your wealth, even as the goddess of splendour attends upon the sun while rising at day-break after having dispelled darkness, his enemy—the sun who poor-rayed and dim on account of the loss of his brilliance was

sunk into the bottomless deep owing to the regulation of providence and time.

Sl. 46. विधि—समय when taken with Dharma may also mean the condition imposed at the time of gambling; नियोग the irrevocable decree of. अगाधे—गाध: fr. गाध् 1. A. to plunge into or dive, + अ (अच्) आपत्प०—आपदेव पयोधि: ; पक्षे आपद्भूत: पयोधि पयांसि धीयन्ते अस्मिन् इति पयोधि: ।

दीप्ति०—दीप्ति: (1) majesty, power or greatness तस्या संहार: loss; (2) contraction of light, loss of heat or brightness. जिह्म—(1) gloomy-looking, (2) dim. Mark this meaning of जिह्म which properly means 'crooked' hence unifit to look at. शिथिल०—(1) शिथिल वसु wealth यस्य; (2) शिथिला वसव: rays यस्य तम् रिपु०—in the second case रिपुभूतं तिमिरं darkness, his enemy. शिथिल fr. श्लथ् 10 P. A. to be loose or weak + इर (किरच्) irregularly formed (श्लथ् मोचने उपधाया इत्वं रेफलोप:, प्रत्ययरेफस्य लत्वं Sid. Kau.). See Unādi I. 53 अजिरशिशिरशिथिल &c.

उदीयमान—pre. p. of ई 4 A. to go with उद. दिन०—दिनं करोतीति दिनकृत् लक्ष्मी:—the goddess of (1) wealth; (2) of splendour. This being the concluding sloka contains the auspicious word Lakshmi; see Malli.'s remarks, The metre of the last two slokas is changed to meet the requrement of a Mahàkavya. See Introduction.

ADDITIONAL NOTES.

Sl. 15. उपाया:—Sometimes seven *Upāyas* are mentioned, three more being added to the list; these are माया or deceit, उपेक्षा trick or neglect and इन्द्रजाल or conjuring, magic; according to others these are मन्त्र, औषध and इन्द्रजाल. *Cf.* कच्चित् राजगुणै: षड्भि सप्तोपायाँस्तथाऽनघ । बलाबलं तथा सम्यक् चतुर्दश परीक्षसे । Sab. P. ch. 5. 21.

Sl.s 31-33. *Cf.* यो न दर्शयते तेज: क्षत्रिय: काल आगते । सर्वभूतानि तं पार्थ सदा परिभवन्त्युत ॥ Van. P. ch. 27.

Sl. 42. *Cf.* तत्त्वया न क्षमा कार्या शत्रून्प्रति नकथं च। तेजसैव हि ते शक्या विहन्तुं नात्र संशयः । *ibid.*

Sl. 45. *Cf.* तदहं तेजसः कालं तव मन्ये नराधिप । धार्तराष्ट्रेषु लुब्धेषु सततं चापकारिषु ॥ *ibid.*

इति महामहोपाध्यायकोलाचलमल्लिनाथसूरिविरचितया घण्टापथसमाख्यया व्याख्यया समेतः कविश्रीभारविकृतौ किरातार्जुनीये महाकाव्ये व्यवसायदीपनो नाम प्रथमः सर्गः ।

द्वितीयः सर्गः

विहितां प्रियया मनः प्रियामथ निश्चित्य गिरं गरीयसीम् ।
उपपत्तिमदूर्जिताश्रयं नृपमूचे वचनं वृकोदरः ॥१॥

अन्वयः—अथ वृकोदरः प्रियया विहितां मनःप्रियां गिरं गरीयसीं निश्चित्य नृपम् उपपत्तिमत् ऊर्जिताश्रयं वचनम् ऊचे ॥१॥

विहितामिति ॥ अथ वृकोदरो भीमः प्रियया द्रौपद्या । प्रियाग्रहणमस्या हितोपदेशसूचनार्थम् । विहिताम् । अभिहितामित्यर्थः । विपूर्वस्य दधातेः क्रियासामान्यवाचिनो योग्यविशेषपर्यवसानात् । मनःप्रियामभिमतार्थयोगान्मनोहराम् । विशेषणद्वयेनापि गिरो ग्राह्यत्वमुक्तम् । गिरं गरीयसीं सारवत्तरां निश्चित्य नृपं धर्मराजमुपपत्तिमद्युक्तियुक्तमूर्जिताश्रयमुदारार्थं वचनमूचे उक्तवान् ॥ कर्तरि लिट् । ब्रुवो वचिरादेशः । "ब्रुविशासि—" इत्यादिना द्विकर्मकत्वम् । "अकथितं च" इति नृपस्य कर्मत्वम् ॥ (अस्मिन्सर्गे । वियोगिनी सुन्दरी वा छन्दः)

अन्वयार्थः—(**अथ**) इस के बाद (**वृकोदरः**) भीम (**प्रियया**) प्रिया से (**विहिताम्**) कही हुई (**मनःप्रियाम्**) मन को प्रिय लगने वाली (**गिरम्**) वाणी को (**गरीयसीम्**) सारयुक्त (**निश्चित्य**) निश्चित करके (**नृपम्**) राजा को (**उपपत्तिमत्**) युक्ति-युक्त (**ऊर्जिताश्रयम्**) उदार अर्थ वाले (**वचनम्**) वचन को (**ऊचे**) बोला ।

तत्पश्चात्, द्रौपदी के मनोभिराम भाषण को सारगर्भित मानता हुआ भीम, युक्तियुक्त एवं प्रबल अर्थयुक्त वाणी को युधिष्ठिर से बोला :

1. Then having concluded that the speech, charming to the mind (or after his own heart) delivered by his beloved wife, was a very weighty one, Bhima addressed the king the following words, full of reasoning and enfolding lofty sense (or, spirited).

Sl. I. **वृकोदर:**—see I. 34. विहितां—धा with वि means to do which has a wide range of meaning and as speaking is a *Kriyā*, it is used here in the particular sense of uttering or speaking. See com. मन:प्रियां—मनस: प्रिया ताम । प्रिय प्रिया, fr. प्री to please and aff. अ (क). उपपत्तिमत्—उपपत्ति establishing a matter by giving a reason; hence reasoning, argument; -मत् argumentative, *Cf.* further sl. 28. ऊर्जिता०—ऊर्जित p. p. p. of ऊर्ज् a den. verb (ऊर्जयति) meaning to strengthen, to get strong. ऊर्जत: आश्रय: यस्य । आश्रीयते वाचा इति आश्रय: अर्थ: sense. ऊर्जिताशयं would be a simpler reading as आशय directly means intention. ऊचे—वच् being substituted for ब्रू governs two accusatives. Mark the alliterations in the 1st half of the sloka.

किं तद्वचनं तदाह—

यदवोचत वीक्ष्य मानिनी परितः स्नेहमयेन चक्षुषा ।
अपि वागधिपस्य दुर्वचं वचनं तद्विदधीत विस्मयम् ॥२॥

अन्वय:—मानिनी स्नेहमयेन चक्षुषा परितः वीक्ष्य यत् अवोचत केनापि दुर्वचं तद् वचनं वागधिपस्य अपि विस्मयं विदधीत । (अथवा) तद् वचनं वागधिपस्यापि दुर्वचं (अतः सर्वस्य) विस्मयं विदधीत ॥२॥

यदिति ॥ मानिनी क्षत्रियकुलाभिमानवती द्रौपदी स्नेहमयेन स्नेहप्रचुरेण । "तत्प्रकृतवचने मयट्" । चक्षुषा ज्ञानचक्षुषा । एतेनाप्तत्वमुक्तम् । परितो वीक्ष्य समन्ताद्विविच्य यद्वचनमवोचत ॥ ब्रुवोर्वचेर्वा लुङ । "वच उम्" इत्युमागमः ॥ वागधिपस्य बृहस्पतेरपि दुर्वचं वक्तुमशक्यम् ॥ शेषे षष्ठीयं न कृद्योगलक्षणा । अतो "न लोक—" इत्यादिना षष्ठीनिषेधो नास्ति ॥ तद्वचनं विस्मयं विदधीत । सर्वस्यापीति शेषः । अथवा वागधिपस्यापि विस्मयं विदधीतेति सम्बन्धः । दुर्वचम् । केनापीति शेषः । यतः स्त्रैणमपि वचः शास्त्रमनुरुणद्धि हितं चानुबध्नाति अतो विस्मयकरं ग्राह्यं चैतद्वचनमिति तात्पर्यार्थः ॥

अन्वयार्थ:—(**मानिनी**) मानयुक्त [द्रौपदी] (**स्नेहमयेन चक्षुषा**) स्नेहयुक्त आँख से (**परितः**) चारों ओर (**वीक्ष्य**) विचार कर (**यत्**) जो (**अवोचत्**) बोली है (**केनापि**) किसी के भी द्वारा (**दुर्वचम्**) बोलने में कठिन (**तद्**) उस

(वचनम्) वचन ने (वागधिपस्य अपि) वाणी के अधिपति के भी (विस्मयम्) आश्चर्य को (विधास्यति) किया है।

क्षत्रियकुलाभिमानी द्रौपदी ने सस्नेह सोच-विचार कर जो कहा है वह दूसरों के सामर्थ्य से परे की बात है। अत एव वागधिपति बृहस्पति के लिए भी यह भाषण विस्मयकारी है।

2. The speech which the lady (Draupadi), justly proud of her Kshatriya race, has just spoken, having taken into consideration all points with an eye full of affection, and (1) which it is difficult for any one to make, will excite the admiration of even the lord of speech (Bṛhaspati); or (2) which is difficult even for Bṛhaspati to make is capable of exciting the admiration of all.

Sl. 2. मानिनी—having a high sense of the exalted position of her family. स्नेहमयेन—The aff. मय indicates प्राचुर्य—'abounding in, full of. The word प्रकृतवचन in the Sūtra means—प्राचुर्येण प्रस्तुतं प्रकृतं तस्य वचनं प्रतिपादनम्। Sid. Kau. He means—In the speech made by Draupadi, affection was the guiding principle परितः—fr. परि and तस् meaning 'all sides'; पर्यभिभ्यां च (तसिल्) Pān. V. 3. 9. सर्वोभयार्थाभ्यामेव Vārt. वीक्ष्य—Taking into consideration all particulars. अवोचत—The Aor. is properly used here. It indicates the recent performance of an act. The speech was completed just then.

दुर्वचं—दुःखेन उच्यते इति; fr. दुर्वच्—अ (खल्) difficult to be spoken. The subject to this is केनापि. वागधिपस्य—वाचामधिपः वागधिपस्तस्य If दुर्वच be taken with वागधिपस्य then the Gen. must be taken as शेषे or as indicating सम्बन्ध and not as subject to it. as that is forbidden by the Sūtra न लोकाव्ययनिष्ठाखलर्थतृनाम्। Păn. II. 3. 69. Here दुर्वचम् is formed by the aff. खल्

The fig. of speech here is अतिशयोक्ति Bṛhaspati was not likely to be astonished at the speech of Draupadi and it is said that he would be so.

विस्मयकरत्वे हेतुमाह—

विषमोऽपि विगाह्यते नयः कृततीर्थः पयसामिवाशयः।
स तु तत्र विशेषदुर्लभः सदुपन्यस्यति कृत्यवर्त्म यः ॥३॥

अन्वयः—विषमः अपि नयः पयसाम् आशय इव कृततीर्थः (सन्) विगाह्यते। तु तत्र स विशेषदुर्लभः यः कृत्यवर्त्म सत् उपन्यस्यति ॥३॥

विषम इति ॥ विषमोऽपि दुर्बोधोऽपि। अन्यत्र दुष्प्रवेशोऽपि। नयो नीतिशास्त्रम्। पयसामाशयो ह्रद इव। कृततीर्थः कृताभ्यासाद्युपायः सन् ॥ "तीर्थं शास्त्राध्वरक्षेत्रोपायोपाध्यायमन्त्रिषु। योनौ जलावतारेषु मन्त्राद्यष्टादशस्वपि ॥" इति विश्वः। अन्यत्र कृतजलावतारः सन् ॥ "तीर्थं योनौ जलावतारे च" इति हलायुधः। विगाह्यते गृह्यते प्रविश्यते च। किंतु तत्र नये जलाशये च स तादृशः पुरुषो विशेषदुर्लभः यः कृत्यं सन्धिविग्रहादि कार्यं स्नानादिकं च तस्य वर्त्म सत्साधु देशकालाद्यविरुद्धम्। यथार्थमित्यर्थः। अन्यत्र च गर्तग्राहपाषाणादिरहितम्। उपन्यस्यत्युदाहरति। "उपन्यासस्तु वाङ्मुखम्। उपोद्घाते उदाहरः" इत्यमरः। यथा केचित्कृततीर्थे पयसि गम्भीरेऽपि प्रवेष्टारः सन्ति। तीर्थंकरस्तु विरलः। तद्वन्नीतावपि निगूढमपि तत्त्वं सति वक्तरि बोद्धारः सन्ति। वक्ता तु न सुलभः। त्वं च साधु वक्तीति युज्यते विस्मय इति तात्पर्यार्थः ॥

अन्वयार्थः—(**विषमः अपि**) दुर्बोध भी (**नयः**) नीति-विद्या (**विषमः अपि**) कठिनाई से प्रविष्ट होने योग्य भी (**पयसाम्**) जलों के (**आशयः इव**) आश्रय [तालाब] की तरह (**कृततीर्थः** [सन्] [विद्याभ्यासादि] उपाय की हुई, घाट बनाया हुआ (**विगाह्यते**) ग्रहण की जाती है, प्रवेश किया जाता है। (**तु**) परन्तु (**तत्र**) वहाँ (**सः**) वह (**विशेषदुर्लभः**) विशेष दुर्लभ है (**यः**) जो (**कृत्यवर्त्म**) सन्धिविग्रहादि कार्य-मार्ग को, स्नानादि कार्य-मार्ग को (**सत्**) भलीभाँति (**उपन्यस्यति**) प्रस्तुत करता है।

जिस प्रकार दुष्प्रवेश जलाशय भी घाट बन जाने पर सरलता से प्रवेश-योग्य हो जाता है इसी प्रकार दुर्बोध नीति-विद्या भी अभ्यास से समझी जा सकती है। परन्तु सन्धिविग्रह आदि के ठीक-ठीक प्रयोग को तथा स्नानादि करने के लिए उचित स्थान को बनाने वाला व्यक्ति वस्तुतः दुर्लभ है।

3. The science of politics, though intricate, can be dived into (well grasped) when a passage to it is made (by close study), just as a body of water (a lake, river &c.) can be entered into when a descent (flight of steps) to it is made but in such a case (तत्र) it is exceedingly difficult to find that person who can well set forth the path of action to be pursued.

Sl. 3. विषम:—विगत: विरुद्धो वा सम: इति (1) intricate, hard to follow or pursue; (2) difficult to enter into. आशय—a reservoir of. आशी+अ (अच्) added अधिकरणे. कृततीर्थ:—कृतं तीर्थं यस्य. तरति, तीर्यते वा अनेन इति तीर्थं fr. तॄ—थ (थक्) The aff. थ is added to roots पा (पीथं), तॄ and others; see Unādi. II. 7. It means (1) उपाय or means of understanding it, such as study &c. (2) a flight of steps leading to water (घाट in Marăthi). विगाह्यते—(1) is well understood or grasped; (2) is entered into. सत्—is used as an adv. here; in a proper or good way. उपन्यस्यति—puts forth, by (1) furnishing a solution of the intricate problems showing the proper time for conciliation &c. (2) by pointing out the proper places of bathing, the rites to be performed &c. Fig.—Upamā and ślesha.

अथ ग्राह्यत्वे हेतुमाह—

परिणामसुखे गरीयसि व्यथकेऽस्मिन्वचसि क्षतौजसाम् ।
अतिवीर्यवतीव भेषजे बहुरल्पीयसि दृश्यते गुणः ॥४॥

अन्वयः—परिणामसुखे गरीयसि क्षतौजसां व्यथके अल्पीयसि (अपि) अस्मिन् वचसि अतिवीर्यवति अल्पीयसि भेषजे इव बहुः गुणः दृश्यते ॥४॥

परिणामेति ॥ परिणामः फलकालः । परिपाकावस्था च । तत्र सुखे हिते ॥ "शस्तं चाथ त्रिषु द्रव्ये पापं पुण्यं सुखादि च ।" इत्यमरः ॥ सुखशब्दस्य विशेष्य-लिङ्गत्वम् ॥ गरीयसि गुर्वर्थप्रतिपादकेऽर्थभूयिष्ठे श्रेष्ठे च । क्षतौजसामुभय-त्रापि क्षीणशक्तीनां व्यथके युद्धोपोद्बलकत्वाद्भयङ्करे । अन्यत्रादौ सन्तापादिदुःख-जनके । अल्पीयस्यल्पाक्षरेऽल्पमात्रे च । उक्तं च, "स्वल्पा च मात्रा बहुलो गुणश्च" इति । अस्मिन्वचसि द्रौपदीवाक्ये । अतिवीर्यवत्यत्यन्तसामर्थ्यवति भेषजे

औषध इव । "भेषजौषधभैषज्यम्" इत्यमरः ॥ बहुरधिको गुणो मानत्राणराज्यलाभादिरारोग्यबलपोषादिश्च दृश्यते । अतो ग्राह्यमस्या वचनमिति भावः ॥

अन्वयार्थः—(**परिणामसुखे**) अन्त में हितकारी, (**गरीयसि**) अर्थ में बहुल, (**क्षतौजसाम्**) क्षीण हो गया है तेज जिनका उन के लिए (**व्यथके**) पीड़ादायक (**अल्पीयसि**) [अपि] अति संक्षिप्त भी (**अस्मिन्**) इस (**वचसि**) वाणी में (**अतिवीर्यवति**) अत्यन्त शक्तिशाली (**भेषजे इव**) औषध की भांति (**बहुः**) अत्यधिक (**गुणः**) गुण (**दृश्यते**) दिखायी देता है ।

औषध पक्ष में—(**परिणामसुखे**) परिपाकावस्था में सुखदायी (**गरीयसि**) श्रेष्ठ (**क्षतौजसां व्यथके**) निर्बलों के लिए [असह्य होने से] कष्टदायक (**अल्पीयसि** [अपि] बहुत थोड़ी भी (**अतिवीर्यवति भेषजे**) सशक्त औषध में .... ।

निर्बल व्यक्ति के लिए असह्य होने के कारण कष्टकर, परन्तु परिणाम में हितकारी, श्रेष्ठ, अल्पमात्रा में सेवन की गई सशक्त औषध की भाँति यह द्रौपदी का भाषण, निस्तेज व्यक्ति के लिए युद्ध-मार्ग दर्शाने के कारण दुःखदायी, परन्तु परिणाम में हितकारी, अर्थ-गौरव से युक्त एवं अति संक्षिप्त होता हुआ भी गुणों से भरपूर है ।

4. Great virtue or (efficacy) is seen in this speech which is short (as compared with the vastness of the subject), of high significance, beneficial in the end though painful to those who have lost their spirit, as is observed in a highly potent medicine, though very small in quantity, which is repugnant to the weak put productive of good in the end.

Sl. 4. परिणाम०—परिणामे सुखं तस्मिन्; सुखयति इति सुखं; fr. सुखय् a denom. from सुख (सुखं करोति)—अच्. क्षतौजसां—क्षतमोजः येषां ते तथा तेषां; ओजस् in one case means spirit, majesty; in the other intrinsic strength, virile power. व्यथकं—व्यथयतीति; व्यथ् cau.+ अक (ण्वुल्). अतिवी०—अतिशयेन वीर्यवत् तस्मिन्. भेषजे-भेषं रोगं जयति इति भेषजं; fr. भेष+जि+अ (डः) The comparison here between Draupadī's short but stirring speech and a powerful medicine is very effective. Draupadī's advice, being strong-worded, was not likely to command itself to a man of peaceful policy like

Dharma just as strong but bitter medicine is not liked by weak persons. The advice, like medicine, was productive of good in the end.

सत्यमेवं तथापि मह्यं न रोचते । किं करोमीत्यत्राह—

इयमिष्टगुणाय रोचतां रुचिरार्था भवतेऽपि भारती ।
ननु वक्तृविशेषनिःस्पृहा गुणगृह्या वचने विपश्चितः ॥५॥

अन्वयः—रुचिरार्था इयं भारती इष्टगुणाय भवतेऽपि रोचताम् । गुणगृह्या विपश्चितः वचने वक्तृविशेषनिःस्पृहा ननु ॥५॥

इयमिति ॥ रुचिरार्था हितार्थसंपन्नेति रुचिहेतूक्तिः । इयं भारती द्रौपदीवाक्यमिष्टगुणायाभिमतगुणाय । गुणग्राहिण इत्यर्थः । भवते तुभ्यमपि ॥ "रुच्यर्थानां प्रीयमाणः" इति संप्रदानत्वाच्चतुर्थी ॥ रोचतां स्वदताम् ॥ विध्यर्थे लोट् ॥ हितवचने बलादरुचिं कुर्यादौषधवदिति भावः । तथापि स्त्रैणे वचसि का श्रद्धा, तत्राह—नन्विति । गुणानां गृह्या गुणगृह्याः । गुणपक्षपातिन इत्यर्थः ॥ "पदास्वैरिबाह्यापक्षेषु च" इति ग्रहेः क्यप् ॥ विपश्चितो विद्वांसः ॥ "विद्वान्विपश्चिद्दोषज्ञः" इत्यमरः ॥ वचने विषये वक्तृविशेष स्त्रीपुंसादिलक्षणे निःस्पृहा ननु निरास्थाः खलु । "बालादपि सुभाषितं ग्राह्यम्" इति न्यायादिति भावः ॥

अन्वयार्थः—(**रुचिरार्था**) सुन्दर अर्थ वाली (**इयं भारती**) यह वाणी (**इष्टगुणाय**) प्रिय हैं गुण जिसे ऐसे (**भवतेऽपि**) आप को भी (**रोचताम्**) अच्छी लगे। (**गुणगृह्याः**) गुणों के पक्षपाती (**विपश्चितः**) विद्वान् (**वचने**) भाषण-विषय में (**वक्तृविशेषनिःस्पृहा ननु**) निश्चय से वक्ताविशेष में स्पृहारहित होते हैं ।

हम सब इस द्रौपदी के भाषण से प्रभावित हुए हैं । गुणानुरागी आप को भी यह भाषण प्रभावित करे । गुणग्राहक विद्वान् लोग भाषण सुनते हुए यह नहीं विचारते कि वक्ता कौन है ।

5. May this speech, charming in sense, commend itself to *you* also who are a lover of noble virtues. As regards (the acceptation of) a speech, wise men who are drawn to (appreciate) merits, are surely indifferent as to the individulality of the speaker (be he a man or a woman).

Sl. 5. रुचिरार्था—रुचिं राति इति रुचिरः flavoury, charming; fr. रुचि+रा+अ(क); or रोचते इति by affixing इर (किरच्) by the Unădi sutra इषिमदि...रुचिरुधिबन्धिशुषिभ्यः। I. 51; so इषिरोऽग्निः, मदिरा सुरा, रुधिरं, बधिरः, शुषिरं छिद्रम्। Sid. Kau. रुचिरः अर्थो यस्याः। भारती—speech; बिभर्ति इति भरतः fr. भृ—अत (अतच् Unādi. III. 110); तस्येयं; by affixing अण् and the fem. ङीष्. इष्टगुणाय—इष्टः गुणः यस्य (and not येन). Here इष्ट has the sense of the present tense by मतिबुद्धिपूजार्थेभ्यश्च and so takes the Gen. by क्तस्य च वर्तमाने। भवतेपि—To you also (as it has been to me).

गुणगृह्या:—Gen. Tat. गृह्य a partisan of (पक्ष्यः). क्यप् (य) is added to गृह in the sense (see Sūtra quoted by Malli.)—पद as प्रगृह्य; अस्वैरी or having no voluntary notion, as गृह्यकाः शुकाः पञ्जरादिबन्धेन परतन्त्रीकृताः इत्यर्थः। बाह्य as ग्रामगृह्या सेना ग्रामबहिर्भूता इत्यर्थः। स्त्रीलिंगनिर्देशात्पुंनपुंसकयोर्न। पक्षे भवः पक्ष्यः। आर्यैर्गृह्यते आर्यगृह्यः (Rag. II. 28. तत्पक्षाश्रित इत्यर्थः। Sid. Kau.) so गुणैर्गृह्यते गुणगृह्यः। विपश्चितः—विप्रकृष्टं चिनोति, चेतति, चिन्तयति वा। fr. चि or चित or चिन्त् with वि and प्र; a comp. of the पृषोदरादि class. वक्तृवि०—वक्तृणां विशेषः the distinction of; now see Malli. *cf.* for a somewhat similar idea स्त्रीपुमानित्यनास्थैषा वृत्तं हि महितं सताम्। Kum. VI. 12. Fig. Kăvyalinga in the first half as the हेतु is stated, and Arthăntara in the 2nd.

संप्रति स्वयमुपालभते—

चतसृष्वपि ते विवेकिनी नृप विद्यासु निरूढिमागता।
कथमेत्य मतिर्विपर्ययं करिणी पङ्कमिवावसीदति ॥६॥

अन्वयः—हे नृप! चतसृष्वपि विद्यासु निरूढिम् आगता (अत एव) विवेकिनी ते मतिः कथं करिणी पङ्कमिव विपर्ययम् एत्य अवसीदति ॥६॥

चतसृष्विति ॥ हे नृप! चतसृष्वपि विद्यास्वान्वीक्षिक्यादिषु ॥ "आन्वीक्षिकी त्रयी वार्ता दण्डनीतिश्च शाश्वती। विद्या ह्येताश्चतस्रस्तु लोकसंस्थितिहेतवः ॥" इति कामन्दकः ॥ निरूढिमागता प्रसिद्धिं गता। अतएव विवेकिनी सदसद्विवेकवती। यथाह मनुः—"आन्वीक्षिक्यां तु विज्ञानं धर्माधर्मौ त्रयीस्थितौ। अर्था-

नयों च वार्तायां दण्डनीत्यां नयानयौ ॥" इति ॥ ते मतिः कथं करिणी पङ्कमिव विपर्ययं वैपरीत्यमविवेकरूपमेत्यावसीदति नश्यति । तन्न युक्तमिति भावः ॥

अन्वयार्थः—(**नृप**) हे राजन् ! (**चतसृष्वपि**) चारों भी (**विद्यासु**) विद्याओं में (**निरुढिम्**) प्रसिद्धि को (**आगता**) प्राप्त हुई-हुई (**अत एव**) (**विवेकिनी**) विवेकयुक्त (**ते**) तुम्हारी (**मतिः**) बुद्धि (**कथम्**) क्यों कर (**पङ्कम्**) दलदल को [प्राप्त हुई] (**करिणी इव**) हथिनी की तरह (**विपर्ययमेत्य**) विपरीतता को प्राप्त करके (**अवसीदति**) नष्ट होती है ।

सभी विद्याओं में निष्णात होने से तुम्हारी बुद्धि सदसद्-विवेकवती है । ऐसा होते हुए भी दलदल में फंसी हथिनी जैसे नष्ट होती है ऐसे ही तुम्हारी बुद्धि अविवेक में पड़कर क्यों नष्ट हो रही है ?

6. How does your intellect, O king, which being well grounded in all the four lores had attained discrimination, now come to be the reverse of itself and sink low liean elephantess on getting stuck in the mud.

Sl. 6. चतसृषु विद्यासु—The four branches of knowledge referred to here are—(1) आन्वीक्षिकी logic and metaphysics; (2) त्रयी the three Vedas (with their branches); (3) वार्ता the science of economic; and (4) दण्डनीति the science of government, politics. Generally fourteen *Vidyas* are mentioned. See Rag. V. and Malli. on it. निरूढि—fr. रुह् with नि—ति (क्तिन् added भावे); growth, hence proficiency. It also means celebrity. विवेकिनी—विवेक power of discrimination ; taking a correct view of things ; fr. विच with वि—अ (घञ्); विवेकः अस्या अस्तीति. विपर्यय—change; fr. विपरि—इ to go—अ (अच). अवसीदति—(1) becomes torpid or dull, gets confused; (2) perishes. Fig. Upamā; मति is compared to a करिणी and विपर्यय to पङ्क.

किं नश्छिन्नमिदानीं येनेत्थमुपालभ्यते तत्राह—

विधुरं किमतः परं परैरवगीतां गमिते दशामिमाम् ।
अवसीदति यत्सुरैरपि त्वयि सम्भावितवृत्ति पौरुषम् ॥७॥

अन्वयः—त्वयि परैः इमाम् अवगीतां दशां गमिते [सति] सुरैरपि सम्भावितवृत्ति पौरुषं अवसीदति यत् इति अतः परं विधुरं किम् ॥७॥

विधुरमिति ॥ त्वयि परैः शत्रुभिरिमामीदृशीमवगीतां गर्हिताम् ॥ "अवगीतं तु निर्वादे मुहुर्दृष्टे च गर्हिते ।" इति विश्वः ॥ दशां गमिते प्रापिते सति । सुरैरपि सम्भावितवृत्ति बहुकृतप्रसारम् । अथवा निश्चितसद्भावम् । पौरुषं पुरुषकारः । युवादित्वादण्प्रत्ययः । अवसीदति नश्यतीति यत् । अतः परं अतोऽन्यदधिकं किं विधुरं किं कष्टम् । न किंचिदित्यर्थः ॥ "विधुरं प्रत्यवाये स्यात्कृष्टविश्लेषयोरपि ।" इति वैजयन्ती ॥ अस्तीति शेषः ॥ "अस्तिर्भवन्तीपरः प्रथमपुरुषेऽप्रयुज्यमानोऽप्यस्ति" इति भाष्यकारः । भवन्तीति लटः पूर्वाचार्याणां संज्ञा ॥ यद्वा,—पुरुषकारस्य दुर्दशा सा च शत्रुकृता इति महत्कष्टं तच्च त्वदुपेक्षयेत्युपालम्भ्यसे इत्यर्थः ॥

अन्वयार्थः—(**त्वयि**) तुम्हारे (**परैः**) शत्रुओं से (**इमाम्**) इस (**अवगीताम्**) गर्हित (**दशाम्**) अवस्था को (**गमिते**) [सति] प्राप्त कराया हुआ होने पर (**सुरैरपि**) देवताओं के द्वारा भी (**सम्भावित वृत्ति**) सम्मानित है स्थिति जिसकी ऐसा (**पौरुषम्**) पुरुषार्थ (**यत् अवसीदति**) जो नष्ट हो रहा है (**इति**) इस प्रकार (**अतः परम्**) इससे अधिक (**विधुरम् किम्**) कष्ट क्या है ?

शत्रुओं द्वारा तुम्हारी यह निन्दित अवस्था कर दी गई है । तुम्हारा वह पौरुष, जिस का देवता भी सम्मान करते हैं, नष्ट हो रहा है । भला इस से बढ़कर भी कष्टकर कुछ हो सकता है ।

7. What can be more lamentable (or painful) than this that the prowess which was highly spoken of (or, thought to exist in you) should thus deteriorate when you are reduced to this deplorable condition by your enemies ?

Sl. 7. अवगीता—Cried down, spoken as low; hence contemptible, low. सम्भावित०—सम्भाविता वृत्तिर्यस्य । सम्भावित may mean highly thought of or thought to be possible. पौरुषं—See I. 9. विधुरं—विगता धूर्यस्य; अ is added to धुर at the end of a comp. Lit. not able to bear a yoke ; hence, miserable, distressed, painful. In the quotation from महाभाष्य given by Malli. भवन्तीपरः means—referring to the present tense (भवन्ती वर्तमाना वृत्तिः).

अथापेक्षाकालत्वादियमुपेक्षेत्याशङ्क्य नायमुपेक्षाकाल इति वक्तुं तदेव तावच्छ्लोकद्वयेन विविनक्ति—

द्विषतामुदयः सुमेधसा गुरुरस्वन्ततरः सुमर्षणः ।
न महानपि भूतिमिच्छता फलसम्पत्प्रवणः परिक्षयः ॥८॥

अन्वयः—भूतिमिच्छता सुमेधसा गुरुः [अपि] अस्वन्ततरः द्विषताम् उदयः सुमर्षणः । महानपि परिक्षयः फलसम्पत्प्रवणः न (सुमर्षणः) ॥८॥

द्विषतामिति ॥ भूतिमुदयमिच्छता । शोभना मेधा यस्य तेन सुमेधसा सुधिया ॥ "नित्यमसिच्प्रजामेधयोः" इत्यसिच्प्रत्ययः । गुरुर्महानप्यस्वन्ततरः अत्यन्तदुरन्तः । क्षयोन्मुख इत्यर्थः । द्विषतामुदयः । सुखेन मृष्यत इति सुमर्षणः सुसहः । उपेक्ष्य इत्यर्थः । स्वतश्च दुर्मर्षण इति भवः ॥ "भाषायां शासि—" इत्यादिना खलर्थे युच् ॥ महानपि फलसंपत्प्रवणः फलसिद्ध्युन्मुखः ॥ "प्रनिरन्तर्" इत्यादिना णत्वम् । परिक्षयो न सुमर्षणः । नोपेक्ष्य इत्यर्थः । अन्यथा तूपेक्ष्य इति भावः । न ह्युदय एव प्रतीकार्यो न च क्षय एवोपेक्ष्यः । किंतु स्वन्तत्वास्वन्तत्वाभ्यामुभावपि प्रतीकार्यावुपेक्ष्यौ च भवत इत्यर्थः ॥

अन्वयार्थः—(**भूतिमिच्छता**) ऐश्वर्य को चाहने वाले (**सुमेधसा**) बुद्धिमान् के द्वारा (**अस्वन्ततरः**) अत्यन्त बुरे परिणाम वाला (**द्विषताम्**) शत्रुओं का (**गुरु**) [अपि] महान् भी (**उदयः**) अभ्युदय (**सुमर्षणः**) सरलता से सह्य होता है । [परन्तु] (**फलसंपत्प्रवणः**) फलसिद्धि की ओर उन्मुख (**महानपि**) महान् होता हुआ भी (**परिक्षयः**) ह्रास (**न**) [सह्य] नहीं है ।

ऐश्वर्येच्छु बुद्धिमान के लिए, शत्रु का ऐसा अभ्युदय जिस का परिणाम बुरा हो, कितना ही अधिक क्यों न हो, उपेक्ष्य होता है । परन्तु परिणाम में सिद्धि देने वाला बहुत अधिक क्षय भी उपेक्षा के योग्य नहीं होता ।

8. By a wise man desiring his own prosperity, the rise of his enemies although great may well be tolerated (overlooked) if it is to have a verybad end, but never their loss of powers (or fall) if likely to lead to a blissful result (prosperity again).

Sl. 8. सुमेधसा—One having good *i. e.* discerning intellect. The words प्रजा् and मेधा add अस् when forming adj. compounds with नञ्, दुस् and सु; so अमेधस्, दुर्मेधस् See Malli. ; the words नञ्, दुःसुभ्यः follow from the preceding Sūtra (Păn. V. 4. 121). अस्वन्ततरः—सुशोभनः अन्तः यस्य स्वन्तः, न स्वन्तः अस्वन्तः । अतिशयेनास्वन्तः अस्वन्ततरः । तर does not express comparison here but merely indicates excess. सुमर्षणः—can well be borne or overlooked; fr. सु—मृष्—अन (युच्). Here the aff. युच् is used in the sense of खल् Hence its subject उदय is put in the Nom. case, the Gen. being barred by the rule न खलर्थं &c.; see *supra* notes on sl. 2.

फलसम्पत्प्र०—फलमेव फलस्य वा सम्पत फलसम्पत् तत्र प्रवणः inclined or leading to. The न of वन is changed to ण after प्र, निर्, अन्तः &c. even when it does not mean a name (संज्ञा) The whole Sūtra is प्रनिरन्तःशरेक्षुप्लक्षाम्रकार्ष्यखदिरपीयूक्षाभ्योऽसंज्ञायामपि । VIII. 4. 5.

अथोभयोरपि मध्य एकतरस्योदयक्षययोर्गतिमुक्त्वेदानीं युगपत्परिक्षयागमे गतिमाह—

अचिरेण परस्य भूयसीं विपरीतां विगणय्य चात्मनः ।
क्षययुक्तिमुपेक्षते कृती कुरुते तत्प्रतिकारमन्यथा ॥९॥

अन्वयः—कृती परस्य क्षययुक्तिम् अचिरेण भूयसीम् आत्मनः [क्षययुक्ति] विपरीतां [च] विगणय्य उपेक्षते, अन्यथा तत्प्रतिकारं [अचिरेण] कुरुते ॥९॥

अचिरेणेति ॥ कृतमनेनेति कृती । कुशल इत्यर्थः ॥ "इष्टादिभ्यश्च" इतीनिप्रत्ययः ॥ परस्य शत्रोः क्षययुक्ति क्षययोगमचिरेणाशुभाविनीं भूयसीं दुरन्तां च तथात्मनः क्षययुक्ति विपरीतां चिरभाविनीमल्पीयसीं स्वल्पां च विगणय्य विचार्य ॥ "ल्यपि लघुपूर्वात्" इत्ययादेशः ॥ उपेक्षते । अन्यथा उक्तवैपरीत्ये परस्य क्षययुक्तावल्पीयस्याम् । स्वस्य च भूयस्यामित्यर्थः । तत्प्रतिकारं तस्याः क्षययुक्तेः प्रतिकारमचिरेणाशु कुरुते । एवं सति यदा शत्रोरभ्युदयः स्वस्य

चातिपरिक्षयो यथास्माकं तदा किं वक्तव्यमित्यर्थः। सद्यः प्रतिकारं कुरुत इत्यर्थात्सिद्धमनुसन्धेयम् ॥

अन्वयार्थः—(**कृती**) किया है जिसने ऐसा अर्थात् चतुर [व्यक्ति] (**परस्य**) शत्रु के (**क्षययुक्तिम्**) विनाशयोग को (**अचिरेण**) शीघ्र होने वाला, [तथा] (**भूयसीम्**) अधिक होने वाला (**विगण्य**) विचार कर (**आत्मनः च**) और अपने [क्षय-योग को] (**विपरीताम्**) इससे विपरीत [विचार कर] (**उपेक्षते**) उपेक्षा करता है। (**अन्यथा**) इससे विपरीत होने पर (**तत्प्रतिकारं कुरुते**) उस के प्रतिकार को करता है।

यदि शत्रु का विनाश शीघ्र एवं अतिमात्रा में होने वाला हो और अपना क्षय बहुत समयोपरान्त एवं न्यून मात्रा में होने वाला हो तो समझदार व्यक्ति उस की उपेक्षा करता है। परन्तु यदि विनाश-क्रम इसके विपरीत हो तो वह तुरन्त उसे रोकने का उपाय करता है।

9. A shrewd man, carefully calculating that the destruction of his enemy is near at hand and of serious consequence and that with regard to himself it is the reverse, overlooks that; but if otherwise, he takes measures to remedy it.

Sl. 9. कृती—कृतमस्यास्तीति ; a man of experience; skilful, wise. क्षययुक्ति—क्षयेण युक्तिः क्षययुक्तिः ताम्। Here युक्ति means योग his being joined with; his going to destruction. अचिरेण—may also be taken with भाविनीम्. भूयसीं—Here also ईयस् has no comparative force but indicates degree of intensity. विपरीत—p. p. p. of इ with वि and परि. प्रतिकार—fr. कृ with प्रति+अ (घञ्); optionally प्रतीकार also by the rule उपसर्गस्य घञि अमनुष्ये बहुलम्।

तथाप्युपेक्षायामनिष्टमाचष्टे—

अनुपालयतामुदेष्यतीं प्रभुशक्तिं द्विषतामनीहया।
अपयान्त्यचिरान्महीभुजां जननिर्वादभयादिव श्रियः ॥१०॥

अन्वयः—उदेष्यतीं द्विषतां प्रभुशक्तिम् अनीहया अनुपालयतां महीभुजां श्रियः जननिर्वादभयात् इव अचिरात् अपयान्ति ॥१०॥

अनुपालयतामिति ॥ उदेष्यतीं वर्धिष्यमाणाम् ॥ "आच्छीनद्योर्नुम्" इति

विकल्पान्नुमभावः ॥ द्विषतां प्रभुशक्ति कोशदण्डजं तेजः ॥ "स प्रभावः प्रतापश्च यत्तेजः कोशदण्डजम् ।" इत्यमरः ॥ अनीहयानुत्साहेनानुपालयतामुपेक्ष माणानां महीभुजां श्रियः सम्पदो जननिर्वादभयान्निकृष्टपुरुषानुरागाल्लोकापवाद-भयादिवेति हेतूत्प्रेक्षा । अचिरादपयान्त्यपसरन्ति । यथाह कामन्दकः—"स्त्रीभिः षण्ठ इव श्रीभिरलसः परिभूयते ।" इति । अतः पराक्रमितव्यमिति भावः ॥

अन्वयार्थः—(**उदेष्यतीम्**) बढ़ते हुए (**द्विषताम्**) शत्रुओं के (**प्रभुशक्तिम्**) प्रताप की (**अनीहया**) अनुत्साह के कारण (**अनुपालयताम्**) उपेक्षा करते हुए (**महीभुजाम्**) राजाओं की (**श्रियः**) राज्य-लक्ष्मियाँ (**जननिर्वादभयात् इव**) मानो लोकापवाद के भय के कारण (**अचिरात्**) शीघ्र ही (**अपयन्ति**) छोड़ जाती हैं ।

जो राजा शत्रु की बढ़ती हुई शक्ति की उपेक्षा अपनी कमजोरी के कारण करता है उस की राज्य-लक्ष्मी शीघ्र ही उसे छोड़ देती है, मानो उसे लोकापवाद का भय हो कि वह एक निर्बल में आसक्त है ।

10. The riches of those kings who overlook, with indifference (lit. without any effort on their part), the increasing power of their enemies, soon pass away as if afraid of public censure (for being attached to an imbecile king).

Sl. 10. उदेष्यती—Fut. p. of इ with उद् The fut. p. has no terminations of its own ; it takes those of the pres., *viz.* शतृ (अत्) and शानच् (मान) joined to स्य; स्यत् takes न् optionally before ई in the fem.; so उदेष्यती also. प्रभुशक्ति—प्रभुशक्ति is one of the three powers possessed by a king; see *infra.* sl. 37 and notes thereon. प्रभो शक्तिः प्रभुशक्तिः ; शक्यते जेतुमनया इति शक्तिः । It is the power due to good treasury and an efficient army or government. See Malli. अनहीया—न ईहा अनीहा want of active exertion; ईहा चेष्टा fr. ईह चेष्टायाम् I A., +अ (आ fem.) जननिर्वाद०—निर्वाद public censure or scandal. The censure may be due to their sticking on to a spiritless man (निकृष्टपुरुषानुराग).

ननु परिक्षीणः कथं प्रबलेनाभियुज्यत इत्यत्राह—

क्षययुक्तमपि स्वभावजं दधतं धाम शिवं समृद्धये ।
प्रणमन्त्यनपायमुत्थितं प्रतिपच्चन्द्रमिव प्रजा नृपम् ॥११॥

अन्वयः—क्षययुक्तमपि स्वभावजं शिवं धाम दधतं समृद्धये उत्थितम् अनपायं नृपं प्रजाः प्रतिपच्चन्द्रमिव प्रणमन्ति ॥११॥

क्षयेति ॥ क्षययुक्तमपि तथा क्षीणमपि सन्तं स्वभावजं सहजं शिवं सर्वलोकाह्लादकं धाम क्षात्रं तेजः प्रकाशं च दधतं समृद्धये वृद्ध्यर्थमुत्थितमुद्युक्तम् । उत्सहमानमिति यावत् । अन्यत्रोत्थितमुदितमत एवानपायमविनाशिनम् । वर्धिष्णुमत्यर्थः । नृपं प्रजाः । प्रतिपच्चन्द्रं द्वितीयाचन्द्रमिवेत्यर्थः । प्रतिपच्छब्देन द्वितीयाग्रहणं प्रतिपदि तस्यादृश्यत्वादिति । प्रणमन्ति प्रह्वीभावेन वर्तन्त इति भावः । चन्द्रं तु नमस्कुर्वन्ति । क्षीणस्याप्युत्साहः कार्यसिद्धेर्निदानमित्यर्थः ॥ "श्रियं [जयं] हि सततोत्साही दुर्बलोऽपि समश्नुते ।" इति कामन्दकः ॥

अन्वयार्थः—(**क्षययुक्तमपि**) क्षीण भी (**स्वभावजम्**) स्वभाविक (**शिवम्**) कल्याणकारी (**धाम**) तेज को (**दधतम्**) धारण किये हुए, (**समृद्धये उत्थितम्**) समृद्धि के लिए उठे हुए, [अत एव] (**अनपायम्**) विनाश से रहित (**नृपम्**) राजा को (**प्रजाः**) प्रजाएँ (**प्रतिपच्चन्द्रमिव**) प्रतिपदा [द्वितीया] के चन्द्रमा की तरह (**प्रणमन्ति**) प्रणाम करती हैं ।

सभी विशेषण चन्द्र पक्ष में भी लगेंगे—

(**धाम्**) प्रकाश को (**उत्थितम्**) उदित हुए-हुए । अन्य शब्दों का अर्थ पूर्ववत् रहेगा ।

जैसे लोग अत्यन्त क्षीण, तथापि कल्याणकारी स्वाभाविक प्रकाश को धारण किये हुए, समृद्धि के लिए उदित हुए, अतएव विनाशरहित द्वितीया के चाँद को नमस्कार करते हैं उसी प्रकार क्षययुक्त राजा को भी नमस्कार करते हैं, यदि उसने अपना स्वाभाविक कल्याणकारी क्षात्र-तेज नहीं छोड़ा हो, समृद्धि के लिए प्रयत्नशील हो, तथा विनाशरहित है ।

11. The subjects bow down to that king, who though grown weak in power, possesses his innate and beneficial majesty, who makes efforts to gain greatness and who thereby goes on ever rising (lit. never suffers decay), just as they do to the moon of the first day of a month, who though it has waned,

possesses its intrisic natural lustre and who, ever bound to increase, rises to wax again.

Sl. 11. चययुक्तम् चयेण युक्तः चययुक्तस्तम्; qualifies नृपं and चन्द्रं. स्वभावजं—स्वः स्वस्य वा भावः स्वभावस्तस्माज्जायते तत्। समृद्धये—(1) For increasing his power; (2) for waxing. उत्थितं—(1) making efforts, striving; (2) rising. अनपायं—न विद्यते अपायः यस्य तम्. प्रतिप०—प्रतिपदः चन्द्रस्तम् By प्रति० is meant here the first day after new moon. But as the lunar digit is scarcely visible on the first day we are to understand by प्रति० द्वितीया by Lakshanā (mere transference). Fig. Upamā.

The gist of the sl. is that people respect a king who does not sit idle but makes strenuous efforts to regain his lost power.

ननु प्रभुशक्तिशून्यस्योत्साहः कुत्रोपयुज्यत इत्यत्राह—

प्रभवः खलु कोशदण्डयोः कृतपञ्चाङ्गविनिर्णयो नयः ।
स विधेयपदेषु दक्षतां नियतिं लोक इवानुरुध्यते ॥१२॥

अन्वयः—कृतपञ्चाङ्गविनिर्णयः नयः कोशदण्डयोः प्रभवः खलु स विधेयपदेषु लोकः नियतिमिव दक्षतामनुरुध्यते ॥१२॥

प्रभव इति । कर्मणामारम्भोपायः पुरुषद्रव्यसम्पद्देशकालविभागो विनिपातप्रतीकारः कार्यसिद्धिश्चेति पञ्चाङ्गानि । यथाह कामन्दकः—"सहायाः साधनोपाया विभागो देशकालयोः । विनिपातप्रतीकारः सिद्धिः पञ्चाङ्ग इष्यते ॥" इति । पञ्चानामङ्गानां विनिर्णयः ॥ "तद्धितार्थ—" इत्यादिनोत्तरपदसमासः ॥ कृतः पञ्चाङ्गविनिर्णयो यस्य येन वा स तथोक्तः । नयो नीतिशास्त्रमिति यावत् । कोशोऽर्थराशिः ॥ "कोशोऽस्त्री कुड्मले खड्गपिधानेऽर्थौघदिव्ययोः ।" इत्यमरः ॥ दण्डश्चतुरङ्गसैन्यम् ॥ "दण्डोऽस्त्री शासने राज्ञां हिंसायां लगुडे यमे । यात्राज्ञायां सैन्यभेदे" इति वैजयन्ती ॥ तयोः कोशदण्डयोः प्रभुशक्तेरित्यर्थः । प्रभवत्यस्मादिति प्रभवः कारणम् ॥ "ऋदोरप्" ॥ स नयो नीतिशास्त्रं विधेयपदेषु कार्यवस्तुषु ॥ "पदं व्यवसितत्राणस्थानलक्ष्माङ्घ्रिवस्तुषु" इत्यमरः ॥ दक्षतां क्षिप्रकारित्वम् । उत्साहमित्यर्थः । लोकः कृष्यादिप्रवृत्तो जनः । नियतिं दैवमिव ॥ "नियतिर्नियमे दैवे" इति विश्वः ॥ अनुरुध्यतेऽनुसरति ॥ रुधेर्दैवादिकात्कर्तरि लट् । मन्त्र-

स्यापि मूलमुत्साहस्तन्मूलाया: प्रभुशक्तेर्मूलमिति किमु वक्तव्यम् । अत: स एवाश्रयणीय: । यतो नक्तंदिवं मन्त्रयतोपि प्रभोर्निरुत्साहस्य न किंचित्सिद्ध्यतीति ।

अन्वयार्थ:—(**कृतपञ्चाङ्गविनिर्णय:**) किया है पाँचों अङ्गों का निर्णय जिसने ऐसा (**नय:**) नीतिशास्त्र (**कोशदण्डयो:**) वित्त एवं सैन्य [शक्ति] का (**प्रभव: खलु**) निश्चय से निमित्त है । (**स:**) वह (**विधेयपदेषु**) कार्य-स्थलों में, (**लोक:**) लोग (**इव**) जैसे (**नियतिम्**) भाग्य की [उसी प्रकार], (**दक्षताम्**) चातुर्य की (**अनुरुध्यते**) कामना करता है ।

पञ्चाङ्ग का निर्णय करने वाला नीतिशास्त्र वित्त-शक्ति एवं सैन्य-शक्ति का निमित्त है । वह नीतिशास्त्र प्रयोग में चातुर्य एवं उत्साह की अपेक्षा रखता है जैसे कृषक आदि लोग दैव की अपेक्षा करते हैं ।

12. Policy having its five constituents well-determined (and secured) is the source of treasure and power (lit. army). This policy, however, depends (for success) on prompt and energetic action in matters to be executed as people depend on (the fixed working of) destiny.

Sl. 12. कृतपञ्चाङ्ग०—The five constituent parts or members of political science or polity are.—(1) securing the means to commence operations or of beginning an undertaking by securing allies &c.; (2) securing of an efficient army and a good treasury; (3) the proper discrimination of favourable time and place ; (4) means to meet emergencies or to avert dangers that may befall and (5) the accomplishment of the final object.

Malli. takes the compound as an Uttarapada Tat. (here द्विगु which is a Tat. also) under तद्धितार्थोत्तरपद—समाहारे च Pān. II. 1. 51. The sutra means—When the sense is that of a Taddita affix (*i. e.* affixes added to nouns) or when an additional member comes after the comp. or when the idea of an aggregate is to be expressed, then a word signifying a direction or a numeral enters into composition with another case-inflected word in apposition with it and the comp. is called Tat. But later grammarians object to this way of taking the comp. saying a त्रिपद Tat. is inadmissible, though an उत्तर पदद्विगु may find a place in a Bah. According to these the comp. must be dissolved as पञ्चसंख्याकानि अङ्गानि पञ्चाङ्गानि a Madhyamapadalopi ; तेषां विनिर्णय: and then कृत: पञ्चा० यस्य or if पञ्चाङ्ग is taken as a संज्ञा in works on policy, the comp. may fall under the preceding *Sutra* दिक्संख्ये संज्ञायाम्.

विनिर्णय—Fr. नी with वि निर्+अच् (अ) by एरच् Pān. III. 3. 56. नय:—by the rule श्रीणीभुवोनुपसर्गे (III. 3. 24.) नी ought to take घञ् (अ which occasions वृद्धि), when not preceded by a preposition; and we get नाय: (with प्र प्रणय:); so ito get नय we must have recourse to the rule एरच् *i. e.* Roots ending in इ or ई take the aff. अ in the sense of the action (भावे) or when the derivative forms a name but not in that of the agent (अकर्तरि) under the authority of बाहुलक. कथं राज्ञो नय इति । बाहुलकात् Sid. Kau. विधेयपदेषु—विधेयानि to be done or achieved पदानि things, objects तेषु । दक्षता—दक्षते इति दक्ष: one who takes emergetic and prompt action ; fr. दक्ष् 1 A (दक्ष वृद्धौ शीघ्रार्थे च) +अच्; तस्य भाव:; दक्षता, ताम् । Fig. उपमा and अनुप्रास. In this sl. दक्षता and नियति are compared. नियति or कर्म is the sum of a man's actions in a previous birth governing the circumstances of his present life. दक्षता also means clever and timely action on the part of a man; and like Niyati it is necessary to give him success in life. *Cf.* यथा मृत्पिण्डत:कर्ता कुरुते यद्यदिच्छति । एवमात्मकृतं कर्म मानव: प्रतिपद्यते ॥ Hit.

ननु सोत्साहस्यासहायस्य कथमर्थसिद्धिरित्यत्राह—

अभिमानवतो मनस्विन: प्रियमुच्चै: पदमारुरुक्षत: ।
विनिपातनिवर्तनक्षमं मतमालम्बनमात्मपौरुषम् ॥१३॥

अन्वय:—अभिमानवत: प्रियम् उच्चै: पदम् आरुरुक्षत: मनस्विन: आत्मपौरुषं विनिपातनिवर्तनक्षमम् आलम्बनं मतम् ॥१३॥

अभिमानवत इति ।। अभिमानवतो मानधनस्य प्रियमिष्टमुच्चैरुन्नतं पदं स्थानं राज्यादिकमारुरुक्षत आरोढुमिच्छतः प्राप्तुकामस्य मनस्विनो धीरस्यात्मपौरुषं स्वपुरुषकार एव विनिपातनिवर्तनक्षममनर्थप्रतीकारसमर्थमालम्बनं सहकारि मतमिष्टम्। यथा कस्यचित्तुङ्गमारोहतः किंचित्पतनप्रतिबन्धकानुचरहस्तादिकमालम्बनं तद्वदिति ध्वनिः। किं पौरुषादन्यैः सहायैः शूराणामिति भावः ।।

अन्वयार्थः—(**अभिमानवतः**) स्वाभिमानी, (**प्रियम्**) इष्ट (**उच्चैः**) उन्नत (**पदम्**) पद पर (**आरुरुक्षतः**) चढ़ना चाहते हुए (**मनस्विनः**) मनस्वी का (**आत्मपौरुषम्**) अपना पुरुषकार (**विनिपातनिवर्तनक्षमम्**) अनर्थों के प्रतिकार में समर्थ (**आलम्बनम्**) सहारा (**मतम्**) माना गया है।

आत्माभिमानी व्यक्ति, जो राज्य-जैसे उन्नत पद को पाना चाहता है, उस मनस्वी के लिए उसका अपना पुरुषार्थ ही, गिरने से बचाने के लिए, सब से बड़ा सहारा है।

13. In the case of a highminded man possssed of self-repect and desirous of attaining a cherished lofty position, his own prowess is considered to be his support capable of averting a downfall.

Sl. 13. **आरुरुक्षतः**—Gen. of the pre. p. of the desi. of **रुह्** with **आ**. विनिपात°—निवर्तने क्षमम्। निवर्तनं fr. वृत् cau. with नि+अन (ल्युट्) that which repels or wards off आलम्बनं—stay, support; fr. लम्ब् with आ+अन (ल्युट्) added कर्मणि by कृत्यल्युटो बहुलम् (*i. e.* the affixes called कृत्य and ल्युट् are used also in senses other than those specified).

मतम्—In some editions the reading तमं with इष्टतमं in the com. is found. In this case Malli. seems to take it in the sense of इष्टतमं *i. e.* adding इष्ट as required by the context to the superlative affix तम as we add सत्य to भामा when required by the context. तम by itself in the sense of इष्ट derived from तम् of the fourth class by अच्, is not supported by usage.

Fig.—As the expression उच्चैः पदमारुरुक्षतः and विनिपात° suggest the parallel instance of a man ascending a lofty place the figure समासोक्ति is implied; see com.

पौरुषानङ्गीकारे दोषमाह—

विपदोऽभिभवन्त्यविक्रमं रहयत्यापदुपेतमायतिः ।

नियता लघुता निरायतेरगरीयान्न पदं नृपश्रियः ॥१४॥

अन्वयः—अविक्रमं विपदः अभिभवन्ति आपदुपेतम् आयतिः रहयति निरायतेः लघुता नियता अगरीयान् नृपश्रियः पदं न ॥१४॥

विपद इति ॥ अविक्रमं पौरुषहीनं विपदोऽभिभवन्ति आक्रामन्ति । आपदुपेतं विपन्नमायतिरुत्तरकालः ॥ "उत्तरः काल आयतिः" इत्यमरः ॥ रहयति त्यजति । निरायतेः आसन्नक्षयस्येत्यर्थः । लघुता अगौरवं नियतावश्यंभाविनी । न कश्चिदेनमाद्रियत इत्यर्थः । अगरीयांल्लघीयान्नृपश्रियः पदं राजलक्ष्म्या आस्पदं न भवति । यद्वा नृपेति पदच्छेदः । तस्मात्पौरुषं कर्तव्यमेवेत्यर्थः ॥ अत्र पूर्वपूर्वस्याविक्रमत्वादेरुत्तरोत्तरं विपदादिकं प्रति कारणत्वात्कारणमालाख्योऽलंकारः । तथा च सूत्रम्—"पूर्वपूर्वस्योत्तरोत्तरहेतुत्वे कारणमाला" इति ॥

अन्वयार्थः—(**अविक्रमम्**) पौरुषहीन को (**विपदः**) आपत्तियाँ (**अभिभवन्ति**) अभिभूत करती हैं। (**आपदुपेतम्**) आपत्ति से युक्त को (**आयतिः**) उत्तर काल (**रहयति**) छोड़ देता है। (**निरायतेः**) फल-रहित की (**लघुता**) तुच्छता (**नियता**) निश्चित है (**अगरीयान्**) गौरव रहित (**नृपश्रियः**) राज्य-लक्ष्मी का (**पदम् न**) स्थान नहीं होता।

उद्यम-रहित व्यक्ति को आपत्तियाँ घेर लेती हैं, आपद्-युक्त को सौभाग्यमय फल प्राप्त नहीं होता, फलरहित का गौरवरहित होना निश्चित है। एवं इस प्रकार का लघु व्यक्ति राज्य-लक्ष्मी का पात्र नहीं होता।

14. Calamities overwhelm a man devoid of prowess; (blissful) future forsakes one smitten by calamities; degradation is the certain lot of one who has no bright future before him; one degraded cannot be the abode of royal fortune (or of wealth, O king).

Sl. 14. अविक्रमं—अविद्यमानः विक्रमः यस्य तम् । devoid of valour or prowess, weak. आपद०—आपदमुपेतः । or आपदा उपेतः if pass., आयतिः—prosperous or bright future. निरायतेः—निर्गता आयतिर्यस्य । This sl. is cited in K. P. VII. as an instance of भग्नप्रक्रमत्व or violation of Uniformity. Here first the uniformity of a preposition is violated; as first the prep. वि has been employed and then आ in connection with the same word (आपद). Again the uniformity of synonymity has been violated by the use of अगरीयान् for लघुता. He suggests the reading— ......तदभिभवः-कुरुते निरायतिम् । लघुतां भजते निरायतिर्लघुतावाञ्च पदं नृपश्रियः । But here the metre is violated.

फलितमाह—

तदलं प्रतिपक्षमुन्नतेरवलम्ब्य व्यवसायवन्ध्यताम् ।
निवसन्ति पराक्रमाश्रया न विषादेन समं समृद्धयः ॥१५॥

अन्वयः—तत् (तस्मात्) उन्नतेः प्रतिपक्षं व्यवसायवन्ध्यताम् अवलम्ब्य अलम् । पराक्रमाश्रयाः समृद्धयः विषादेन समं न निवसन्ति ॥१५॥

तदिति ॥ तत्तस्मात् । उपेक्षायां दोषसंभवादित्यर्थः । उन्नतेरभ्युदयस्य प्रतिपक्षमन्तरायं व्यवसायवन्ध्यतामुद्योगशून्यतामवलम्ब्यालम् । उद्योगशून्यतावलम्बनेनालमित्यर्थः ॥ "अलंखल्वोः प्रतिषेधयोः प्राचां क्त्वा" इति क्त्वाप्रत्ययः । तस्य ल्यबादेशः ॥ तथाहि । पराक्रम आश्रयः कारणं यासां तास्तथोक्ताः समृद्धयः संपदो विषादेन सममनुत्साहेन सह न निवसन्ति । पौरुषसाध्याः संपदो नानुत्साहसाध्याः । उभयोः सहावस्थानविरोधादित्यर्थः ॥ वैधर्म्येण कार्यकारणरूपोऽर्थान्तरन्यासः ॥

अन्वयार्थः—(**तत्**) इसलिए (**उन्नतेः**) उन्नति के (**प्रतिपक्षम्**) बाधक (**व्यवसायवन्ध्यताम्**) उद्योगाभाव के (**अवलम्ब्य अलम्**) आश्रय से बस । (**पराक्रमाश्रयाः**) पराक्रम ही है कारण जिन का ऐसी (**समृद्धयः**) समृद्धियाँ (**विषादेन समम्**) अनुत्साह के साथ (**न निवसन्ति**) नहीं रहती हैं ।

उन्नति में रुकावट डालने वाले अनुद्योग को आप ने पर्याप्त आश्रय बना लिया, अब इसे छोड़िये । पराक्रम से पैदा होने वाली समृद्धियाँ कभी आलस्य के साथ नहीं रहा करतीं ।

15. Enough, therefore, of having recourse to inactivity (lit. want of active exertion) which is an impediment to greatness: prosperity which depends on valour does not abide with despondency (inactivity).

Sl. 15. प्रतिपक्षं—प्रत्यर्थी पक्षः प्रतिपक्षस्तम् । One on the opposite side; an impediment to. व्यवसाय०—व्यवसाये वन्ध्यः तस्य भावस्ताम्.

The state of being without exertion. वन्ध्य fr. बन्ध्+य by ऋहलोर्ण्यत्; or by the Unădi aff. य (यक्); बवयोरैक्यात्; lit. what is fettered; hence unproductive, barren. अलं—अलं and खलु may be used with the gerund in त्वा (*i. e.* य or त्य also). निवसन्ति &c.—*i. e.* fortune favours the brave.

ननु समयः प्रतीक्ष्यते। किं वेगेनेत्यत्राह—

अथ चेदवधिः प्रतीक्ष्यते कथमाविष्कृतजिह्मवृत्तिना।
धृतराष्ट्रसुतेन सुत्यजाश्चिरमास्वाद्य नरेन्द्रसंपदः ॥१६॥

अन्वयः—अथ अवधिः प्रतीक्ष्यते चेत् आविष्कृतजिह्मवृत्तिना धृतराष्ट्रसुतेन चिरम् आस्वाद्य नरेन्द्रसम्पदः (अथवा) हे नरेन्द्र सम्पदः कथं सुत्यजाः ॥१६॥

अथेति ॥ अथावधिः कालः प्रतीक्ष्यते चेत् ॥ "अवधिस्त्ववधाने स्यात्सीम्नि-काले बिलेऽपि च" इति विश्वः ॥ आविष्कृतजिह्मवृत्तिना प्रकटितकपटव्यवहारेण धृतराष्ट्रसुतेन दुर्योधनेन नरेन्द्रसंपदो राज्यसंपदः। नरेन्द्रेति वा पदच्छेदः। चिरं चतुर्दशवर्षाण्यास्वाद्यानुभूय कथं सुत्यजाः। ज्ञातास्वादेन तेन पश्चादपि सुखेन युद्ध-क्लेशं विना न त्यक्ष्यन्त एवेत्यवधिप्रतीक्षणं व्यर्थमित्यर्थः ॥

अन्वयार्थः—(**अथ चेत्**) और यदि (**अवधिः प्रतीक्ष्यते**) अवधि की प्रतीक्षा है [तो] (**आविष्कृत जिह्मवृत्तिना**) प्रकट किया है कपट-व्यवहार जिसने ऐसे (**धृतराष्ट्रसुतेन**) धृतराष्ट्र के पुत्र से (**चिरम्**) चिर काल तक (**आस्वाद्य**) स्वाद लेकर (**नरेन्द्र**) हे राजन्! (**सम्पदः**) संपत्तियाँ (**कथं**) क्योंकर (**सुत्यजाः**) सुखपूर्वक त्याज्य होंगी ?

यदि आप तेरह वर्ष की अवधि की प्रतीक्षा कर रहे हैं तो, कपट-व्यवहारी वह दुर्योधन इतने दिनों तक राज्यलक्ष्मी का स्वाद लेकर सरलता से कैसे छोड़ देगा?

16. If you wait for the expiration of the period (agreed upon), how can the son of Dhṛtarāshṭra (Duryodhana), who has manifested his wicked conduct (be expected to) easily (to) give up the royal fortune after having enjoyed it for a long time!

Sl. 16. अवधिः—Fr. धा with अव+इ (कि); उपसर्गे धोः किः; the roots दा and धा take कि when preceded by a preposition. आविष्कृत०—जिह्मा चासौ वृत्तिः जिह्मवृत्तिः; आविष्कृता जिह्मवृत्तिर्येन। धृतराष्ट्र०—Bhima disdains to mention the name of Duryodhana.

By using this expression he wishes prominently to draw Dharma's attention to Dhṛtarāshtra's evil deeds also. Duryodhana is the son of his father and will not easily part with royalty. नरेन्द्र—नरेषु इन्द्र इव । सुत्यजाः—सुखेन त्यज्यन्ते इति; fr. सु—त्यज्—य (खल्).

अथवा तदा दैववशात्स्वयमेव दुर्योधनः संपदो दास्यति चेत्तथापि तत्कथं रोचयेमहीत्याह—

द्विषता विहितं त्वयाऽथवा यदि लब्धा पुनरात्मनः पदम् ।
जननाथ तवानुजन्मनां कृतमाविष्कृतपौरुषैर्भुजैः ॥१७॥

अन्वयः—अथवा द्विषता विहितं पुनः आत्मनः पदं यदि लब्धा जननाथ तव अनुजन्मनाम् आविष्कृतपौरुषैर्भुजैः कृतम् ॥१७॥

द्विषतेति ॥ अथवा द्विषता दुर्योधनेन विहितम् । समर्पितमित्यर्थः । आत्मनः पदं राज्यं पुनरपि त्वया लब्धा लप्स्यते यदि ॥ लभेः कर्मणि लुट् ॥ हे जननाथ ! तव अनुजन्मनामनुजानामाविष्कृतपौरुषैः प्रकटितपराक्रमैर्भुजैः कृतमलम् । व्यर्थमिति यावत् । अस्मद्भुजैर्न किंचित्साध्यमित्यर्थः । राज्यदानादानयोर्द्विषतामेव स्वातन्त्र्येऽस्मद्भुजनैष्फल्यात् । "क्षत्रियस्य विजितव्यम्" इति शास्त्रात्क्षात्रेणैव राज्यं ग्राह्यमिति भावः ॥ कृतमिति प्रतिषेधार्थमव्ययं चादिषु पठ्यते । "कृतमिति निवारणनिषेधयोः" इति गणव्याख्याने । भुजैरिति गम्यमानसाधनक्रियापेक्षया करणत्वात्ततीया । उक्तं च न्यासोद्द्योते—"न केवलं श्रूयमाणैव क्रिया निमित्तं कारकभावस्यापि तु गम्यमानापि" इति ॥

अन्वयार्थः—(**अथवा**) अथवा (**द्विषता**) शत्रु से (**विहितम्**) सौंपा हुआ (**आत्मनः**) अपना (**पदम्**) पद [राज्य] (**यदि त्वया**) यदि तुम से (**पुनः**) फिर से (**लब्धा**) प्राप्त किया जायेगा, [तो] (**जननाथ**) हे राजन् ! (**तव**) (**अनुजन्मनाम्**) तुम्हारे पश्चात् उत्पन्न होने वालों की [छोटे भाइयों की] (**आविष्कृतपौरुषैः**) प्रकट किया है पराक्रम जिन्होंने, ऐसी (**भुजैः**) भुजाओं से (**कृतम्**) क्या ?

वनवास की अवधि के बाद यदि दुर्योधन से सौंपे हुए राज्य को तुम ने पा लिया तो फिर तुम्हारे छोटे भाइयों की सबल भुजाएं किस काम आयेंगी ।

17. If on the other hand you get back your kingdom being restored to you by your enemy (after the expiry of the

term), then, O lord of men, vain will be the arms of your younger brothers which have (already) displayed their valour.

Sl. 17. विहितं—is here used in the sense of 'given back.' लब्धा—1st fut. pass. जननाथ—The lord of men ; by this he appeals to his heart. You can do what you like but you must consider what the state of our mind will be if you accept your share of the kingdom as a gift. This idea is forcibly explained in the next sloka. अनु॰—अनु जन्म येषां तेषाम्.

ननु साम्नैव कार्यसिद्धौ किं क्षात्रेण ? यथाह मनुः—"साम्ना दानेन भेदेन समस्तैरथवा पृथक्। विजेतुं प्रयतेतारीन्न युद्धेन कदाचन ॥" इति । तत्किमाग्रहेणेत्याशङ्क्याह—

मदसिक्तमुखैर्मृगाधिपः करिभिर्वर्तयते स्वयंहतैः ।
लघयन्खलु तेजसा जगन्न महानिच्छति भूतिमन्यतः ॥१८॥

अन्वयः—मृगाधिपः स्वयंहतैः मदसिक्तमुखैः करिभिः वर्तयते । [तथाहि] तेजसा जगत् लघयन् महान् अन्यतः भूमिं न इच्छति खलु ॥१८॥

मदेति ॥ मृगाधिपः सिंहो मदसिक्तमुखैः । मदवर्षिभिरित्यर्थः । स्वयं स्वेनैव हतैः करिभिर्वर्तयते वृत्तिं करोति । तैरेव जीवतीत्यर्थः ॥ चौरादिकाद्वृतेर्लट् । भौवादिकस्य तु "अणावकर्मकाच्चित्तवत्कर्तृकात्" इति परस्मैपदनियमादिति ॥ तथाहि । तेजसा प्रभावेण ॥ 'तेजो बले प्रभावे च ज्योतिष्यर्चिषि रेतसि ।" इति वैजयन्ती ॥ जगल्लघयँल्लघूकुर्वन्महांस्तेजस्व्यन्यतोऽन्यस्मात्पुरुषात् भूतिं वृद्धिं नेच्छति खलु । नहि तेजस्विनः परायत्तवृत्तित्वं युक्तम् । मनुवचनं तु "अशूरविषयम्" इति भावः ॥ विशेषेण वक्ष्यमाणसामान्यसमर्थनरूपोऽर्थान्तरन्यासः ॥

अन्वयार्थः—(**मृगाधिपः**) सिंह (**स्वयंहतैः**) स्वयं से मारे गये (**मदसिक्तमुखैः**) मद जल से सिंचित है मुख जिन का ऐसे (**करिभिः**) हाथियों से (**वर्तयते**) निर्वाह करता है । (**खलु**) निश्चय से (**तेजसा**) प्रभाव से (**जगल्लघयन्**) संसार को लघु करता हुआ (**महान्**) तेजस्वी (**अन्यतः**) दूसरे से (**भूतिम्**) ऐश्वर्य को (**न इच्छति**) नहीं चाहता है ।

सिंह मदस्रावी हाथियों को स्वयं मार कर अपना निर्वाह करता है । तेजस्वी

व्यक्ति अपने प्रभाव से संसार को छोटा करता हुआ किसी दूसरे व्यक्ति से ऐश्वर्य की प्राप्ति नहीं करना चाहता ।

18. The monarch of the beasts (lion subsists on elephants, with their faces besprinkled with ichor, killed by himself. A great man, overpowering (lit. eclipsing the valour of) the world by his might, does not indeed, wish to attain prosperity at another's hands.

Sl. 18. मदसिक्त०—मदेन सिक्तं मुखं येषां तैः । करिभिः—करः trunk अस्ति येषां ते करिणस्तैः । वर्तयते—According to Malli. this is the form of the root वृत् of the 10th class which means 'to live or subsist upon' ; and not of the Cau. वृत् 1 A.; for वृत् 1 A. will take Par. in the causal by the rule अणा &c. *i. e.* a root, intransitive in its non-causal form, takes Par. terminations provided it has a being endowed with चित्त or the faculty of knowledge for its agent. Some however, hold that वृत् of the 10th class is conjugated Par. only.

लघयन्—लघु करोति लघयति; by affixing इ (णिच्) which is added in the sense of तत्करोति or तदाचष्टे before this words undergo the same change as before इष्ठ of the superlative. लघयन् pre. p.; making small, eclipsing, casting into the shade. न महान् &c. —A spirited man gains supremacy by the might of his own arms and does not seek it as a favour.

ननु युद्धात्पाक्षिको लक्ष्मीलाभः । उपायान्तरैस्तु न तथेत्याशङ्क्याह—

अभिमानधनस्य गत्वरैरसुभिः स्थास्नु यशश्चिचीषतः ।
अचिरांशुविलासचञ्चला ननु लक्ष्मीः फलमानुषङ्गिकम् ॥१९॥

अन्वयः—अभिमानधनस्य (अत एव) गत्वरैः असुभिः स्थास्नु यशः चिचीषतः अचिरांशुविलासचञ्चला लक्ष्मीः आनुषङ्गिकं फलं ननु ॥१९॥

अभिमानेति ॥ अभिमानधनस्य वैरनिर्यातनमात्रनिष्ठस्य । अतएव गत्वरैर्गमनशीलैरस्थिरैः ॥ "गत्वरश्च" इति क्वरबन्तो निपातः ॥ असुभिः प्राणैः । करणैः ॥ "पुंसि भूम्न्यसवः प्राणाः" इत्यमरः ॥ स्थास्नु स्थिरम् ॥ "ग्लाजिस्थश्च ग्स्नुः" इति ग्स्नुप्रत्ययः ॥ यशश्चिचीषतश्चेतुं संगृहीतुमिच्छतः ॥ चिनोतेः

सन्नन्ताच्छतृप्रत्ययः॥ अचिरमंशवो यस्याः साचिरांशुर्विद्युत्तस्या विलासः स्फुरणं तद्वच्चञ्चला। क्षणिकेत्यर्थः। लक्ष्मीः संपदनुषङ्गादागतमानुषङ्गिकमन्वाचयशिष्टमल्पं फलम्। मानत्राणजं यश एव मुख्यं फलमभ्युच्चयस्तु लक्ष्मीरिति मानिनामिदमेव श्लाघ्यमित्यर्थः॥ अत्रास्थिरप्राणत्यागेन स्थिरयशःस्वीकाराभिधानान्न्यूनाधिकविनिमयाख्यः परिवृत्त्यालङ्कारः। उक्तं च काव्यप्रकाशे—"परिवृत्तिर्विनिमयो योऽर्थानां स्यात्समासमैः।" इति॥

अन्वयार्थः—(**अभिमानधनस्य**) अभिमान ही है धन जिस का ऐसे [अतएव] (**गत्वरैः**) गमनशील (**असुभिः**) प्राणों से (**स्थास्नु यशः**) स्थिर यश को (**चिचीषतः**) इकट्ठा करना चाहने वाले को (**अचिरांशुविलासचञ्चला**) बिजली की चमक की तरह चञ्चल (**लक्ष्मीः**) राज्य-लक्ष्मी (**ननु**) निश्चय से (**आनुषङ्गिकम्**) गौण (**फलम्**) फल है।

अभिमानी अत एव अस्थिर प्राणों से स्थिर यश को संजोते हुए व्यक्ति के लिए विद्युत की चमक-जैसी अस्थिर लक्ष्मी निश्चय ही गौण है।

19. To a man regarding self-respect as his wealth and seeking imperishable (lasting) glory by (at the cost of) perishable life, wealth which is unsteady like a flash of lightning is but an object of secondary consideration.

Sl. 19. अभिमान०—अभिमान एव धनं यस्य तस्य। गत्वरैः गन्तुं शीलं येषां ते गत्वराः; fr. गम्+क्वरप् (वर) the म् is dropped irregularly. Pān. has a special sūtra for this—गत्वरश्च। स्थास्नु—lasting, permanent, see com.; so ग्लास्नु, जिष्णु. चिचीषतः—pre. p. of the desid. base of चि.

अचिरांशु०—see com. विलास—flashing चञ्चला fr. चञ्च् to go + अल (बाहुलकादलच्) or चञ्चं गतिं लाति इति चञ्चला. आनुषङ्गिकं अनुसङ्गः fr. सञ्ज् with अनु+अ (घञ्) connection; अनुसङ्गात्प्राप्तमानुषङ्गिकं by adding इक (ठक्) ननु—surely, simply; is used to emphasise the statement.

नन्वल्पस्य मानस्य हेतोः कथं प्राणत्यागः शक्यते कर्तुं यतो "जीवन्नरो भद्रशतानि पश्येत्" इत्याशङ्क्याह—

ज्वलितं न हिरण्यरेतसं चयमास्कन्दति भस्मनां जनः।
अभिभूतिभयादसूनतः सुखमुज्झन्ति न धाम मानिनः॥२०॥

अन्वयः—जनः भस्मनां चयम् आस्कन्दति ज्वलितं हिरण्यरेतसं न । [अतः] मानिनः अभिभूतिभयात् असून् (एव) सुखं उज्झन्ति धाम न ॥२०॥

ज्वलितमिति ॥ जनो भस्मनां चयं पुञ्जमास्कन्दति पादादिनाक्रामति । अदाहकत्वादिति भावः । ज्वलितं ज्वलन्तम् ॥ कर्तरि क्तः । "मतिबुद्धि—" इत्यादिसूत्रे चकाराद्वर्तमानार्थत्वम् ॥ हिरण्यं रेतो यस्य तं हिरण्यरेतसमग्निं नास्कन्दति । दाहकत्वादिति भावः । अतो हेतोर्मानिनोऽभिभूतिभयात्प्राणलोभेन तेजस्त्यागे परिभवो भविष्यतीति भयादसूनेव सुखमक्लिष्टमुज्झन्ति त्यजन्ति । धाम तेजस्तु नोज्झन्ति । मानहानिकराज्जीवनात्स्वतेजसा मरणमेव वरमित्यर्थः ॥ पूर्वतरश्लोकवदर्थान्तरन्यासः ॥

अन्वयार्थः–(**जनः**) लोग (**भस्मानां चयम्**) भस्मों के समूह को (**आस्कन्दति**) लांघते हैं, (**ज्वलितम्**) प्रज्वलित (**हिरण्यरेतसम्**) आग को (**न**) नहीं । (**मानिनः**) मानी (**अभिभूतिभयात्**) तिरस्कार-भय से (**असून** [एव] प्राणों को ही (**सुखम्**) सुखपूर्वक (**उज्झति**) छोड़ते हैं (**धाम न**) तेज को नहीं ।

लोग राख के ढेर को लांघा करते हैं, प्रज्वलित आग को नहीं । स्वाभिमानी लोग कहीं तिरस्कार न हो अतः प्राणों को सुखपूर्वक छोड़ देते हैं तेज को नहीं ।

20. People tread not upon blazing fire, but they do so upon a heap of ashes : hence from fear of (rather than suffer) insult, men of self-respect easily (willingly) give up their life but not their natural lustre (spirit).

Sl. 20. ज्वलितं—here has the sense of the pres. tense; see Malli.; the च in the sūtra मतिबुद्धिपूजार्थेभ्यश्च provides for the inclusion of such roots as are not actually mentioned in it. हिरण्यरेतसं—see I. 22. अभिभूति०— अभिभूतेः भयमभिभूतिभयं तस्मात् Ab. Tat. *cf.* बलवानपि निस्तेजाः कस्य नाभिभवास्पदम् । निःशंकं दीयते लोकैः पश्य भस्मचये पदम् ॥

अथवा किमत्र प्रयोजनं चिन्तया ॥ किंतु तेजस्विनामयं स्वभावएव यज्जिगीषुत्वमित्याशयेनाह—

किमपेक्ष्य फलं पयोधरान्ध्वनतः प्रार्थयते मृगाधिपः ।
प्रकृतिः खलु सा महीयसः सहते नान्यसमुन्नतिं यया ॥२१॥

अन्वयः—मृगाधिपः किं फलम् अपेक्ष्य ध्वनतः पयोधरान् प्रार्थयते? महीयसः सा प्रकृतिः खलु यथा अन्यसमुन्नतिं न सहते ॥२१॥

किमिति ॥ मृगाधिपः सिंहः किं फलं प्रयोजमपेक्ष्य ध्वनतो गर्जतः। धरन्तीति धराः। पचाद्यच् ॥ पयसां धरास्तान्पयोधरान्मेघान्प्रार्थयतेऽभियाति ॥ "याञ्चायामभियाने च प्रार्थना कथ्यते बुधैः।" इति केशवः ॥ अथवा प्रार्थयते अवरुणद्धीत्यर्थः॥ "प्रा स्याद्याञ्चावरोधयोः" इत्यभिधानात्। प्रा अवरोधेन। प्रा इति तृतीयान्तम्। आकारान्तस्य प्राशब्दस्य योगविभागात् 'आतो धातोः' इत्यालोपः। तथाहि। महीयसो महत्तरस्य सा प्रकृतिः खलु स्वभावो यया प्रकृत्या अन्यसमुन्नतिं परवृद्धिं न सहते। महतः परभञ्जनमेव पुरुषार्थं इत्यर्थः॥ पूर्ववदलङ्कारः ॥

अन्वयार्थः—(**मृगाधिपः**) सिंह (**किम्**) किस (**फलमपेक्ष्य**) फल की अपेक्षा से (**ध्वनतः पयोधरान्**) गरजते हुए मेघों की ओर (**प्रार्थयते**) आक्रमण करता है (**महीयसः**) महान् का, (**खलु सा प्रकृतिः**) निश्चय से वह स्वभाव है (**यया**) जिस से (**अन्यसमुन्नतिम्**) दूसरे की उन्नति को (**न सहते**) नहीं सहता है।

तेजस्वी व्यक्ति स्वभाव से ही दूसरे की उन्नति को नहीं सह सकता। गरजते हुए बादलों पर जो शेर उछल पड़ता है भला वह किसी फल की दृष्टि से होता है ?

21. With what object in view does the lion (seek to) attack the roaring clouds ? It is but the nature of the mighty which does not allow them to suffer the superiority (rise to power) of others.

Sl. 21. प्रार्थयते—Challenges to fight, attacks, *Cf.* अनुहुँकुरुते घनध्वनिं Sis. V. 25. महीयस्—One very great. सहते नान्यसमु०—*Cf.* गर्जन्हरिः साम्भसि शैलकुञ्जे प्रतिध्वनीनात्मकृतान्निशम्य। क्रमं बबन्ध क्रमितुं सकोपः प्रतर्कनन्यमृगेन्द्रनादान् Bhatti. II. 9. *Cf.* for a similar idea न तेजस्तेजस्वीप्रसृतमपरेषां विषहते, स तस्य स्वो भावः प्रकृतिनियतत्वादकृतकः मयूखैरश्रान्तं तपति यदि देवो दिनकरः; किमाग्नेयो ग्रावा निकृत इव तेजांसि वमति। Uttar. Vi. 14.

निगमयति। उक्तार्थोपसंहरणं निगम उच्यते।

कुरु तन्मतिमेव विक्रमे नृप निर्धूय तमः प्रमादजम्।
ध्रुवमेतदवेहि विद्विषां त्वदनुत्साहहता विपत्तयः ॥२२॥

अन्वयः—हे नृप ! तत् प्रमादजं तमः निर्धूय विक्रमे मतिं कुरु । विद्विषां विपत्तयः त्वदनुत्साहहताः एतद् ध्रुवं अवेहि ॥२२॥

कुरु तदिति ॥ हे नृप ! तत्तस्मादुक्तरीत्या पराक्रमावसरत्वाद्धेतो [पराक्रमोत्साहयोर्हेतुत्वाद्धेतोः इ. पा०] ॥ "यत्तद्यतस्ततो हेतौ" इत्यमरः ॥ प्रमादजं तमो मोहं निर्धूय निरस्य विक्रमे पौरुष एव मतिं कुरु । विक्रममेवाङ्गीकुरु न तूपायान्तरमित्यर्थः ॥ न च विक्रमवैफल्यशंका कार्येत्याह ध्रुवमिति ॥ विद्विषां विपत्तयस्त्वदनुत्साहहतास्तवानुत्साहेनाव्यवसायेन हताः प्रतिबद्धाः । अन्यथा प्रागेव विपद्येरन्निति भावः । इत्येतद् ध्रुवं निश्चितमवेहि विद्धि ॥ "ध्रुवं नित्ये निश्चिते च" इति शाश्वतः ॥

अन्वयार्थः—(**हे नृप**) हे राजन् (**तत्**) इस कारण से (**प्रमादजं तमः**) आलस्य से उत्पन्न मोह को (**निर्धूय**) समाप्त कर के (**विक्रमे**) पुरुषार्थ में (**मतिम्**) बुद्धि को (**कुरु**) करो । (**विद्विषाम्**) शत्रुओं की (**विपत्तयः**) आपत्तियाँ (**त्वद्**) तुम्हारे (**अनुत्साह हताः**) अनुत्साह के कारण ही मृत हैं (**एतद् ध्रुवमवेहि**) यह निश्चयपूर्वक जानो ।

अतः, हे महाराज ! इस सुस्ती से होने वाले मोह को छोड़ कर आप पुरुषार्थ की सोचिये। अबतक शत्रुओं पर विपत्तियाँ नहीं आ रही हैं, यह तुम्हारे अनुत्साह का ही परिणाम है । आप निश्चय जानिये, ज्यों ही आपने उद्यम किया शत्रुओं पर विपत्तियाँ घहराने लगेंगी ।

22. Having shaken off, therefore, your apathy due to negligence (or misapprehension), set your heart, O king, on exploit (making active efforts). Know it for certain that calamities are debarred from (befalling) your enemies only by your inaction (or by want of active exertion on your part.)

Sl. 22. प्रमादजं—प्रमाद carelessness, negligence; fr. प्रमद्—अ (घञ्); when not preceded by a prep. मद् takes अप्; as मदः; but with a prep. it takes घञ् as प्रमाद, उन्मादः &c. प्रमद meaning joy is a Prădi. comp. प्रकृष्टो मदः. तमः—lethargy, dulness; lit. darkness obscuring mental vision. अनुत्साह—want of energetic action or exertion. हता—kept back. obstructed. Cf. त्वदाच्छान्तरितानि सम्प्रति विभो तिष्ठन्ति साध्यानि नः । Mudra.

न च नः पराजयशङ्का कार्येत्याह—

द्विरदानिव दिग्विभावितांश्चतुरस्तोयनिधीनिवायतः ।
प्रसहेत रणे तवानुजान्द्विषतां कः शतमन्युतेजसः ॥२३॥

अन्वयः—दिग्विभावितान् आयतः चतुरः द्विरदान् इव (तथा चतुरः) तोयनिधीन् इव रणे दिग्विभावितान् शतमन्युतेजसः चतुरः तव अनुजान् द्विषतां- कः प्रसहेत ॥२३॥

द्विरदानिति ॥ दिग्विभावितान्दिक्षु प्रसिद्धांस्तानायत आगच्छतः ॥ आङ्पूर्वादिण्धातोः शतृप्रत्ययः ॥ चतुरो द्विरदान्दिग्गजानिव तथोक्तविशेषणांश्चतुरस्तोयनिधीनिव रणे दिग्विभाविताञ्छतमन्युतेजस इन्द्रविक्रमांश्चतुरस्तवानुजान्द्विषतां मध्ये कः प्रसहेत । सोढुं शक्नुयादित्यर्थः ॥ "शकि लिङ् च" इति शक्यार्थे लिङ् ॥ अतो निःशङ्कं प्रवर्तस्वेति भावः ॥

अन्वयार्थः—(**दिग्विभावितान्**) दिशाओं में प्रसिद्ध (**आयतः**) आते हुए (**चतुरः द्विरदान् इव**) चार हाथियों की तरह [तथा] **चतुरः तोयनिधीन् इव**) चार समुद्रों की तरह (**शतमन्युतेजसः**) इन्द्र-जैसे पराक्रमी (**तवानुजान्**) तुम्हारे छोटे भाइयों को (**रणे**) युद्ध में (**द्विषतां कः**) शत्रुओं में कौन (**प्रसहेत**) सह सकता है ?

युद्ध में, आते हुए दिग्गजों की तरह, एवं चार समुद्रों की तरह इन्द्र-जैसे पराक्रमी दिक्-प्रसिद्ध तुम्हारे भाइयों को, शत्रुओं में, कौन है जो सह सकता है ?

23. Which of your enemies will be able to withstand in battle (bear the furious charge of) your four brothers, renowned in all the quarters, and having the might of Indra, rushing forward like the four well-known elephants (of the quarters) or (like the four oceans) ?

Sl. 23. दिग्विभावितान्—दिक्षु विभाविता दिग्विभावितास्तान् qualifies द्विरदान्, तोयनिधीन् and अनुजान् विभावित p. p. p. of विभू Cau. means well thought of, hence well known; referring to oceans and elephants, it might also mean 'discerned or seen to exist in. आयतः—Acc. pl. of the pre. p. of इ with आ (1) striding on, advancing ; (2) rushing forward; (3) rolling or surging on. द्विरदान्— द्वौ रदौ येषां ते द्विरदस्तान् । रदतीति रदः fr. रद्

to cut—श्रच्. शतमन्यु०—Having the lvstre *i. e.* might of Indra. शतं मन्यवो यज्ञा अस्य; Indra is regarded as the performer of a hundred sacrifices ; or शते दैत्येषु मन्युः क्रोधोऽस्य In the Veda मन्यु (fr. मन् to know or think) means 'knowledge, wisdom and the term शत० originally meant the god of hundred wisdoms or intelligences. The Pauranic conception of Indra was due to a misunderstanding of the real sense of the original epithet.

The comparison to the quarter elephants and seas implies extraordinary physical strength in the four brothers as well as the extreme hugeness of their bodies. Nakula and Sahadeva have already been compared to elephants. See I. 36. प्रसह्देत—The Pot. indicates power.

आशीर्वादव्याजेन फलितमाह—

ज्वलतस्तव जातवेदसः सततं वैरिकृतस्य चेतसि ।
विदधातु शमं शिवेतरा रिपुनारीनयनाम्बुसन्ततिः ॥२४॥

अन्वयः—तव चेतसि सततं ज्वलतः वैरिकृतस्य जातवेदसः शिवेतरा रिपुनारीनयनाम्बुसन्ततिः शमं विदधातु ॥२४॥

ज्वलत इति ॥ तव चेतसि सततं ज्वलतो वैरिकृतस्य जातवेदसः क्रोधाग्नेः शिवेतरा अशिवा अमङ्गला । वैधव्यदुःखजनकत्वादिति भावः । रिपुनारीनयनाम्बुसन्ततिः वैरिवनिताश्रुप्रवाहः शमं विदधातु । वैरिकृतस्य क्रोधस्य वैरिवधमन्तरेण शान्त्यसंभवादवश्यं तद्वधस्त्वया कर्तव्य इत्यर्थः ॥ क्रोधस्य विषयनिगरणेन विषयिणो जातवेदस एवोपनिबन्धनादतिशयोक्तिरलङ्कारः । तदुक्तम्—"विषयस्यानुपादानाद्विषय्युपनिबध्यते । यत्र सातिशयोक्तिः स्यात्कवेः प्रौढोक्तिजीविता ॥" इति । तत्रापि क्रोधस्य जातवेदसो भेदेऽप्यभेदाध्यवसायाद्भेदेऽभेदरूपा । तत एवाम्बुनिर्वाप्यत्वोक्तिश्च घटते । तथा च यथाम्बुसेकेनाग्निः सम्यक्शाम्यति तथा शत्रुवधेन क्रोध इत्यौपम्यं गम्यते ॥

अन्वयार्थः—(**तव चेतसि**) तुम्हारे चित्त में (**सततम्**) निरन्तर (**ज्वलतः**) प्रज्वलित (**वैरिकृतस्य**) शत्रु द्वारा की गई (**जातवेदसः**) अग्नि का, (**शिवेतरा**)

अमाङ्गलिक (**पुरिनारीनयनाम्बुसंततिः**) शत्रु की स्त्रियों की आंखों की जलधारा (**शमम्**) शमन (**विदधातु**) करे।

तुम्हारे चित्त में शत्रु द्वारा जलाई गई निरन्तर प्रज्वलित आग को, शत्रु-स्त्रियों के अशुभ आंसू बुझाएं।

24. Let the inauspicious uninterrupted flow of tears from the eyes of the wives of your enemies extinguish the fire (of anger) kindled.

Sl. 24. शिवेतरा— शिवाया इतरा। रिपुनारी०— रिपूणां नार्यः रिपुनार्यः नयनानामम्बूनि नयनाम्बूनि रिपुनारीणां नयनाम्बूनि रिपु०नि तेषां सन्ततिः the continuous or uninterrupted flow of. जातवेदस्— fire, विद्+Unădi aff. अस् (असुन्). This is variously derived— जातं वेदो धनं यस्मात् जाते जाते विद्यते exists इति वा जातं वेद वेदयते वा। *Cf.* Yāska's Nir. जातवेदाः कस्मात्— जातानि वेद जातानि वैनं विदुः जाते जाते विद्यते इति वा जातविक्तो वा जातधनो जातविद्यो वा जातप्रज्ञानो यत्तज्जातः पशूनविन्दतेति तज्जातवेदसो जातवेदस्त्वमिति ब्राह्मणम्।

In the verse कोप is spoken of as Agni; but the comparison is not expressed; the Upameya is identified with it so completely that it is lost in the other being swallowed up by it as it were; hence the fig. is अतिशयोक्ति (or hyperbole) of the first kind. There is also Upamā implied. See com.

इति दर्शितविक्रियं सुतं मरुतः कोपपरीतमानसम्।
उपसान्त्वयितुं महीपतिर्द्विरदं दुष्टमिवोपचक्रमे ॥२५॥

अन्वयः—इति दर्शितविक्रियं कोपपरीतमानसं मरुतः सुतं महीपतिः दुष्टं द्विरदमिव उपसान्त्वयितुम् उपचक्रमे ॥२५॥

इतीति॥ इत्युक्तरीत्या दर्शिता विक्रिया विकारो वागारंभात्मको येन तं कोपपरीतमानसं कोपाक्रान्तचित्तम्। इदं विशेषणद्वयं द्विरदेऽपि योज्यम्। मरुतः सुतं भीमं महीपतिर्युधिष्ठिरो दुष्टं द्विरदमिव। एतेनास्य शौर्यमेव न बुद्धिरस्तीति गम्यते। उपसान्त्वयितुमनुनेतुमुपचक्रमे प्रवृत्तः॥ "प्रोपाभ्यां समर्थाभ्याम्" इत्यात्मनेपदम्॥ राज्ञा भाव्युपकारविशेषापेक्षया कथंचिदवशो जनः शनैः शनैः द्विरदवद्वशीकरणीयो न तु त्याज्य इति भावः॥

अन्वयार्थः—(**इति**) इस प्रकार (**दर्शितविक्रियम्**) प्रकट किया है विकार जिस ने ऐसे (**कोपपरीतमानसम्**) क्रोध से घिरे हुए चित्त वाले (**मरुतः सुतम्**) पवन-पुत्र को, (**महीपतिः**) राजा, (**दुष्टं**) दुष्ट (**दर्शित विक्रियं कोप परीतमानसम्**) प्रकट किया है विकार जिस ने ऐसे [एवं] क्रोधाभिभूत चित्त वाले (**द्विरदमिव**) हाथी की तरह (**उपसान्त्वयितुम्**) सान्त्वना देने के लिए (**उपचक्रमे**) प्रवृत्त हुआ ।

उपर्युक्त भाषण में भीम के चेहरे में विकार आ गया था एवं उसका मन क्रोधाभिभूत था। दुष्ट हाथी जैसे उस भीम को सान्त्वना देते हुए युधिष्ठिर बोला :

25. The king (Dharma) proceeded to appears the son of Marut (Bhima) who had thus manifested his excitement and whose mind was over-powered by anger, as one would do an infuriated elephant.

Sl. 25. दर्शित०—विक्रिया change of the natural state of the mind, excitement. परीत—lit. surrounded by; completely possessed by. मरुत्—the wind-god and the regent of the norh—west. म्रियन्ते अनेन वर्द्धेन विना वा इति मरुत् fr. मृ + उत् (उति Unādi. 1. 95.) दुष्ट—excited, infuriated. उपचक्रमे—क्रम् with प्र and उप is Atm. in the sense of 'beginning. Fig. Upamă. See Mallis.'s remarks on this.

प्रथमं तावत्स्तुत्यादिभिः प्रसादयति—

अपवर्जितविप्लवे शुचौ हृदयग्राहिणि मङ्गलास्पदे ।
विमला तव विस्तरे गिरां मतिरादर्श इवाभिदृश्यते ॥२६॥

अन्वयः—अपवर्जितविप्लवे शुचौ (अत एव) हृदयग्राहिणी मङ्गलास्पदे तव गिरां विस्तरे मतिः आदर्श इव विमला अभिदृश्यते ॥२६॥

अपवर्जितेति ॥ विप्लवः प्रमाणाबाधः । अन्यत्र बाह्यमलसंक्रमः । सोऽपवर्जितो यस्य तस्मिन्नपवर्जितविप्लवे । शुचौ । शब्दसौष्ठवं लौहशुद्धिश्च शुचित्वं तद्वति । अतएव हृदयग्राहिणि मनोरमे मङ्गलास्पदे । एकत्र हितार्थप्रतिपादकत्वादन्यत्र मङ्गलवस्तुत्वाच्च श्रेयस्करे । "रोचनं चन्दनं हेम मृदङ्गं दर्पणं मणिम् । गुरूनग्निं तथा सूर्यं प्रातः पश्येत्सदा बुधः ॥" इति पुराणवचनात् । तव गिरां विस्तरे वाक्यप्रपञ्चे ॥ "प्रथने वावशब्दे" इति घञ्प्रतिषेधात् "ऋदोरप्" इत्यप् । अतएव

विस्तारो विग्रहो व्यासः स तु शब्दस्य विस्तरः।" इत्यमरः ॥ मतिस्त्वद्बुद्धिरादर्शे दर्पण इव॥ "दर्पणे मुकुरादर्शौ" इत्यमरः ॥ विमला विशदाभिदृश्यते । वाग्वैशद्यादेव मतिवैशद्यमनुमीयते । तत्पूर्वकत्वात्तस्येत्यर्थः ॥

अन्वयार्थः—(अपवर्जित विप्लवे) हट गया है तर्क-बाध जिस का [तर्क से जिसे बाधित नहीं किया जा सकता] ऐसे, **(शुचौ)** शब्द-सौन्दर्य से युक्त **(अत एव) (हृदयग्राहिणि)** हृदय को हरने वाले **(मङ्गलास्पदे)** मङ्गलकारी, **(तव)** तुम्हारे **(गिरां विस्तरे)** वाक्यप्रपञ्च में, **(मतिः)** [तुम्हारी] बुद्धि **(इव)** यथा **(आदर्शे)** दर्पण में, **(विमला)** सुस्पष्ट **(अभिदृश्यते)** दिखाई देती है।

आदर्श पक्ष में—**(अपवर्जितविप्लवे)** दूर हो गई है धूल जिस की ऐसे **(शुचौ)** स्वच्छ (अतएव) **(हृदयग्राहिणि)** मनोभिराम **(मङ्गलास्पदे)** माङ्गलिक **(आदर्शे)** दर्पण में...... ।

धूलरहित, स्वच्छ, सुन्दर माङ्गलिक शीशे में जैसे कोई भी वस्तु स्पष्ट प्रतिबिम्बत होती है उसी प्रकार, युक्तियों से पुष्ट, शब्द-सौन्दर्य से युक्त, हृदयहारी एवं मङ्गल करने वाले तुम्हारे भाषण में तुम्हारी सुबुद्धि स्पष्ट लक्षित हो रही है।

26. Your pure (honest) intention is fully (clearly) seen reflected in your speech, which is free from arguments contrary to reasoning and proof, lucid (or elegant), attractive to the heart and salutary, as in a mirror, which is free from the coating of dust, transparent, charming to the mind and auspicious.

Sl. 26. अपवर्जितः—applies to both speech and mirror. अपवर्जितः avoided (free from) विप्लवः यस्य यस्मिन्वा विप्लव (1) opposition to reasoning and proof; (2) being covered with dirt or dust (setting on its surface). शुचौ—(1) elegant, lucid and beautiful. हृदय०—हृदयं गृह्णाति attracts, touches, इति हृदयग्राही तस्मिन् (1) attractive to the heart, impressive; (2) beautiful, मङ्गला०—Because the speech was meant for the good of Dharma. A mirror is also looked upon as an auspicious thing. See Malli. आस्पदं—आपद्यतेऽस्मिन्; fr. पद् with आ+अ (घ) the स् comes in irregularly in the sense of प्रतिष्ठा or place for a thing. आस्पदं प्रतिष्ठायाम् । Păn. VI. 1. 146. विस्तर—fr. स्तृ with वि+अप् when the extent meant refers to speech or words; in other cases घञ्

is added and we get विस्तार: magnitude, extention; see com. We have a third derivative from the same, *viz*. विष्टर in the sense of a seat or tree; वृक्षासनयोर्विष्टरः । आदर्शः— आदृश्यते रूपमत्र; fr. दृश्+घञ् (अ) अधिकरणे. Fig. Upamă with ślesha.

अथ युग्मेनाह—

स्फुटता न पदैरपाकृता न च न स्वीकृतमर्थगौरवम् ।
रचिता पृथगर्थता गिरां न च सामर्थ्यमपोहितं क्वचित् ॥२७॥

अन्वयः—पदैः स्फुटता न अपाकृता अर्थगौरवं च न स्वीकृतम् [इति] न गिरां पृथगर्थता रचिता; (तथा) क्वचित् (अपि) गिरां सामर्थ्यं च न अपोहितम् ॥२७॥

स्फुटतेति । उपपत्तिरिति च ॥ पदैः सुप्तिङन्तशब्दैः स्फुटता विशदार्थता नापाकृता न त्यक्ता । अर्थगौरवमर्थभूयस्त्वं च न न स्वीकृतम् । स्वीकृतमेवेत्यर्थः ॥ "वैशद्यप्रसक्तार्थगौरवाभावनिवर्तनार्थं नञ्द्वयम् । "संभाव्यनिषेधनिवर्तने द्वौ प्रतिषेधौ" इति वामनः ॥ गिरां पदानामवान्तरवाक्यानां च पृथगर्थता भिन्नार्थता ॥ अपुनरुक्तार्थतेति यावत्, रचिता कृता । तथा क्वचिदपि सामर्थ्यं गिरामन्योन्यसामर्थ्यं साकाङ्क्षत्वं नापोहितं न वर्जितम् । अन्यथा दशदाडिमादिशब्दवदेकवाक्यता न स्यात् । यथाहुः—"अर्थैकत्वादेकवाक्यं सापेक्षा चेद्विभागे स्यात्" इति ॥ नन्वर्थगौरवमित्यत्र कथं षष्ठीसमासः । "पूरणगुण—" इत्यादिना प्रतिषेधात्नैष दोषः, ये शुक्लादयः शब्दा गुणे गुणिनि च वर्तन्ते । यथा पटस्य शौक्ल्यं शुक्लः पट इति च तेषामेवात्र निषेधात् ये पुनः स्वतः गुणमात्रवचनाः यथा गौरवं प्राधान्यं रसो गन्धः स्पर्श इत्येवमादयः । तेषामनिषेधात् । तथा "तत्स्थैश्च गुणैः षष्ठी समस्यते" इति वचनाद् बुहुलमभियुक्तप्रयोगदर्शनाच्च । बलाकाया शौक्ल्यमित्यादौ तु भाष्यकारवचनादसमासः । अतएवाह वामनः— "पत्त्रपीतिमादिषु गुणवचनसमासो बालिश्यात्" इति ॥

अन्वयार्थः—(**पदैः**) पदों से (**स्फुटता**) स्पष्टता (**न अपाकृता**) दूर नहीं की, (**अर्थगौरवम् च**) और अर्थ-गाम्भीर्य (**न स्वीकृतम्**) नहीं स्वीकार किया [इति] (**न**) ऐसा नहीं; (**गिराम्**) वाक्यों की (**पृथगर्थता**) भिन्नार्थकता (**रचिता**) बनाई, (**च**) और (**क्वचित्**) [अपि] कहीं भी (**सामर्थ्यम्**) [वाक्यों की परस्पर] आकांक्षा को (**न अपोहितम्**) नहीं छोड़ा ।

इस भाषण में प्रत्येक पद स्पष्ट है एवं अर्थ-गाम्भीर्य से युक्त है। प्रत्येक वाक्य भिन्न अर्थ को कहता है—कहीं भी पुनरुक्ति-दोष नहीं है—तथा वाक्य एक-दूसरे से सम्बद्ध हैं।

27. (A speech) in which perspicuity of the inflected words has not been done away with, nor has depth of meaning been unattended to (lit. not brought in); distinctness of sense of the different parts has been brought out and the power of expression of the words has nowhere been neglected (lit. dropped out of consideration).

Sl. 27. पद— सुबन्तं (inflected forms of declinable bases) तिङन्तं (verbal forms) च पदसंज्ञं स्यात्। Sid. Kau. स्फुटता— Perspicuity, clearness of sense. अर्थगौरवम्— अर्थस्य गौरवं depth, loftiness of. Malli. thus discusses the propriety of this comp. How is the Gen. comp. formed here ? for the Sūtra. पूरणगुणसुहितार्थ॰ (Pān. 11. 2. 11) prohibits the comp. of words denoting a quality or attribute &c. with nouns in the Gen. This objection will not do. The sutra prohibits compounds of such words only as denote a quality as also the concrete objects having that quality; e.g. ब्राह्मणस्य शुक्ला दन्ताः or पटस्य शुक्ल, शुक्लः पटः &c. and not of such words as connote a quality only, as गौरवं (as here), प्राधान्यं (as in बुद्धिप्राधान्यं) &c. Such compounds are allowed by the rule तत्स्थैश्च गुणैः षष्ठी समस्यते (a noun in the Gen. is compounded with words expressive of qualities inherent in those objects) and also by wide usage. All this discussion is unnecessary. The Sid. Kau. gives a simple defence of such cases. It says—अनित्योयं not always obligatory गुणेन निषेधः which can be inferred from तदशिष्यं संज्ञाप्रमाणत्वात् (where Pǎn. himself has used such comp.) इत्यादिनिर्देशात् तेनार्थगौरवं बुद्धिमान्द्यमित्यादि सिद्धम्।

स्वीकृतं—न स्वमस्वम्, अस्वं स्वं सम्पद्यमानं कृतं स्वीकृतम्। न च न— the two negatives result in a strong affirmative (स्वीकृतमेव) The words संभाव्यनिषेध &c. in the quotation mean for a possible negation being negatived.

पृथग॰—पृथग् अर्थः यासां ताः पृथगर्थाः तासां भावः पृथगर्थता (the state of having a distinct meaning); ताम्. सामर्थ्यं— समर्थानां भावः

सामर्थ्यं तत् । the power to express a meaning or to convey a particular sense or connected meaning by mutual dependence and connection. अपोहितं—done away with; removed; p. p. p. of ऊह् 1. A. (sometimes P.) to guess &c. With prepositions it is P. A.; अपोहति-ते.

In this verse all the excellences and requisites of a good speech (composition) are mentioned.

उपपत्तिरुदाहृता बलादनुमानेन न चागमः क्षतः ।
इदमीदृगनीदृगाशयः प्रसभं वक्तुमुपक्रमेत कः ॥२८॥

अन्वयः—(किं च) बलात् उपपत्तिः उदाहृता अनुमानेन च आगमः न क्षतः ईदृक् इदम् [वचनम्] । अनीदृगाशयः कः प्रसभं वक्तुं उपक्रमेत ॥२८॥

उपपत्तिरिति ॥ किं च बलात्स्वबलमाश्रित्य । कर्मणि ल्यब्लोपे पंचमी वक्तव्या । उपपत्तिर्युक्तिरुदाहृता । पराक्रमपक्ष एव श्रेयानिति युक्तिरुक्तेत्यर्थः ।– उचितं चैत-
उपपत्तिर्युक्तिरुदाहृता । पराक्रमपक्ष एव श्रेयानिति युक्तिरुक्तेत्यर्थः । उचितं चैत-
न्महावीरस्येति भावः । तथानुमानेन युक्त्यागमः शास्त्रं न क्षतो न हतः । किंत्वागमाविरुद्धमेवोक्तम् । अन्यथा तद्विरोधादनुमानस्यैव प्रामाण्यभङ्गप्रसङ्गादिति भावः । ईदृगित्थं क्षात्रयुक्तमिदं वचनमविद्यमान ईदृगाशय इत्थं क्षात्रयुक्ताभिप्रायो यस्य सोऽनीदृगाशयः ॥ "अभिप्रायश्छन्द आशयः" इत्यमरः ॥ कः प्रसभं हठाद्वक्तुम् उपक्रमेत । न कोऽपीत्यर्थः । इत्थं वक्तुमुपक्रमितैव नास्ति । वक्ता तु दूरापास्त एवेति भावः ॥ केचिदेतच्छ्लोकत्रयं निन्दापरत्वेनापि योजयन्ति । तदसत् । हितोपदेशमात्रतत्परस्यातिवत्सलस्य राज्ञो मत्सरिण इव महावीरे भ्रातरि विघेये सर्वानर्थमूलभूतनिन्दातात्पर्यकल्पनानौचित्यादिति ॥

अन्वयार्थः—(**बलात्**) स्वपक्ष [में] (**उपपत्तिः**) युक्ति (**उदाहृता**) प्रस्तुत की (**अनुमानेन च**) और अनुमान [प्रमाण] से (**आगमः**) [नीति] शास्त्र का (**न क्षतः**) हनन नहीं किया (**ईदृग् इदम्**) ऐसे इस (**वचनम्**) वचन को (**अनीदृगाशयः**) ऐसे [क्षात्र] अभिप्रायं से रहित (**कः**) कौन (**प्रसभम्**) हठपूर्वक (**वक्तुम्**) कहने के लिए (**उपक्रमेत**) तैयार हो सकता है ?

परात्रम के पक्ष में तुम ने युक्तियाँ प्रस्तुत कीं; तथा तर्क में नीति-शास्त्र का

उल्लंघन नहीं किया। क्षात्र-भाव से रहित भला कौन व्यक्ति बलपूर्वक ऐसा भाषण दे सकता है !

28. Arguments have been adduced from a hero's standpoint (or, having hostile operations in view), and the (teaching of the) science of politics has not been set aside by (contradictory) inference. Who that has not such high motives (or aspirations) can make such a speech as this (couched in such terms) on the spur of the moment ?

Sl. 28. बलात्—forcibly; or it may mean बलमाश्रित्य taking your stand on heroic spirit, from a hero's standpoint. अनुमान—inference or deduction; fr. मा with अनु + अन (ल्युट्). आगमः—The Vedas; here the authority of the Vedas. क्षत—contradicted, overriden. The authority of the Vedas has ever been regarded in India as the first प्रमाण and a system of philosophy to be acceptable had to conform to the teachings of the Veda in the main. Doctrines that ran counter to the Śruti were looked upon as heretic and rejected. Or rather may be taken to mean here the political science or Śăstra.

अनीदृगा॰—ईदृग् आशयः ; intention, thought यस्य स ईदृगाशयः; न ईदृ॰ अनीदृगाशयः। ईदृक् इदमिव दृश्यते fr. इदम् + दृश् + क्विन् (०). ई and की are substituted for इदं and किम् respectively before दृश् दृश or दृक्ष (all derived from the root दृश्). प्रसभं—without previous thought; or it may mean 'forcible.' उपक्रमेत—For the A. See sl. 25. See Malli.'s remarks.

यदि साधूक्तं तर्हि तथैव क्रियतामित्याशङ्क्याह—

अवितृप्ततया तथापि मे हृदयं निर्णयमेव धावति।

अवसाययितुं क्षमाः सुखं न विधेयेषु विशेषसंपदः ॥२९॥

अन्वयः—तथापि मे हृदयम् अवितृप्ततया निर्णयमेव धावति। विधेयेषु विशेषसंपदः सुखम् अवसाययितुं न क्षमाः ॥२९॥

अवितृप्ततयेति ॥ तथापि त्वया सम्यङ्निर्णीतेऽपि मे हृदयमवितृप्ततयासंतुष्टतया। अद्यापि संशयगतत्वेनेत्यर्थः। निर्णयमेव धावत्यनुसरति। अपेक्षत इति

यावत् । अद्यापि निर्णयस्यानुदयादिति भावः ॥ निर्णयानुदये हेतुमाह—**अवेति** ॥ विधेयेषु संधिविग्रहादिकर्तव्यार्थेषु या विशेषसंपदोऽवान्तरभेदानां समृद्धयो बाहुल्यानि ताः सुखमक्लेशेनावसययितुम् । पुरुषान्प्रत्यानुकूल्येन स्व स्वरूपं स्वयमेव शीघ्रं प्रत्याययितुमित्यर्थः ॥ स्यतेर्ण्यन्तादणि कर्मकर्तृकात्तुमुन् । णेरनादिसूत्रस्यायं विषयः ॥ क्षमन्त इति क्षमाः ॥ पचाद्यच् ॥ शक्ता न भवन्ति ॥ "क्षमं शक्ते हिते त्रिषु" इत्यमरः ॥ विधेयमात्रस्य सुगमत्वेऽपि तद्विशेषाणां सौक्ष्म्याद्बाहुल्याच्च दुर्ज्ञेयत्वादद्यापि निर्णयाकाङ्क्षेति तात्पर्यार्थः ॥ अत्र निर्णयधावनं प्रति उत्तरवाक्यार्थस्य हेतुत्वाभिधानाद्वाक्यार्थहेतुकं काव्यलिङ्गमलङ्कारः । तदुक्तम्—"हेतोर्वाक्यपदार्थत्वे काव्यलिङ्गमुदाहृतम् । " इति ॥

अन्वयार्थः—(**तथापि**) भी तो (**मे हृदयम्**) मेरा मन (**अवितृप्ततया**) पूर्णतः असंतुष्ट होने से (**निर्णयमेव**) निर्णय की ही ओर (**धावति**) दौड़ता है—अपेक्षा करता है । (**विधेयेषु**) सन्धि-विग्रह आदि करणीय कार्यों में (**विशेष सम्पदः**) अवान्तर भेदों का बाहुल्य विविधता एवं विस्तार (**सुखम्**) सुखपूर्वक (**अवसाययितुम**) (**पुरुषों के प्रति अपने स्वरूप को अनुकूलता से**) स्वयमेव ज्ञात कराने में (**न क्षमाः**) समर्थ नहीं है ।

तुम्हारे सुन्दर भाषण के बावजूद मेरा मन पूर्णतः असन्तुष्ट है और मैं किसी निर्णय पर नहीं पहुँचा हूँ । सन्धि-विग्रहादि नीति के कार्यों के भेद इतने अधिक एवं विविध हैं कि सरलता से उनका स्वरूप स्पष्ट नहीं होता ।

29. Yet my mind, not being fully satisfied, runs after (still seeks) decision alone. In respect of matters to be undertaken the multiplicity of the policies to be adopted as different circumstances arise cannot make itself easily understood.

Sl. 29. अवितृप्ततया—वि means completely, entirely, तथापि—*i. e.* inspite of your conclusive speech as to the advisability of speedy action. विधेयेषु—things to be done ; विधा+यत् (कर्मणि). The Gen. would have been better. धावति—yet pursues (seeks) decision *i. e.* I have not yet come to any decision as to the line of action to be adopted. So Malli. It seems better, however, to take निर्णय in the sense of 'decision' already formed, *viz.* not to do any thing rashly but to stick to the condition accepted at the time of gambling. *Cf.* Dharma's reply to Bhîma— मम प्रतिज्ञां च निबोध सत्यां वृणे धर्मममृताज्जीविताच्च ॥ राज्यं च पुत्राश्च यशो धनं च सर्वं न सत्यस्य कलामुपैति ॥ Van. p. ch. 34. The following speech of Dharma also supports this view. विशेष°— विशेषाणां particular policies to be followed सम्पद : the richness *i. e.* variety of. अवसाययितुं—Inf. of the cau. of सो with अव. The root सो takes the augment य् (युक्) instead of प् (पुक्) before the इ of the Cau. (णिच्). The meaning here is 'to make themselves intelligible or to make their nature understood, 'a sense which is virtually equal to the non-causal sense. विशेषसम्पद: the original object of अवसो is put in the Nom. case in the Causal form— पुरुषा विधेयेषु विशेषसम्पदः अवस्यन्ति Cau.— विशेष सम्पदः पुरुषान् स्वयमेव अवसाययन्ते । अवसो being a बुद्ध्यर्थं root पुरुष take the Acc. case in the Cau. construction. This falls within the province of the sutra णेरणौयत्कर्म णौचेत्स कर्ताऽनाध्याने । Pān. I. 3. 67. See Malli. on I 10; and notes.

वस्तुविशेषावधारणमन्तरेणैव प्रवृत्तिरित्याशङ्कयाह—

सहसा विदधीत न क्रियामविवेकः परमापदां पदम् ।

वृणते हि विमृष्यकारिणं गुणलुब्धाः स्वयमेव संपदः ॥३०॥

अन्वयः—सहसा क्रियां न विदधीत अविवेकः आपदां परं पदम् (हि) विमृश्यकारिणं गुणलब्धाः सम्पदः स्वयमेव वृणते ॥३०॥

सहसेति ॥ क्रियत इति क्रिया कार्यं तां सहसा । अविमृष्येत्यर्थः । "सहसेत्याकस्मिकाविमर्षयोः" इति गणव्याख्याने स्वरादिपाठादव्यम् ॥ न विदधीत न कुर्वीत । कुतः । अविवेकोऽविमृष्यकारित्वं परमत्यन्तमापदां पदं स्थानम् । विपत्तिकारणमित्यर्थः ॥ व्यतिरेकेणोक्तमर्थमन्वयेनाह—वृणत इति ॥ गुणल्लुब्धा गुणगृह्याः । गुणगृघ्रव इति स्वयंवरणहेतूक्तिः । संपदः श्रियः । विमृष्य करोतीति विमृष्यकारी ॥ "उपपदमतिङ" इति समासः । तं स्वयमेव वृणते भजन्ते हि ॥ "वृञ संभक्तौ" इति धातुः ॥ तस्माद्विमृष्यैव प्रवर्तितव्यमित्यर्थः ॥ अत्र सहसा विधाननिषेधलब्धविमृष्यकारित्वरूपकारणस्यापद्रूपव्यतिरेककार्येण समर्थनाद्वैधर्म्येणार्थान्तरन्यासः । द्वितीयार्धेन च स एव साधर्म्येणेति ज्ञेयम् ॥

अन्वयार्थः—(**क्रियाम्**) कार्य को (**सहसा**) बिना विचारे (**न विदधीत**) नहीं करे। (**अविवेकः**) अज्ञान (**आपदाम्**) आपत्तियों का (**परं पदम्**) परम धाम है। (**विमृश्यकारिणम्**) सोच-विचारकर कार्य करने वाले को (**गुण-लुब्धाः**) गुणों की लोभी (**सम्पदः**) सम्पत्तियों (**स्वयमेव वृणते**) स्वयं ही सेवन करती हैं।

बिना विचारे सहसा कोई कार्य न करे। अज्ञान में ही आपत्ति का वास है। गुणलोलुप सम्पदाएँ विवेक-पूर्व कार्य करने वाले को स्वयं ही वर लेती हैं।

30. One should not do any thing precipitately; want of deliberation is a great source of calamities : fortunes that are ever attached to merits, seek, of their own motion, one who acts with circumspection (proper thought).

Sl. 30. सहसा—Properly Inst. sing of सहस् meaning 'strength, force; used as an indeclinable particle; suddenly, thoughtlessly. गुणलुब्धा—गुणेषु लुब्धाः coveting or attracted by merits; लुभित is the p. p. when लुभ् means 'to be perplexed.' विमृश्यका—An irregular Upapada Samāsa. *Cf.* महापापानि कर्माणि यानि केवलसाहसात्। आरभ्यन्ते भीमसेन व्यथन्ते (व्यथयन्ति) तानि भारत॥ सुमन्त्रिते सुविक्रान्ते सुकृते सुविचारिते। सिध्यन्त्यर्था महाबाहो दैवं च प्रदक्षिणमम्॥ Van. p. ch. 36.

ननु साहसिकस्यापि फलसिद्धिर्दृश्यत एव। तत्किं विवेकेनेत्यत्राह—

अभिवर्षति योऽनुपालयन्विधिबीजानि विवेकवारिणा।
स सदा फलशालिनीं क्रियां शरदं लोक इवाधितिष्ठति॥३१॥

अन्वयः—यः विधिबीजानि विवेकवारिणा अनुपालयन् अभिवर्षति सः लोकः (फलशालिनीं) शरदमिव फलशालिनीं क्रियां सदा अधितिष्ठति॥३१॥

अभीति— य पुमान्। विधीयन्त इति विधयः कृत्यवस्तूनि बीजानीवेत्युपमितसमासः। शरदं लोक इवेति वाक्यगतोपमानुसारात्। तानि विधिबीजानि। विवेको वारीव विवेकवारि तेन विवेकवारिणा॥ पूर्ववत्समासः॥ अनुपालयन्प्रतीक्षमाणः संरक्षन्नभिवर्षति सिञ्चति। स पुमान्। फलं साधननिष्पाद्योऽर्थः सस्यं च॥ "सस्ये हेतुकृते फलम्" इत्युभयत्राप्यमरः॥ तच्छालिनीं क्रियां कर्म लोको जनः। "लोकस्तु भुवने जने" इत्यमरः॥ शरदमिव सदा नित्यमधितिष्ठति। सदा क्रियाफलं प्राप्नोत्येव। न कदाचिद्व्यभिचरतीत्यर्थः। साहसिकस्य काकतालीयन्या-

यन फलासिद्धिर्विवेकिनस्तु नियतेति भावः ॥ अत्र फलशब्देन सस्यहेतुकृतयोरर्थ-योरभेदाध्यवसायात्श्लेषमूलातिशयोक्तिस्तदनुग्रहीता चोपमेत्यनुसंधेयम् ॥

अन्वयार्थः—(**यः**) जो (**विधिबीजानि**) करणीय-कार्य रूप बीजों को, (**विवेकवारिणा**) सम्यक् विचार रूप जल से (**अनुपालयन्**) रक्षा करता हुआ, (**अभिवर्षति**) सुशोभित (**क्रियाम्**) क्रिया को (**इव**) जैसे (**लोकः**) लोग **अन्नफल से सुशोभित**) (**शरदम्**) शरद् ऋतु को, (**अधितिष्ठति**) प्राप्त करता है।

जैसे कृषक लोग धान्य से सुशोभित फसल को शरद् ऋतु में प्राप्त करते हैं उसी प्रकार जो व्यक्ति अपने करणीय कर्तव्यों के बीज को विवेक जल से, संरक्षित रखते हुए, सींचता है वह फल-सिद्धि को प्राप्त होता है।

31. He, who nourishes the seeds of the objects to be achieved with the water of deliberation, preserving them (till the time of fruition), has mastery over his labour rich with fruit (*i. e.* reaps with certainty the fruits of his labour) as people (husbandmen) have power over the autumn majestic with its harvest (*i. e.* reap the harvest in autumn).

Sl. 31. विधि—what is done, an undertaking ; fr. विधा + इ (कि). अनुपालयन्—taking care of them and waiting till they bear fruit. ्वारिणा अभिवर्षयत—अयि all round, thoroughly. The roots सिच्, वष् &c. govern the instrumental of the liquid used when the idea is that of thorough wetting; when mere sprinkling is meant the Acc. is used (as (वृक्षे वारि सिञ्चति).

फलशालिनीं—फलेन शालते इति ताम् qualifies both क्रियां and शरदम. The word फल is *shilshta*; it means—(1) the attainment of the object desired; (2) the fruit. अधितिष्ठति—स्था with अधि is trans.; it means to have mastery over, to lord it over; *cf.* sl. 38 further on; hence to obtain with certainly here. The fig. here is Upamă. supported by अतिशयोक्ति based on Ślesha. विवेक 'cautious proceeding' is compared with वारि, बीज with विधि and a king with a farmer.

नियता विवेकिनः फलसिद्धिरित्युक्तम्। संप्रति तामेव रुच्यर्थं स्तौति—

शुचि भूषयति श्रुतं वपुः प्रशमस्तस्य भवत्यलंक्रिया।
प्रशमाभरणं पराक्रमः स नयापादितसिद्धिभूषणः ॥३२॥

अन्वयः—शुचि श्रुतं वपुः भूषयति प्रशमः तस्य अलंक्रिया भवति । पराक्रमः प्रशमाभरणं, (भवति) सः नयापादितसिद्धिभूषणः ॥३२॥

शुचीति ॥ शुचि संप्रदायशुद्धं श्रुतं शास्त्रश्रवणम् ॥ कर्तृ ॥ वपुर्भूषयति । अन्यथा विद्वान्पुरुषः शोच्य इति भावः । तस्य श्रुतस्य प्रशमः क्रोधोपशान्तिरलंक्रिया भूषणं भवति । अन्यथा श्रुतवैफल्यादिति भावः । पराक्रमः सत्यवसरे शौर्यं प्रशमस्याभरणं भवति । अन्यथा सर्वैः परिभूयत इति भावः । स पराक्रमः । नयापादिता नीतिसंपादिता । विवेकपूर्विकेति यावत् । सा चासौ सिद्धिश्च सैव भूषणं यस्य स तथोक्तः । अन्यथा साहसिकस्य सिद्धेः काकतालीयत्वेन पक्षे पराक्रमवैयर्थ्यादिति भावः ॥ वपुषो भूष्यतैवात्र सिद्धेर्भूषणतैव तु । उभयं मध्यमानां तु तत्पूर्वोत्तरपक्षयोः (तेषां पूर्वोत्तरेच्छया इ.पा.) ॥ इति विवेकः । एवं विशिष्टासिद्धेरनन्यभूषितायाया एव भूषणत्वोक्त्या सर्वाभरणतया (सर्वोत्तरतया–इ. पा.) स्तुतिर्गम्यते ॥ अत्रोत्तरोत्तरस्य पूर्वपूर्वविशेषणत्वादेकावल्यलंकारः । तदुक्तम्—"यत्र विशेषणभावं पूर्वं पूर्वं प्रतिक्रमेणैव । भजति परंपरमेषालंकृतिरेकावलीकथिता। ।" इति ॥

अन्वयार्थः—(**शुचिः**) शुद्ध (**श्रुतम्**) शास्त्र-ज्ञान (**वपुः**) शरीर को (**भूषयति**) शोभित करता है। (**प्रशमः**) शान्ति (**तस्य**) उस [शास्त्र-ज्ञान] की (**अलङ्क्रिया**) आभूषण (**भवति**) होती है। (**पराक्रमः**) पराक्रम (**प्रशमाभरणम्**) शान्ति का आभूषण है। (**सः**) वह (**पराक्रम**) (**नयापादितसिद्धि भूषणः**) नीति से प्राप्त सिद्धि है आभूषण जिसकी, ऐसा है।

पवित्र शास्त्र-ज्ञान शरीर का आभूषण है। शक्ति से वह शास्त्र-ज्ञान सुशोभित होता है। शान्ति का आभूषण पराक्रम है और पराक्रम विवेकपूर्वक प्राप्त सफलता से सुशोभित होता है।

32. Correct knowledge of the Śāstras adorns the person; self possession becomes its embellishment; timely (display of) valour is the ornament of self-possession; and valour has for its ornament success brought on by right policy.

Sl. 32. शुचि—pure, correct, being handed down in a proper way by tradition; hence able to shed its light on the dark problems of policy. श्रुतं—श्रूयते इति श्रुतं lit. knowledge got by oral trainsmission; hence knowledge of a Śāstra in general ; here of the science of policy. This is explained in the next Śloka (सुकृतिः परिशुद्ध आगमः &c.). प्रशमः—This is not used in its Vedāntic sense here; it means here restraint over the passions (especially क्रोध or restlessness) and keeping the mind at peace or not allowing it to be ruffled or agitated; self possession. This is explained further in slokas 35 and 37. *Cf.* ज्ञानस्योपशमः श्रुतस्य विनयः (भूषणं) &c. Bhar. Nit. प्रशमा०—प्रशमस्य आभरणं; Gen. Tat. (and not a Bah.); mere tranquillity is useless; it must be embellished by a timely display of valour. नयापा०—नय a right course of policy; नयेन अपादिता; (secured, brought about) नयापादिता now see com. This is explained in sl. 38. Fig.—Ekāvalī, as each succeeding statement qualifies each preceding statement.

विमृष्य कुर्यादिति स्थितम् । तत्र विमर्षोपायः क इत्युक्ते शास्त्रमेवेत्याह—

मतिभेदतमस्तिरोहिते गहने कृत्यविधौ विवेकिनाम् ।
सुकृतः परिशुद्ध आगमः कुरुते दीप इवार्थदर्शनम् ॥ ३३ ॥

अन्वयः—मतिभेदतमस्तिरोहिते गहने कृत्यविधौ विवेकिनां सुकृतः परिशुद्ध आगमः दीप इव अर्थदर्शनं कुरुते ॥३३॥

मतीति ॥ मतिभेदः कार्यविप्रतिपत्तिः । मतिभेदस्तम इवेत्युपमितसमासः । दीप इवेत्युपमानुसारात् । तेन तिरोहित आच्छन्नेऽतएव गहने दुरवगाहे कृत्यविधौ कार्यानुष्ठाने विवेकिनां सुकृतः सदभ्यस्तोऽतएव परिशुद्धो निश्चितोऽन्यत्र सुविहितः प्रवातादिदोषरहितश्च आगमः शास्त्रम् ॥ "आगमः शास्त्र आयाते" इति विश्वः ॥ दीप इवार्थदर्शनं कार्यज्ञानं वस्तुप्रतिभासनं च कुरुते ॥

अन्वयार्थः—(**मतिभेदतमस्तिरोहिते**) बुद्धि-भेद रूपी अन्धकार में छिपे हुए (**अत एव**) (**गहने**) दुरधिगम्य (**कृत्यविधौ**) कार्यानुष्ठान में (**विवेकिनाम्**) ज्ञानियों का (**सुकृतः**) भली भांति [अभ्यास] किया हुआ (**अत एव**) (**परिशुद्धः**) निश्चित (**आगमः**) शास्त्र-ज्ञान (**दीप इव**) दीपक की भांति (**अर्थदर्शनम्**) कार्य-ज्ञान को (**कुरुते**) कराता है।

दीपक-पक्ष में—(**सुकृत**) वातादि विघ्नों से सुरक्षित (**दीपः**) दीपक (**अर्थदर्शनम् कुरुते**) वस्तु-प्रतीति कराता है।

जैसे हवा के झोंके से सुरक्षित दीपक पदार्थों को दिखाता है उसी प्रकार विवेकी

व्यक्तियों को, भलीभांति अभ्यस्त एवं सुनिश्चित शास्त्र-ज्ञान, गहन अन्धकार में भी छिपे हुए कर्तव्य-मार्ग को दिखाता है ।

33. In the matter of the execution of duties which is hidden in the darkness of conflicting opinions and therefore difficult to be brought about, correct and definite knowledge of the *Śāstras* acquired by keep study shows to discriminating men like a bright and well-placed lamp (the way to obtain their object.

Sl. 33. मतिभेद०—मतेः भेदः मतिभेदः divergence of opinion as regards the achivement of objects; now see Mal. तिरोहित—concealed by ; Gatisamas'a; Păn. I. 4. 71. The comp. is necessary; so तिरोभूय. The comp. ०तमस्तिरोहित is grammatically inaccurate ; properly it ought to be तमसातिरोहिते there being aluk of the Inst. ending bh the rule ओजःसहोम्भस्तमसस्तृतीयायाः Pān. VI. 3. 3. To avoid the gramatical difficulty we may take it as a loc. Tat.; ०तमसि तिरोहिते तिरोहित being taken in an active sense. For the intran. use of धा *cf* अभितृष्य मरुत्सस्यं कृष्णमेघस्तिरोदधे । Rag. X 48.

गहन—difficult to penetrate (understand) or grasp). Fr. गाह् +युच (अन), the आ being irregularly shortened to अ. कृत्यविधौ-कृत्यस्य विधिस्तस्मिन् । सुकृतः—acquired by careful study. परिशुद्धः—correctly grasped and definite. दीपः—दीप्यते इति; दीप् + अ (क). अर्थदर्शनम्—अर्थ्यते इति अर्थः: an object desired; also a thing in the case of दीप fr. अर्थ + अ (घञ्) added कर्मणि । तस्य दर्शनम् the showing of; fr. दृश् cau. + अन (ल्युट्) भावे The fig. here is उपमा, आगम and दीप being compared.

एवं विमृष्य कुर्वतो दैवादर्थागमेऽपि न कश्चिदपराध इत्याह—

स्पृहणीयगुणैर्महात्मभिश्चरिते वर्त्मनि यच्छतां मनः ।
विधिहेतुरहेतुरागसां विनिपातोऽपि समः समुन्नतेः ॥३४॥

अन्वयः—स्पृहणीयगुणैः महात्मभिः चरिते वर्त्मनि मनः यच्छतां विधिहेतुः आगसाम् अहेतुः विनिपातः अपि समुन्नतेः समः ॥३४॥

स्पृहणीयेति ।। स्पृहणीयगुणैर्लोकश्लाघ्यगुणैर्महात्मभिः सज्जनैश्चरितेऽनुष्ठिते वर्त्मन्याचारे मनो यच्छतां निदधताम् । सन्मार्गेण व्यवहरतामित्यर्थः । विधिहेतुर्दैवनिमित्तकः ।। "विधिर्विधाने दैवे च" इत्यमरः ।। अतएवागसामपराधानामहेतुर्विनिपातोऽपि दैविकानर्थोऽपि ।। "विनिपातोऽवपाते स्याद्दैवादिव्यसनेऽपि च ।" इति विश्वः ।। समुन्नतेरतिवृद्धेः समस्तुल्यः । दैविकेषु पुरुषस्यानुपालम्भ्यत्वादिति भावः । यथाह कामन्दकः—"यत्तु सम्यगुपक्रान्तं कार्यमेति विपर्ययम् । पुमांस्तत्रानुपालम्भ्यो दैवान्तरितपौरुषः ।।" इति ।।

अन्वयार्थः—(**स्पृहणीय गुणैः**) श्लाघनीय हैं गुण जिनके ऐसे (**महात्मभिः**) महात्माओं से (**चरिते**) आचरण किये गये (**वर्त्मनि**) मार्ग में (**मनः**) मन (**यच्छताम्**) लगाते हुओं का, (**विधिहेतुः**) भाग्य है निमित्त जिस का ऐसा, [अत एव] (**आगसाम् अहेतुः**) अपराधों का अकारण (**विनिपातः अपि**) दुर्भाग्य भी (**समुन्नतेः समः**) उन्नति के समान है ।

गुणी महापुरुषों के पद-चिह्नों पर चलते हुए व्यक्ति का, दुर्भाग्य से होने वाला पतन भी अपराध नहीं होता । उसके लिए तो यह दुर्भाग्य भी उन्नति सरीखा ही है ।

34. In the case of men who set their minds on the path (course of conduct) followed by high—souled persons of enviable virtues, even the downfall which is due to adverse fate and is (therefore) no cause for blame, is equal to (as good as) rise (prosperity).

Sl. 34. विधिहेतुः—विधिर्हेतुर्यस्य brought on or caused by adverse fate. आगस्—fault, blame, एति इति; fr. इ+अस् (असुन् Unădi. IV. 212) आग being irregularly substituted. विनिपातः—a misfortune (destruction &c.) coming from the gods and not of one's own making. समुन्नतेः—also समुन्नत्या words meaning 'equal', except तुल्य and उपमा, are construed with the Gen. or the Inst., by तुल्यार्थैरतुलोपमाभ्यां तृतीयान्यतरस्याम्.

संप्रति यद्विमृष्यं तदाह—

शिवमौपयिकं गरीयसीं फलनिष्पत्तिमदूषितायतीम् ।
विगणय्य नयन्ति पौरुषं विजितक्रोधरया जिगीषवः ।।३५।।

अन्वयः— जिगीषवः विजितक्रोधरयाः गरीयसीं फलनिष्पत्तिम् अदूषितायतीं विगणय्य पौरुषं शिवं औपयिकं नयन्ति ॥३५॥

शिवमिति ॥ जिगीषवो जयेच्छवो नृपा विजितक्रोधरया जितक्रोधवेगाः सन्तो गरीयसीं प्रभूतामदूषितायतीमक्षतोत्तरकालाम्। स्वन्तामित्यर्थः। फलनिष्पत्तिं फलसिद्धिं विगणय्य। फलवत्त्वं निश्चित्येत्यर्थः। पौरुषं पुरुषकारं शिवमनुकूलमौपयिकमुपायम् ॥ विनयादित्स्वात्स्वार्थे ठक्। उपायाद्ध्रस्वत्वं च ॥ नयन्ति प्रापयन्ति। पौरुषमुपायेन योजयन्तीत्यर्थः। नानिश्चितफलं कर्म कुर्वत इति भावः। यथाह कामन्दकः—"निष्फलं क्लेशबहुलं संदिग्धफलमेव च। न कर्म कुर्यान्मतिमान्सदा वैरानुबन्धि च" इति ॥ नयतिः प्रापणार्थे द्विकर्मकः। अत्र पौरुषस्य कर्तृस्थकर्मत्वेऽप्युपायस्यातथात्वात्क्रोधं विनयत इत्यादिवत् ॥ "कर्तृस्थे चाशरीरे कर्मणि" इत्यात्मनेपदं न भवति ॥

अन्वयार्थः—(**जिगीषवः**) विजय को चाहने वाले (**विजितक्रोधरयाः**) जीता है क्रोध के आवेग को जिन्होंने ऐसे, (**फलनिष्पत्तिम्**) फल सिद्धि को (**गरीयसीम्**) अत्यधिक [तथा] (**अदूषितायतीम्**) दोष रहित परिणाम-कालिक (**विगणय्य**) जान कर (**पौरुषम्**) पुरुषार्थ को (**शिवम्**) कल्याणकारी (**औपयिकम्**) उपाय को (**नयन्ति**) प्राप्त कराते हैं।

क्रोधाभिभूत न होने वाले विजयेच्छु लोग, प्रचुर फलसिद्धि को, परिणाम में निर्दोष समझ कर ही पुरुषार्थ को उपाय से युक्त करते हैं। अर्थात् जब तक फल के विषय में निश्चय न हो तब तक कार्य नहीं करते।

35. Men desirous of conquest overcome the (overbearing) force of anger, and having well ascertained that the accomplishment of their desired end will be very great and will have no adverse future, direct their prowess to the favourable means.

Sl. 35. जिगीषु—n. in उ from the desid. base of जि to conquer. विजित०—विजितः क्रोधस्य रयः overpowering impulse or force of यैः ते। This is equal to ते क्रोधरयं विजयन्ते *i. e.* they do no yield to the impulse of anger but wait for a favourable opportunity. अदूषितायतीम्—दूषिता आयतिर्यस्याः सा दूषितायतिः, न दूषि० अदूषितायतीम्। दुष् in the cau. lengthens its उ; in the sense of 'to make depraved' it takes guṇa substitute optionally; दूषयति दोषयति. निष्पत्तिः—production, accomplishment विगणय्य

or ascertained. **औपयिकं**—उपाय एव औपयिकः तम्; उपाय fr. इ with उप+अ (घञ्) The word उपाय, being one of the विनयादि group, takes इक (ठक्) स्वार्थे *i. e.* in its own sense. इक causes वृद्धि of the initial vowel; the आ of उपाय is shortened into अ, see com. नयन्ति—Here the Atm. is not used as in क्रोधं विनयते For the rule (कर्तृस्थे &c.) requires that the object of नी (the fruit of the action) should refer to the agent and must not be a limb of the body; here पौरुष refers to the agent is not a part of the body, but the indirect object औपयिकं does not refer of the agent and the conditions of the Sūtra not being wholly fulfilled Atm. is not used. Bhaṭṭoji Diks meets the difficulty by saying —कथं तर्हि विगणय्य नयन्ति पौरुषमिति कर्तृगामित्वाविवक्षार्था भविष्यति। Dharma means—Men really bent on conquest do not take a leap in the dark, but carefully clculating the time when they would get lasting success, display their valour making use of the most favourable of the means.

यदुक्तं विजितक्रोधरया इति तदावश्यकमित्याह—

अपनेयमुदेतुमिच्छता तिमिरं रोषमयं धिया पुरः ।
अविभिद्य निशाकृतं तमः प्रभया नांशुमताप्युदीयते ॥३६॥

अन्वयः—उदेतुम् इच्छता पुरः रोषमयं तिमिरं धिया अपनेयम् । अंशुमता अपि प्रभया निशाकृतं तमः अविभिद्य न उदीयते ॥३६॥

अपनेयमिति ॥ उदेतुमभ्युदेतुमिच्छता पुरुषेण पुरः प्रथमं रोषमयं रोषादागतम् ॥ "मयट् च" इति मयट् । तिमिरमज्ञानं धिया विवेकबुद्धया । करणेन । अपनेयमपोद्यम् । तथाहि । अंशुमतापि । कर्त्रा । प्रभया तेजसा । करणेन । निशाकृतं तमो ध्वान्तमविभिद्य नोदीयते । किंतु विभिद्यैवेत्यर्थः । सूर्यस्याप्येवं किमुतान्येषामित्यपिशब्दार्थः ॥ इणो भावे लट् ॥

अन्वयार्थः—(**उदेतुमिच्छतः**) अभ्युदय चाहने वाले के द्वारा (**पुरः**) पहले (**रोषमयम्**) क्रोध से होने वाले (**तिमिरम्**) अज्ञान को (**धिया**) बुद्धि से (**अपनेयम्**) दूर किया जाना चाहिए। (**अंशुमता अपि**) सूर्य के द्वारा भी (**प्रभया**) तेज से (**निशाकृतम्**) रात्रि द्वारा उत्पन्न (**तमः**) अन्धकार को (**अविभिद्य**) बिना भेदे (**न उदीयते**) नहीं उदय हुआ जाता।

उन्नति चाहने वाले व्यक्ति को, पहले अपनी बुद्धि पर से क्रोधोत्पन्न अज्ञान को दूर करना चाहिए। देखो ! सूर्य भी पहले रात के अंधकार को अपने तेज से दूर करता है और फिर उदय होता है।

36. By a man wishing to rise the darkness of anger must first be dispelled by (the light of) his intellect. Even the sun does not rise without having dispersed by his light (rays) the darkness caused by night.

Sl. 36. रोषमयं—Here मय (ट्) has the sense of identity or तादात्म्यं. अंशुमता अपि—even by the sun, what of others then. अविभिद्य—without having penetrated *i. e* completely chased away.

ननु दुर्बलस्यैवमस्तु। बलीयसस्तु क्रोधादेव कार्यसिद्धिरित्यत आह—

बलवानपि कोपजन्मनस्तमसो नाभिभवं रुणद्धि यः ।
क्षयपक्ष इवैन्दवीः कलाः सकला हन्ति स शक्तिसंपदः ॥३७॥

अन्वयः—बलवानपि यः कोपजन्मनः तमसः अभिभवं न रुणद्धि स क्षयपक्ष ऐन्दवीः कला इव सकलाः शक्तिसंपदः हन्ति ॥३७॥

बलवानिति ॥ बलवाञ्छूरोऽपि यः। कोपाज्जन्म यस्य तस्य कोपजन्मनः ॥ "अवर्ज्यो बहुव्रीहिर्व्यधिकरणो जन्माद्युत्तरपदः।" इति वामनः ॥ तमसो मोहस्य ॥ कृद्योगात्कर्तरि षष्ठी ॥ अभिभवमाक्रान्ति न रुणद्धि न निवारयति। स नृपः। क्षयस्य पक्षः क्षयपक्षः कृष्णपक्ष ऐन्दवीरिन्दुसंबन्धिनीः कला इव ॥ "कला तु षोडशो भागः" इत्यमरः ॥ सकला समग्राः शक्तिसंपदः प्रभुमन्त्रोत्साहशक्तीस्तिस्रोऽपि हन्ति नाशयति। अन्धस्य जङ्घाबलमिव क्रोधान्धस्य लोकोत्तरमपि सामर्थ्यं व्यर्थमेवेत्यर्थः। अत्र कालस्य सर्वकारणत्वात्क्षयपक्षस्य कलाक्षयकारित्वमस्त्येव। तमसस्तु तत्कालविजृम्भणात्तथा व्यपदेशः ॥

अन्वयार्थः—(**बलवानपि**) शूरवीर भी (**यः**) जो (**कोपजन्मनः**) क्रोध से उत्पन्न (**तमसः**) अन्धकार के (**अभिभवम्**) दमन को (**न रुणद्धि**) नहीं रोकता है, (**सः**) वह (**क्षयपक्षे**) घटाव-पक्ष में [कृष्ण पक्ष में] (**ऐन्दवीः**) चन्द्रमा की (**कलाः इव**) कलाओं की भांति (**सकलाः**) सम्पूर्ण (**शक्तिसंपदः**) शक्ति-संपद् को (**हन्ति**) नष्ट कर देता है।

क्रोध से उत्पन्न अन्धकार से स्वकीय अभिनव को जो नहीं रोकता वह बलवान् होता हुआ भी अपनी समग्र शक्ति को खो देता है जैसे कृष्ण-पक्ष में चन्द्रमा अन्त में सभी कलाओं से रहित हो जाता है।

37. He, who, although powerful, does not resist the attack of ignorance (clouding reason) born of (sprung from) anger, destroys (the benefits from) all the regal powers, as the dark half (of a month) does all the digits of the moon.

Sl. 37. कोपजन्मनः—such a Vyad. Bah. is unavoidable says Vaman (see com.) तमसः—caused by the darkness of ignorance; a factitive Gen. (कर्तरि). अभिभवं—attack, the being overpowered by ऐन्दवीः—इन्दोः इमा ऐन्दव्यः, fr. इन्दु + अण + ई. इन्दु—उनत्ति wets चन्द्रिकया भुवनमिति; the उ of उन्द is changed to इ by Unădi. 1. 12. (उन्देरिच्चादेः). इन्दु in Vedic Sans. signified a bright drop of Soma (सुतास इन्दवः Rg. I. 16, 6) and then became a name of the moon (Soma coming to signify the moon). शक्तिसं०—शक्तय एव सम्पदः शक्तीनां सम्पदः excellence of इति वा। The Śaktis are three शक्तयस्तिस्रः प्रभावोत्साहमन्त्रजाः। Amara. (1) प्रभुशक्ति; see sl. 10; (2) उत्साहश० or the power arising from the king's personal energy or enthusiasm; and (3) मन्त्रश० or that arising from good counsel (having a good ministry).

विमृष्य कुर्वतः क्रियाप्रकारमाह—

समवृत्तिरुपैति मार्दवं समये यश्च तनोति तिग्मताम् ।
अधितिष्ठति लोकमोजसा स विवस्वानिव मेदनीपतिः ॥३८॥

अन्वयः—यः समवृत्तिः (सन्) समये मार्दवम् उपैति, तिग्मतां च तनोति, स मेदिनीपतिः विवस्वानिव ओजसा लोकम् अधितिष्ठति ॥३८॥

समेति ॥ यः समा नातिमृदुर्नातितिग्मा वृत्तिर्यस्य स समवृत्तिः सन्समये सत्यवसरे मार्दवं मृदुवृत्तित्वमुपैति तिग्मतां तीक्ष्णवृत्तित्वं च तनोति। स मेदिनीपतिर्विवस्वानिव। ओजसा तेजसा लोकमधितिष्ठत्याक्रामति। सूर्योऽपि ऋतुभेदेन समवृत्तिरित्यादि योज्यम्।

अन्वयार्थ—**(यः)** जो **(समवृत्तिः)** समान है [नीति] व्यवहार जिसका

ऐसा (**सन्**) हुआ हुआ (**समये**) अवसर [आने] पर (**मार्दवम्**) कोमलता को (**उपैति**) प्राप्त करता है (**तिग्मतां च**) और तीक्ष्णता को (**तनोति**) विस्तृत करता है। (**स मेदिनीपतिः**) वह भूमिपति (**विवस्वान् इव**) सूर्य की भाँति (**ओजसा**) तेज से (**लोकम्**) संसार को (**अधितिष्ठति**) आक्रान्त करता है।

जैसे सूर्य न तो सदा बहुत प्रखर होता है और न ही सदा बहुत मन्द होता है इसी प्रकार जो राजा समव्यवहार नीति का आचरण करता है तथा समय आने पर कोमल और आवश्यकता होने पर तीक्ष्ण हो जाता है वही संसार पर अनुशासन करता है ।

38. That king, who maintains an even course of conduct (is neither too mild nor too severe) and assumes mildness or displays severity at the proper time, presides over (brings under his sway) the whole world, like the sun, by his lustre (majesty).

Sl. 38. समवृत्तिः—also applies to the sun—that is neither always severely burning nor very mild. तिग्मतां—तिग्म fr. तिज् (तेजयति इति)—म (मक्) by युजिरुजितिजां कुश्च Uṇādi I. 146; the ज् is changed to ग् तीक्ष्ण is also derived fr. the same root. विवस्वान्—विवः रश्मिः अस्य विद्यते; विवस्—वत्; विविधं वस्ते आच्छादयति इति विव; fr. विवस्—क्विप् (०) . मेदिनी०——For a similar sentiment *of* स हि सर्वस्य लोकस्य युक्तदण्डतया मनः। आददे नातिशीतोष्णो नभस्वानिव दक्षिणः ॥ Rag. IV. 8; also न खरो न भूयसा मृदुः....स पुरस्कृतमध्यमक्रमो नमयामास नृपाननुद्धरन् ॥ Rag. VIII. 9; Mahābhārata—मृदुर्भवत्यवज्ञातस्तीक्ष्णादुद्विजते जनः। काले काले तु सम्प्राप्ते मृदुस्तीक्ष्णोऽथवा भवेत् ॥

उक्तान्यथाकरणेऽनिष्टमाह—

क्व चिराय परिग्रहः श्रियां क्व च दुष्टेन्द्रियवाजिवश्यता।
शरदभ्रचलाश्चलेन्द्रियैरसुरक्षा हि बहुच्छलाः श्रियः ॥३९॥

अन्वयः—श्रियां चिराय परिग्रहः क्व दुष्टेन्द्रियवाजिवश्यता च क्व । (हि) शरदभ्रचला बहुच्छलाः श्रियः चलेन्द्रियैः असुरक्षाः ॥३९॥

क्वेति ॥ श्रियां संपदां चिराय बहुकालं परिग्रहः स्वायत्तीकरणं क्व । इन्द्रियाणि

वाजिन इवेत्युपमितसमासः । दुष्टानाममार्गधाविनामिन्द्रियवाजिनां वश्यो वशंगतस्तस्य भावस्तत्ता क्व । नोभयमेकत्र तिष्ठतीत्यर्थः । कुतः । हि यस्माच्छरदभ्रवच्चलाश्चञ्चलाः । किंच बहुच्छला बहुव्याजाः । बहुरन्ध्रा इति यावत् ॥ "छलं तु स्खलिते व्याजे" इति विश्वः । श्रियो संपदः । चलेन्द्रियैरजितेन्द्रियैरसुरक्षा रक्षितुमशक्याः । कथंचित्प्राप्ता अपि श्रियः नाविनीतेषु तिष्ठन्तीत्यर्थः ॥ वाक्यार्थहेतुकं काव्यलिङ्गमलंकारः ॥

अन्वयार्थः— (**श्रियाम्**) सम्पदाओं का (**चिराय**) चिर काल तक (**परिग्रहः क्व**) अपने आधीन रखना कहाँ, (**दुष्टेन्द्रियवाजिवश्यता च क्व**) और दुष्ट इन्द्रिय-रूप घोड़ों का वश में रखना कहाँ ! [हि] क्यों कि (**शरदभ्रचलाः**) शरद्-कालीन मेघों-जैसी चंचल (**बहुच्छलाः**) बहुत कपटी (**श्रियः**) लक्ष्मियाँ (**चलेन्द्रियैः**) चञ्चल हैं इन्द्रियाँ जिन की ऐसों से (**असुरक्षाः**) असुरक्षित होती है।

देर तक वैभव का उपभोग करने वाला व्यक्ति इन्द्रिय-रूपी घोड़ों को वश में नहीं रख सकता। और जो जितेन्द्रिय नहीं उसके पास शारद् मेघों की तरह चञ्चल एवं छलिया-रूप वाली लक्ष्मी सुरक्षित नहीं रह सकती।

39. Where is retaining into possession riches (royalty for a long time and where subjection to (yielding to the influence of) the horse-like senses ! (how difficult to reconcile the two !) fortunes flitting like the autumnal clouds and full of pretexts (to pass away) cannot be well retained by those whose senses are unsteadly (*i. e.* who have no control over their senses).

Sl. 39. दुष्टेन्द्रिय०... इन्द्रियाणि वाजिन इव इन्द्रियवाजिनः Upmitaa samăsa; दुष्टा इन्द्रि० दुष्टेन्द्रियवाजिनः तेषां वश्यता । वशं गतः वश्यः fr. वश्—य (यत्) the state of being subject to the influence of the senses which are like unruly horses. The senses are again compared to horses further on.— मा भूवन्नपथहरास्तवेन्द्रियाश्वाः । V. 50. वाजिन्—अवश्यं वजति गच्छति इति; fr. वज् 1 P. to go+इन् (णिनिः) It may beter be derived as वाज strength (which meaning it has in the Veda) +इन् having इन्द्रिय is derived as इन्द्रस्य आत्मनः लिङ्गं the sign of *i. e.* leading to the inference of. Pān. gives various derivations; he has इन्द्रियमिन्द्रलिङ्गमिन्द्रदृष्टमिन्द्रसृष्टमिन्द्रजुष्टमिन्द्रदत्तमिति वा । on which Vămana thus comments इन्द्रस्य लिंगमिन्द्रियम् । इन्द्र आत्मा । स चक्षुरादिना करणेनानुमीयते । नाकर्तृकं करणमस्ति । इन्द्रेणात्मना दृष्टम् । इन्द्रेण सृष्टम् । आत्माना सृष्टं तत्कृतेन शुभाशुभकर्मणोत्पन्नमिति कृत्वा । इन्द्रेण जुष्टमात्मना सेवितम् । तद्द्वारेण विज्ञानोत्पादनात् । इन्द्रेण दत्तम् । आत्मना विषयेभ्यो दत्तं यथायथं ग्रहणाय । इन्द्र is derived from the root इन्द्+र (Uṇădi) इन्दति परमैश्वर्यं भुंक्ते इति. According to the Bṛh. Upanishad इन्द्र is the same as इन्ध (fr. इन्ध् to kindle, to light), the Supreme Soul which lights up the whole world.

इन्द्रियवाजि०—The organs of sense are compared to horses in Vedāntic works. *Cf.* इन्द्रियाणि हयानाहुर्विषयांस्तेषु गोचरान् । आत्मेन्द्रियमनोयुक्तं भोक्तेत्याहुर्मनीषिणः । Kaṭhopanishad, 3rd Valli.

शरदभ्र०—शरदः अभ्राणि शरदभ्राणि तानीव चलाः । The autumnal clouds are taken because they are lighter and are more at the mercy of the wind than the rain-clouds. अभ्र is derived as न भ्रश्यतीति; fr. भ्रंश्+अ (डः) or अपः बिभर्तीति fr. अप्+भृ+अ (क). बहुच्छलाः—बहूनि छलानि यासां which slip away through various pretexts (loop-holes). For the pretexts *Cf.* तीक्ष्णादुद्विजते मृदौ परिभवत्रासान्न सन्तिष्ठते । मूर्खान्द्वेष्टि न गच्छति प्रणयितामत्यन्तविद्वत्स्वपि । शूरेभ्योप्यधिकं बिभेत्युपहसत्येकान्तभीरूनपि श्रीर्लब्धप्रसरेव वेशवनिता दुःखोपचर्या भृशम् ॥ Mud. III. 5. *Cf.* also श्रियमवेद्यसरन्ध्रचलामभूदनलसोनलसोमसमद्युतिः ॥ Rag. IX. 15.

चलेन्द्रियैः—चलानि इन्द्रियाणि येषां तैः । असुरक्षाः—सुष्ठु रक्ष्यन्ते इति सुरक्षाः; fr. रक्ष+अ (खल्)+आ. न सुरक्षाः असुरक्षाः ।

The fig. of speech here is *Kāvyaliṅga* (see com.) which is mixed with *Vishama* in the first two lines and *Upamā* implied in इन्द्रियवाजि and शरदभ्रचला (समासगा).

क्रोधस्य दुष्टतामुक्त्वा तस्य त्यागमुपदिशति—

किमसामयिकं वितन्वता मनसः क्षोभमुपात्तरंहसः ।
क्रियते पतिरुच्चकैरपां भवता धीरतयाधरीकृतः ॥४०॥

अन्वयः—उपात्तरंहसः मनसः असामयिक क्षोभं वितन्वता भवता (पुरा) धीरतया अधरीकृतः अपां पतिः । (अधुना) किम् उच्चकैः क्रियते ॥४०॥

किमिति ॥ उपात्तरंहसः प्राप्तत्वरस्य मनसः । समयोऽस्य प्राप्तः सामयिकः ॥ "समयस्तदस्य प्राप्तम्" इति ठञ् ॥ स न भवतीत्यसामयिकस्तमप्राप्तकालं क्षोभं वितन्वता भवता धीरतया धैर्यगुणेन । "मनसो निर्विकारत्वं धैर्यं सत्स्वपि हेतुषु ।"

इति रसिकाः । अधरीकृतस्तिरस्कृतः । प्रागिति शेषः । अपां पतिः समुद्रः किं किमर्थमुच्चकैरधिकः क्रियते । न पराजितं पुनरुच्चकैः कुर्यादिति भावः । अत्र वितन्वतेति भीमविशेषणत्वेन पदार्थस्योच्चैःकरणे हेतुत्वात्काव्यलिङ्गमलंकारः ॥

अन्वयार्थः—(**उपात्तरंहसः**) प्राप्त किया है वेग जिसने ऐसे (**मनसः**) मन के (**असामयिकम्**) अनवसर प्राप्त (**क्षोभम्**) क्षोभ को (**वितन्वता**) विस्तृत करते हुए (**भवता**) आप के द्वारा [पुरा] पहले (**धीरतया**) धैर्य से (**अधरीकृतः**) तिरस्कृत (**अपां पतिः**) सागर [अधुना] अब (**किम्**) क्यों (**उच्चकैः**) उन्नत (**क्रियते**) किया जा रहा है ।

धैर्य में, पहले आप सागर को भी मात दे चुके हैं । अब बिना किसी उपयुक्त अवसर के उग्र मन के क्षोभ को प्रकट करके उसी पूर्व तिरस्कृत सागर को अपनेसे बड़ा क्यों बना रहे हैं ।

40. Why by you, manifesting the agitation of your mind wild with commotion, is the ocean, once surpassed by you in steadiness, now allowed to be your superior (in that respect) ?

Sl. 40. उपात्त०—उपात्तं (p. p. of दा with उप and आ) रंहः velocity, speed येन तस्य. असाम०—सामयिक that of which the time is come. ठञ् (इक) is added to words expressive fo time. असा०—inopportune, untimely. धीरतया—धियं राति इति धीरः fr. रा+अ (क) or धियम् ईरयति fr. ईर् to go+अण् (अ) properly a wise man able to guide others; hence patient. अधरी—न अधरः, (lower, inferior) अनधरः; अनधरः अधरः सम्पद्यमानः कृतः अधरीकतः excelled, vanquished. उच्चकैः—*indce.* used as *adj.* here; fr. उच्चकैः+अक (अकच्); अक is inserted immediately before the final vowel of a word ; उच्च्+अक+ऐस्. It is added to pronominal bases. verbal forms, indeclinables &c. in various senses.

श्रुतमप्यधिगम्य ये रिपून्विनयन्ते न शरीरजन्मनः ।
जनयन्त्यचिराय संपदामयशस्ते खलु चापलाश्रयम् ॥४१॥

अन्वयः—ये श्रुतम् अधिगम्य अपि शरीरजन्मनः रिपून् न विनयन्ते ते अचिराय संपदां चापलाश्रयम् अयशः जनयन्ति खलु ॥४१॥

श्रुतमिति ॥ किञ्च । ये श्रुतं शास्त्रमधिगम्यापि शरीरजन्मनः शरीरप्रभवा-

न्रिपून्कामक्रोधलोभमोहमात्सर्यादीन्न विनयन्ते न नियच्छन्ति ॥ "कर्तृस्थे चाशरीरे कर्मणि" इत्यात्मनेपदम् ॥ ते खल्वचिराय झटिति संपदां श्रियां चापलाश्रयमस्थैर्यनिबन्धनमयशो दुष्कीर्ति जनयन्ति । आश्रयदोषादस्थैर्यं संपदां न स्वदोषादित्यर्थः । अजितारिषड्वर्गस्य कुतः संपद इति भावः ॥

अन्वयार्थः—(**य**) जो (**श्रुतम्**) शास्त्र को (**अधिगम्य अपि**) प्राप्त कर के भी (**शरीरजन्मनः**) शरीर से है जन्म जिन का ऐसे (**रिपून्**) शत्रुओं को (**न विनयन्ते**) वश में नहीं करते हैं, (**ते**) (**अचिराय**) शीघ्र (**संपदाम्**) सम्पत्तियों के (**चापलाश्रयम्**) अस्थिरता है आश्रय जिसका ऐसे (**अयशः**) अपयश को (**खलु**) निश्चय से (**जनयन्ति**) उत्पन्न करते हैं ।

शास्त्र पढ़ कर भी जो लोग काम-क्रोध आदि शारीरिक शत्रुओं पर नियन्त्रण नहीं रखते हैं, वास्तव में वे ही लोग सम्पदाओं में 'अस्थिरता' के अपयश को उत्पन्न करते हैं ।

41. Verily those, who, even after having acquired Śāstric knowledge, do not check their passions (lit. the enemies sprung from the body), quickly bring on the goddess of wealth the infamy due to fickleness (her being unsteady).

Sl. 41. शरीर०—शृणाति शीर्यते वा; fr. शॄ+ईरन्; that which decays or is sent into pieces. विनयन्ते—For the Atm. see notes on sl. 35. चापला०—चपलस्य भावः चापलं by affixing अण्; चापलमाश्रयः यस्य तत् । strangely enough, चपल is derived from the root चुप् which means 'to go slowly' (मन्दायां गतौ)+अल (कल) the penultimate उ being changed to अ by चुपेरच्चोपधायाः । Uādi. I. III. *Cf.* येन श्रियः संश्रयदोषरूढं स्वभावलोलेत्ययशः प्रमृष्टम् । Rag. VI. 41.

तथा क्रोधात्कार्यहानिरित्याशयेनाह—

अतिपातितकालसाधना स्वशरीरेन्द्रियवर्गतापनी ।
जनवन्न भवन्तमक्षमा नयसिद्धेरपनेतुमर्हति ॥४२॥

अन्वयः—अतिपातितकालसाधना स्वशरीरेन्द्रियवर्गतापनी अक्षमा भवन्तं जनवत् नयसिद्धेः अपनेतुं न अर्हति ॥४२॥

अतिपातितेति ।। अतिपातितान्यतिक्रान्तानि कालः समयोऽनन्तरूपा साधनानि सहायादीनि च यया सा तयोक्ता । तापयतीति तापनी ।। कर्तरि ल्युट् । टित्वात् ङीप् ।। स्वस्य यच्छरीरमिन्द्रियवर्गश्च तयोस्तापन्यक्षमा क्रोधो भवन्तं जनवत्पृथग्जनमिव ।। "तेन तुल्यम्—" इति वतिप्रत्यय तेनेवार्थो लक्ष्यते ।। "तद्धितश्चासर्वविभक्तिः" इत्यव्ययम् ।। नयसिद्धेर्नयसाध्यफलादपनेतुं पृथक्कर्तुं नार्हति । असमयक्रोधस्यात्मसंतापातिरिक्तं फलं नास्तीत्यर्थः ।।

अन्वयार्थः—(**अतिपातितकालसाधना**) अतिक्रम किया है समय एवं [मित्र-रूप] साधनों का जिसने ऐसा, (**स्वशरीर-इन्द्रिय-वर्ग-तापनी**) अपने शरीर एवं इन्द्रियसमूह को कष्ट पहुंचाने वाली, (**अक्षमः**) असहिष्णुता (**भवन्तम्**) आप को (**जनवत्**) सामान्य व्यक्ति की तरह (**नयसिद्धेः**) नीति से [प्राप्त] होने वाले फल से (**अपनेतुम्**) दूर करने में (**न अर्हति**) नहीं योग्य है ।

असहिष्णु व्यक्ति समय एवं सहायक मित्रवर्ग से हाथ धो बैठता है । यह उसके अपने देह एवं इन्द्रियों को हानि पहुंचाती है । एक सामान्य व्यक्ति की भांति आप को इस असहिष्णुता के कारण, नीति से प्राप्त होने वाली सफलता से वञ्चित नहीं होना चाहिए ।

42. Anger, which makes one trangress proper time and means and which inflames one's body and the group of senses, should not have the power to lead you away, like an ordinary man from success to be achieved by sound policy.

Sl. 42. अतिपातित—making one pass over or trangress. साधनं may mean here an army or friends (allies) or the means of doing a thing. वर्ग fr. वृज् +अ (धञ्); a collection तापनी —तापयतीति fr. तप्+अन (ल्युट् कर्तरि)+ई. जनवत्—*indec.* जनेन तुल्यं जनवत् like an ordinary man. Words formed with such Taddihta affixes as do not take all the case terminations are indeclinables. See com. नयसिद्धेः नयेन साध्या नयसाध्या सिद्धिः नयसिद्धिः । शाकपार्थिवादिवत्समासः ।

दुष्टः क्रोध इत्युक्तम् । अथ क्षमया गुणानाह—

उपकारकमायतेर्भृशं प्रसवः कर्मफलस्य भूरिणः ।
अनपायि निबर्हणं द्विषां न तितिक्षासममस्ति साधनम् ।।४३।।

अन्वयः—आयतेः भृशम् उपकारकं भूरिणः कर्मफलस्य प्रसवः अनपायि द्विषां निबर्हणं तितिक्षासमं साधनं न अस्ति ॥४३॥

उपकारकमिति ॥ आयतेरुत्तरकालस्य भृशमत्यन्तमुपकारकम् । स्थिरफलहेतुरित्यर्थः । भूरिणः प्रभूतस्य कर्मफलस्य । प्रसूयतेऽनेनेति प्रसवः कारणम् । अपायि न भवतीत्यनपायि स्वयमविनश्यदेव द्विषां निबर्हणं विनाशकमेवंगुणकं साधनं तितिक्षासमं क्षमातुल्यं नास्ति ॥ "क्षान्तिः क्षमा तितिक्षा च" इत्यमरः ॥ "तिज् निशाने" इति धातोः "गुप्तिज्किद्भ्यः सन्" इति क्षमार्थे सन्प्रत्ययः ॥ तितिक्षासममित्यनुक्तोपमेया समास आर्थी लुप्तोपमा भृशायत्यनपायिशब्दैः साधनान्तरवैलक्षण्याद्व्यतिरेकश्च व्यज्यते । भेदप्राधान्य उपमानादुपमेयस्याधिक्ये विपर्यये च व्यतिरेकः ॥

अन्वयार्थः—(**आयते**) उत्तर काल का (**भृशम्**) अत्यधिक (**उपकारकम्**) उपकारी (**भूरिणः**) प्रचुर (**कर्मफलस्य**) कर्मफल का (**प्रसवः**) कारण, (**अनपायि**) नाश-रहित (**द्विषाम्**) शत्रुओं का (**निबर्हणम्**) विनाशक, (**तितिक्षा समम्**) सहिष्णुता-सदृश (**साधनम्**) साधन (**नास्ति**) नहीं है ।

सहिष्णुता परिणाम में अत्यन्त उपकारी, प्रचुर कर्म-फल की निमित्त तथा स्वयं अविनाशी होते हुए भी शत्रुओं को नष्ट करने वाली है । वास्तव में सहिष्णुता जैसा अन्य उपाय है ही नहीं ।

43. There is no means equal to forgiveness, which is highly conducive to future prosperity, which is the great source of success in undertakings, and which is an unfailing destroyer of enemies.

Sl. 43. प्रसवः—fr. प्रसू+अ (अप्) added करणे; source, case. Usually the aff. is added कर्मणि; what is produced, a product. निबर्हण—बर्हते बर्हयति वा that which destroys; fr. बर्ह्+अन (ल्युट्).

तितिक्षा०—तितिक्षा fr. the Desid. base of तिज्+आ; but the aff. सन् is not desiderative here, but has the sense of 'forgiving', क्षमायां सन् Păn. III. 1. 15. तितिक्षायाः क्षया वा समम्; Gen. or Inst. Tat.

ननु तितिक्षया कालक्षेपे दुर्योधनः सर्वान्राज्ञो वशीकुर्यादित्यत्राह—

प्रणतिप्रवणान्विहाय नः सहजस्नेहनिबद्धचेतसः ।
प्रणमन्ति सदा सुयोधनं प्रथमे मानभृतां न वृष्णयः ॥४४॥

अन्वयः—सहजस्नेहनिबद्धचेतसः मानभृतां प्रथमे वृष्णयः प्रणतिप्रवणान् नः विहाय सुयोधनं सदा न प्रणमन्ति ॥४४॥

प्रणतीति ॥ सहजस्नेहेनाकृत्रिमप्रेम्णा निबद्धचेतसोऽस्मासु गाढं लग्नचित्ताः ॥ सुयोधने तु न तथेति भावः । किं च मानभृतामहंकारिणां प्रथमेऽग्रेसराः । सुयोधनस्यापीति भावः । वृष्णयो यादवाः प्रणतिप्रवणान्प्रणामपरान् । सुयोधनस्तु न तथेति भावः । नोऽस्मान्विहाय सुयोधनं सदा न प्रणमन्ति न नमन्ति नानुसरन्ति । किंतु कार्यकाले त्यक्ष्यन्त्येवेत्यर्थः । सति यादवविग्रहे न किंचिदस्माकमसाध्यं भवेदिति भावः ॥ अनेकपदार्थहेतुकं काव्यलिङ्गमलंकारः ।

अन्वयार्थः—(**सहजस्नेहनिबद्धचेतसः**) स्वभाविक प्रेम से (**हम में**) बंधा हुआ है चित्त जिन का ऐसे (**मानभृताम्**) स्वाभिमानियों में (**प्रथमे**) श्रेष्ठ (**वृष्णयः**) यादव (**प्रणतिप्रवणान्**) नमस्कार में प्रवृत्त (**नः**) हमें (**विहाय**) छोड़कर (**सुयोधनम्**) सुयोधन को (**सदा न प्रणमन्ति**) सदा प्रणाम नहीं करेंगे ।

अति स्वाभिवमानी, अभिन्न हृदय यादव लोग भी, जिन्हें हम सदा नमस्कार करते हैं, अधिक समय तक दुर्योधन के सामने नहीं झुकते रहेंगे ।

44. The descendants of Vrishṇi (Yādavas), the foremost among those possessed of self-respect and whose minds are linked to us by (the ties of) natural affection; will not always bow to Suyodhana, leaving us (ever) inclined (or ready) to bow down to them.

Sl. 44. सहज०—सह जायते असौ सहजः । सहजश्चासौ स्नेहश्च तेन निबद्धं चेतः येषां ते (or तान् if taken with नः). मानभृतः—मानं बिभ्रतीति; full of self respect, proud of their race. वृष्णयः—वृष्णेः गोत्रापत्यानि पुमांसः वृष्णयः; the descendants of Vṛshṇi; the Yădavas. The तद्धित aff. अण् is dropped; see Păn. II. 4. 63. वृष्णि—the ancesstor of Kṛshaṇa, was the chief of the hundred sons of Madhu, a descendant of Yadu. The family had various appelations—*cf.* Vishṇu P. ततो विष्णुसंज्ञामेतगोत्रमवाप । मधुसंज्ञाहेतुश्च मधुरभवत् । यादवाश्च यदुनामोपलक्षणात् । प्रणतिप्रवणान्—प्रणतौ प्रवणास्तान् ।

किंच कारणान्तरमाह—

सुहृदः सहजास्तथेतरे मतमेषां न विलङ्घयन्ति ये ।
विनयादिव यापयन्ति ते धृतराष्ट्रात्मजमात्मसिद्धये ॥४५॥

अन्वयः—एषां (वृष्णीनां) ये सहजा सुहृदः तथा इतरे मतं न विलङ्घयन्ति ते आत्मसिद्धये धृतराष्ट्रात्मजं विनयादिव यापयन्ति ॥४५॥

सुहृय इति ॥ किं च एषां वृष्णीनां ये सहजाः सहजाताः । मातृपितृपक्षा इत्यर्थः ॥ "अन्येष्वपि दृश्यदे" इति डप्रत्ययः ॥ सुहृदो मित्राणि तथेतरे कृत्रिमसुहृदश्चैषां मत वृष्णिपक्षं न विलङ्घयन्ति नातिक्रामन्ति । ते द्वयेऽपि नृपाः । दुर्योधनोपजीविनोऽपीति भावः । आत्मसिद्धय आत्मजीवनार्थं धृतराष्ट्रात्मजं दुर्योधनं विनयादानुकूल्यादिव यापयन्ति कालं गमयन्ति । कार्यकाले तु वृष्णिपक्षप्रवेशिन एवेत्यर्थः ॥ यातेर्ण्यन्ताल्लट् । "अर्तिहि—" इत्यादिना पुगामम: ॥

अन्वयार्थः—(**एषाम्**) इन (**यादवों**) के (**ये**) जो (**सहजाः**) सगे (**सुहृदः**) मित्र हैं (**तथा**) और (**इतरे**) अन्य [जो] (**मतम्**) [**यादव**] पक्ष का (**न विलङ्घयन्ति**) उल्लङ्घन नहीं करते हैं, (**ते**) वे [दोनों प्रकार के मित्र] (**आत्मसिद्धये**) अपनी [**आजीविका**] सिद्धि के लिए (**धृतराष्ट्रजम्**) धृतराष्ट्र के पुत्र के पास (**विनयादिव**) अनुकूल की भांति (**यापयन्ति**) समय बिताते हैं ।

इन यादवों के जो मातृपक्ष या पितृपक्ष के अपने सगे हैं वे तथा इन का कभी भी विरोध न करने वाले जो मित्र हैं वे सब अपनी आजीविका के कारण दुर्योधन के अनुकूल-से बन कर अपना समय व्यतीत कर रहे हैं । वास्तव में वे उसके पक्ष में नहीं हैं ।

45. Their natural friends, and those others who never go contrary to (*i.e.* act in conformity with) their wishes, doing obeisance to (or acting favourably towards) the son of Dhṛtaráshtra in order gain their ends, allow him go to (pass time) on that supposition.

Sl. 45. सहजाः—friends by birth; the relatives of father and mother. There are two other classes of friends, कृत्रिमः (कार्येण निर्वृत्तः) सुहृत् is one so by conduct (*i. e.* by doing some service or a beneficial act), and प्राकृत (प्रकृत्या सिद्धः) is one whose property is not close to that of ours (so that there is no chance of a quarrel taking place with him). Similarly enemies also are of three kinds. *Cf.* सखा गरीयान् शत्रुश्च कृत्रिमस्तौ हि कार्यतः । स्यातामभित्रौ मित्रे च सहजप्राकृतावपि ll Sis. II. 36 and Malli. on it.

आत्म०—आत्मन: सिद्धि: आत्मसिद्धि: । विनयात्—is equivalent to विनयमाश्रित्य l ल्यब्लोपे पञ्चमी when the sense of an absolutive is supressed the object of the absolutive is put in the Ab. case. यापयन्ति—Duryodhana goes on the supposition that they are attached to him; and they allow him to pass his days that supposition.

किंच नायमभियोगकाल इत्याशयेनाह—

अभियोग इमान्महीभुजो भवता तस्य कृतः कृतावधेः।

प्रविघाटयिता समुत्पतन्हरिदश्वः कमलाकरानिव ॥४६॥

अन्वयः—कृतावधेः तस्य भवता कृतः अभियोगः इमान् महीभुजः हरिदश्वः कमलाकरान् इव समुत्पतन् प्रविघाटयिता ॥४६॥

अभियोग इति ॥ कृतावधेः परिभाषितकालस्य ॥ "अवधिस्त्ववधाने स्यात्सीम्नि काले बिलेऽपि च ।" इति विश्वः ॥ तस्य सुयोधनस्य ॥ कर्मणि षष्ठी ॥ भवता कृतः । अवधिमनपेक्ष्येति शेषः । अभियोगः । आर्द्राभिभव इति यावत् ॥ "अभियोगस्तु शपथे स्यादार्द्रे च पराभवे" इति विश्वः ॥ इमान्पूर्वोक्तान्महीभुजो राज्ञो हरिदश्व उष्णरश्मिः कमलाकरानिव समुत्पतन्नुद्यन्नेव प्रविघाटयिता भेत्स्यति ॥ घाटयतेर्भौवादिकाल्लुट् । चौरादिकस्य तु "मितां ह्रस्वः" इति ह्रस्वत्वं स्यात् ॥

अन्वयार्थः—(**कृतावधेः**) किया है अवधि को जिसने ऐसे (**तस्य**) उस पर (**भवता**) आप के द्वारा (**कृतः**) किया हुआ (**अभियोगः**) आक्रमण, (**इमान्**) इन (**महीभुजः**) राजाओं को (**हरिदश्वः**) सूर्य (**समुत्पतन् एव**) उदय होते ही (**कमलाकरानिव**) जैसे कमल-समूहों को, (**प्रविघाटयिता**) भेदन करने वाला होगा ।

दुर्योधन ने अवधि का निश्चय किया और हम ने उसे स्वीकार कर लिया । यदि हम अवधि से पहले ही उस पर आक्रमण करेंगे तो जैसे उदय होते ही सूर्य कमलों का भेदन कर देता है (उन्हें खिला देता है), उसी प्रकार तुम्हारा यह आक्रमण उपर्युक्त राजाओं का विघटन कर देगा ।

46. An attack on him who has not down a limit of time

made by you (before its expiry) will at the very outset separate these kings (from one another or from us) as does the sun the (petals of) lotuses just on rising.

Sl. 46. कृतावधेः—कृतः laid down, fixed अवधिर्येन तस्य. See *supra* I. 45. अभियोगः—a fresh attack. हरिदश्वः—हरितः अश्वा यस्य. The horses of the sun are called Harit in the Ṛg. Veda, see I. 50. 8; 115. 4. They are seven in number, being the seven principal rays of the sun personified. *Cf.* the name सप्ताश्व, सप्तरश्मि. हरति तमः स्वतेजसा इतिहरित्; fr. हृ+इत् (इति Uṇādi I. 97). समुत्पतन्—qualifies both अभियोगः and हरिदश्वः meaning taking its course; at the outset; (2) rising प्रविघाटयिता—Ist. Fut. of घट् of the 10th class, and not the Cau. of घट् of the first class which has घटयति in the Cau.; see com.

There is some uncertainty as to the exact meaning of this verse. Malli.'s Com. is not clear enough. In some editions the reading is भवता कृतः । अवधिमनपेक्ष्येति शेषः । and अभियोगः is translated by आद्यभिभवः. So the meaning seems to be—If you lead an attack against Duryodhana without waiting for the expiry of the time agreed upon, your action will have no justification and will alienate the sympathy of the Yădavas and their friends from us. But then the simile becomes inappropriate. The sun rises at stated times (not before the expiry of the night). In the new edition of the Nir. press we have अवधितः for अवधिमनपेक्ष्य; the real meaning and one which better accords with the context, is—If you take hostile action against Duryodhana having waited for *i. e.* at the end of, the stipulated time, it will make the Yădavas and their allies break from their apparent allegiance to Duryodhan's party. Fig:—*Upamā*. The sun opens the lotus flourers which means the parting asunder of their petals which before were in union, as it were.

अथ न ये वृष्णिपक्षास्तान्प्रत्याह—

उपजापसहान्विलङ्घयन्स विधाता नृपतीन्मदोद्धतः ।
सहते न जनोऽप्यधःक्रियां किमु लोकाधिकधाम राजकम् ॥४७॥

अन्वयः—मदोद्धतः स नृपतीन् विलङ्घयन् उपजापसहान् विधाता । जनः अपि अधःक्रियां न सहते, लोकाधिकधाम राजकं किमु ॥४७॥

उपजापेति ॥ महोद्धतः स दुर्योधनो नृपतीवन्यान्नृपान्विलङ्घयन्मदादवमानयन् । सहन्त इति सहाः । पचाद्यच् ॥ उपजापस्य सहान्भेदयोग्यान् ॥ "समौ भेदोपजापौ" इत्यमरः ॥ विधाता विधास्यति ॥ विपूर्वस्य दधातेर्लुट् ॥ अवमानितो जनः सुभेद्य इति भावः । न च ते सहिष्णव इत्याह—जनः प्राकृतोऽप्यधःक्रियामपमानं न सहते । लोकाधिकधाम लोकोत्तरप्रतापं राजकं राजसमूहः ॥ "गोत्रोक्षोष्ट्र—" इत्यादिना वुञ्प्रत्ययः ॥ किमु । न सहत इति किं वक्तव्यमित्यर्थः । तथा सति कृत्स्नमेव राजमण्डलमस्मानेवावलम्बिष्यत इति भावः ।

अन्वयार्थः—(**मदोद्धतः सः**) मद से उद्धत हुआ-हुआ वह (**नृपतीन्**) राजाओं का (**विलङ्घयन्**) तिरस्कार करता हुआ (**उपजायसहान्**) फूट के योग्य (**विधाता**) बनायेगा । (**जनः अपि**) सामान्य व्यक्ति भी (**अधःक्रियाम्**) अपमान को (**न सहते**) नहीं सहन करता है, (**लोकाधिकधाम**) लोकोत्तर तेज युक्त (**राजकम्**) राजाओं का समुदाय (**किमु**) क्यों (**सहेगा**) ?

मदोद्धत दुर्योधन इन राजाओं का तिरस्कार करने से नहीं रुक सकता । तिरस्कृत होने पर इन में भेद-नीति का प्रयोग सरल होगा । एक सामान्य व्यक्ति भी तिरस्कार को नहीं सहता फिर अति तेजस्वी राजाओं का तो कहना ही क्या ।

47. Inflated with vanity he, insulting the (other) kings, will make them suscetible to dissension. Even an ordinary person does not suffer (or put up with) an insult (or being slighted); how much less then the multitude of kings wose prowess transcends that of the world (is extraordinary) !

Sl. 47. मदोद्धतः—मदेन उद्धतः haughty or elated with vanity. उपजापस०—उप उपांशु (near) जपनं (whispering into the ear) उपजापः; fr. उप+जप्+अ (घञ्) It means secret overtures or negotiations with the enemy's friends; sowing the seeds of dissension ; or causing discord among them; **तस्य सहाः susceptible** to. That is—If we make overtures to them they will be ready to come over to our side leaving that of Duryodhana. *Cf.* अपि सहन्ते अस्मदुपजापं प्रजा; । Mud. Act II. लोकाधिक०—लोकेभ्यः अधिकं लोकाधिकं धाम यस्य । राजकं—a collection of kings; fr. राजन् + अक (वुञ्).

ननु सखीनिवेत्यादिवनेचरोक्त्या तस्य मदसंभावनापि कथमित्यत्राह—

असमापितकृत्यसंपदां हतवेगं विनयेन तावता ।

प्रभवन्त्यभिमानशालिनां मदमुत्तम्भयितुं विभूतयः ॥४८॥

अन्वयः—असमापितकृत्यसंपदाम् अभिमानशालिनां विभूतयः तावता विनयेन हतवेगं मदम् उत्तम्भयितु प्रभवन्ति ॥४८॥

असमापितेति ॥ असमापितकृत्यसंपदामकृतकृत्यानामभिमानशालिनामहंकारिणां विभूतयः संपद एव तावता स्वल्पेन विनयेन । कार्यवशादारोपितेनेति शेषः । हतवेगं प्रतिबद्धवेगं नतु स्वरूपतो हतं मदमुत्तम्भयितुं वर्धयितुं प्रभवन्ति । सर्वथा दुर्जनं संपदो विकारयन्तीति भावः ॥

अन्वयार्थः—(**असमापितकृत्यसंपदाम्**) नहीं समाप्त किया है कृत्य सम्पत्तियों को जिन्होंने ऐसे—अकृतकार्य—(**अभिमानशालिनाम्**) अहंकारियों की (**विभूतयः**) सम्पदाएँ, (**तावता**) उतने मात्र (**विनयेन**) विनय से (**हतवेगं मदम्**) रुक गया है वेग जिसका ऐसे मद को (**उत्तम्भयितुम्**) बढ़ाने में (**प्रभवन्ति**) समर्थ होती हैं ।

अकृतकार्य एवं अहंकारी व्यक्तियों की सम्पदाऐं उन के मद को फिर से उभारने में समर्थ होती हैं; क्यों कि अल्प विनय से वह मद कम भले ही हो जाये, मूलतः नष्ट नहीं होता ।

48. The prosperity of those who have not done all that is necessary to be done (for the permanency of their rule) and who are conspicuous by their pride has power to call up (again) their arrogance, the force of which was checked by humility just sufficient to do it (for a while).

Sl. 48. असमापित &c.—कृत्यानां सम्पदः कृत्यसम्पदः । समापिताः कृत्यसम्पदो यैस्ते समा०दः; न समा० असमापितकृत्यसम्पदः तेषाम् । अभिमान० —अभिमानेन शालन्ते ते अभिमानशालिनस्तेषाम् । तावता—तत्परिमाणमस्य तावान् तेन fr. तत्+वत् (वतुप्). हतवेगं—हतः checked, restrained वेगः outburst, force यस्य तम् । उत्तम्भयितुम्—To raise up. The स् of स्था and स्तम्भ् is dropped after the prep. उद्; Pān. VIII. 4. 61. *Cf.* स्तम्भते पुरुषः प्रायो यौवनेन धनेन च । Kavirahasya.

अथ मदस्यानर्थहेतुतां युग्मेनाह—

मदमानसमुद्धतं नृपं न वियुङ्क्ते नियमेन मूढता ।
अतिमूढ उदस्यते नयान्नयहीनादपरज्यते जनः ॥४९॥

अन्वयः—मदमानसमुद्धतं नृपं मूढता नियमेन न वियुंक्ते, अतिमूढः नयात् उदस्यते, नयहीनात् जनः अपरज्यते ॥४९॥

मदेति । अपरागेति च ॥ मदमानाभ्यां दर्पाहंकाराभ्यां समुद्धतं नृपं मूढता कार्यापरिज्ञानं नियमेनावश्यं न वियुंक्ते न विमुञ्चति । अतिमूढो नयान्नीतिमार्गादुदस्यत उत्क्षिप्यते ॥ कर्मकर्तरि लट् ॥ नयहीनाज्जनो लोकोऽपरज्यतेऽपरक्तो भवति ॥ "स्वरितञितः—"इत्यादिनात्मनेपदम् ॥

अन्वयार्थः--(**मदमानसमुद्धतम्**) दर्प एवं अहंकार के कारण उद्धत (**नृपम्**) राजा को (**मूढता**) मूर्खता (**नियमेन**) नियम से--अवश्यम्भावी रूप से--(**न विमुक्ते**) नहीं छोड़ती है । (**अतिमूढ**) अति मूर्ख (**नयात्**) नीति से (**उदस्यते**) फेंक दिया जाता है । (**नयहीनात्**) नीति-रहित से (जनः) लोक (**अपरज्यते**) विरक्त होता है ।

दर्प एवं अहंकार के कारण उद्धत हुआ-हुआ व्यक्ति निश्चित रूप से मूर्ख होता है । मूर्ख नीति-मार्ग का अनुसरण नहीं कर सकता और नीति-च्युत में लोगों की आस्था समाप्त हो जाती है ।

49. Imprudence (want of good sense) does not, as a rule, leave off (is always found with) a king puffed up wih arrogance and conceit; one extreme imprudent is thrown off (or falls off) from the path of right policy; and one not following the right course of conduct is disliked by the people.

Sl. 49. This and the following sl. convey one idea. *viz.* मदस्यानर्थहेतुता. मूढता—In ability to know what is right or wrong; folly. नियमेन—As a rule, certainly. वियुंक्ते—युज् 7 cl. with any preposition beginning or ending with a vowel is used in the Atm. स्वराद्यन्तोपसर्गादिति वक्तव्यम् । vārt. उदस्यते—see com.; or this may be taken intransitively in the active voice, the Atm. being due to the rule 'उपसर्गादस्यत्यूह्योर्वेति वक्तव्यम्।'

Fig.—कारणमाला.

अपरागसमीरणेरितः क्रमशीर्णाकुलमूलसंततिः ।
सुकरस्तरुवत्सहिष्णुना रिपुरुन्मूलयितुं महानपि ॥५०॥

अन्वयः—अपरागसमीरणेरितः क्रमशीर्णाकुलमूलसंततिः रिपुः महान् अपि तरुवत् सहिष्णुना उन्मूलयितुं सुकरः ॥५०॥

अपरागोऽप्रीतिः । द्वेष इति यावत् । समीरण इव । तेनेरितश्चोदितः । अतएव क्रमेण शीर्णा शीर्णीभूता आकुला चला च मूलसंततिः प्रकृत्यादिस्वजनवर्गः शिफासंघातश्च यस्य स तथोक्तः ॥ "मूलं वशीकृते स्वीये शिफातारान्तिकादिषु ।" इति वैजयन्ती ॥ रिपुर्महानपि तरुवद् वृक्ष इव सहिष्णुना क्षमावतोन्मूलयितुमुद्धर्तुं सुकरः सुसाध्यः । सुकरोन्मूल इत्यर्थः ॥ अत्र (श्लोकद्वये) महादेः पूर्वपूर्वस्योत्तरोत्तरं प्रति कारणत्वात्कारणमाला तरुवदित्युपमा चेति द्वयोः संसृष्टिः ॥

अन्वयार्थः—(**उपरागसमीरणेरितः**) अपरक्ति-रूप हवा से प्रेरित, (**क्रमशीर्णाकुलमूलसंततिः**) क्रम से क्षीण एवं विचलित हो गया है अमात्य तथा सगे-संबन्धियों का वर्ग जिस का ऐसा (**रिपुः**) शत्रु (**महानपि**) महान् भी, (**क्रमशीर्णाकुलमूलसंततिः**) क्रमशः जर्जरित एवं चलायमान हो गया है जड़-समूह जिस का ऐसे (**तरुवत्**) वृक्ष की भाँति, (**सहिष्णुना**) सहनशील के द्वारा (**उन्मूलयितुं सुकरः**) उखाड़ने के लिए सरल है ।

आंधी से क्रमशः जर्जरित एवं हिली हुई जड़ों वाला वृक्ष जैसे सरलता से उखाड़ा जा सकता है, उसी प्रकार अपरक्ति-रूप हवा के झोंके से क्षीण एवं विचलित हुए अमात्यों से युक्त शत्रु भी सहनशीलता की नीति से सरलता से उखाड़ा जा सकता है ।

50. Tossed by the wind of disaffection and with the ministers and other friends gradually estranged (lit. undermined), an enemy, even though very great, is, like a tree shaken by the wind and with its stretching roots gradually shattered, easy to uprooted by one having patience.

Sl. 50. अपराग—Fr. अप्+रञ्ज्+अ (घञ्), the nasal of रञ्ज्

is dropped before (घञ्) used भावे or करणे क्रमशीर्णा०—आकुल disordered, shaky. मूलानां संततिः मूलसंततिः । मूल is Ślishta and means—(1) ministers and relatives ; (2) the roots. तरुवत्—तरुः इव this is against Păn. (तत्र तस्येव V. 1. 116.) as वति cannot be used with the उपमान in the Nom. सहिष्णु—सहनशीलः patient by nature; सह्+इष्णु (इष्णुच्).

नन्वन्तर्भेदमात्रेण कथं सुसाध्यस्तत्राह—

अणुरप्युपहन्ति विग्रहः प्रभुमन्तःप्रकृतिकोपजः ।
अखिलं हि हिनस्ति भूधरं तरुशाखान्तनिघर्षजोऽनलः ॥५१॥

अन्वयः—अन्तःप्रकृतिप्रकोपजः विग्रहः अणुः अपि प्रभुम् उपहन्ति । तरुशाखान्तनिघर्षजः अनलः अखिलं भूधरं हिनस्ति हि ॥५१॥

अणुरिति ॥ अणुरल्पोऽप्यन्तःप्रकृतिप्रकोपजोऽन्तरङ्गामात्याद्यपरागसमुत्थः ॥ "प्रकृतिः पञ्चभूतेषु स्वभावे मूलकारणे । छन्दःकारणगुह्येषु जन्त्वमात्यादिकेष्वपि ॥" इति वैजयन्ती ॥ विग्रहो वैरं प्रभुमुपहन्ति नाशयति ॥ अत्र दृष्टान्तमाह—तरुशाखान्तानां निघर्षो घर्षणं तज्जोऽनलोऽग्निः । भूधरं गिरिमखिलं साकल्येन हिनस्ति हि । दहतीत्यर्थः ॥ अत्रोपमानोपमेयसमानधर्माणां प्रतिबिम्बतया निर्देशेन दृष्टान्तालंकारः ॥

अन्वयार्थः—(**अन्तःप्रकृतिकोपजः**) अन्तरङ्ग अमात्यादि के क्रोध से उत्पन्न (**विग्रहः**) वैर (**अणुरपि**) स्वल्प भी (**प्रभुमुपहन्ति**) स्वामी को नष्ट कर देता है । (**तरु शाखान्तनिघर्षजः**) वृक्ष की शाखाओं के शिखर के संघर्ष से उत्पन्न (**अनलः**) आग (**हि**) निश्चय से (**अखिलम्**) सम्पूर्ण (**भूधरम्**) वृक्ष को (**हिनस्ति**) नष्ट कर देती है ।

जिस प्रकार वृक्ष की अपनी शाखाओं से उत्पन्न अग्नि उसे भस्म कर देती है उसी प्रकार अन्तरङ्ग अमात्यादि में उत्पन्न वैर भी, स्वल्प होता हुआ भी, स्वामी को नष्ट कर देता है ।

51. Even a very small distursbanse (revolt) caused by the disaffection of the internal constituents of a kingdom kills a king. The fire produced by the friction of the points of the branches of a tree burns the whole mountain.

Sl. 51. अन्तःप्र०—अन्तर्गताः प्रकृतयः अन्तः प्रकृतयः तासां प्रकोपः

तस्माज्जायते ऽसौ । प्रकोप disturbance of feelings, discontent, disaffection. For fig. see com. Here विग्रह is aptly compared with fire and a king surrounded by his ministers and other officers with a mountain with trees growing on its sides. In both cases the cause of destruction is not external but internal.

तथापि कथं वर्धमानं शत्रुमुपेक्षेतेत्याशङ्क्य दुर्विनीतत्वादित्याह—

मतिमान्विनयप्रमाथिनः समुपेक्षेत समुन्नतिं द्विषः ।
सुजयः खलु तादृगन्तरे विपदन्ता ह्यविनीतसंपदः ॥५२॥

अन्वयः—विनयप्रमाथिनः द्विषः समुन्नतिं मतिमान् उपेक्षेत । तादृक् अन्तरे सुजयः हि अविनीतसंपदः विपदन्ताः ॥५२॥

मतिमानिति ॥ मतिमान्प्राज्ञः । विनयं प्रमथ्नाति त्यजतीति विनयप्रमाथिनो दुर्विनीतस्य द्विषः समुन्नतिं वृद्धिं समुपेक्षेत । उपेक्षायाः फलमाह—तादृगविनीतोऽन्तरे क्वचिद्रन्ध्रे सुजयः सुखेन जेतुं शक्यः खलु । हि यस्मादविनीतसंपदो विपदन्ता अनर्थोदर्काः ॥

अन्वयार्थः—(**विनयप्रमाथिनः**) विनय का त्याग करने वाले (**द्विषः**) शत्रु की (**समुन्नतिम्**) उन्नति की (**मतिमान्**) बुद्धिमान् (**उपेक्षेत**) उपेक्षा कर दे। (**तादृक्**) वैसा (**अन्तरे**) [किसी न किसी] दोष में [के कारण] (**सुजयः**) आसानी से जीता जा सकता है। (**हि**) निश्चय से (**अविनीतसम्पदः**) विनय-रहित की सम्पदाएं (**विपदन्ताः**), विपत्ति है अन्त जिन का, ऐसी होती हैं।

शत्रु यदि अविनीत है तो उस की उन्नति उपेक्षा के योग्य है। उस में कोई न कोई दोष होगा, अत एव उसे सरलता से जीता जा सकता है। अविनीत की सम्पदाएं भी अन्त में उसे अनर्थ की ही प्राप्ति कराने वाली होती हैं।

52. A man of foresight should overlook the rise of his enemy outraging (setting at naught) right conduct. Such ia person can be easily vanquished when there is a weak point. For surely the fortune (or prosperity) of an ill-behaved arrogant person has misery for its end.

Sl. 52. प्रमाथिन्—one who tramples down. सुजयः—fr. जि+अ (खल्). अन्तर—a loop-hole, a weak point. विपद०—विपद् अन्तः यासां ताः । Fig. अर्थान्तरन्यास (कारणेन कार्यसमर्थनरूपः).

कथं दुर्विनीतस्य शत्रोः सुजयत्वमित्याशङ्क्य भेदजर्जरितत्वादित्याह—

लघुवृत्तितया भिदां गतं बहिरन्तश्च नृपस्य मण्डलम् ।

अभिभूय हरत्यनन्तरः शिथिलं कूलमिवापगारयः ॥५३॥

अन्वयः—लघुवृत्तितया बहिः अन्तः च भिदां गतं नृपस्य मंडलम् अनन्तरः आपगारयः शिथिलं कूलम् इव अभिभूय हरति ॥५३॥

लघ्विति ॥ लघुवृत्तितया स्वस्य दुर्वृत्तरूपतया बहिर्मित्रादिजनपदेष्वन्तरमात्यादिषु च भिदां भेदं गतम् ॥ "षिद्भिदादिभ्योऽङ्" इत्यङ्प्रत्ययः ॥ नृपस्य मण्डलं राष्ट्रमनन्तरः संनिहितो जिगीषुरापगारयो नदीवेगः शिथिलमन्तर्भेदजर्जरं कूलमिवाभिभूयाक्रम्य हरति ॥

अन्वयार्थः—(**लघुवृत्तितया**) क्षुद्र आचरण के कारण (**बहिः**) बाहर (**अन्तः च**) और अन्दर (**भिदां गतम्**) भेद को प्राप्त (**नृपस्य**) राजा के (**मण्डलम्**) राज्य को (**अनन्तरः**) समीपवर्ती (**राजा**) (**आपगारयः**) नदी-वेग (**शिथिलम्**) [अन्तर-भेद से] ढीले हुए (**कूलमिव**) किनारे की भाँति, (**अभिभूय**) आक्रमण कर के (**हरति**) ले लेता है।

जैसे नदी-प्रवाह ढीले किनारे को गिरा देता है, उसी प्रकार अपने ओछे आचरण के कारण अन्दर-बाहर की फूट से व्याप्त राजा के राज्य को पड़ौसी राजा आक्रमण करके छीन लेता है।

53. A neighbouring king (ambitious of conquest) attacks and seizes the dominion of a king, the constituent members, external as well as internal (*viz.* ministers, subjects and friendly kings) of which are affected with dissension owing to his ill behaviour (towards them), as the current of a river overruns and sweeps away its loose bank broken through inside and outside.

Sl. 53. लघु॰—लघुः mean, insulting वृत्तियस्य स लघुवृत्तिस्तस्य भावः लघुवृत्तिता तया may also be taken with कूलं—split up owing to the swift motion of the current. भिदा—alienotion; spllitting up. मण्डलं—The circle of the seven constituents of a kingdom. *Cf.* अमात्यराष्ट्रदुर्गाणि कोषो दण्डश्च पञ्चमः । एताः प्रकृतयस्तज्ज्ञैर्विजिगीषोरुदाहृताः ॥ एताः पञ्च तथा मित्रं (friendly kings) सप्तमः पृथिवीपतिः । सप्तप्रकृतिकं राज्यमित्युवाच बृहस्पतिः ॥ Kām. Nit. VIII. 4, 5. अनन्तरः —The immediate neighbouring king wishing to conquer (desirous of self-agrandisement). आपगा—अपां समूहः आपं (fr. अप्+अण्); आपेन गच्छति इति; आप+गम्+अ (डः). Fig. *Upamā.*

अनुशासतमित्यनाकुलं नयवर्त्माकुलमर्जुनाग्रजम् ।
स्वयमर्थ इवाभिवाञ्छितस्तमभीयाय पराशरात्मजः ॥५४॥

अन्वयः—इति आकुलम् अर्जुनाग्रजं नयवर्त्म अनाकुलम् अनुशासतं तं पराशरात्मजः स्वयम् अभिवांछितः अर्थ इव अभीयाय ॥५४॥

अन्विति ॥ इतीत्थमाकुलमरिनिकरस्मरणात्क्षुभितमर्जुनाग्रजं भीमसेनं नयवर्त्म नीतिमार्गमनाकुलमसंकीर्णं यथा तथानुशासतमुपदिशन्तम् ॥ "जक्षित्यादयः षट्" इत्यभ्यस्ताच्छतुर्नुमभावः ॥ तं युधिष्ठिरं पराशरात्मजो वेदव्यासः । स्वयमभिवाञ्छितोऽर्थ इव । साक्षान्मनोरथ इवेत्युत्प्रेक्षा । अभीयाय प्राप्तः ॥

अन्वयार्थः—(**इति**) इस प्रकार (**आकुलम्**) व्याकुल (**अर्जुनाग्रजम्**) अर्जुन के बड़े भाई [भीम] को (**नयवर्त्म**) नीति-मार्ग का (**अनाकुलम्**) असङ्कीर्ण रूप से (**अनुशासतम्**) उपदेश देते हुए (**तम्**) उसके पास (**पराशरात्मजः**) पराशर-पुत्र [वेदव्यास] (**स्वयम्**) स्वयं (**अभिवाञ्छितः अर्थः इव**) चाहे गये पदार्थ की तरह (**अभीयाय**) प्राप्त हुए ।

विक्षुब्ध भीम को उपर्युक्त प्रकार से नीति-शास्त्र का विशद् उपदेश देते हुए युधिष्ठिर के पास स्वयमेव वेदव्यासजी साक्षात् अभिलषित पदार्थ की भाँति आये ।

54. As he (Dharma) was thus explaining unmistakable term the right line of policy to the elder brother Arjuna agitated at heart, there came to him of his won accord, the son of Parāśara (Vyasa) like his desired object (incarnate).

Sl. 54. अनाकुलं:—in which there was no confusion, with a clear exposition. पराशरात्मजः:—Parāśare was the grandson of Vasishṭha and the father of Vyāsa. He was a great sage. The Smṛti (code of religious law) written by him is considered to to have chief authority in Kali age. आत्मजः:—Vyāsa, the son of Pariśara and Satyavati (before her marriage). Being born on an island (द्वीप) and of a dark complexion, he was called कृष्णद्वैपायन. He came to be called Vyāsa or Vedavyāsa on account of his having arranged the Vedas in their present form.

Cf. यो व्यस्य वेदांश्चतुरस्तपसा भगवानृषिः । लोके व्यासत्वमापेदे कार्ष्ण्यात्कृष्णत्वमेव च ॥ Mahābhārata, Like Bhishma, he was also the grandfather of the Kauravas and the Pāṇḍavas. He is the author of the great epic, the Mahābhārata, which he is said to have written in three years. The eighteen Purāṇas, the Brahmasūtras and several other works are ascribed to him. He is one of the seven Chirajivins or persons living for ever. Fig. *Upamá*. *Cf.* तयोः संवदतोरेवं तदा पाण्डवयोर्द्वयोः । आजगाम महायोगी व्यासः सत्यवतीसुतः । Van. p. ch. 36. sl. 22.

अथ युग्मेनाह—

मधुरैरवशानि लम्भयन्नपि तिर्यञ्चि शमं निरीक्षितैः ।
परितः पटु बिभ्रदेनसां दहनं धाम विलोकनक्षमम् ॥५५॥

अन्वयः—मधुरैः निरीक्षितैः अवशानि तिर्यञ्चि शमं लम्भयन् परितः एनसां दहनं विलोकनक्षमं पटु धाम बिभ्रत् ॥५५॥

मधुरैरिति ॥ मधुरैः शान्तैर्निरीक्षतैरवलोकनैः ॥ नपुंसके भावे क्तः ॥ न विद्यते वशमायत्तत्वं येषां तान्यवशानि प्रतिकूलानि ॥ "वशमायत्ततायां च" इति विश्वः ॥ तिर्यञ्चि मृगपक्ष्यादीनि शमं शान्ति लम्भयन्प्रापयन् ॥ "लभेश्च" इति नुमागमः । "गत्यर्थ—"इत्यादिना द्विकर्मकत्वम् । परितः पटूज्ज्वलमेनसाम् । दह्यतेऽनेनेति दहनं निवर्तकं तथापि विलोकनक्षमं दर्शनीयम् । वह्न्यादिविलक्षणमिति भावः । धाम तेजो बिभ्रत् ॥

अन्वयार्थः—(**मधुरैः**) [अपने] सौम्य (**निरीक्षितैः**) दर्शनों से (**अवशानि**) स्वच्छन्द (**तिर्यञ्चि**) पशु-पक्षियों को (**शमम्**) शान्ति (**लम्भयन्**) प्राप्त कराते हुए (**परितः**) चारों ओर (**एनसां दहनम्**) पापों को भस्म करने वाले, (**विलोकनक्षमम्**) देखने के योग्य (**पटु**) उज्जवल (**धाम**) तेज को (**बिभ्रत्**) धारण किये हुए......

55-56. Making even the savage (lit. of uncontrolled nature) animals (beasts, birds &c.) get a peaceful disposition by his sweet looks having about him a brilliant effulgence able to destroy all sins and capable of being looked at, the sage, who came unexpctedly, who was the source of asceticism and no source a remover) of calamities, was beheld by the king with wonder like a (or is) store of religious merit having a bodily form (incarnate).

Sl. 55. मधुरैः:—charming pleasing. See *infra.* III. 3. निरीक्षित— here is added to form a *neu.* abs. noun. तिर्यञ्चि—तिरः अञ्चति इति तिर्यक्; fr. तिरस् changed to तिरि before the अ of अञ्च्+क्विन्; तिर्यञ्चि is in the Obj. case. लभ् being a गत्यर्थ root governs its Nom. in the Obj. in the Cau. तिर्यञ्चि शमं लभन्ते; स तानि शमं लम्भयति । विलोकनस्य क्षमम्.

सहसोपगतः सविस्मयं तपसां सूतिरसूतिरापदाम् ।

ददृशे जगतीभुजा मुनिः स वपुष्मानिव पुण्यसंचयः ॥५६॥

अन्वयः—सहसा उपगतः तपसां सूतिः आपदाम् असूतिः स मुनिः वपुष्मान् पुण्य-संचय इव जगतीभुजा सविस्मयं ददृशे ॥५६॥

सहसेति ॥ पुनः सहसोपगतोऽकस्मादागतस्तपसां सूतिः प्रसव आपदामसूतिरप्रभवः । निवर्तक इति यावत् । स मुनिर्व्यासो वपुष्मान्देहधारी पुण्यसंचयः पुण्यराशिरिवेत्युत्प्रेक्षा । जगतीभुजा राज्ञा सविस्मयं ददृशे दृष्टः ॥

अन्वयार्थः—(**सहसा**) अकस्मात् (**उपगतः**) आये हुए (**तपसां सूतिः**) तपस्याओं के उत्पादक (**आपदाम् सूतिः**) आपत्तियों के अनुत्पादक (**स मुनिः**) वह मुनि (**वपुष्मान् पुण्यसंचयः इव**) मानो शरीरधारी पुण्य-समूह हो, ऐसे, (**जगतीभुजा**) राजा के द्वारा (**सविस्मयम्**) आश्चर्य के साथ (**ददृशे**) देखे गये ।

अपने सौम्य दर्शन से वे मुनि वेदव्यास वन के स्वच्छन्द पशु-पक्षियों को भी शान्त करने वाले थे । उन के चारों ओर पापों को भस्म करने वाला होते हुए भी देखा जा सकने वाला उज्ज्वल तेज विद्यमान था । वे तपस्याओं के उत्पादक तथा आपत्तियों के विनाशक थे । इस प्रकार उन मुनि व्यास को युधिष्ठिर ने साश्चर्य ऐसे देखा मानो साक्षात् शरीर धारण करके पुण्य-समूह ही उपस्थित हो गया हो ।

Sl. 56. सूतिः—सूयते अनया इति; fr. सू+ति (क्तिन्); source. जगती॰—जगतीं भुङ्क्ते इति जगतीभुक् तेन । पुण्यसंचयः—the sage was so holy and majestic that he looked like an embodied mass of religious merit; or **पुण्यसञ्चय** may refer to Dharma. He was as it were the store of Dharma's religious merit come there to oblige him.

अथोच्चकैरासनतः परार्ध्यादुद्यन्स धूतारुणवल्कलाग्रः ।
रराज कीर्णाकपिशांशुजालः शृङ्गात्सुमेरोरिव तिग्मरश्मिः ॥५७॥

अन्वयः—अथ उच्चकैः परार्ध्यात् आसनतः उद्यन् धूतारुणवल्कलाग्रः स (नृपः) कीर्णाकपिशांशुजालः सुमेरो शृङ्गात् उद्यन् तिग्मरश्मिः इव रराज ॥५७॥

अथेति ॥ अथ दर्शनानन्तरम् । उच्चकैरुन्नतापराध्यार्च्छ्रेष्ठात् ॥ "अर्घाद्यत्" "परावराधमोत्तमपूर्वाच्च" इति यत्प्रत्यय ॥ आसनतः सिंहासनादुद्यन्नुत्तिष्ठन्नतएव धूतानि कम्पितान्यरुणानि वल्कलाग्राणि यस्य स तथोक्तः । स नृपः कीर्णं विस्तृतमाकपिशमंशुजालं यस्य स तथोक्तः । सुमेरोः शृङ्गादुद्यंस्तिग्मरश्मिरिव । रराज ॥ (उपजातिच्छन्दः ।)

अन्वयार्थः—(**अथ**) इस के बाद (**उच्चकैः**) ऊंचे (**परार्ध्यात्**) (**आसनतः**) आसन से (**उद्यन्**) उठता हुआ (**अत एव**) (**धूतारुणवल्कलाग्रः**) हिला है लाल वल्कल (**वस्त्र**) का अग्रभाग जिस का ऐसा (**सः**) वह, [युधिष्ठिर], (**सुमेरोः शृङ्गात्**) सुमेरुपर्वत के शिखर से (**उद्यन्**) उदय होते हुए (**कीर्णाकपिशांशुजालः**) बिखेरा है किञ्चित् सुनहरा किरण समूह जिसने ऐसे (**तिग्मरश्मिः इव**) सूर्य की तरह (**रराज**) सुशोभित हुआ ।

मुनि वेदव्यास को आया देख युधिष्ठिर उन्नत एवं श्रेष्ठ आसन से उठ खड़ा हुआ । उठते समय उसके वल्कल वस्त्र हिल रहे थे । इस प्रकार वह ऐसे सुशोभित हो रहा था जैसे सुनहरी किरणों के समूह को बिखेरता हुआ सूर्य, सुमेरुपर्वत से उदय होते समय सुशोभित होता है ।

57. Then rising from his lofty and magnificent seat, he, with the ends of his purple bark garments shaken, shone like the hot-rayed (sun) rising from the peak of Sumeru with the mass of his rosy rays spread all round.

Sl. 57. परार्ध्य—परः श्रेष्ठः अर्धः परार्धः परार्धे भवं पदार्ध्यं; य (यत्) is added to अर्घ and also when preceded by पर &c. ; see com. सुमेरोः—Sumeru or Meru is a mountain of gold, gems &c.; see notes on III. 32. The comparison to the peak of Meru shows that Dharma was seated on a gold throne decked with gems. But from the tenor of Draupadi's speech it appears that Dharma was leading the life of a poor exile in the forest and it is not possible that he had a costly throne alone with him. See *supra* I. 40. Perhaps the poet forgot the fact; or perhaps it may be that the seat on which Dharma sat, illumined by his natural lustre as it was, was in the poet's eyes as good as a throne of gold set with gems.

अवहितहृदयो विधाय सोऽर्हामृषिवदृषिप्रवरे गुरूपदिष्टाम् ।
तदनुमतमलंचकार पश्चात्प्रशम इव श्रुतमासनं नरेन्द्रः ॥५८॥

अन्वयः—स अवहितहृदयः (सन्) ऋषिप्रवरे ऋषिवत् गुरूपदिष्टाम् अर्हां विधाय पश्चात् तदनुमतम् आसनं प्रशमः श्रुतम् इव अलंचकार ॥५८॥

अवहितेति ॥ स नरेन्द्रोऽवहितहृदयोऽप्रमत्तचित्तः सन् ॥ "चित्तं तु चेतो हृदयं स्वान्तं हृन्मानसं मनः ।" इत्यमरः ॥ ऋषिप्रवरे मुनिश्रेष्ठे । ऋषिवदृष्यर्हाम् ॥ अर्हत्यर्थे वतिप्रत्ययः । गुरूपदिष्टाम् । शास्त्रीयामित्यर्थः । अर्हां पूजाम् ॥ "गुरोश्च हलः" इत्यकारप्रत्ययः ॥ विधाय पश्चादनन्तरं तदनुमतं तेनानुज्ञातमासनम् । प्रशमः शान्तिः श्रुतं शास्त्रश्रवणमिव । अलंचकार । उक्तं च पूर्वम्—"प्रशमस्तस्य भवत्यलंक्रिया" इति । मुन्याज्ञयोपविष्टवानित्यर्थः ॥ (पुष्पिताग्रा वृत्तम् ।)

अन्वयार्थः—(सः) वह (अवहितहृदयः) [सन्] एकाग्र है चित्त जिस का ऐसा हुआ-हुआ (**ऋषिप्रवरे**) मुनि-श्रेष्ठ की (**ऋषिवत्**) ऋषि के योग्य (**गुरूपदिष्टाम्**) गुरु [शास्त्र] से बताई गई (**अर्हाम्**) पूजा को (**विधाय**) करके (**पश्चात्**) बाद में (**तदनुमतम्**) उससे अनुमति मिल गई है जिस की ऐसे (**आसनम्**) आसन को, (**प्रशमः श्रुतम् इव**) शान्ति जैसे शास्त्र को, (**अलञ्चकार**) सुशोभित किया ।

युधिष्ठिर ने एकाग्र-चित्त से शास्त्रोक्त विधि के अनुसार व्यास की ऋषियों के योग्य पूजा की । बाद में मुनि की अनुमति पाकर उसने आसन को ऐसे ही सुशोभित किया जैसे शान्ति शास्त्र को सुशोभित करती है ।

58. Having offered with an attentive mind worship befitting

a sage to him, worthiest of ascetics, as directed by his spiritual guide, the king adorned the seat being asked to occupy it by him (the sage as tranquility mind does knowledge of the Śaśtras.

Sl. 58. अवहित०—अवहितं हृदयं यस्य, Here हृदय is the agent of अवधा used intransitively, त being added in an active sense. *Cf.* अवहितोस्मि I am attentive. Or we may dissolve—अवहितं हृदयं येन. ऋषिप्र०—ऋषिषु प्रवर: तस्मिन्. Properly this should have been in the Gen. case, being the object of the root noun अर्हा. But this may be defended by the principle विवक्षावशात् सप्तमी. ऋषिवत्—वत् is added in the sense of 'befitting', ऋषिमर्हति. अर्हा—fr. अर्ह् to worship, + अ (with the *fem.* aff. आ). A root ending in a consonant with a penultimate long vowel takes the aff. अ in the sense of भाव or the action implied by the root, (provided it takes इ before त or त्वा). तदनुमतं—तेन अनुमतं; here अनुमत is not used in the sense of the present tense by मतिबुद्धि &c. see sl. 1.; for in that case अनुमतं could not have been compounded as the role क्तेन च पूजायां (मतिबुद्धीत्यादिना विहितो य: क्तस्तदन्तेन षष्ठी न समस्यते Sid. Kau.) Pān. II. 2. 12, forbids such a compound. प्रशम:—&c. ; *cf. supra* sl. 32.

व्यक्तोदितस्मितमयूखविभासितोष्ठ
स्तिष्ठन्मुनेरभिमुखं स विकीर्णधाम्नः ।
तन्वन्तमिद्धमभितो गुरुमंशुजालं
लक्ष्मीमुवाह सकलस्य शशाङ्कमूर्तेः ॥५९॥

अन्वय:—व्यक्तोदितस्मितमयूखविभासितोष्ठः विकीर्णधाम्नः मुनेः अभिमुखं तिष्ठन् स इद्धम् अंशुजालं तन्वन्तं गुरुम् अभितः (तिष्ठतः) सकलस्य शशांकमूर्तेः लक्ष्मीम् उवाह ॥५९॥

व्यक्तेति ॥ व्यक्तोदितैः स्फुटोद्गतोः स्मितमयूखैर्विभासितावोष्ठौ यस्य स तथोक्तः । विकीर्णधाम्नो विस्तृततेजसो मुनेरभिमुखं तिष्ठन्स नृपः । इद्धं समृद्धम् । दीप्तमिति यावत् । अंशुजालं तन्वन्तं गुरुं गीष्पतिम् ॥ "गुरुर्गीष्पतिपित्रादौ" इत्यमरः ॥ "अभितः परितः—" इत्यादिना द्वितीया ॥ अभितोऽ-

भिमुखम् । तिष्ठत इति शेषः । सकलस्य संपूर्णस्य शशाङ्का मूर्तिर्यस्य तस्येन्दोर्लक्ष्मीमुवाह वहति स्म ।। अत्रोपमेयस्य राज्ञ उपमानेन्दुधर्मेण लक्ष्म्याः साक्षात्संबन्धासंभवात्सदृशीं लक्ष्मीमिवेति प्रतिबिम्बकरणाक्षेपादसंभवद्वस्तुसंबन्धात्पदार्थवृत्तिर्निदर्शनालंकारः । तदुक्तम्—"प्रतिबिम्बस्याकरणं संभवता यत्र वस्तुयोगेन । तत्साम्यमसंभवता निदर्शना सा द्विधाभिमता ।।" इति ।। (वसन्ततिलका वृत्तम्)।।

अन्वयार्थः—(व्यक्तोदितस्मितमयूखविभासितोष्ठ) स्पष्ट उठी हुई मुस्कराहट की किरणों से प्रकाशित हैं ओष्ठ जिस के ऐसा, (**विकीर्णधाम्नः**) विस्तृत किया है तेज जिसने ऐसे (**मुनेः**) मुनि के (**अभिमुखम्**) सामने (**तिष्ठन्** बैठा हुआ (**सः**) वह (**इद्धम्**) उद्दीप्त (**अंशुजालम्**) किरण-समूह को (**तन्वन्तम्**) विस्तृत करते हुए (**गुरुम् अभितः**) बृहस्पति के सम्मुख (**तिष्ठतः**) बैठे हुए (**सकलस्य**(सम्पूर्ण (**शशाङ्कमूर्तेः**) चन्द्रमा की (**लक्ष्मीम्**) शोभा को (**उवाह**) धारण करता था ।

युधिष्ठिर, जिस के ओठों पर मुस्कराहट सुशोभित हो रही थी, तेजस्वी मुनि व्यास के सम्मुख बैठा हुआ ऐसे सुशोभित हो रहा था जैसे अपनी दीप्त किरणों को चतुर्दिक फैलाते हुए बृहस्पति के सम्मुख पूर्णिमा का चाँद शोभित होता है ।

59. He, with his lips illumined by the clearly shining rays of his smile and seated in front of the sage shedding his lustre all round, possessed the beauty of the full moon risen opposite to Jupiter diffusing a bright flood of rysa light.

Sl. 59. व्यक्तोदितः०—व्यक्तं clearly उदिताः व्यक्तोदिताः । सुप् सुपेति समासः; स्मितस्य मयूखाः स्मितमयूखाः; ०दिताश्च ते स्मितमयूखाश्च तैः see com. ०तौष्ठ also—तौष्ठः by ओत्वोष्ठयोः समासे वा Vārtika on Pān I. 1. 64. In a comp. with ओतु a cat, or ओष्ठ for its latter member the Sandhi is optionally पररूप *i. e.* ओ or औ ; but तवौष्ठः alone.

स्मित—fr. स्मि+त (क्त) added भावे; a smile. Although Dharma was greatly pleased he, as a great man, expressed his joy by a gentle smile. *cf.* ईषद्विकसितैर्दन्तैः कटाक्षैः सौष्ठवान्वितम् । अलक्षितद्विजद्वारमुत्तमानां स्मितं भवेत् ।।

विकीर्ण०—विकीर्णं धाम येन स विकीर्णधामा तस्य । **गुरु**—here the planet Jupiter. **शशाङ्क**—शशः अङ्कः यस्य स शशाङ्कः; the spot on the moon is supposed by some to be a hare.

इति महोमहापाध्यायकोलाचलमल्लिनाथसूरिविरचितया घण्टापथसमाख्यया व्याख्यासमेतः कविश्रीभारविकृतौ किरातार्जुनीये महाकाव्ये व्यासागमनो नाम द्वितीयः सर्गः ।

तृतीयः सर्गः

अथ त्रिभिर्मुनिं विशिषंश्चतुर्भिः कलापकमाह। तदुक्तम्—"द्वाभ्यां युग्ममिति प्रोक्तं त्रिभिः श्लोकैर्विशेषकम्। कलापकं चतुर्भिः स्यात्तदूर्ध्वं कुलकं स्मृतम् ॥" इति।

ततः शरच्चन्द्रकराभिरामैरुत्सर्पिभिः प्रांशुमिवांशुजालैः।

बिभ्राणमानीलरुचं पिशङ्गीर्जटास्तडित्वन्तमिवाम्बुवाहम् ॥ १ ॥

अन्वयः—ततः शरच्चंद्रकराभिरामैः उत्सर्पिभिः अंशुजालैः प्रांशुम् इव [स्थितम्], आनीलरुचं, पिशङ्गीः जटाः बिभ्राणम्, (अत एव) तडित्वन्तम् अम्बुवाहम् इव [च स्थितम्] ॥ १ ॥

तत इति ॥ तत उपवेशनानन्तरं शरच्चन्द्रकराभिरामैः। प्राह्लादकैरित्यर्थः। उत्सर्पिभिरूर्ध्वं प्रसारिभिरंशुजालैः प्रभापटलैः प्रांशुमुन्नतमिव स्थितमित्युत्प्रेक्षा। पुनरानीलरुचं कृष्णवर्णं पिशङ्गीः पिङ्गलवर्णाः। गौरादित्वात् ङीष्। जटा बिभ्राणं धारयन्तमतएव तडित्वन्तं विद्युद्युक्तमम्बुवाहमिव स्थितमित्युत्प्रेक्षा। धर्मात्मजो युधिष्ठिर एतादृशं मुनिमाबभाषे इति चतुर्थश्लोकेनान्वयः ॥

अन्वयार्थः—(**ततः**) उस के बाद (**शरच्चन्द्रकराभिरामैः**) शरद् ऋतु के चन्द्रमा की किरणों के समान मनोहर (**उत्सर्पिभिः**) ऊपर उठते हुए (**अंशुजालैः**) किरणसमूहों के कारण (**प्रांशुमिव**) मानों लम्बे हों, (**आनीलरुचं**) चारों ओर नीली है आभा जिसकी ऐसे, (**पिशङ्गीः**) पीले वर्ण की (**जटाः**) जटाएँ (**बिभ्राणम्**) धारण किए हुये (अत एव) (**तडित्वन्तम्**) विद्युत् से युक्त (**अम्बुवाहमिव**) मानों बादल हों—

बैठने के बाद (युधिष्ठिर ने मुनि के आगमन के कारण को पूछा)। बैठे हुए व्यास मुनि के चारों ओर एक प्रकाश-पुञ्ज बना हुआ था। इस प्रकाश-पुञ्ज के कारण वे अपने वास्तविक आकार की अपेक्षा अधिक बड़े दिखाई दे रहे थे। नील-वर्ण की आभा उन के शरीर के चारों ओर व्याप्त थी, सिर पर पीत-वर्ण

जटाएँ धारण की हुई थीं, इस प्रकार वे बिजली से युक्त मानो मेघ हों ऐसे दिखाई देते थे।

1-4. Then the son of Dharma (Yudhishthira), wishing to know the object of his unexpected visit, thus addressed the sage when comfortably seated—the sage who looked as if raised high (magnified) by the effulgent brilliance (lit. up-shooting streams of rays) of his body delightful like the autumnal moon-light, who having a dark complexion and wearing matted hair of a bright yellow resembled a cloud accompanied by flashing lightning, who by the supreme excellence of his person surpassing that of all other men possessed all the grace of serenity of form (the charm that serenity lends), who gave rise to an overpowering (lit. forcibly) feeling of affection in the hearts of even those who did not know him; who by his modest demeanour indicated the purity of his mind (lit. the condition of his mind as being pure, being free from all foulness); [so Malli; or who on account of his gentle appearance produced in the (beholder's) mind a state of purity]; who appeared already to have conversed (or offered consolation) by his look peculiarly or exceedingly) sweet and confidence inspiring; and who (above all) was the origin (author of the compilation) of the Vedas that set forth religious law and dispel sin.

Sl. 1. Slokas 1—4 form what is technically called a *Kalàpaka* (four ślokas forming one grammatical sentence); see com. Here the epithets in the first three ślokas qualify मुनिं in the fourth.

शरच्चन्द्र०—शारदः चन्द्रः शरच्चन्द्रः तस्य करास्तद्वदभिरामैः attractive or delightful like the rays &c. Autumnal moon-light is bright and not dazzling; the lustre of the sage also was attracting and not repelling; *cf.* विलोकनक्षमं *supra* II, 55. उत्सर्पि०— उत्सर्प्तुं शीलं येषां तैः spreading upwards, effulgent. अंशुजालैः by the streams of rays. प्रांशु—lofty, higher in stature than he really was. Mark the derivation (प्रकृष्टा अंशवो अत्र) and the alliteration, आनील०— आ समन्तान्नीला त्वक् यस्य स० त्वक् तम्. Vyāsa was of a dark complexion and so he was called कृष्णद्वैपायन.

तडित्वन्तं—तडितः सन्त्यस्मिन् तम्; this by itself means 'a cloud'

'धाराधरो जलधरस्तडित्वान्' । Amara but here it means 'having lightning. अम्बु०—अम्बु वहतीति अम्बुवाहस्तमिव, fr. वह् + अ by कर्मणि अण् Pán. III. 2. 1. *Cf.* दधानमम्भोरुहकेसरद्युतीर्जटाः शरच्चन्द्रमरीचिरोचिषम् । Sis. I. 5. (description of Nārada). The sloka begins with त which indicates fulfilment of one's wishes; *cf.* Bṛhaspati— तकारे अर्थसिद्धिश्च प्राप्यते विपुलं धनम् । सर्वश्रेयो भवेत्तस्य सुस्थितं चोपजायते ।।

प्रसादलक्ष्मीं दधतं समग्रां वपुःप्रकर्षेण जनातिगेन ।
प्रसह्य चेतःसु समासजन्तमसंस्तुतानामपि भावमार्द्रम् ॥ २ ॥

अन्वयः—समग्रां प्रसादलक्ष्मीं दधतम् (अत एव) जनातिगेन वपुःप्रकर्षेण असंस्तुतानामपि चेतःसु आर्द्रभावं प्रसह्य समासजन्तम् ।। २ ।।

प्रसादेति ।। पुनः समग्रां संपूर्णां प्रसादः सौम्यता तस्य लक्ष्मीं संपदं दधतम् । अतएव जनमतिगच्छतीति जनातिगेन लोकातिशायिना ।। "अन्येष्वपि दृश्यते" इति डप्रत्ययः ।। वपुःप्रकर्षेणाकारसंपदा असंस्तुतानामपिरिचितानामपि । व्यासोऽयमित्यजानतामित्यर्थः ।। "संस्तवः स्यात्परिचयः" इत्यमरः ।। चेतःसु चित्तेष्वार्द्रभावं स्नेहार्द्रभावमभिप्रायं प्रसह्य बलात्समासजन्तम् । लगयन्तमिति यावत् ।। "दंशसञ्जस्वञ्जां शपि" इत्युपधालोपः ।। प्रसन्नाकारेषु सर्वोऽपि स्निह्यतीति भावः ।।

अन्वयार्थः—(**समग्राम्**) सम्पूर्ण (**प्रसादलक्ष्मीम्**) सौम्यता के ऐश्वर्य को (**दधतम्**) धारण करते हुए [अत एव] (**जनातिगेन**) लोकोत्तर (**वपुः प्रकर्षेण**) आकृति की उत्कृष्टता से (**असंस्तुतानामपि**) अपरिचितों के भी (**चेतःसु**) मनों में (**आर्द्रभावम्**) स्नेहभाव को (**प्रसह्य**) हठपूर्वक (**समासजन्तम्**) उत्पन्न करते हुए ।

अत्यन्त सौम्य व्यास मुनि अपने अलौकिक शरीरोत्कर्ष से अपरिचितों के भी मन में साग्रह श्रद्धा उत्पन्न कर रहे थे ।

Sl. 2. समग्रां—सङ्गतमग्रमस्याः सा तथोक्ता ताम् with the extremities i. e. the whole of, complete. प्रसाद—calm or serene appearance, composure; लक्ष्मी—dignity, beauty of. जनातिगेन—surpassing that of all other men; extraordinary, supremely great. अतिग fr. गम् + ड: (अ) The aff. ड is added to the root जन्

(see Pān. III. 2. 97-100); but Pān. remarks **अन्येष्वपि** on which the Kau. runs as **अन्येषूपपदेषु जनेर्डः स्यात् । अजः । द्विजो ब्राह्मणः । अपिशब्दः सर्वोपाधिव्यभिचारार्थः, तेन धात्वन्तरादपि कारकान्तरेष्वपि क्वचित्, परितः खाता परिखा । वपु०—वपुष:** of bodily form **प्रकर्ष:** excellence, grace. **असंस्तुत**—not acquainted or familiar with. **प्रसह्य**—properly absol. fr. **सह्** with **प्र**—having borne great strain, used as an *indec.* meaning 'with great force,' 'powerfully.' **आर्द्रभावं**—thoughtfull of love.; a feeling of affection, **समासजन्तं**—Lit. fixing in, attaching to; hence giving rise to.

अनुद्धताकारतया विविक्तां तन्वन्तमन्तःकरणस्य वृत्तिम् ।
माधुर्यविस्रम्भविशेषभाजा कृतोपसंभाषमिवेक्षितेन ॥ ३ ॥

अन्वयः—अनुद्धताकारतया अन्तःकरणस्य वृत्तिं विविक्तां तन्वन्तम् माधुर्य-विस्रम्भविशेषभाजा ईक्षितेन कृतोपसंभाषमिव ॥ ३ ॥

अनुद्धतेति ॥ पुनरनुद्धताकारतया शान्ताकारत्वेन लिङ्गेनान्तःकरणस्य वृत्तिं विविक्तां पूताम् । शान्तामिति यावत् ॥ "विविक्तौ पूतविजनौ" इत्यमरः ॥ तन्वन्तं प्रकटयन्तम् । आकृतिरेवास्य चित्तशुद्धिं कथयतीत्यर्थः । पुनर्माधुर्यं निसर्ग-सौम्यता विस्रम्भो विश्वासः ॥ "समौ विस्रम्भविश्वासौ" इत्यमरः ॥ तयो-र्विशेषमतिशयं भजतीति तथोक्तेनेक्षितेन दर्शनेनैव कृता उपसंभाषा संभाषणं येनतमिवेत्युत्प्रेक्षा । दृष्टिविशेषेणैवोपसंभाषमाणमिव स्थितमित्यर्थः ॥ काशिकायां तु "उपसंभाषणमुपसान्त्वनम्" इति भासनादिसूत्रेण ॥

अन्वयार्थः—(**अनुद्धताकारतया**) शान्त आकृति से (**अन्तःकरणस्य**) अन्तःकरण की (**वृत्तिम्**) प्रवृत्ति को (**विविक्ताम्**) पवित्र (**तन्वन्तम्**) प्रकट करते हुए (**माधुर्य-विस्रम्भविशेषभाजा**) स्वाभाविक सौम्यता एवं विश्वास के आधिक्य से युक्त (**ईक्षितेन**) दृष्टि से [ही] (**कृतोपसंभाषम्िव**) मानो किया है वार्तालाप जिन्होंने, ऐसे—

उन की शान्त आकृति से उन के अन्तःकरण का पवित्र व्यवहार प्रकट हो रहा था । अत्यधिक सौम्य एवं विश्वास उत्पन्न करने वाली दृष्टि-मात्र से ही मानो वे दूसरों से बात चीत कर रहे थे ।

Sl. 3. **अनुद्धताका०**—न उद्धत: haughtly **अनु०** त: **अनुद्धतश्चासौ आकार:** तस्य भाव: **अनु०** ता तया on account of his modest, serene appearance, modest demeanour. **अन्त:करण**—the innder instrument of communication with the external world of the soul; the mind. **वृत्ति**—state or condition of. **विविक्त**—pure, free from taint or sin. माधुर्य—Ab. *n.* fr. मधुर which may be derived as मधु sweetness राति fr. रा to take+aff, **अ (क)** or **मधु अस्त्यस्मिन्** fr. मधु+र a *Matub* aff. by **ऊषसुषिमुष्कमधो र:** (Păn. V. 2. 107, so **ऊषर सुषिर** &c.); sweetness or loveliness, agreeableness. '**स्वादुप्रियौ च मधुरौ ।**' Amara. विशेषभाजा—possessed of an excess of. ईहितेन—P. p. p. used as a noun. उपसंभाषा—Conversation; or friendly persuasion, conciliation, winning over; see Kaśikă or Kau. on Păn. I. 3. 47.

धर्मात्मजो धर्मनिबन्धिनीनां प्रसूतिमेनःप्रणुदां श्रुतीनाम् ।
हेतुं तदभ्यागमने परीप्सुः सुखोपविष्टं मुनिमाबभाषे ॥ ४ ॥

अन्वय:—धर्मनिबन्धिनीनाम् एन:प्रणुदां श्रुतीनां प्रसूतिं सुखोपविष्टं मुनिं तदभ्यागमने हेतुं परीप्सु: धर्मात्मज: आबभाषे ॥ ४ ॥

धर्मेति ॥ पुनर्धर्मं निबनन्तीति धर्मनिबन्धिनीनामग्निहोत्रादिधर्मप्रतिपादिकानाम् ॥ एन:प्रणुदामघच्छिदाम् ॥ क्विप् ॥ श्रुतीनां वेदानाम् ॥ "श्रुति: स्त्री वेद आम्नाय:" इत्यमर: ॥ प्रसूतिं प्रभवं सुखेनोपविष्टं मुनिं तदभ्यागमने तस्य मुनेरागमने हेतुं कारणं परीप्सुर्जिज्ञासु: ॥ आप्नोते: सन्नन्तादुप्रत्यय: । "आप्ज्ञप्यृधामीत्" इतीकार: । अत्र "लोपोऽभ्यासस्य" इत्यभ्यासलोप: ॥ आबभाष उवाच ॥

अन्वयार्थ:—(**धर्मनिबन्धिनीनाम्**) धर्म के प्रतिपादक (**एन:प्रणुदाम्**) पाप के नाशक (**श्रुतीनाम्**) वेदों के (**प्रसूतिम्**) जन्म-स्थान (**सुखोपविष्टम्**) सुखपूर्वक बैठे हुए (**मुनिम्**) मुनि को (**तदभ्यागमने**) उस के आगमन में (**हेतुम्**) कारण को (**परीप्सु:**) जानने के इच्छा वाला (**धर्मात्मज:**) युधिष्ठिर (**आबभाषे**) बोला ।

धर्म के प्रतिष्ठापक तथा पाप के नाशक वेदों के जन्म स्थान मुनि व्यास से, उन के आने के कारण को जानने की इच्छा से, युधिष्ठिर बोले—

Sl. 4. धर्मात्मज:—The son of Dharma or Yama; Yudhishṭhira. धर्मनिब०—enfolding in them, containing ; hence setting forth, laying down religious rites and ordinances. ०प्रणुदां—एन: sin प्रणुदन्ति इति—एन: प्रणुदस्तासां removing, driving away sin. श्रुतीनां—of the Vedic texts. प्रसूति—see II. 56. *Cf*. Rag. II. 63.; producer or author of; he having arranged the Vedas; or 'author' of holy precepts, rising to the dignity of Vedic precepts, scattered throughout the Mahābhārata which, on this account, is called the fifth Veda. परीप्सु—*Noun* in उ fr. the Desi. base of आप् with परि (परीप्सति); wishing to know.

अनाप्तपुण्योपचयैर्दुरापा फलस्य निर्धूतरजाः सवित्री ।
तुल्या भवद्दर्शनसंपदेषा वृष्टेर्दिवो वीतबलाहकायाः ॥ ५ ॥

अन्वयः—अनाप्तपुण्योपचयैः दुरापा फलस्य सवित्री निर्धूतरजाः एषा भवद्दर्शनसंपत् वीतबलाहकायाः दिवः वृष्टेः तुल्या ॥ ५ ॥

अनाप्तेति ॥ अनाप्तपुण्योपचयस्कृतपुण्यसंग्रहैर्दुरापा दुर्लभा । फलस्य सवित्री श्रेयस्करीत्यर्थः । निर्धूतरजा हतरजोगुणा । अन्यत्र निरस्तधूलिः । "रजो रजोगुणे धूलौ परागार्तवयोरपि ।" इति शाश्वतः ॥ एषा भवद्दर्शनसंपत्संपत्तिः । लाभ इति यावत् ॥ संपदादिभ्यः क्विपो भावार्थत्वात् ॥ वीतबलाहकाया गतमेघाया दिव आकाशस्य संबन्धिन्या वृष्टेस्तुल्येत्युपमालंकारः । अनभ्रवृष्टिवदतर्कितोपपन्नं भवद्दर्शनं सर्वथा कस्यचिच्छ्रेयसो निदानमित्यर्थः ॥ वारि वहतीति बलाहकः पृषोदरादित्वात्साधुः ॥

अन्वयार्थः—(**अनाप्तपुण्योपचयैः**) नहीं किया है पुण्य संग्रह जिन्होंने, उन के लिए (**दुरापा**) दुर्लभ (**फलस्य**) फल की (**सवित्री**) उत्पादक (**निर्धूतरजः**) समाप्त किया है रजोगुण को जिस ने ऐसी (**एषा**) यह (**भवद्दर्शनसंपत्**) आप की दर्शन रूप सम्पत्ति, (**वीतबलाहकायाः दिवः**) हट गये हैं बादल जिसके ऐसे दिन की (**वृष्टेः**) वर्षा के (**तुल्या**) समान है ।

वह आपकी दर्शन-सम्पत्ति पुण्य-संग्रह से रहित लोगों के लिए दुर्लभ है । यह रजोगुण की नाशक एवं सिद्धिजनक है । हमें इसकी प्राप्ति ठीक ऐसी ही है जैसे बिना बादल के वर्षा हो जाय ।

5. Difficult to be obtained by those who have not secured a stock of religious merit and productive of the desired result, this your blissful visit, which entirely removes the effects of the *rajas* quality (expels all passion), is like (as much to be hailed as) a shower that sweeps away dust, from the sky free from clouds (*i.e.* out of the rainy season when it is unexpected).

Sl. 5. अनाप्त०—न आप्तः अनाप्तः; पुण्यस्योपचयः (a store of) पुण्योपचयः; अनाप्तः पुण्योपचयः यैस्तैः । दुरापा—दुःखेनाप्यते; fr. दुस् + आप् + अ (खल्); Pān. III. 3. 126. See *supra* दुर्बोधं I. 6. *Cf.*—गृहानुपैतुं प्रणयादभीप्सवो भवन्ति नापुण्यकृतां मनीषिणः I Sis. I. 14. निर्धूतरजा—निर्धूतं रजः यया applies both, to दर्शनसंपत् and वृष्टि. रजस् in the first case means the quality of Rajas or foulness, the cause of activity, energy, passion &c. *Cf.* रजो रागात्मकं विद्धि तृष्णासंगसमुद्भवम् । तन्निबध्नाति कौन्तेय कर्मसंगेन देहिनम् ॥ Bg. XIV. 7. In the second case it means 'dust.' ०संपद् wealth *i.e.* good fortune; hence a coverable event. वतो०—वीता वलाहकाः (a comp. of the पृषोदरादि class) यस्याः सा तस्याः । from which the clouds have passed away. He means—This your unexpected visit is indicative of some future good.

अद्य क्रियाः कामदुघाः क्रतूनां सत्याशिषः संप्रति भूमिदेवाः ।
आसंसृतेरस्मि जगत्सु जातस्त्वय्यागते यद्बहुमानपात्रम् ॥ ६ ॥

अन्वयः—अद्य क्रतूनां क्रियाः कामदुघाः, संप्रति भूमिदेवाः सत्याशिषः यत् त्वयि आगते (अहं) आसंसृतेः जगत्सु बहुमानपात्रं जातः अस्मि ॥ ६ ॥

अद्येति ॥ अद्य क्रतूनां क्रिया अनुष्ठानानि । कामान्दुहन्तीति कामदुघाः । फलदा इत्यर्थः । "दुहः कब्घश्च" इति कप्प्रत्ययो घादेशश्च । संप्रत्यद्य भूमिदेवा ब्राह्मणाः ॥ "द्विजात्यग्रजन्मभूदेववाडवाः । विप्रश्च ब्राह्मणः" इत्यमरः ॥ सत्याशिषो जाताः । ब्राह्मणाशिषोऽद्य फलिता इत्यर्थः । यद्यतः कारणात्त्वय्यागते सति । त्वदागमनेन निमित्तेनेत्यर्थः । अस्मीत्यहमर्थेऽव्ययम् ॥ "अस्मीत्यस्मदर्थानुवादेऽहमर्थेऽपि" इति गणव्याख्याने । "दासे कृतागसि भवत्युचितः प्रभूणां पादप्रहार इति सुन्दरि नास्मि दूये ।" इति प्रयोगाच्च । आसंसृतेरासंसारात् । यावत्संसारमित्यर्थः । अभिविधावाङ्विकल्पादसमासः । जगत्सु बहुमानपात्रं

बहुयोग्यताभाजनं जातः । सकलसत्कर्मफलभूतं त्वदागमनं येन मे जगन्मान्यतेति भावः ॥

अन्वयार्थः—(**अद्य**) आज (**क्रतूनाम् क्रियाः**) यज्ञों के अनुष्ठान (**कामदुघाः**) कामनाओं को देने वाले हुए हैं, (**सम्प्रति**) अब (**भूमिदेवाः**) ब्राह्मण (**सत्याशिषः**) सत्य है आशीर्वाद जिनका ऐसे हुए हैं, (**यत् त्वयि आगते**) जो तुम्हारे आने पर [मैं] (**आसंसृतेः**) जब तक संसार है तब तक (**जगत्सु**) जगत् में (**बहुमानपात्रम्**) अत्यधिक सम्मान का भाजन (**जातः अस्मि**) हो गया हूँ ।

आज हमारे यज्ञानुष्ठान सफल हुए । अब ब्राह्मणों के आशीर्वाद सत्य सिद्ध हुए । आप के यहाँ आने पर मैं संसार की स्थिति-पर्यन्त अत्यधिक सम्मान का पात्र बन गया हूँ ।

6. To-day have the sacrificial rites performed (by me) yielded all desires; now the Bráhmanas have their blessings come true (fulfilled); since by your coming (to see me) I have become an object of great respect in the world till the course of worldly life lasts (to the end of the world).

Sl. 6. क्रतु—a sacrifice. करोति क्रियते वा इति क्रतुः fr. कृ + the Unădi aff. क्रतु lit. what man does or is done and as nothing done by man is so important as a sacrifice it means 'a sacrifice.' Dharma had performed the Ràjasùya sacrifice before he lost every thing by gambling. भूमि०—भूमौ भूम्या वा देवा इव. आसंसृतेः—as long as the course of the world continues, to the end of the world. By 'आङ् मर्यादाभिविध्योः' Pán. II. 1. 13. आ in the sense of मर्यादा (limit *i.e.* exclusion) and अभिविधि (inclusion) is optionally compounded in an Avya., and also not compounded as here (see Malli.). अस्मि—Malli. takes this as an indec. in the sense of 'I', or we may construe जातोऽस्मि.

श्रियं विकर्षत्यपहन्त्यघानि श्रेयःपरिस्नौति तनोति कीर्तिम् ।
संदर्शनं लोकगुरोरमोघं तवात्मयोनेरिव किं न धत्ते ॥ ७ ॥

अन्वयः—आत्मयोनेः इव लोकगुरोः तव अमोघं संदर्शनं श्रियं विकर्षति,

अघानि अपहन्ति, श्रेयं परिस्नौति, कीर्तिं तनोति। (किंबहुना) किं न धत्ते ? ॥ ७ ॥

श्रियमिति ॥ आत्मयोनेर्ब्रह्मण इव लोकगुरोस्तवामोघमविफलं संदर्शनं श्रियं विकर्षत्याकृष्य ददाति। अघानि दुःखान्यपहन्ति ॥ "अंहोदुःखव्यसनेष्वघम्" इत्यमरः ॥ श्रेयः पुरुषार्थं परिस्नौति स्रवति ॥ "परिस्तौति" इति पाठेऽपि स एवार्थः ॥ धातूनामनकार्थत्वात्। कीर्तिं तनोति। किं बहुना किं न धत्ते किं न करोति। सर्वं करोतीत्यर्थः ॥

अन्वयार्थः—(**आत्मयोनेः इव**) स्वजन्मा ब्रह्मा की तरह (**लोकगुरोः तव**) जगद्-गुरु तुम्हारा (**अमोघम्**) कभी निष्फल न होने वाला (**संदर्शनम्**) दर्शन, (**श्रियम्**) ऐश्वर्य को (**विकर्षति**) चारों ओर से खींचकर देता है, (**अघानि**) पापों को (**अपहन्ति**) नष्ट करता है, (**श्रेयः**) पुरुषार्थ को (**परिस्नौति**) प्रवाहित करता है, (**कीर्तिं तनोति**) यश को फैलाता है—[किं बहुना] अधिक कहने से क्या—(**किं न धत्ते**) क्या नहीं करता ?

ब्रह्मा की तरह हे जगद्गुरु ! आप का यह सफल दर्शन क्या नहीं करता ? यह ऐश्वर्य लाने वाला, पापनाशक, कल्याणदायक एवं यश को बढ़ाने वाला है।

7. What good does the sight of you, the teacher of the world, like that of the self-born (Brahman), never failing in its effect, does not bring (to men)? It draws (brings) prosperity in its train, destroys sin, (or, misery) pours down blessings and spreads fame. [Or the sight of you..............forcibly drags wealth..............; in fact what good is it not productive of?]

Sl. 7. आत्मयोनेः—आत्मा योनिः source यस्य the self-born. लोकगुरोः—may also be taken with आत्मयोनेः the creator (गुरु) of the world. अमोघं—न मोघममोघं unfailing, ever productive of some good. मुह्यत्यस्मिन् इति मोघं fr. मुह् + अ (घञ्) ह् being changed to घ्. *Cf.* Kṛshṇa's address to Nārada—हरत्यघं संप्रति हेतुरेष्यतः शुभस्य पूर्वाचरितैः कृतं शुभैः। शरीरभाजां भवदीयदर्शनं व्यनक्ति कालत्रितयेपि योग्यताम् ॥ Sis. I. 26.

श्च्योतन्मयूखेऽपि हिमद्युतौ मे ननिर्वृतं निर्वृतिमेति चक्षुः ।

समुज्झितज्ञातिवियोगखेदं त्वत्सन्निधावुच्छ्वसतीव चेतः ॥ ८ ॥

अन्वयः—श्च्योतन्मयूखे हिमद्युतौ अपि ननिर्वृतं मे चक्षुः त्वत्सन्निधौ निर्वृतिम् एति । (तथा) समुज्झितज्ञातिवियोगखेदं चेतः समुच्छ्वसतीव ॥ ८ ॥

श्च्योतदिति ॥ हे भगवन् । श्च्योतन्मयूखे सुधास्राविकरे हिमद्युताविन्दावपि-विषये ननिर्वृतम् ॥ नञर्थस्य नञ्शब्दस्य सुप्सुपेति समासः ॥ मे चक्षुस्त्वत्सन्निधौ निर्वृतिं सुखमेति ॥ तथा चेतश्च समुज्झितज्ञातिवियोगखेदं त्यक्तबन्धुविरहदुःखं समुच्छ्वसतीवानुपरोधेन प्राणितीवेत्युत्प्रेक्षा ॥ पूर्वार्धे तु निर्वृतिकारणे सत्य-पीन्दावनिर्वृतिकथनाद्विशेषोक्तिः । तदुक्तम्—" तत्सामग्र्यामनिर्वृतिर्विशेषोक्ति-र्निगद्यते ।" इति ॥

अन्वयार्थः—(**श्च्योतन्मयूखे**) प्रस्रवित हैं किरणें जिस की ऐसे (**हिमद्युतौ अपि**) चन्द्रमा में भी (**न निर्वृतिम्**) निवृत्ति को नहीं पाया है जिसने ऐसी (**मे चक्षुः**) मेरी आंख (**त्वत्सन्निधौ**) तुम्हारे समीप (**निर्वृतिमेति**) निवृत्ति को प्राप्त करती है [और] (**समुज्झितज्ञाति वियोगखेदम्**) छोड़ा है बन्धु-बान्धवों के वियोग के दुःख को जिसने ऐसा (**चेतः**) चित्त (**समुच्छ्वसतीव**) मानो जीवित हो उठा है ।

अमृतवर्षी शीतरश्मि चन्द्रमा में भी आनन्द को न पाने वाली मेरी आंख आप के सामीप्य से आनन्दित हो रही है तथा वन्धु-बान्धवों के वियोग को भूल-कर मेरा चित्त पुनः जीवित हो उठा है ।

8. If your presence my eye, which found no delight even in the moon with her rays shedding ambrosia, feels completely comforted; and my mind forgetting all grief at the separation from relatives, as if breathes with relief.

Sl. 8. श्च्योतन्म०—श्च्योतन्तो मयूखा यस्य तस्मिन् । हिम०—हिमा द्युतिर्यस्याः the cool-rayed one; the moon. समुज्झित०—ज्ञातिभिर्वियोगः ज्ञातिवियोगस्तस्मात्तस्य वा खेदः ज्ञा०खेदः समुज्झितो ज्ञाति०दो येन तत् ।

निरास्पदं प्रश्नकुतूहलित्वमस्मास्वधीनं किम् निःस्पृहाणाम् ।

तथापि कल्याणकरीं गिरं ते मां श्रोतुमिच्छा मुखरीकरोति ॥ ९ ॥

अन्वयः—प्रश्नकुतूहलित्वं निरास्पदम्, निस्पृहाणाम् अस्मासु अधीनं किमु । तथापि कल्याणकरीं ते गिरं श्रोतुम् इच्छा मां मुखरीकरोति ॥ ९ ॥

निरास्पदमिति ॥ प्रश्नकुतूहलित्वं निरास्पदम् । आगमनप्रयोजनप्रश्नो निरास्पद इत्यर्थः ॥ "आस्पदं प्रतिष्ठायाम्" इति निपातः ॥ प्रश्नानवकाशे हेतुमाह—निःस्पृहाणाम् । युष्मत्सदृशामित्यर्थः । अस्मास्वधीनमायत्तं किमु । न किंचिदस्मत्तो लभ्यमित्यर्थः ॥ आधारत्वविवक्षायां सप्तमी । तथापि कल्याणकरीम् । अस्मद्धितैकहेतुमित्यर्थः ॥ निःस्पृहवृत्तेः पारार्थ्यादिति भावः ॥ "कृञो हेतु--" इति टप्रत्यये ङीप् ॥ अतस्ते गिरं श्रोतुमिच्छा माम् । मुखं वागस्यास्तीति मुखरो निरन्तरभाषी ॥ "मुखकुञ्जेभ्यो रो वक्तव्यः" इति रः ॥ "दुर्मुखे मुखराबद्धमुखौ" इत्यमरः ॥ ततश्च्विप्रत्ययः ॥ मुखरीकरोति । व्यापारयतीत्यर्थः । निःस्पृहस्यापि ते वाक्यमस्मद्धितकरत्वाच्छ्रोतव्यमिति भावः ॥

अन्वयार्थः—(**प्रश्नकुतूहलित्वम्**) प्रश्न-विषयक उत्सुकता (**निरास्पदम्**) निराधार है । [क्यों कि] (**निःस्पृहाणाम्**) निरभिलाष [व्यक्तियों] का (**अस्मासु**) हमारे (**अधीनम् किमु**) आधीन क्या है ? (**तथापि**) तो भी (**कल्याणकारीम्**) कल्याण करने वाली (**ते**) तुम्हारी (**गिरम्**) वाणी को (**श्रोतुमिच्छा**) सुनने की इच्छा (**माम्**) मुझे (**मुखरीकरोति**) वाचाल कर रही है ।

मेरी जिज्ञासा निरर्थक है क्योंकि आप-सदृश निस्पृह व्यक्तियों का हम से भला क्या कार्य हो सकता है ? तो भी आप की कल्याणमयी वाणी को सुनने की इच्छा से मैं पूछ रहा हूँ ।

9. There is no room for entertaining curiosity to ask you (about the object of your visit). For what is there that those who are free from all worldly desires have to seek of us ? Still the desire to bear your salutary advice prompts me to speak.

Sl. 9. प्रश्नकुतू० प्रश्ने कुतूहलं तदस्यास्तीति प्रश्नकुतूहली तस्य भावः प्र०त्वम् having curiosity to ask a question. निरास्पदम्—निर्गतमास्पदं यस्मात् without room for it. निस्पृहाणां—These free from all desire, who have nothing to wish for. अधीनं in the power of (अधिगतः इनमधीनः) depending on. *Cf.* गतस्पृहोऽप्यागमनप्रयोजनं वदेति वक्तुं व्यवसीयते यया । तनोति नस्तामुदितात्मगौरवो गुरुस्तवैवागम एव

धृष्टताम् ॥ Sis. I. 30.

मुखरी०—मुखर fr. मुख+र (a possessive aff.), see Malli.; one who talks unceasingly ; or मुखं मुखव्यापारं राति fr. रा+क (अ) न मुखरः अमुखरः; अमुखरः मुखरः संपद्यते तं करोति मुखरीकरोति makes one speak.

इत्युक्तवानुक्तिविशेषरम्यं मनः समाधाय जयोपपत्तौ ।
उदारचेता गिरमित्युदारां द्वैपायनेनाभिदधे नरेन्द्रः ॥ १० ॥

अन्वयः—इति उक्तिविशेषरम्यम् उक्तवान् उदारचेता नरेन्द्रः द्वैपायनेन जयोपपत्तौ मनः समाधाय इति उदारां गिरम् अभिदधे ॥ १० ॥

इतीति ॥ इतीत्थमुक्तिविशेषरम्यमुक्तिवचिञ्यचारु यथा तथोक्तवान् । उदारचेता महामना नरेन्द्रो द्वैपायनेन व्यासेन । द्वीपमयनं स्थानं जन्मभूमिर्यस्य स द्वीपायनः । स एव द्वैपायनः । "प्रज्ञादिभ्यश्च" इति स्वार्थेऽण्प्रत्ययः । नापत्यार्थे "नडादिभ्यः फक्"। तेष्वेव पाठाद्बाधितार्थत्वाच्च ॥ जयोपपत्तौ मनः समाधाय । जयसिद्धिमपेक्ष्येत्यर्थः । इति वक्ष्यमाणप्रकारामुदारामर्थवतीं गिरमभिदध उक्तः ॥ दुहादित्वादप्रधाने कर्मणि लिट् । "प्रधानकर्मण्याख्येये लादीनाहुर्द्विकर्मणाम् । अप्रधाने दुहादीनां ण्यन्ते कर्तुश्च कर्मणः ॥" इति वचनात् ॥

अन्वयार्थः—(**इति**) इस प्रकार (**उक्तिविशेषरम्यम्**) उक्तिविशेष के कारण सुन्दर (**उक्तवान्**) कहा है जिसने ऐसा (**उदारचेता**) उदार चित्त वाला (**नरेन्द्रः**) राजा, (**द्वैपायनेन**) व्यास के द्वारा, (**जयोपपत्तौ**) विजय की प्राप्ति में (**मनः समाधाय**) मन लगाकर (**इति**) इस प्रकार (**उदाराम्**) उदार (**गिरम्**) वाणी को (**अभिदधे**) कहा गया।

उपर्युक्त सुन्दर स्वागत-भाषण युधिष्ठिर ने दिया । इसके बाद पाण्डवों के विजय-लाभ को ध्यान में रखकर व्यास मुनि उदार वाणी बोले।

10. The magnanimous king wo had thus spoken in a manner charming on account of the variety of (or peculiarly happy) expressions used, was addressed the following significant (or fine) speech by Vyāsa, having firmly set his mind on the means of securing success (to him).

Sl. 10. उक्तिविशे०—उक्तेर्विशेषः उक्तिविशेषस्तेन रम्यं charming on account of the chosen or happy turns of expressions used.

द्वैपायनः—Vyăsa, so called because he was born in an island. We have first द्वीपायन and then अण् (अ) being added स्वार्थे (in the sense of the original word) we get द्वैपायन; अण् is added to प्रज्ञ and the other words of the group; as प्रज्ञ एव प्राज्ञ &c. *Cf.* Mahăbhārata—जज्ञे च यमुनाद्वीपे पाराशर्यः स वीर्यवान् । न्यस्तो द्वीपे स यद्बालस्तस्माद् द्वैपायन स्मृतः ॥

जयोपपत्तौ—the way to secure or bring about success, or his attainment of success. For the various meaning of उपपत्ति comp. further on sl. 52 and *supara* II, 1. 28. मनः समाधाय—having well set un *i. e.* having in contemplation. नरेन्द्रः अभिदधे—धा with अभि being a synonym of ब्रू the secondary object is put in the Nom. case the cons. being passive.

आदौ तावत्तस्य मध्यस्थताभङ्गदोष युग्मेन परिहरति—

चिचीषतां जन्मवतामलघ्वीं यशोवतंसामुभयत्र भूतिम् ।
अभ्यर्हिता बन्धुषु तुल्यरूपा वृत्तिर्विशेषेण तपोधनानाम् ॥ ११ ॥

अन्वयः—अलघ्वीं यशोवतंसाम् उभयत्र भूतिं चिचीषता जन्मवतां बंधुषु तुल्यरूपा वृत्तिः अभ्यर्हिता । तपोधनानां (तु) विशेषेण अभ्यर्हिता ॥ ११ ॥

चिचीषतामिति ॥ अलघ्वीं गुर्वीम् ॥ "वोतो गुणवचनात्" इति ङीप् ॥ यशोवतंसां कीर्तिभूषणाम् । उभयत्रेह चामुत्र च भूतिं श्रेयश्चिचीषतां संचेतुं संग्रहीतुमिच्छताम् । चिनोतेः सन्नन्ताच्छतृप्रत्ययः ॥ जन्मवतां शरीरिणां बन्धुषु विषये तुल्यरूपा एकविधा वृत्तिर्व्यवहारोऽभ्यर्हिता उचिता तपोधनानां त्वस्मत्सदृशां विशेषेण नियमेनाभ्यर्हिता ॥

अन्वयार्थः—(**अलघ्वीम्**) महान् (**यशोवतंसाम्**) कीर्ति के आभूषण (**उभयत्र**) इस लोक एवं परलोक में (**भूतिम्**) ऐश्वर्य का (**चिचीषताम्**) संग्रह करना चाहते हुए (**जन्मवताम्**) प्राणियों की (**बंधुषु**) बांधवों के विषय में (**तुल्यरूपा**) एक जैसे रूप वाला (**वृत्तिः**) व्यवहार (**अभ्यर्हिता**) उचित है। (**तपोधनानाम्**) [तु] तपस्वियों को तो (**विशेषेण**) विशेष रूप से (**अभ्यर्हिता**) उचित है।

महान् तथा कीर्ति के शोभावर्धक ऐश्वर्य का भूलोक एवं परलोक में जो

संग्रह करना चाहते हैं उन्हें अपने बन्धुओं के प्रति समान व्यवहार का आचरण करना चाहिए और मुझ-जैसे तपस्वियों को तो विशेष रूप से समव्यवहार करना चाहिए।

11. A conduct of equanimity towards relatives is commendable to those born beings who wish to attain in both the worlds prosperity, great and embellished (exalted) with glory, and especially towards those who regard enance as their wealth (asctics like myself).

Sl. 11. **यशोवतंसां**—यशः अवतंसः ornament यस्या सा तथोक्ता ताम्. चिचीषतां—see II. 19. तुल्यरूपा—तुल्यं रूपं यस्याः of the same form. अभ्यर्हिता—fit, suitable. तपो—तप एव धनं येषां ते तेषाम्.

तथापि निघ्नं नृप तावकीनैः प्रह्वीकृतं मे हृदयं गुणौघैः ।
वीतस्पृहाणामपि मुक्तिभाजां भवन्ति भव्येषु हि पक्षपाताः ॥ १२ ॥

अन्वयः तथापि (हे) नृप ! तावकीनैः गुणौघैः प्रह्वीकृतं मे हृदयं निघ्नं (हि) वीतस्पृहाणां मुक्तिभाजाम् अपि भव्येषु पक्षपाताः भवन्ति ॥ १२ ॥

तथापीति ॥ तथापि तुल्यवृत्तौ चित्तेऽपि । हे नृप ! तावकीनैस्त्वदीयैः ॥ "युष्मदस्मदोरन्यतरस्यां खञ्च" इति खञ्प्रत्ययः । "तवकममकावेकवचने" इति तवकादेशः ॥ गुणौघैः प्रह्वीकृतमावर्जितं मे हृदयं निघ्नं त्वदायत्तम् ॥ "अधीनो निघ्न आयत्तः" इत्यमरः ॥ ननु निःस्पृहस्य कोऽयं पक्षपात इत्यत्राह वीतेति ॥ वीतस्पृहाणां विरक्तानां मुक्तिभाजाम् । मुमुक्षूणामपीत्यर्थः । भवन्तीति भव्याः साधवः ॥ "भव्यगेय—" इत्यादिना कर्तरि निपातः । तेषु पक्षपाताः स्नेहा भवन्ति । न तु साध्वनुग्रहो महतां माध्यस्थ्यभञ्जक इति भावः ॥

अन्वयार्थः—(नृप) हे राजन् ! (**तावकीनैः**) तुम्हारे (**गुणौघैः**) गुणसमूहों से (**प्रह्वीकृतम्**) आकृष्ट किया हुआ (**मे हृदयम्**) मेरा हृदय (**निघ्नम्**) तुम्हारे आधीन है । [क्योंकि] (**वीतस्पृहाणाम्**) त्याग दिया है अभिलाषाओं को जिन्होंने ऐसे (**मुक्तिभाजाम् अपि**) मुक्ति चाहने वालों के भी (**भव्येषु**) सज्जनों में (**पक्षपाताः भवन्ति**) पक्षपात होते हैं ।

हे युधिष्ठिर, तुम्हारे गुणों ने मेरे हृदय को जीत लिया है । मैं तुम्हारे वश में हूँ । निःस्पृह एवं मुमुक्षु लोगों का भी सज्जनों में पक्षपात होता है ।

12. Still, O King, my heart won over by your manifold merits, is drawn (or attached) to you; for even those, who are free from desires and seek absolution (or, are free from worldly ties), love the good.

Sl. 12. तावकीन—of thee; also तावकं; तवक is substituted for युष्मद in the sing. before the aff. खञ् (ईन) and अण्; see Malli. प्रह्वीकृतं—प्रह्व inclined, bent; न प्रह्वं अप्रह्वं, प्रह्वं सम्पद्यते तथा कृतम् deawn to; hence won over. निघ्न—in the power of, subdued by. मुक्तिभाजां—of those desiring absolution (Malli.); or मुक्ति may mean जीवन्मुक्ति liberated though living *i. e.* entirely free from worldly ties or its concerns. भव्य Lit. that which preeminently is or exists; hence good, noble.

अथ नृपस्य गुणवत्तां प्रकटयितुं धृतराष्ट्रस्य दुश्चेष्टामुद्घाटयति—

सुता न यूयं किमु तस्य राज्ञः सुयोधनं वा न गुणैरतीताः ।
यस्त्यक्तवान्वः स वृथा बलाद्वा मोहं विधत्ते विषयाभिलाषः ॥ १३ ॥

अन्वयः—यूयं तस्य राज्ञः सुताः न किमु, गुणैः सुयोधनं न अतीताः वा, यो वः वृथा त्यक्तवान् । स विषयाभिलाषः बलात् वा मोहं विधत्ते ॥ १३ ॥

सुता इति ॥ यूयं तस्य राज्ञो धृतराष्ट्रस्य सुताः पुत्रा न किमु अपि तु सुता एवेत्यर्थः । गुणैः शान्तिदानदाक्षिण्यादिभिः सुयोधनं नातीताः नातिक्रान्ता वा । अतीता एवेत्यर्थः ॥ कर्तरि क्तः ॥ असुतत्वमगुणत्वं च त्यागे हेतुः । युष्मासु तन्नास्तीत्यर्थः । उपालम्भे कारणमाह—य इति । यो धृतराष्ट्रो वो युष्मान्वृथा निष्कारणमेव त्यक्तवान् ॥ यदि वयं सुता गुणाधिकाश्च तर्हि कथमत्याक्षीत्तत्राह—बलादिति ॥ स विषयाभिलाषो भोगतृष्णा बलाद्वाबलात्कारादिव ॥ "वा स्याद्विकल्पोपमयोरेवार्थेऽपि समुच्चये ।" इति विश्वः ॥ मोहमविवेकं विधत्ते । विषयाभिलाषातिरिक्तो न कश्चिद्युष्मत्त्यागहेतुरस्तीत्यर्थः ॥ अत्र कार्यकारणसमर्थनरूपोऽर्थान्तरन्यासः ॥

अन्वयार्थः—(**यूयम्**) तुम (**तस्य**) उस (**राज्ञः**) राजा के (**सुताः न किमु**) पुत्र नहीं हो क्या ? (**वा**) अथवा (**गुणैः**) गुणों से (**सुयोधनम्**) सुयोधन को (**न अतीताः**) अतिक्रान्त नहीं किया है क्या ? (**यो वः**) जिसने तुम्हें (**वृथा**) बिना

कारण के (**त्यक्तवान्**) छोड़ दिया, (**स**) वह [धृतराष्ट्र] (**विषयाभिलाषः**) भोग की है तृष्णा जिसे ऐसा (**बलात् वा**) मानो हठपूर्वक (**मोहम्**) अविवेक को (**विधत्ते**) धारण करता है ।

आप लोग क्या धृतराष्ट्र के पुत्र नहीं हो ? या दुर्योधन से अधिक गुणवान् नहीं हो ? धृतराष्ट्र ने बिना कारण आप को त्याग दिया, विषयेच्छु वह धृतराष्ट्र मानो जान-बूझकर अज्ञानी बना हुआ है ।

13. Are you not the sons of that King (Dhṛtarăshta), or have you not excelled Suyodhna in qualities, that he should have abandoned you for nothing (without a fault of yours)? Or it is that (well-known) desire for the enjoyment of pleasures which as if by force produce infatuation (or mental aberration).

Sl. 13. यस्त्यक्तवान् यः &c.—This may also be construed as स वः वृथा बलात् because he had the power to do so त्यक्तवान्; वा अथवा or why?

अथ राज्ञ उत्साहवर्धनाय शत्रोर्हानिं सूचयति—

जहातु नैनं कथमर्थसिद्धिः संशय्य कर्णादिषु तिष्ठते यः ।
असाधुयोगा हि जयान्तरायाः प्रमाथिनीनां विपदां पदानि ॥ १४ ॥

अन्वयः—यः संशय्य कर्णादिषु तिष्ठते एनम् । (तम्) अर्थसिद्धिः कथं न जहातु । (हि) असाधुयोगाः जयान्तरायाः प्रमाथिनीनां विपदां पदानि ॥ १४ ॥

जहात्विति ॥ एनं धृतराष्ट्रमर्थसिद्धिः कथं न जहातु । जहात्वेवेत्यर्थः ॥ "प्रैषातिसर्गप्राप्तकालेषु कृत्याश्च" इति प्राप्तकाले लोट् ॥ तस्य हानिकालः प्राप्त इत्यर्थः । कुतः । यो धृतराष्ट्रः संशय्य संदिह्य कर्णादिषु तिष्ठते । कर्णादीन्दुर्मन्त्रिणः संदिग्धार्थे निर्णेतृत्वेनावलम्बत इत्यर्थः ॥ "प्रकाशनस्थेयाख्ययोश्च" इति स्थेयाख्यायामात्मनेपदम् । "प्रकाशस्थेयाख्ययोश्च" इति तङ ॥ तिष्ठतेऽस्मिन्निति स्थेयो विवादपदनिर्णेता । तथाहि । असाधुयोगा दुर्जनसंसर्गा जयान्तराया जयविघातकाः । किंच प्रमाथिनीनामुन्मूलनशीलानां विपदां पदानि स्थानानि ॥ "पदं व्यवसितत्राणस्थानलक्ष्माङ्घ्रिवस्तुषु ।" इत्यमरः । न केवलं

जयघातिनः किं त्वनर्थकारिणश्चेत्यर्थः। धृतराष्ट्रोऽपि दुर्जनविधेयत्वाद्विनङ्क्षयतीति भावः ॥

अन्वयार्थः—(**यः**) जो (**संशय्य**) सन्देह करके (**कर्णादिषु तिष्ठते**) कर्ण आदि पर निर्भर रहता है, (**एनम्**) इस को (**अर्थसिद्धिः**) अभीप्सित-सिद्धि (**कथं न जहातु**) कैसे नहीं छोड़ेगी ? [हि] क्योंकि (**असाधुयोगाः**) दुर्जनों के सम्पर्क (**जयान्तरायाः**) विजय के विघातक [होते हैं तथा] (**प्रमाथिनीनाम्**) नाश करने वाली (**विपदाम्**) विपत्तियों के (**पदानि**) स्थान [होते हैं]।

संदिग्ध स्थलों पर यह दुर्योधन कर्ण इत्यादि दुष्ट मन्त्रियों से सलाह करता है अतः इसे सफलता निश्चित रूप से छोड़ेगी। क्योंकि दुर्जनों का सम्पर्क विजय में बाधक तथा विपत्तियों का स्थान होता है।

14. How will success in the objects to be gained not fail him who, when in doubt, depends upon Karṇa and others for decision ? Verily associations with the wicked, being obstacles to success, are the seat cauees) of crushing calamities.

Sl. 14. अर्थसिद्धिः—अर्थ्यते असौ अर्थः (what is desired to be gained, an object or end wished to be accomplished) तस्मिन्सिद्धिः success in policy. संशय्य—when having a doubt or when he is in suspense as to the adoption of a particular measure or when an intricate point of policy arises. तिष्ठते—स्था is Atm. in the sense of प्रकाशन (disclosing one's feelings or intention) and approaching one as an umpire *i. e.* for decision; hence acts upon the advice of, follows the decision of. असाधु—असाधुभियोगाः association or keeping company with, जया —जयस्य अन्तरायाः obstacles in the way of, impediments to. प्रमाथिनीनां—प्रमथितुं शीलं यासां ताः crushing, overwhelming.

एवं शत्रोरनर्थं सूचयित्वा राज्ञोऽर्थसिद्धिं सूचयति—

पथश्च्युतायां समितौ रिपूणां धर्म्यां दधानेन धुरं चिराय।
त्वया विपत्स्वप्यविपत्तिरम्यमाविष्कृतं प्रेम परं गुणेषु ॥ १५ ॥

अन्वयः—रिपूणां समितौ पथः च्युतायां चिराय धर्म्यां धुरं दधानेन त्वया विपत्सु अपि अविपत्तिरम्यं गुणेषु परं प्रेम आविष्कृतम् ॥ १५ ॥

पथ इति ॥ रिपूणां समितौ सभायाम् । "सभासमितिसंसदः" इत्यमरः । पथश्च्युतायां मार्गाद्भ्रष्टायाम् । दुरात्मनो दुःशासनस्य स्त्रीग्रहणसाहसमङ्गी-कृतवत्यामित्यर्थः । चिराय धर्म्यां धर्मादनपेताम् ॥ "धर्मपथ्यर्थन्यायादनपेते" इति यत्प्रत्ययः ॥ धुरं भारं दधानेन । कृच्छ्रेष्वपि धर्मादचलतेत्यर्थः । त्वया विपत्स्वपि । अविपत्ति अविनाश्यत एव रम्यं गुणेषु शान्त्यादिषु विषये परमुत्कृष्टं प्रेमाविष्कृतं प्रकटीकृतम् । दुःसहमपि सोढवता त्वया साधु कृतमिति भावः ॥

अन्वयार्थः—(**रिपूणाम्**) शत्रुओं की (**समितौ**) सभा के (**पथश्च्युतायाम्**) मार्ग-भ्रष्ट होने पर (**चिराय**) चिरकाल-पर्यन्त (**धर्म्याम्**) धर्म से युक्त (**धुरम्**) भार को (**दधानेन त्वया**) धारण करते हुए तुम से (**विपत्सु अपि**) विपत्तियों में भी (**अविपत्तिरम्यम्**) अविनाशी होने के कारण सुन्दर, (**गुणेषु**) गुणों में (**परं प्रेम आविष्कृतम्**) उत्कृष्ट प्रेम प्रकट किया ।

(द्रौपदी के वस्त्रापहरण के समय) शत्रु-सभा के मार्ग-भ्रष्ट हो जाने पर भी तुमने अपने धर्म को नहीं त्यागा । विपत्ति-काल में भी गुणों के प्रति स्थायी अतएव सुन्दर एवं उत्कृष्ट प्रेम प्रकट किया ।

15. When the assembly of your enemies swerved from the right path, (or path of duty) by you long bearing the yoke of righteousness (ever acting righteously) was manifested the highest love for virtues, charming by its remaining steady (lit undestroyed, unshaken) even in difficulties.

Sl. 15. समिति—an assembly; fr. स सह मितिः (discussion for correct knowledge) यस्याम्. धर्म्या—धर्मात् अनपेता not departing from, consistent with religious duty or righteousness; विप-पत्ति०—नास्ति विपति विपत्तिर्यस्य तदविपत्ति; now see Malli.; delightful on account of its not being diminished or destroyed *i. e.* ever remaining unshaken.

विधाय विध्वंसमनात्मनीनं शमैकवृत्तेर्भवतश्छलेन ।
प्रकाशितत्वन्मतिशीलसाराः कृतोपकारा इव विद्विषस्ते ॥ १६ ॥

अन्वयः—शमैकवृत्तेः भवतः छलेन अनात्मनीनं विध्वंसं विधाय प्रकाशित-त्वन्मतिशीलसाराः ते विद्विषः कृतोपकारा इव (जाताः) ॥ १६ ॥

विधायेति ।। किंच शम एवैका मुख्या वृत्तिर्यस्य तस्य। अपरोपतापिन इत्यर्थ:। भवतश्छलेन कपटेन। आत्मने हित आत्मनीन:। स न भवतीत्यनात्मनीन:। स्वस्यैवानर्थहेतुरित्यर्थ:। तम् ।। "आत्मन्विश्वजनभोगोत्तरपदात्ख:" इति खप्रत्यय: ।। विध्वंसमपकारं विधाय कृत्वा। प्रकाशित: प्रख्यापितस्त्वन्मतिशीलयोस्तव प्रज्ञास्वभावयो: सार: प्रकर्षो यैस्ते तथोक्ता:। ते तत्र विद्विष: कृतोपकारा इवोपकृतवन्त इव। जाता इति शेष:। अपकारोपि उपकारायैव संवृत्त:। यदेषां दौर्जन्यं युष्मत्सौजन्यं च जगति सुव्यक्तमासीदित्यर्थ:। विद्यमानस्यापि सुजनस्य चन्दनदारुण इव गुणा: परिभव एव प्रकटीभवन्तीति भाव: ।।

अन्वयार्थ::—(**शमैकवृत्ते:**) शान्ति ही है मुख्य वृत्ति जिसकी ऐसे (**भवत:**) आपके, (**छलेन**) कपट से (**अनात्मनीनम्**) अपने लिए अहितकर (**विध्वंसम्**) अपकार को (**विधाय**) करके, (**प्रकाशितत्वन्मतिशीलसारा:**) प्रकट किया है तुम्हारी बुद्धि तथा आचरण की उत्कृष्टता को जिन्होंने ऐसे (**विद्विष:**) शत्रु, (**कृतोपकारका: इव**) उपकार करने वालों की भांति [**जाता:**] हो गये ।

शान्तिप्रिय, तुम्हारा कपट से अहित करके शत्रुओं ने अपना ही अहित किया है। इससे तुम्हारी बुद्धि एवं आचरण की उत्कृष्टता प्रकट हो गई और इस प्रकार स्वयं शत्रु तुम्हारा उपकारी बन गया।

16. Working ruin upon you who always act peacefully by means of a fraudulent scheme, but to their own detriment, your enemies, in as much as they have prominently brought into light the excellence of your wisdom and character, have, as it were, conferred an obligation upon you (or done you a service).

Sl. 16. शमैक —शम: tranquil disposition, peacefulness of the mind. वृत्ते:—always acting peacefully. छलेन—by fraud, by means of a fraudulent scheme. विध्वंस—ruin, destruction, injury. अनात्म०—आत्मनीन beneficial to one's self; fr. आत्मन्—ख (ईन) which is added also to विश्वजन and comp. words having भोग for their latter member; विश्वजनीन, राजभोगीन, see Malli. मति—wisdom, or thought, way of action. कृतो —कृत उपकार:

यैः. The meaning of Malli.'s remark विद्यमानस्यापि &c. is that although a good man may be near, his virtues are brought into preminence only when maltreated by his enemies or when under difficulty as the fragrance of sandal is when rubbed.

अथ प्रयोजनान्तरमाह—

लभ्या धरित्री तव विक्रमेण ज्यायांश्च वीर्यास्त्रबलैर्विपक्षः ।

अतः प्रकर्षाय विधिर्विधेयः प्रकर्षतन्त्रा हि रणे जयश्रीः ॥ १७ ॥

अन्वयः—तव (त्वया) धरित्री विक्रमेण लभ्या, विपक्षः च वीर्यास्त्रबलः ज्यायान् । अतः प्रकर्षाय विधिः विधेयः । [हि] रणे जयश्रीः प्रकर्षतन्त्रा ॥१७॥

लभ्येति ॥ तव त्वयेत्यर्थः ॥ "कृत्यानां कर्तरि वा" इति षष्ठी ॥ धरित्री विक्रमेण लभ्या प्राप्या । न च सुलभ्या तं विनेत्याहः । विपक्षश्च शत्रुरपि । वीर्यं शौर्यमस्त्राण्याग्नेयादीनि बलानि सैन्यानि तैर्ज्यायान्प्रशस्यतरः । अधिकतर इति यावत् ॥ ज्येष्ठस्य "ज्यादादीयसः" इति ज्यादेशः ॥ अतः प्रकर्षायाधिक्याय विधिरुपायो विधेयः कर्तव्यः । हि यस्माद्रणे जयश्रीः प्रकर्षतंत्रा प्रकर्षप्रधाना । उत्कर्षायत्तेत्यर्थः ॥ "तन्त्रं प्रधाने सिद्धान्ते" इत्यमरः ॥ बलिन एव जयो न तु दुर्बलस्येति भावः ॥

अन्वयार्थः—(**तव**) तुम्हें (**धरित्री**) पृथ्वी (**विक्रमेण**) पराक्रम से (**लभ्याः**) प्राप्त करती है (**विपक्षः** च) और शत्रु (**वीर्यास्त्रबलैः**) शौर्य, शस्त्रास्त्र तथा सेना से (**ज्यायान्**) श्रेष्ठ है, (**अतः**) इस लिए (**प्रकर्षाय**) श्रेष्ठता के लिए (**विधिः**) उपाय (**विधेयः**) करना चाहिए (हि) क्योंकि (**रणे**) युद्ध में (**जयश्रीः**) विजय-लक्ष्मी (**प्रकर्षतन्त्रा**) उत्कर्ष के आधीन है ।

पराक्रम से ही तुम्हें राज्य प्राप्त करना है । शत्रु बल, शस्त्रास्त्र एव सेना की दृष्टि से अपेक्षाकृत अधिक बलवान् है अतः अपने उत्कर्ष के लिए प्रयत्न करना चाहिए; क्योंकि युद्ध में विजय उसी की होती है जो उत्कृष्ट होता है अर्थात् शस्त्र एवं सैन्य शक्ति में अधिक होता है ।

17. The earth (your kingdom) is to be regained by you by valour alone; (the enemy, however, is stronger than you) in valour, missiles and the army; measures, therefore, must

be taken to gain superiority; for, success, in battle depend, on superiority (in men and means).

Sl. 17. तव—The Gen. for Inst. by the rule.—In the case of Pot p. participles (कृत्यानां) the agent is put in the Gen. or the Inst. case. See Malli. विपक्षः—विरुद्धः पक्षः अस्य the enemy. च—but, however. वीर्यं—Valour of, and the knowledge of missiles possessed by, Bhishma, Droṇa, Karṇa &c. *Cf.* भीष्मे द्रोणे कृपे कर्णे द्रोणपुत्रे च भारत । धनुर्वेदश्चतुष्पाद एतेष्वद्य प्रतिष्ठितः ॥ दैवं ब्राह्मं मानुषं च सयत्नं सचिकित्सितम् । सर्वास्त्राणां प्रयोगं च अभिजानन्ति कृत्स्नशः ॥ Sab. p. ch. 37. प्रकर्ष—Superiority, excess of power. प्रकर्षः तन्त्रं यस्या सा depending on.

अथ "त्रिः"—इत्यादिना श्लोकचतुष्टयेन विपक्षज्यायस्त्वं वर्णयति—

त्रिःसप्तकृत्वो जगतीपतीनां हन्ता गुरुर्यस्य स जामदग्न्यः ।

वीर्यावधूतः स्म तदा विवेद प्रकर्षमाधारवशं गुणानाम् ॥ १८ ॥

अन्वयः—त्रिःसप्तकृत्वः जगतीपतीनां हन्ता स गुरुः जामदग्न्यः यस्य वीर्यावधूतः सदा गुणानां प्रकर्षम् आधारवशं विवेद स्म ॥ १८ ॥

त्रिःसप्तेति ॥ त्रिरावृत्तान्सप्तवारांस्त्रिःसप्तकृत्वः । एकविंशतिकृत्व इत्यर्थः ॥ त्रिःसप्तशब्दयोः सुप्सुपेति समासः । "संख्यायाः क्रियाभ्यावृत्तिगणने कृत्वसुच्" इति कृत्वसुच्प्रत्ययः ॥ जगतीपतीनां महीपतीनां हन्ता नाशको गुरुरस्त्रवेदोपदेष्टा सः । प्रसिद्ध इत्यर्थः ॥ अतएव यच्छब्दानपेक्षत्वम् । तदुक्तं काव्यप्रकाशे—"अप्रसिद्धानुभूतार्थविषयस्तच्छब्दोपादानं नापेक्षते" इति ॥ जमदग्नेरपत्यं पुमाञ्जामदग्न्यः ॥ "गर्गादिभ्यो यञ्" इति यञ्प्रत्ययः ॥ यस्य भीष्मस्य वीर्यावधूतो विक्रमाभिभूतः । अम्बिकास्वयंवर इत्यर्थः । तदा भङ्गप्राप्तिसमये गुणानां शौर्यादीनां प्रकर्षमतिशयं वीर्यातिशयमाधारवशमाश्रयाधीनं विवेद जज्ञे स्म । स्वविद्यायाः स्वशिष्ये भीष्मे स्वस्मादपि प्रकर्षाधानदर्शनादिति भावः ॥ "स्म पादपूरणे भूतेऽर्थे च" इति विश्वः ॥

अन्वयार्थः—(**त्रिःसप्तकृत्व**) तीन बार सात की आवृत्ति करके (**जगतीपतीनाम्**) राजाओं का (**हन्ता**) विनाशक (**स गुरुः**) वह अस्त्रवेद का शिक्षक (**जामदग्न्यः**) जमदग्नि-पुत्र (**यस्य**) जिस के (**वीर्यावधूतः**) पराक्रम से अभिभूत हुआ (**तदा**) तब (**गुणानां प्रकर्षम्**) शौर्यादि गुणों के अतिशय को (**आधार-**

वशम्) आश्रय के आधीन (विवेद) जाना। (स्म) पादपूरक शब्द, अतः निरर्थक।

धनुर्वेद के शिक्षक परशुराम ने इक्कीस बार क्षत्रिय राजाओं का संहार किया। स्वयं अपनी सिखायी हुई विद्या से वे भीष्म से अम्बिका के स्वयंवर में परास्त हुए। इस पराजय से उन्होंने जाना कि शौर्य आदि गुण उचित आधार को पाकर अतिशय को प्राप्त होते हैं। (परशुराम ब्राह्मण थे, अतः वही विद्या क्षत्रिय-आधार, भीष्म, को पाकर ब्राह्मण आधार-परशुराम की अपेक्षा अधिक फलीभूत हुई।)

18-19. Shabong his bour rellong its ends vibrating fiercely in battle, whose mind will not Bhīshma, make susceptible to terror (fill with terror,—Bhishma whose preceptor, the redoutable, Jāmadagnya, the destroyer of kings (the Kshatriyas) twentyone times, knew when overpowered by his valour, that supereminence of qualities depends upon proper substratum or their being in the proper element), and from whom even the Destroyer (god of death) seems to have sustained defeat, he having the chagrin of having no power over him ?

Sis. 18. 19. जामदग्न्यः—Better known as परशुराम, the youngest of the five sons of Jamadagni, Paraśuráma's hostility to the Kshatriyas and his clearing the earth of them twenty one times is well-known to the Indian student. गुरुः—Gangā was forced to come down to the earth as a mortal by the curse of Brahmā and became the wife of king Śantanu. She bore him eight sons of whom Bhîshma was the youngest and the only son who was allowed to live by her. When young he was placed by her under Parśurāma who taught him the military art and the use of missiles.

वीर्यात्र०—वीर्येणावधूतः overpowered (vanquished) by valour. प्रकर्ष—the attainment of highest excellence. आधार—आधारस्य वशः तम् dependent on its right substratum. स्म—used here as an expletive. The science of arms is the proper province of the Kshatriyas. Now Bhîsma was a Kshatriya fully, while Parashurāma was a Kshatriya on his mother's side only. So the same Vidyā when possessed by the former naturally attained a superior excellence in him. अनैश्वर्य—न

ईश्वरः अनीश्वरः; now see Malli.; when the five words शुचि and others come after the neg. particle their initial vowel takes Vṛddhi, नञ् optionally taking it before such terminations as य, अ &c. So अशौचं-आशौचं, अनैश्वर्यं, आनैश्वर्यं &c. अनैश्वर्येण कृतं व्यलीकं shame यस्य. On account of a boon conferred on him by his father Bhîshma's death depended on his will and Yama had no control over him. अन्तकः—अन्तयतीति fr. अन्तय् deri. fr. अन्त—अक (ण्वुल्). भीष्मः—Son of Śantanu and Gáṅgā, also called Śăntanava, Gāṅgeya &c. One day as Śaṇtanu was walking by a river side he beheld a charming damsel, Satyavati by name, the daughter of a fisherman and though old, conceived a passion for her. He sent his son Bhîshma to negotiate the marriage, but the parents of the girl objected to the marriage on the ground that if their daughter bore sons they would not succeed to the throne he being the rightful heir. But Śántanava, to gratify his father's desire, made a vow to the girl's parents that he would never accept the throne, nor marry a wife, nor become the father of children by any other woman. This dreadful vow soon became known to the public and thenceforth he came to be called Bhîshma. For this singular act of philial piety his father conferred upon him a boon that he would have the power of choosing his own time of death. After the death of his father he set Vichitravirya, the son of Satyavati, on the throne, got him married to the two daughters of the King of Kăśi, and on his death became the guardian of his sons and grandsons. He also directed the training of the Kauravas and the Păṇḍavas and engaged Droṇa to teach them the science of war. When the war broke out he fought on the side of the Kauravas and was made the commander-in-chief of their forces. When mortally wounded by Arjuna he lay on a couch of arrows for 58 days till the sun had entered the vernal equinox and then gave up his soul. In the interval he delivered several didactic discourses. He was remarkable for his continence, wisdom, firmness of resolve and unflinching devotion to God.

यस्मिन्ननैश्वर्यकृतव्यलीकः पराभवं प्राप्त इवान्तकोऽपि ।
धुन्वन्धनुः कस्य रणे न कुर्यान्मनो भयैकप्रवणं स भीष्मः ॥ १९ ॥

अन्वयः—यस्मिन् अनैश्वर्यकृतव्यलीकः अन्तकोपि पराभवं प्राप्त इव स भीष्मः रणे धनुः धुन्वन् कस्य मनः भयैकप्रवणं न कुर्यात् ॥ १९ ॥

यस्मिन्निति ॥ यस्मिन्भीष्मे विषये । अनीश्वरस्य भावोऽनैश्वर्यमसामर्थ्यम् । "नञः शुचीश्वरक्षेत्रज्ञकुशलनिपुणानाम्" इति विकल्पान्नञः पूर्वपदवृद्ध्यभावः ॥ तेन कृतव्यलीको जनितवैलक्ष्यः ॥ "दुःखे वैलक्ष्ये व्यलीकम्" इति यादवः ॥ अन्तकोऽपि यमोऽपि पराभवं प्राप्त इव । भीष्मस्येच्छामरणत्वादन्तकोऽपि पराजित इवास्ते किमुतान्य इति भावः । स भीष्मो रणे धनुर्धुन्वन्कस्य मनो भयैकप्रवणं भय एकप्रवणमेकोन्मुखम् ॥ शिवभागवतवत्समासः ॥ न कुर्यात् । सर्वस्यापि मनसि भयं कुर्यादेवेत्यर्थः ।

अन्वयार्थः—(**यस्मिन्**) जिस (**भीष्म**) के विषय में (**अनैश्वर्यकृतव्यलीकः**) असामर्थ्य से उत्पन्न हुई है लज्जा जिसे ऐसा (**अन्तकः अपि**) यमराज भी (**पराभवं प्राप्तः इव**) पराजय को प्राप्त-सा हुआ (**सः**) वह (**भीष्मः**) भीष्म (**रणे**) युद्ध में (**धनुः धुन्वन्**) धनुष को कंपाता हुआ (**कस्य**) किसके (**मनः**) मन को (**भयैकप्रवणम्**) एक मात्र भयोन्मुख (**न कुर्यात्**) न करेगा ?

अपने असामर्थ्य के कारण लज्जित यमराज भी जिस भीष्म से पराजित-सा हुआ (उन की मृत्यु इच्छाधीन थी) उस का सर्वथा अभाव नहीं था । युद्ध में धनुष से बाण बरसाता हुआ वह भीष्म किस को भयाक्रान्त नहीं करेगा ?

Sl. 19. धनुः धुन्वन्—Shaking fiercely (as he will be discharging arrows in rapid succession). The bow used by Bhishma was of the measure of a palm tree (तालदघ्नं धनुधुन्वन् Mah. Bhăr.) and the arrows shot by him were as long as long as a *yuga* or yoke. भयैक०—This should properly be एकभय०; so the comp. is to be explained like शिवभागवतं see *supra*, notes on अरिषड्वर्ग I, 9.

सृजन्तमाजाविषुसंहतीर्वः सहेत कोपज्वलितं गुरुं कः ।
परिस्फुरल्लोलशिखाग्रजिह्वं जगज्जिघत्सन्तमिवान्तवह्निम् ॥ २० ॥

अन्वयः—आजौ इषुसंहतीः सृजन्तं कोपज्वलितम् (अत एव) परिस्फुरल्लोलशिखाग्रजिह्वं जगत् जिघत्सन्तम् अन्तर्वह्निमिव (स्थितं) गुरुं कः सहेत ॥ २० ॥

सृजन्तमिति ॥ आजौ रण इषुसंहतीर्बाणसंघान्सृजन्तं वर्षन्तं कोपज्वलितमतएव परिस्फुरन्त्यो लोलाश्च शिखाग्राण्येव जिह्वा यस्य तं तथोक्तं जगल्लोकं जिघत्सन्तमत्तुमिच्छन्तम् ॥ अदेः सन्नताच्छतृप्रत्ययः । "लुङ्सनोर्घस्लृ" इति घस्लृआदेशः ॥ अन्तर्वह्नि कालाग्निमिव स्थितं गुरुं द्रोणं वो युष्माकं मध्ये कः सहेत सोढुं शक्नुयात् । न कोऽपीत्यर्थः ॥ "शकि लिङ् च" इति शक्यार्थे लिङ् ॥

अन्वयार्थः—(**आजौ**) युद्ध में (**इषु संहतीः**) बाण-समूह को (**सृजन्तम्**) बरसाते हुए (**कोपज्वलितम्**) क्रोध से जलते हुए, [अत एव] (**परिस्फुरल्लोलशिखाग्रजिह्वम्**) चारों ओर चमकती हुई चंचल शिखा-सी है जिह्वा जिस की ऐसी (**जगत जिघत्सन्तम्**) संसार को खाना चाहती हुई (**अन्तर्वह्निमिव**) प्रलयाग्नि की भाँति [स्थित] (**गुरुम्**) गुरु [द्रोणाचार्य को] (कः) **कौन** (**सहेत**) सह सकेगा ?

युद्ध में बाण-वर्षा करते हुए, क्रोध के कारण, लपलपाती शिखा-रूप जिह्वा से समग्र संसार को भस्म कर देना चाहती हुई प्रलयाग्नि की भांति स्थित द्रोणाचार्य का कौन सामना कर सकेगा ?

20. Who of you will be able to withstand the preceptor (Droṇa) burning with anger and pouring blazing showers of arrows in battle, as if he were the fire of final destruction wishing to consumet he world with its tongues of tapering flames quivering and blazing all around ?

Sl. 20. आजौ—in battle, अजन्त्यस्यां fr. अज् to go and इ (इण्); see Pān. III. 3. 108. and Vārt. संहति—a collection; volleys of arrows. सृजन्तं—lit. creating, sending forth. The idea is this—Droṇa being a dexterous bowman drew the arrows from the arrow—case, fixed them on the bow—string and discharged them with such quickness that the eye was not able to follow the various actions and fancied Droṇa as creating the arrows. The following sl. will serve as a com. on this—

स दक्षिणं तूणमुखेन वामं व्यापारयन् हस्तमलक्ष्यतयाताजौ । आकर्णकृष्टा सकृदस्य नोद्ध्रुमौर्वीव बाणान्सुषुवे रिपुघ्नान् ॥ Rag. VII. 57. परिस्फुरत् &c.—see Malli. जिघत्सन्तं—wishing to eat up or destroy; pre p. of the desi. of अद् (जिघत्सति pre.) *Cf.* for a similar idea अस्त्रज्वालावलीढप्रतिबलजलधेरन्तरौर्वायमाणे &c. Ven. III. 7.

निरीक्ष्य संरम्भनिरस्तधैर्यं राधेयमाराधितजामदग्न्यम् ।
असंस्तुतेषु प्रसभं भयेषु जायेत मृत्योरपि पक्षपातः ॥ २१ ॥

अन्वयः—संरम्भनिरस्तधैर्यम् आराधितजामदग्न्यं राधेयं निरीक्ष्य मृत्योः अपि असंस्तुतेषु भयेषु प्रसभं पक्षपातः जायेत ॥ २१ ॥

निरीक्ष्येति ॥ संरम्भेण कोपेन निरस्तं त्याजितं धैर्यं निर्विकारचित्तत्वं येन तं तथोक्तम् । आकारेणैव परधैर्यापहारिणमित्यर्थः । आराधितजामदग्न्यं शुश्रूषितभार्गवम् । जामदग्न्यादधिगतास्त्ररहस्यमित्यर्थः । राधेयं राधासुतं कर्णम् ॥"स्त्रीभ्यो ढक्" ॥ निरीक्ष्य मृत्योरप्यसंस्तुतेष्वपरिचितेषु ॥ "संस्तवः स्यात्परिचयः" इत्यमरः ॥ भयेषु प्रसभं पक्षपातः परिचयो जायेत । मृत्युरप्यस्माद्बिभीयात्किमुतान्य इति भावः ॥ संभावनायां लिङ् । अत्र जनिक्रियापेक्षया समानकर्तृकत्वाभावेऽपि पक्षपातक्रियापेक्षया तत्संभवान्निरीक्ष्येति ल्यब्निर्देशः । "समर्थनीयप्रधानोपसर्जनभावस्त्वप्रयोजकः" इति व्यक्तिविवेककारः । अत्र भयसंबन्धरहितस्य मृत्योर्भयसंबन्धाभिधानादसंबन्धे संबन्धरूपातिशयोक्तिरलंकारः ॥

अन्वयार्थः—(**संरम्भनिरस्तधैर्य्यम्**) क्रोध से छुड़ा दिया है धैर्य्य जिसने ऐसे, (**आराधितजामदग्न्यम्**) आराधना की है परशुराम की जिसने ऐसे (**राधेयम्**) राधा-पुत्र [कर्ण को] (**निरीक्ष्य**) देख कर (**मृत्योः अपि**) यम का भी (**असंस्तुतेषु भयेषु**) भय से अपरिचितों में (**प्रसभम्**) हठपूर्वक (**पक्षपातः**) परिचय (**जायेत**) हो जायेगा ।

जिन्होंने आज तक भय को नहीं जाना उन का भी, क्रोध से दूसरों के धैर्य्य को छुड़ा देने वाले परशुराम के शिष्य कर्ण को देख कर, जबरन भय से परिचय हो जायेगा ।

21. On seeing the son of Rádhā (Karṇa) who propitiated Jāmadagnya (for acquiring the know ledge of missiles) and who by is vehemence completely shakes off the courage (of his adversaries), even the God of death will be forcibly led to acquaint himself with fear unknown to him before.

Sl. 21. संरम्भ—vehement anger, impetuosity. धैर्यं properly unruffled state of the mind under any circumstances; hence fortitude, courage. आराधितo—आराधित: served विद्यार्थं जामदग्न्यो येन. राधेयं—Karṇa. Karṇa was born of Kunti when she was yet a virgin residing at her father's house (being begotten on her by Surya). Afraid of the taunts of her relatives and public scandal she threw the child into the Yamunā where he was found by Adhiratha, the charioteer of Dhṛtarāṣṭra. He was brought up as their own son by the charioteer and his wife Rādhā, and thus came to be called Rādheya, Sûtaputra &c. With a desire to attain proficiency in the science of weapons and missiles he, calling himself a Brāhmaṇa boy, went to Paraśu-rāma and learnt that art from him. As a warrior he held equal rank with Arjuna, may in some repects he was the latter's superior and hence Dharma alway feared him.[1] And Arjuna could kill him in the great war that followed as he laboured under some disadvantages, such as the curse of his Guru (that he would forget the charm of Brahmāstra when opposed by a warrior of equal rank), the curse of a Brāhmaṇa whose cow he had unwittingly slain (that the earth would swallow up the wheel of his chariot in the hour of trial) &c.

असंस्तुतेषु—To which he is not used, not known to him, novel प्रसभं—प्रगता सभा विचारो यस्मिन्कर्मणि lit. thoughtlessly; at once; hence also violently; forcibly. Probably सभ is originally सह to endure and प्रसभं may have the same meaning as प्रसक्त पक्षपात:—a strong liking for. See. Malli.'s remarks.

अथानन्तरं करणीयमागमनप्रयोजनं च युग्मेनाह—

यया समासादितसाधनेन सुदुश्चरामाचरता तपस्याम् ।
एते दुरापं समवाप्य वीर्यमुन्मूलितारः कपिकेतन ॥ २२ ॥

अन्वयः—यया सुदुस्तरां तपस्याम् आचरता (अतएव) समासादित-साधनेन कपिकेतनेन (अन्यस्य) दुरापं वीर्यं समासाद्य एते उन्मूलितारः ॥ २२ ॥

ययेति ॥ यया विद्यया ॥ करणेन ॥ सुदुश्चरामतिदुष्करां तपस्यां तपश्चर्याम् ॥ "कर्मणो रोमन्थतपोभ्यां वर्तिचरोः" इति क्यङ् । "अ प्रत्ययात्" इति स्त्रिया-मप्रत्ययः ॥ आचरता । पशुपतिं प्रति तपः कुर्वतेत्यर्थः । अतएव समासादितं साधनं पाशुपतास्त्ररूपं येन तेन । कपिर्हनुमान्केतनं चिह्नं यस्य तेन । अर्जुने-नेत्यर्थः । दुरापमन्यस्य दुर्लभं वीर्यं तेजः समवाप्य । एते पूर्वोक्ता भीष्मादय उन्मूलितार उन्मूलयिष्यन्ते ॥ उन्मूलयतेर्ण्यन्तात्कर्मणि लुट् । अत्र चिण्वदिडा-गमेऽपि तस्य "असिद्धवदत्राभात्" इत्यसिद्धत्वात् "णेरनिटि" इति णिलोपः । तन्निमित्तस्यैव "अनिटि" इति निषेधात् । उक्तं च—"इत्चिण्वद्वृद्धिर्युक्च हन्तेश्च घत्वं दीर्घश्चोक्तो यो मितां वा चिणीति । इट् चासिद्धस्तेन मे लुप्यते णिर्नित्य-श्चायं वल्निमित्तो विघाती ॥" इति ॥

अन्वयार्थः—(यया) जिससे, (सुदुश्चराम्) कठिनाई से की जाने योग्य (तपस्याम्) तपस्या को (आचरता) करते हुए [अत एव] (समासादित-साधनेन) प्राप्त किया है साधन जिस ने ऐसे (कपिकेतनेन) हनुमान है चिन्ह जिसका ऐसे [अर्जुन] से (दुरापम्) [औरों के लिए] दुर्लभ (वीर्यम्) तेज को (समासाद्य) प्राप्त करके (एते) ये (उन्मूलितारः) समाप्त किये जायेंगे.....

जिस वक्ष्यमाण (विद्या) से कठोर तपस्या करके साधन-प्राप्त अर्जुन, असामान्य बल को प्राप्त करके इन पूर्वोक्त कर्णादि को नष्ट करेंगे...

22-23. O King, worthy of the bestowal (of a favour), I have come to impart the knowledge of the mystic lore of great efficacy by virtue of which, Aruna (it. the monkey-bannered one) having practised austerities very difficult to perform and acquired thereby the means for (it the Pāśupatā missile) and extraordinary (lit. difficult to obtain) valour, will uproot these (Bhīshma and others), and which is the means of propitiating deities of mighty power fer the attainment of supreme excellence, as if it were success (incarnate).

Sl. 22. यया—enabled by which. तपश्चर्यां—for the propitiation of Indra and Śiva. ०साधनेन—When Śiva was propitiated he gave him the Pāśupata missile, one of his most powerful weapons. Indra, Varuṇa, Yama and Kubera then came to him and presented him with their own peculiar weapons. See *infra* XVIII. 45 and अथ शशधरमौलेरभ्यनुज्ञामवाप्य त्रिदशपतिपुरोगाः पूर्णकामाय तस्मै । अवितथफलमाशीर्वादमारोपयन्तो विजयिविविधमस्त्रं लोकपाला वितेरुः ॥ 46. see also Intro. Arjuna.

कपिके०—whose emblem or distinguishing mark is the monkey (Hanumat) *i. e.* Arjuna. उन्मूलितारः—1st Fut. pass. of मूल with उद्.

महत्त्वयोगाय महामहिम्नामाराधनीं तां नृप देवतानाम् ।
दातुं प्रदानोचित भूरिधाम्नीमुपागतः सिद्धिमिवास्मि विद्याम् ॥ २३ ॥

अन्वयः—महत्त्वयोगाय महामहिम्नां देवतानाम् आराधनीं भूरिधाम्नीं सिद्धिमिव तां विद्यां (हे) प्रदानोचित नृप ! दातुम् उपागतः अस्मि ॥ २३ ॥

महत्त्वेति ॥ हे नृप ! महत्त्वयोगाय प्रकर्षलाभाय महामहिम्नां महानुभावानां देवतानामिन्द्रादीनाम् । आराध्यतेऽनयेत्याराधनी ताम् । प्रसादयित्रीमित्यर्थः ॥ करणे ल्युट् । ङीप् ॥ भूरिधाम्नीं महाप्रभावाम् ॥ "धाम देशे गृहे रश्मौ स्थाने जन्मप्रभावयोः ।" इति विश्वः ॥ "अन उपधालोपिनोऽन्यतरस्याम्" इति वा ङीप् ॥ विद्यामैन्द्रमन्त्ररूपां सिद्धिं साक्षात्कार्यसिद्धिमिवेति विद्याया अमोघत्वोक्तिः । हे प्रदानोचित दानपात्र! प्रभूतफलभोक्तृत्वादस्य पात्रत्वोक्तिः । दातुमुपागतोऽस्मि ॥

अन्वयार्थः—(**महत्त्वयोगाय**) उत्कर्ष-लाभ के लिए (**महामहिम्नाम्**) महान् महिमाशाली (**देवतानाम्**) देवताओं की (**आराधनीम्**) आराधना की जाती है जिससे ऐसी (**भूरिधाम्नीम्**) बहुत प्रभावयुक्त (**सिद्धिमिव**) साक्षात्-कार्यसिद्धि की भाँति (**तां विद्याम्**) उस [मन्त्र-रूप] विद्या को, (**प्रदानोचित नृप**) हे दान-पात्र राजन् ! (**दातुम्**) देने के लिए (**उपागतः अस्मि**) आया हूँ।

इसी विद्या से उत्कर्ष-प्राप्ति के लिए महामहिमाशाली इन्द्रादि देवताओं की आराधना की जाती है; यह अत्यन्त प्रभावशाली एवं साक्षात् कार्यसिद्धि-जैसी

है। हे राजन् ! आप दान के उपयुक्त पात्र हैं, अतः इस विद्या को देने के लिए मैं यहाँ आया हूँ।

Sl. 23. **महत्त्व०**—महत्त्वेन योगः तस्मै for the attainment of super human power. **महाम०**— महान् महिमा यासां ता महामहिमानः तासां. By अन उपधा०—Pān. IV. 1. 28. and the preceding Sūtra Bah. comps having for their latter members words ending in अन् capable of dropping their अ, optionally take ई or आ in the *fem*; so महामहिम्नी and—महिमा also भूरि०—भूरि धाम power, efficacy यस्यास्ताम्. प्रदा०—प्रदानस्य उचितः प्र०तः *Cf.* गृहाणेमां मया प्रोक्तां सिद्धिं मूर्तिमतीमिव । विद्यां प्रतिस्मृतिं नाम प्रपन्नाय ब्रवीमि ते ॥ Van. P. Ch. 37.

इत्युक्तवन्तं व्रज साधयेति प्रमाणयन्वाक्यमजातशत्रोः।
प्रसेदिवांसं तमुपाससाद वसन्निवान्ते विनयेन जिष्णुः ॥ २४ ॥

अन्वयः—इति उक्तवन्तं प्रसेदिवांसं तं (मुनिं) 'व्रज साधय' इति अजातशत्रोः वाक्यं प्रमाणयन् जिष्णुः अन्ते वसन् इव विनयेन उपाससाद ॥२४॥

इतीति ॥ इत्युक्तवन्तं प्रसेदिवांसं प्रसन्नम् ॥ "भाषायां सदवसश्रुवः" इति क्वसुः ॥ तं मुनिं जिष्णुर्जयनशीलोऽर्जुनः ॥ ग्लाजिस्थश्च—" इति ग्स्नुप्रत्ययः ॥ व्रज साधयानुतिष्ठेत्येवंरूपम्। अजातशत्रोर्धर्मराजस्य। स्वयमविद्वेषणशीलत्वादियं संज्ञा। वाक्यं प्रमाणयन्। तदादिष्टः सन्नित्यर्थः। अन्ते वसंश्छात्र इव ॥ "छात्रान्तेवासिनौ शिष्ये" इत्यमरः ॥ विनयेनानौद्धत्येनोपाससाद समीपं प्राप ॥

अन्वयार्थः—(इति उक्तवन्तम्) इस प्रकार कहा है जिस ने ऐसे **(प्रसेदिवांसम्)** प्रसन्न **(तं)** उस [मुनि] के, **('व्रज साधय' इति)** 'जाओ, सिद्धि प्राप्त करो' इस प्रकार **(अजातशत्रोः)** नहीं उत्पन्न हुआ है शत्रु जिसका ऐसे [युधिष्टिर] के **(वाक्यम्)** वाक्य को **(प्रमाणयन्)** प्रमाण मानता हुआ **(जिष्णुः)** विजय है स्वभाव जिस का ऐसा [अर्जुन] **(अन्ते वसन् इव)** शिष्य की भाँति **(विनयेन)** नम्र भाव से **(उपाससाद)** समीप प्राप्त हुआ।

विजयशील अर्जुन, 'जाओ, सिद्धि प्राप्त करो', अजातशत्रु युधिष्ठिर के इस वाक्य को प्रमाण मानता हुआ शिष्य की तरह नम्र भाव से, विद्या-विषयक बात कहने वाले प्रसन्न-वदन मुनि व्यास के पास आया।

24. Obeying the words--Go, act up to his instructions--of Dharma, who had none for his enemy, Jishṇu (Arjuna) approached with humility like a pupil the sage, who had thus declared his purpose and who was graciously disposed.

Sl. 24. प्रसेदिवांसम्—प्रसेदिवस् Perf. p. of सद् with प्र. अजात॰ —अजात: शत्रुर्यस्य who looked upon no one as an enemy; or अजात शत्रु: who never became the enemy of any one. जिष्णु:—habitually conquering, who always came off victorious fr. जि+स्नु which is also added to ग्लै (ग्लास्नु) and स्था (स्थास्नु) See Malli.

निर्याय विद्याथ दिनादिरम्याद्बिम्बादिवार्कस्य मुखान्महर्षेः ।
पार्थाननं वह्निकणावदाता दीप्तिः स्फुरत्पद्ममिवाभिपेदे ॥ २५ ॥

अन्वय:—अथ दिनादिरम्यात् अर्कस्य बिंबात् दीप्ति: स्फुरत्पद्मम् इव वह्नि-कणावदाता विद्या महर्षे: मुखात् निर्याय पार्थाननम् अभिपेदे ॥ २५ ॥

निर्यायेति ॥ अथ वह्निगणावदाता स्फुलिङ्गवदुज्ज्वला । देवतासान्निध्यादिति भावः । विद्येन्द्रमन्त्ररूपा । दिनादिरम्यादर्कस्य प्रभातभास्करस्य बिम्बादिव महर्षेर्व्यासस्य मुखान्निर्याय निर्गत्य ॥ समासेऽनञ्पूर्वे क्त्वो ल्यप् । दीप्तिरर्कदीधितिः स्फुरद्विकसत्पद्ममिव । पार्थाननमर्जुनस्य मुखमभिपेदे प्रविष्टा ।

अन्वयार्थ:—(**अथ**) इसके बाद (**दिनादिरम्यात्**) दिन के आरम्भ में होने से सुन्दर (**अर्कस्य बिम्बात्**) सूर्य के बिम्ब से (**दीप्तिः**) सूर्य-रश्मि (**स्फुरत्पद्ममिव**) खिले हुए कमल की तरह (**वह्निकणावदाता**) अग्नि-स्फुलिंग की तरह उज्ज्वल (**विद्या**) मन्त्रविद्या (**महर्षे:**) महर्षि के (**मुखात्**) मुख से (**निर्याय**) निकल कर (**पार्थाननम्**) अर्जुन के मुख में (**अभिपेदे**) प्रविष्ट हुई ।

तदनन्तर प्रातःकालीन सूर्य के सुन्दर बिम्ब से निकलकर किरण जिस प्रकार खिले हुए कमल में प्रविष्ट होती है उसी प्रकार आग की चिनगारी की तरह उज्ज्वल वह मन्त्रविद्या महर्षि व्यास के मुख से निकलकर अर्जुन के मुख में प्रविष्ट हुई ।

25. Then the lore (Mantra having Indra for its deity), bright like a spark of fire (on account of the presence of its deity), issuing from the mouth of the great sage passed to that

of Arjuna as spreading lustre does from the sun's disc, attractive in the early morning, to the opening lotus.

Sl. 25. विद्या—*i. e.* here a *Mantra* which has its deity and which being repeated for a stated number of times with the deity duly worshipped proves efficacious and the deity remains subservient to the will of the *Sādhaka*, वह्निकल्पा०—As Vyāsa himself uttered the words of the *Mantra* and made Arjuna request them there was a flash of light on account of the presence of its deity (here Indra). दिनादिरम्याद्—दिनस्यादिस्तत्र रम्यं तस्मात्. The sage being the repository of dazzling Brāhmāṇic lustre his face is compared to the disc of the morning sun, Arjuna's face brightening with hope is aptly compared to a blooming lotus. According to the Van. Vyāsa imparted the Vidyǎ to Dharma, who in his turn communicated it to Arjuna at a suitable time afterwards. See Intro., extracts from the Van. P.

योगं च तं योग्यतमाय तस्मै तपःप्रभावाद्वितताार सद्यः ।
येनास्य तत्त्वेषु कृतेऽवभासे समुन्मिमीलेव चिराय चक्षुः ॥ २६ ॥

अन्वयः—स योग्यतमाय तस्मै तं योगं च तपःप्रभावात् सद्यः विततार; येन तत्त्वेषु अवभासे कृते अस्य चक्षुः चिराय समुन्मिमीलेव ॥ २६ ॥

योगं चेति ॥ स योग्यतमायार्हतमाय तस्मै पार्थाय तं वक्ष्यमाणमहिमान योगं ध्यानं विधिं च ॥ "योगः संनहनोपायध्यानसंगतियुक्तिषु ।" इत्यमरः ॥ तपःप्रभावात्सद्यो विततार ददौ । चिरकालप्राप्यमपीति भावः । येन योगेन तत्त्वेषु प्रकृतिमहदादिषु । तथा च । मूलप्रकृतिर्महानहंकारो मनश्च पञ्च तन्मात्राणि पञ्च बुद्धीन्द्रियाणि पञ्च कर्मेन्द्रियाणि पञ्च महाभूतानीति चतुर्विंशति तत्त्वानि । तत्रावभासे साक्षात्कारे कृते सत्यस्यार्जुनस्य चक्षुरक्षि चिराय समुन्मिमीलेवोन्मिषितमिवेत्युत्प्रेक्षा । तदा तस्य कोऽपि महानखिलाज्ञानभञ्जनस्तत्त्वावभासश्चिरादन्धस्य दृष्टिलाभ इवाभवदिति भावः ॥

अन्वयार्थः—(च) और (सः) उसने (योग्यतमाय) योग्यतम (तस्मै) उस [अर्जुन] को (तं योगम्) उस ध्यान तथा विधि को (तपःप्रभावात्) तप के

प्रभाव से (सद्यः) तुरन्त (वितितार) दे दिया, (येन) जिस के द्वारा (तत्त्वेषु) [मूलप्रकृति-महत् अहंकार आदि] तत्त्वों का (अवभाते कृते) साक्षात्कार कर लेने पर (अस्य चक्षुः) इस [अर्जुन] की दृष्टि (चिराय सद्युन्मिमीलेव) मानो चिरकालोपरान्त खुली हो।

व्यास मुनि ने अपने तप के प्रभाव से तुरन्त उस ध्यान एवं सिद्धि को, योग्यतम शिष्य अर्जुन को दे दिया। इस सिद्धि से अर्जुन को चौबीसों तत्त्वों के यथार्थ स्वरूप का साक्षात्कार हुआ और उसे ऐसा प्रतीत हुआ मानो उसकी दृष्टि बहुत समयोपरान्त खुली हो।

26. And by the power of his penance he (the sage), at the very moment (without the necessary time for practice) imparted to him, the fittest recipient, the powers of contemplation (the knowledge and power attained when perfection in yoga is reached) by which he being enlightened as to the real nature of the cosmic principles his eye seemed to be opened after a long time (of ignorance).

Sl. 26. योगं—Yoga is properly contemplation or concentration of the mind on one object it eing drawn away from others and its functions suspended. When perfection is reached in contemplation one gets superhuman power. Malli. says ध्यानविधिं च *i.e.* the practical part of it for the development of will-power. Vyāsa at once enabled Arjuna to acquire that perfection in the practice of Yoga which others require a long course of contemplation to do.

तत्त्वेषु—Here Malli. refers to the 24 principles or evolutes of the Sāṇkhyas which are also recognised by the Yoga. According to the Sānkhyas there are two primary principles, Prakṛti and Purusha or Soul. Soul is neither a product nor productive, Prakṛti or nature, also called Mulaprakṛti is Pradhāna (chief) from its being the root of seven principles produced from it which are also productive in their turn. Prakṛti gives rise to Mahat or Intellect, from it springs Ahamkāra or Egotism which in its turn gives rise to the five Tanmāntras or subtle rudiments. These again produce 16 others, *viz*. the five organs of parception, the five organs of action, with the mind (as the eleventh) and the five elements. A correct knowledge of these 25 principles leads to *Moksha*. *Cf.* पञ्चविंशतितत्त्वज्ञो यत्र तत्राश्रमे वसेत् । जटी मुण्डी शिखी वापि मुच्यते नात्र संशयः ॥ quoted by Gauḍapāda in his Bhāshsya on Sān. Kār. I.

अवभास—manifestation of the right knowledge of, inspiration.

आकारमाशंसितभूरिलाभं दधानमन्तःकरणानुरूपम् ।
नियोजयिष्यन्विजयोदये तं तपः समाधौ मुनिरित्युवाच ॥ २७ ॥

अन्वयः—आशंसितभूरिलाभम् अन्तःकरणनुरूपम् आकारं दधानं तं मुनिः विजयोदये तपःसमाधौ नियोजयिष्यन् इति उवाच ॥ २७ ॥

आकारमिति ॥ आशंसित आख्यातो भूरिलाभोऽनेकश्रेयः प्राप्तिर्येन तं तथोक्तम् । महाभाग्यसूचकमित्यर्थः । अन्तःकरणशब्देन तद्वृत्तिरुत्साहो लक्ष्यते तदनुरूपं तदनुकूलम् । उत्साहानुगुणव्यापारक्षममित्यर्थः । आकारं मूर्ति दधानं तमजुनं मुनिर्विजयोदये विजयफलके तपःसमाधौ तपोनियमे । "समाधिर्नियमे ध्याने नीवाके च समर्थने" इति विश्वः ।। नियोजयिष्यन् । नियोजयितुमिच्छन्नित्यर्थः ॥ "लृट् शेषे च" इति लृट् । "लृटः सद्वा" इति सत्प्रत्ययः । इति वक्ष्यमाणमुवाच ॥

अन्वयार्थः—(**आशंसितभूरिलाभम्**) कहा है अनेक प्रकार की कल्याण-प्राप्ति को जिसने ऐसी (**अन्तःकरणानुरूपम्**) अन्तःकरण के अनुकूल (**आकारं दधानम्**) आकृति को धारण किये हुए (**तम्**) उस [अर्जुन] को (**मुनिः**) मुनि (**विजयोदये**) विजय का है उदय जिससे उस (**तपःसमाधौ**) तपस्या एवं नियम में (**नियोजयिष्यन्**) नियुक्त करना चाहते हुए (**इति**) इस प्रकार (**उवाच**) बोले ।

चित्त के उत्साह के अनुरूप अर्जुन की आकृति, होने वाले कल्याण की सूचना दे रही थी । ऐसे अर्जुन को विजय प्राप्त कराने वाले तप और नियमों में नियुक्त करते हुए मुनि व्यास बोले—

27. The sage, wishing to direct him to the practice of penance for the attainment of success, thus addressed him whose bodily appearance foreshadowed the acquisition of great

(or varied) success and which was in keeping with the high aspirations (enthusiasm) of his mind.

Sl. 27. आशंसित०—आशंसितः (indicated, foreshadowed) भूरिः (great), भूरीणां (of many things) वा लाभः येन. अतःकरण—has here the seconday sense of 'energy, the high aspiration of his mind.' रूपस्य सदृशः योग्यो वा अनुरूपः; अन्त०स्यानुरूपः तम्. आकार—General appearance, expression of face. विजयो०—विजयस्योदयो यस्मात्. नियोज०—Nom. sing. of the Fut. par. of युज् with नि, Cau.

अनेन योगेन विवृद्धतेजा निजां परस्मै पदवीमयच्छन् ।

समाचराचारमुपात्तशस्त्रो जपोपवासाभिषवैर्मुनीनाम् ॥ २८ ॥

अन्वयः—अनेन योगेन विवृद्धतेजाः निजां पदवीं परस्मै अयच्छन् उपात्तशस्त्रः (सन्) जपोपवासाभिषवैः मुनीनाम् आचारं समाचर ॥ २८ ॥

अनेनेति ॥ अनेन स्वोपदिष्टेन योगेन विवृद्धतेजा निजां पदवीं परस्मै अयच्छन् । परस्य प्रवेशमयच्छन्नित्यर्थः । उपात्तशस्त्रो निगृहीतायुधः सन् । हे अर्जुन ! जपोपवासाभिषवैः स्वाध्यायानशनस्नानैर्मुनीनामाचारं समाचरानुतिष्ठ ॥

अन्वयार्थः—(**अनेन योगेन**) इस योग से (**विवृद्धतेजाः**) बढ़ गया है तेज जिसका ऐसे (**निजां पदवीम्**) अपने स्थान को (**परस्मै**) दूसरे के लिए (**अयच्छन्**) न देते हुए (**उपात्तशस्त्रः**) [सन्] लिये हैं शस्त्र जिसने ऐसे हुए हुए [तुम] (**जपोपवासाभिषवैः**) जाप, उपवास तथा स्नानों से (**मुनीनाम् आचारम्**) मुनियों की वृत्ति को (**समाचर**) करो ।

"...इस योग के प्रभाव से अधिक तेजस्वी तुम, अपने तपस्या के स्थान में अन्य किसी को न आने दो । एवं अपने शस्त्रों सहित मन्त्रजाप, उपवास तथा स्नान करते हुए तपस्वियों की भाँति आचरण करो...

28. With your power increased by this yoga, taking with you your weapons and not allowing any one to approach you, lead the life of ascetics by (regular) bathing, muttering prayers and observing fasts.

Sl. 28. विवृद्ध०—विवृद्धं (greatly increased) तेजः यस्य, पदवीं—the place where you will practise penance; allowing no one to enter the place. पद्यते अनया इति पदवी fr. पद्+अवि by पदडिभ्यामविः; so अटवी fr. अट्. उपात्त०—उपात्तानि (p. p. of दा with उप and आ) हस्तगतानि येन. अभिषव:—a bath.

क्षेत्रविशेषे तपःसिद्धिरित्याशयेन तं निदर्शयन्नाह—

करिष्यसे यत्र सुदुश्चराणि प्रसत्तये गोत्रभिदस्तपांसि ।

शिलोच्चयं चारुशिलोच्चयं तमेष क्षणान्नेष्यति गुह्यकस्त्वाम् ॥ २९ ॥

अन्वयः—यत्र गोत्रभिदः प्रसत्तये सुदुश्चराणि तपांसि करिष्यसे तं चारुशिलोच्चयं त्वाम् एष गुह्यकः क्षणात् नेष्यति ॥२९॥

करिष्यस इति ॥ यत्र शिलोच्चये गोत्रभिद इन्द्रस्य प्रसत्तये प्रसादाय सुदुश्चराणि तपांसि करिष्यसे । चारुशिलोच्चयं रम्यशिखरं तं शिलोच्चयं गिरिमिन्द्रकीलम् ॥ "अद्रिगोत्रगिरिग्रावाचलशैलशिलोच्चयाः ।" इत्यमरः ॥ त्वामेष गुह्यको यक्षः । अनन्तरमेवास्य पुरःप्रादुर्भावादेष इति निर्देशः । क्षणान्नेष्यति प्रापयिष्यति ॥

अन्वयार्थः—(**यत्र**) जहाँ (**गोत्रभिदः**) इन्द्र की (**प्रसत्तये**) प्रसन्नता के लिए (**सुदुश्चराणि**) अत्यन्त कठिनता से आचरण किये जा सकने योग्य (**तपांसि**) तपों को (**करिष्यसे**) तुम करोगे, (**तं**) उस (**चारुशिलोच्चयम्**) सुन्दर हैं चोटियाँ जिस की ऐसे [पर्वत] को (**त्वाम्**) तुम्हें (**एष गुह्यकः**) यह यक्ष (**क्षणात्**) क्षण भर में (**नेष्यति**) प्राप्त करायेगा ।

इन्द्र को प्रसन्न करने के लिए जिस स्थान पर तुम्हें अतिकठोर तप करना है उस सुन्दर शिखरवाले पर्वत पर यह (वक्ष्यमाण) यक्ष तुम्हें क्षण-भर में पहुँचा देगा ।

29. This Yaksha will take you, in an instant, to the mountain with beautiful peaks, where you have to practise a penance, difficult to perform, for the propitiation of Indra the splitter of mountains)

Sl. 29. गोत्रभिदः—गोत्र mountain fr. गो the earth त्र which protects or holds in place (गां त्रायते इति); गोत्रं भिनत्तीति the cleaver of (the wings of) mountains. प्रसत्ति—pleasing, propitiation. शिलोच्चयं—शिलाभिः उच्चीयते a mountain. चारु०—चारवः

शिलोच्चयाः (peaks शिलानामुच्चयाः) बत्र. गुह्यकः—a kind of demigod; the Guhyakas are, like Yakshas, the servants of Kubera.

इति ब्रुवाणेन महेन्द्रसूनुं महर्षिणा तेन तिरोबभूवे ।
तं राजराजानुचरोऽस्य साक्षात्प्रदेशमादेशमिवाधितष्ठौ ॥ ३० ॥

अन्वयः—इति महेन्द्रसूनुं ब्रुवाणेन तेन महर्षिणा तिरोबभूवे । राजराजानुचरः मुनेः साक्षात् आदेशम् इव तं प्रदेशम् अधितष्ठौ (च) ॥ ३० ॥

इतीति ॥ इतीत्थं महेन्द्रसूनुमर्जुनं ब्रुवाणेनोक्तवता ॥ "वर्तमानसामीप्ये" इति भूते वर्तमानवत्प्रत्ययस्तिरोधानस्याविलम्बसूचनार्थः ॥ तेन महर्षिणा व्यासेन तिरोबभूवेऽन्तर्दधे ॥ भावे लिट् । राजराजो यक्षराजः ॥ "राजा प्रभौ नृपे चन्द्रे यक्षे क्षत्रियशक्रयोः ।" इति विश्वः ॥ तस्यानुचरः पूर्वोक्तयक्षोऽस्य मुनेरादेशं साक्षादिव प्रदेशमर्जुनाधिष्ठितस्थानमधितष्ठौ । प्राप्त इत्यर्थः ॥ "स्थादिष्वभ्यासेन चाभ्यासस्य" इति षत्वम् ॥

अन्वयार्थः—(**इति**) इस प्रकार (**महेन्द्रसूनुम्**) इन्द्र पुत्र [अर्जुन] को (**ब्रुवाणेन**) कहते हुए (**तेन महर्षिणा**) उस महर्षि के द्वारा (**तिरोबभूवे**) अन्तर्धान हुआ गया । [और] (**राजराजानुचरः**) यक्षराज का सेवक (**मुनेः**) मुनि के (**साक्षात् आदेशमिव**) साक्षात् आदेश की भाँति (**तं प्रदेशम्**) उस स्थान पर (**अधितिष्ठौ**) प्राप्त हुआ ।

अर्जुन से उपर्युक्त बात कहकर मुनि व्यास अन्तर्धान हो गये और उनकी साक्षात् आज्ञा की तरह वह यक्ष वहाँ प्रकट हुआ ।

30. The great sage, just as he thus addressed the son of Mahendra (Arjuna), disappeared, and the servant of Kubera, as if his injunction incarnate, stood on the spot.

Sl. 30. ब्रुवाणेन—when he had just spoken thus. See Malli तिरो॰—Pass. Perf. of भू with तिरस्. राजराजः—Kubera; राज्ञां यक्षाणां राजा.

कृतानतिर्व्याहृतसान्त्ववादे जातस्पृहः पुण्यजनः स जिष्णौ ।
इयाय सख्याविव संप्रसादं विश्वासयत्याशु सतां हि योगः ॥ ३१ ॥

अन्वयः—स कृतानतिः पुण्यजनः व्याहृतसान्त्ववादे जिष्णौ जातस्पृहः

(सन्) सख्यौ इव संप्रसादम् इयाय । तथाहि सतां योगः आशु विश्वासयति ॥ ३१ ॥

कृतेति ॥ स पुण्यजनो यक्षः कृतानतिः कृतप्रणामः । व्याहृत उक्तः सान्त्ववादः प्रियवचनं येन तस्मिन ॥ "व्याहार उक्तिर्लपितम्" इत्यमरः ॥ जिष्णावर्जुने जातस्पृहो जाता स्पृहाकाङ्क्षा यस्य स जातानुरागः सन् । सख्यौ सुहृदीव । "अथ मित्रं सखा सुहृत्" इत्यमरः ॥ संप्रसादं विश्रम्भमियाय प्राप । तथाहि । सतां साधूनां योगः संगतिराशु विश्वासयति हि विश्वासं जनयति । सामान्येन विशेषसमर्थनरूपोऽर्थान्तिरन्यासः ॥

अन्वयार्थः—(**सः**) वह [यक्ष] (**कृतानतिः**) किया है प्रणाम जिसने ऐसा (**पुण्यजनः**) यक्ष, (**व्याहृतसान्त्ववादे**) कहा है प्रियवचन जिसने ऐसे (**जिष्णौ** जयशील [अर्जुन] में (**जातस्पृहः**) उत्पन्न हो गया है अनुराग जिसका ऐसा [सन्] हुआ-हुआ (**सख्यौ इव**) सुहृद् की भांति (**सप्रंसादम्**) विश्वास को (**इयाय**) प्राप्त हुआ । (**हि**) क्योंकि (**सतां योगः**) साधुजनों की संगति (**आशु**) शीघ्र (**विश्वासयति**) विश्वास को उत्पन्न करती है ।

यक्ष ने उपस्थित होकर प्रणाम किया । वह प्रियभाषी अर्जुन में अनुरक्त हुआ २ मित्र की भांति विश्वस्त हो गया । ऐसा भला क्यों न हो, सज्जनों की संगति तुरन्त विश्वास उत्पन्न करती है ।

31. That Yaksha, on making his obeisance, found himself drawn to Jishnu who addressed sweet words (of welcome) to him and felt confidence in him as in a friend: for the company of good men quickly produces confidence.

Sl. 31. पुण्यजनः— पुण्यश्चासौ जनश्च । अथ पुण्यजनो यक्षे राक्षसे सज्जनेपि च । कृता०—कृता आनतिः lit bending, a bow येन सः सान्त्वस्य वादः सान्त्ववादः agreeable words. संप्रसादः—pleasure; or clearness of the mind (its being free from suspicion or misgivings); hence confidence.

अथोष्णभासेव सुमेरुकुञ्जान्विहीयमानानुदयाय तेन ।
बृहद्द्युतीन्दुःसहतात्मलाभं तमः शनैः पाण्डुसुतान्प्रपेदे ॥ ३२ ॥

अन्वयः—अथ उष्णभासा उदयाय विहीयमानान् बृहद्द्युतीन् सुमेरुकुञ्जान्

तमः इव तेन उदयाय विहीयमानान् बृहद्द्युतीन् पाण्डुसुतान् दुःखकृतात्मलाभ तमः शनैः प्रपेदे ॥ ३२ ॥

अथेति ॥ अथोष्णभासा सूर्येणोदयाय पुनरुद्गमाय विहीयमानांस्त्यज्यमानानिति तमःप्राप्तिकारणोक्तिः । बृहद्द्युतीन् । सौवर्णत्वाद्दीप्यमानानित्यर्थः । इति तमसः संकोचकारणोक्तिः सुमेरुकुञ्जानिव । अत्र सुमेरुग्रहणं कुञ्जानां सौवर्णत्वद्योतनार्थम् । तेनार्जुनेनोदयाय श्रेयसे विहीयमानान्बृहद्द्युतीननेकबुद्धिप्रकाशान् । पूर्ववद्विशेषणद्वयस्य प्रयोजनमनुसंधेयम् ॥ पाण्डुसुतान् । चतुर इति शेषः । दुःखेन कृच्छ्रेण कृत उपपादित आत्मलाभ उत्पत्तिर्यस्य तत्तथोक्तम् । तेषां विवेकित्वात्कथंचिल्लब्धोदयमित्यर्थः । तमः शोकोऽन्धकारश्च ॥ "तमोऽन्धकारे स्वर्भानौ तमशोके गुणान्तरे ।" इत्युभयत्रापि विश्वः ॥ शनैर्मन्दं प्रपेदे । तेषां विवेकित्वाद्भीतमिवेति भावः ॥ अत्र तमःशब्दस्य श्लिष्टत्वाच्छ्लेषानुप्राणितेयमुपमा ॥

अन्वयार्थः—(**अथ**) इसके बाद (**उष्णभासा**) सूर्य के द्वारा (**उदयाय**) उदय होने के लिए (**विहीयमानान्**) छोड़े जाते हुए (**बृहद् द्युतीन्**) बहुत बड़ी है चमक जिनकी ऐसे (**सुमेरुकुञ्जान्**) मेरु-पर्वत के लता-वितानों को (**तमः इव**) अन्धकार की भांति (**तेन**) उस अर्जुन के द्वारा (**उदयाय**) कल्याण के लिए (**विहीयमानान्**) छोड़े जाते हुए (**बृहद् द्युतीन्**) अनेक विध है बुद्धि-चातुर्य जिन का ऐसे (**पाण्डुसुतान्**) पाण्डु-पुत्रों को (**दुःखकृतात्मलाभम्**) कठिनाई से प्राप्त किया है अपनी स्थिति को जिसने ऐसा (**तमः**) दुःख (**शनैः**) धीरे से (**प्रपेदे**) प्राप्त हुआ ।

जिस प्रकार अत्यधिक चमकीले स्वर्ण पर्वत के लतावितानों को फिर से उदय होने के लिए (सायंकाल) सूर्य छोड़ देता है और अन्धकार धीरे से व्याप्त कर लेता है उसी प्रकार अर्जुन से, विजयलाभ के निमित्त छोड़े जाते हुए अत्यन्त चतुर पाण्डवों को कठिनाई से धीरे-धीरे शोक ने आ घेरा ।

(जिस प्रकार अत्यन्त प्रकाशित होने से लतावितानों में अन्धकार कठिनाई से पहुँचा उसी प्रकार बुद्धि-चातुर्य के कारण प्रसन्न रहने वाले पाण्डवों में भी शोक ने कठिनाई से ही अपनी सत्ता बनायी ।)

32. Then like darkness appearing with difficulty and gradually overtaking the arbours of Sumeru emitting great lustre, when being left by the sun to rise, mental gloom (sorrow) which took its rise with difficulty slowly came over the sons of Paṇḍu, of great brilliance, when about to be left by him for acquiring (greater) prosperity.

Sl. 32. उष्णभासा—उष्णा भा यस्य स उष्णभाः—the sun, तेन. सुमेरु—'मेरुः सुमेरुर्हेमाद्री रत्नसानुः सुरालयः ।' Amara. The mountain of gold, gem-peaked, which is in the centre of all *dwipas*, and round which all heavenly bodies revolve. *Cf.* Kālikā P. मेरुर्मध्ये भुवनानां च भर्ता &c.; and Vishṇu P: II. 2. तस्यापि मेरुर्मैत्रेय मध्ये कनकपर्वतः ।। चतुरशीतिसाहस्रो योजनैरस्य चोच्छ्रयः । भूपद्मस्यास्य शैलोसौ कर्णिकाकारसंस्थितः ।। 7, 8. कुञ्ज—*m. n.* a place covered with creepers, an arbour. 'निकुञ्जकुञ्जौ वा क्लीबे लतादिपिहितोदरे ।'Amara.

विहीयमानं—Pre. p. of the pass. of हा with वि to abandan. उदयाय—(1) that he should rise; (2) prosperity, glory. बृह०—बृहती द्युतिर्येषाम्. दुःख—This is explained in the com. तमः—Here the word तमः is *shishṭa* (paronomastic); (2) sorrow (that which clouds the mind).

असंशयालोचितकार्यनुन्नः प्रेम्णा समानीय विभज्यमानः ।
तुल्याद्विभागादिव तन्मनोभिर्दुःखातिभारोऽपि लघुः स मेने ।। ३३ ।।

अन्वयः—असंशयालोचितकार्यनुन्नः (तथापि) प्रेम्णा समानीय विभज्यमानः स दुःखातिभारोपि तन्मनोभिः तुल्यात् विभागात् इव लघुः मेने ।। ३३ ।।

असंशयेति ।। असंशयमसंदिग्धं यथा तथालोचितं विवेचितं यत्कार्यं तेन नुन्नो निरस्त इति लघुत्वहेतूक्तिः ।। "नुदविदोन्दत्राघ्राह्रीभ्योऽन्यतरस्याम्" इति निष्ठानत्वम् ।। कायगौरवमालोच्य निरस्त इत्यर्थः । तथापि प्रेम्णा भ्रातृवात्सल्येन ।। कर्त्रा ।। समानीय पुनराकृष्य विभज्यमानः समशोकभागी क्रियमाणः । तुल्येन प्रेम्णा तुल्यदुःखत्वं भवतीति भावः । स पूर्वोक्तो दुःखमेवातिभारोऽपि । अतिभारभूतमपि दुःखमित्यर्थः । तन्मनोभिस्तेषां चतुर्णां पार्थानां मनोभिस्तुल्याद्विभागादिव । पूर्वोक्तात्प्रेमकृतात्समविभागादिवेत्यर्थः । वस्तुतस्तु विवेकादेवेति भावः । पुनर्विभा-

गग्रहणं तस्य हेतुत्वोत्प्रेक्षार्थमनुवादाददोषः । लघुर्मेनेऽमानि । यथैकोऽनेकधा विभज्य बहुभिरुह्यमानो महानपि भारो लघुर्मन्यते तद्वदित्यर्थः ॥

अन्वयार्थः—(असंशयालोचितकार्यनुन्नः) असंदिग्ध रूप से विवेचना किये गए कार्य से समाप्त हुआ-हुआ [तथापि] तो भी (प्रेम्णा) [भाई के वात्सल्य] प्रेम से (समानीय) पुनः लाकर (विभज्यमानः) विभक्त किया जाता हुआ (सः) वह (दुःखातिभारोऽपि) दुःख का अत्यधिक भार भी (तन्मनोभिः) उन के मनों से (तुल्यात् विभागादिव) मानो बराबर-बराबर विभाग किया हुआ होने से (लघुः मेने) छोटा माना गया ।

सुविवेचित होने से निश्चित साफल्य के कारण वह दुःख समाप्त हुआ । परन्तु भाई के वात्सल्य-प्रेम के कारण पुनः उत्पन्न हुआ वह अत्यधिक दुःख भी मानों चारों में परस्पर बँटा होने से ही उनके मन को अधिक नहीं प्रतीत हुआ ।

33. That excessively heavy burden of grief, though dispelled by the certainty of success in the business determined upon, was brought back by (fraternal) affection and divided so that being equally apportioned as it were, it was thought to be light by their minds (*i. e.* was easily borne).

Sl. 33. असंशया०—अविद्यमानः संशयः यस्मिन्कर्मणि तथथा तथा; now see com.; आलोचित—comprehended, foreseen; about the success of which there was no doubt *i. e.* which was certain. नुन्नः—dispelled by; p. p. p. of नुद् 6 conj.

अथैवं प्रेम्णाकृष्यमाणमपि शोकं विवेको निर्जिगायेत्याह—

धैर्येण विश्वास्यतया महर्षेस्तीव्रादरातिप्रभवाच्च मन्योः ।
वीर्यं च विद्वत्सु सुते मघोनः स तेषु न स्थानमवाप शोकः ॥ ३४ ॥

अन्वयः—धैर्येण, महर्षेः विश्वास्यतया, अरातिप्रभवात् तीव्रात् मन्योश्च मघोनः सुते वीर्यं च विद्वत्सु तेषु (पार्थेषु) स शोकः स्थानं न अवाप ॥ ३४ ॥

धैर्येणेति ॥ धैर्येण तेषां निसर्गतो निर्विकारचित्तत्वेन तथा महर्षेर्व्यासस्य । प्रवर्तकस्येति शेषः । विश्वास्यतया । श्रद्धेयवचनत्वेनेत्यर्थः । अरातिप्रभवादरातिहेतुकात्तीव्राद्दुःसाहन्मन्योः क्रोधाद्धेतोः । तथार्जुनप्रभावपरिज्ञानाच्चेति हेत्वन्तरं विवे-

षण्मुखेनाह—मघोनः सुतेऽर्जुने वीर्यम् ॥ "न लोक—" इत्यादिना षष्ठीप्रतिषेधः ॥ विद्वत्सु ज्ञातवत्स्विति यावत् ॥ "विदेः शतुर्वसुः" इति वैकल्पिको वस्वादेशः ॥ तेषु पार्थेषु स शोकः स्थानं स्थितिं नावाप न प्राप ॥

अन्वयार्थः—(धैर्येण) धैर्य्य के कारण **(महर्षेः विश्वास्यतया)** महर्षि के विश्वासयोग्य होने के कारण, **(च अरातिप्रभवात्)** और शत्रु से है जन्म जिस का ऐसे **(तीव्रात्)** तीव्र **(मन्योः)** क्रोध के कारण **(च मघोनः सुते)** और इन्द्र के पुत्र में **(वीर्यम्)** बल को **(विद्वत्सु)** जानते हुए **(तेषु)** उनमें **(स शोकः)** उस दुःख ने **(स्थानम्)** स्थिति को **(न अवाप)** नहीं प्राप्त किया ।

स्वभावतः वे धैर्य्यशाली थे, महर्षि व्यास में अत्यधिक विश्वास था और शत्रुजन्य तीव्र क्रोध था—तथा अर्जुन के बल का उन्हें ज्ञान था, अतः दुःख को उन पाण्डवों के मन में कोई स्थान नहीं मिला ।

34. On account of their firmness of mind, the confidence the great sage commanded, the intense anger (or worry) caused by (the actions of) their enemies, and the prowess they knew to exist in the son of Indra (Arjuna), sorrow did not (long) find a footing in them.

Sol. 34. धैर्य—धीरस्य भावः धैर्यं; धियं राति इति धीरः one who takes a right view of things and does not lose courage; firmness of mind. विश्वास्यतया—*abs. n.* fr. the Pot. par. of श्वस् with वि, विश्वसितुं योग्यः विश्वास्यः तस्य भावस्तत्ता तया. अराति०—न राति सुखमराति an enemy स प्रभवो यस्य तस्मात्. मघोनः—मह्यते पूज्यते असौ माघवा, fr. मह to adore and the Uṇădi aff. अन् (कनिन्) the ह् being changed to घ् and the aug. व् (वुक्) coming in irregularly by श्वन्नुक्षन् &c. Uṇādi I. 159; other words similarly derived are श्वन्, उक्षन् पूषन् &c.

तान्भूरिधाम्नश्चतुरोऽपि दूरं विहाय यामानिव वासरस्य ।
एकौघभूतं तदशर्म कृष्णां विभावरीं ध्वान्तमिव प्रपेदे ॥ ३५ ॥

अन्वयः—भूरिधाम्नः चतुरः वासरस्य यामान् विहाय कृष्णां विभावरीम् एकौघभूतं ध्वान्तम् इव भूरिधाम्नः चतुरः तान् दूरं विहाय एकौघभूतं तत् अशर्म कृष्णां प्रपेदे ॥ ३५ ॥

तानिति ॥ तत्पार्थत्यागवच्छर्मं सुखम् ॥ "शर्मशातसुखानि च इत्यमरः ॥ तद्विरुद्धमशर्म दुःखम् ॥ "नञ्" इति नञ्समासः । भूरिधाम्नस्तेजस्विन इति हानिहेतुत्वोक्तिः । चतुरस्तान्पार्थानपि वासरस्य भूरिधाम्नश्चतुरोऽपि यामान्प्रहरानिव । दूरं विहाय त्यक्त्वैकौघभूतमेकराशिभूतं सत् ॥ "श्रेण्यादयः कृतादिभिः इत्यर्थे कर्मधारयः । "श्रेण्यादिराकृतिगणः" इति शाकटायनः ॥ कृष्णां विभावरीं कृष्णपक्षरात्रिं ध्वान्तमिव । कृष्णां द्रौपदीं प्रपेदे प्राप ॥

अन्वयार्थः—(**भूरिधाम्नः**) बहुत प्रकाश युक्त (**चतुरः**) चार, (**वासरस्य**) दिन के (**यामान्**) प्रहरों को (**विहाय**) छोड़कर '(**कृष्णां विभावरीम्**) काली रात्रि को (**एकौघभूतम्**) संघीभूत (**ध्वान्तमिव**) अन्धकार की भांति—

(**भूरिधाम्नः**) अत्यधिक तेजस्वी (**चतुरः**) चारों (**तान्**) उनको (**दूरं विहाय**) दूर छोड़कर (**एकौघभूतम्**) संघीभूत (**तत्**) वह (**अशर्म**) दुःख (**कृष्णाम्**) द्रौपदी को (**प्रपेदे**) प्राप्त हुआ ।

जिस प्रकार प्रकाशित दिन के चारों प्रहरों को छोड़कर घना होता हुआ अंधकार अँधियारी रात को प्राप्त होता है, उसी प्रकार अतितेजस्वी उन चारों भाइयों को छोड़कर एकीभूत हुआ-हुआ वह दुःख द्रौपदी को प्राप्त हुआ ।

35. That gloom (sorrow) leaving far off the four brothers of mighty prowess, and collecting into one mass overtook Draupadî, as does darkness thickening into powers for the attainment of supreme excellence, as if it were success (incarnate).

Sl. 35. भूरि०—भूरि धाम lustre, might येषां ते तान्. एकौघ०—एकः ओघः flow यस्य तत् एकौघं, एकौघं भूतं; see Malli. कृष्णां—is a श्लिष्ट word; (1) dark; (2) Draupadī. विभावरी—विभाति नक्षत्रादिभिः fr. भा with वि+वन्. which is added to roots in आ preceded by a prātipadika or a preposition and the fem. aff. before ई which वन् changes its final to र् by वनोर च Pān. IV. I. 7. अशर्म—opposite of शर्मन् or happiness, sorrow, affliction. Grief when it was with the four brothers was divided and so was lightly felt by each. But as it left them now it attacked Draupadī with concentrated force.

तुषारलेखाकुलितोत्पलाभे पर्यश्रुणी मङ्गलभङ्गभीरुः ।
अगूढभावापि विलोकने सा न लोचने मीलयितुं विषेहे ॥ ३६ ॥

अन्वयः—विलोकने अगूढभावापि मङ्गलभङ्गभीरुः सा पर्यश्रुणी (अत एव) तुषारलेखाकुलितोत्पलाभे लोचने मीलयितुं न विषेहे ॥ ३६ ॥

तुषारेति ॥ सा द्रौपदी विलोकनेऽर्जुनावलोकनेऽगूढभावागूढाभिप्रायापि । स्फुटाभिलाषिणीति यावत् ॥ "भावो लीलाक्रियाचेष्टाभूत्यभिप्रायजन्तुषु ।" इति वैजयन्ती ॥ मङ्गलभङ्गभीरुर्मङ्गलहानेर्भीता सती । पर्यश्रुणी परिगताश्रुके । बाष्पावृते इत्यर्थः । अतएव तुषारलेखाकुलितोत्पलाभे हिमबिन्दुसहितेन्दीवरसन्निभे इत्युपमालंकारः । लोचने मीलयितुं न विषेहे न शशाक । अश्रुणोर्दृष्टयावरकत्वेऽपि तन्निपातस्यामङ्गलत्वात्तन्निवर्तकं निमीलनं सा न चकारेत्यर्थः ॥

अन्वयार्थः—(**विलोकने**) [अर्जुन के] दर्शन में (**अगूढभावापि**) नहीं छिपा हुआ है भाव जिसका ऐसी भी (**मङ्गलभङ्गभीरुः**) मङ्गल के भङ्ग होने से डरी हुई (**सा**) वह (**पर्यश्रुणी**) चारों ओर [व्याप्त] है आँसू जिनमें ऐसे, [अत एव] (**तुषारलेखाकुलितोत्पलाभे**) हिम-रेखाओं से व्याप्त कमल के समान है आभा जिनकी ऐसे, (**लोचने**) नेत्रों को (**मीलयितुम्**) बन्द करने में (**न विषेहे**) समर्थ नहीं हुई ।

यद्यपि द्रौपदी अर्जुन को देखना चाहती थी तो भी, आँसू टपकने से कहीं अमंगल न हो जाय—इस भय से अश्रुप्लावित, हिम से व्याप्त कमल-सरीखे सुन्दर, नयनों को वह बन्द नहीं कर सकी ।

36. Although manifestly longing to see him, Draupadī, afraid to violate the auspiciousness (of the hour) could not close her eyes suffused with tears and (thereby) resembling lotuses thickly covered with dew-drops.

Sl. 36. अगूढ०— न गूढः अगूढः भावो यस्याः whose object (desire to look at him) was not concealed *i. e.* was clearly discernible, मङ्गल०—मङ्गलस्य भङ्गः तस्मात् भीरुः To weep when one is about to depart is not auspicious. पर्य०—परिगतानि अश्रूणि ययोः । तुषार०—तुषारस्य लेखाः तुषारलेखाः lines of dew-drops ताभिः आकुलितं च तदुत्पलं च तस्य इव आभा ययोः । मीलयितुं &c.—For that would have caused the dropping of tears.

अकृत्रिमप्रेमरसाभिरामं रामार्पितं दृष्टिविलोभि दृष्टम् ।
मनःप्रसादाञ्जलिना निकामं जग्राह पाथेयमिवेन्द्रसूनुः ॥ ३७ ॥

अन्वयः—इन्द्रसूनुः अकृत्रिमप्रेमरसाभिरामं रामार्पितं दृष्टिविलोभि दृष्टं मनः-प्रसादाञ्जलिना पाथेयमिव निकामं जग्राह ॥ ३७ ॥

अकृत्रिमेति ॥ इन्द्रसूनुर्जुनः । क्रियया निवृत्तः कृत्रिमः ॥ "ड्वितः क्त्रिः" इति क्त्रिः । "क्त्रेर्मम्नित्यम्" इति मम्प्रत्ययः ॥ तद्विरुद्धम् । प्रेमैव रसः । अकृत्रिमेण प्रेमरसेनाभिरामम् । अन्यत्र प्रेमरसेन मधुरादिना चाभिरामम् । रामया रमण्यार्पितम् । दृष्टिं विलोभयतीति दृष्टिविलोभि । दृष्टिप्रियमित्यर्थः । दृष्टं दर्शनम् ॥ "नपुंसके भावे क्त" ॥ मनःप्रसादः । प्रसन्नमन इत्यर्थः । सोऽञ्जलिरिवेत्युपमितसमासः । न मनःप्रसादाञ्जलिना । पथि साधु पाथेयं शम्बलमिव ॥ "पथ्यतिथिवसतिस्वपतेर्ढञ्" ॥ निकाममतिशयेन जग्राह । रामार्पितं पाथेयं पथि क्षेमाय भवतीत्यागमः ॥

अन्वयार्थः—(**इन्द्रसूनुः**) अर्जुन ने (**अकृत्रिमप्रेमरसाभिरामम्**) स्वाभाविक प्रेम-रस के कारण सुन्दर (**रामार्पितम्**) स्त्री से अर्पित (**दृष्टिविलोभि**) दृष्टि को लुभाने वाले (**दृष्टम्**) दर्शन को (**मनःप्रसादाञ्जलिना**) प्रसन्न मन-रूपी अञ्जलि से (**पाथेयमिव**) पाथेय की भाँति (**निकामम्**) अतिशय रूप से (**जग्राह**) लिया ।

अर्जुन ने द्रौपदी के स्वभाविक प्रेम के कारण सुन्दर, आकर्षक दर्शन को पाथेय मानकर मन-रूपी अञ्जलि से स्वीकार किया ।

37. The son of Indra (Arjuna) eagerly received in the cavity (formed by the joining) of his hands in the form of his delighted mind the look of his wife charming to the eyes as provisions for his journey, offered by his beauteous wife and sweet on account of the flavour of unfeigned (sincere) love.

Sl. 37. अकृत्रिम०—कृत्रिम artificial, lit. brought about by an act; see Malli.; the aff. त्रिम is added to a few roots having an indictaory डु (ड्वितः) prefixed to them in the Dhātupāṭha, in the sense of 'brought about by' or the result of the action implied by the root. *Cf.* दत्रिम, विहित्रिम. अकृत्रिम not articial *i. e.* real, genuine. The meaning of अ here is विरोध; see com. रस:—रस्यते आस्वाद्यते इति रस: what is tasted and enjoyed, flavour.

रामा—रमते इति fr. रम्+अ (ण:) +*fem.* आ. lit. the sportive one; hence a beautiful woman. दृष्टि०—enticing of altracting the eye; charming to look at. दृष्टं—an ab. n fr. दृश्; see com. मन प्रसाद:—being clear or free from the dirt of sorrow &c. hence the delight of *i. e.* the delighted mind. निकामं—to his heart's content, as much as he liked. पाथेयं—what is serviceable on the road; provisions for a journey.; fr. पथिन्+एय (ढञ्). See com.

धैर्यावसादेन हृतप्रसादा वन्यद्विपेनेव निदाघसिन्धुः ।
निरुद्धबाष्पोदयसन्नकण्ठमुवाच कृच्छ्रादिति राजपुत्री ॥ ३८ ॥

अन्वयः—वन्यद्विपेन निदाघसिंधुः इव धैर्यावसादेन हृतप्रसादा राजपुत्री निरुद्धबाष्पोदयसन्नकण्ठं कृच्छ्रात् इव उवाच ॥ ३८ ॥

धैर्येति ॥ वन्यद्विपेन । वन्यग्रहणमुच्छृङ्खलत्वद्योतनार्थम् । निदाघसिन्धुर्ग्रीष्मनदीव । निदाघग्रहणं दौर्बल्यद्योतनार्थम् । धैर्यावसादेन धैर्यभ्रंशेन ॥ कर्त्रा ॥ हृतप्रसादा हृतनैर्मल्या । क्षोभं गमितेत्यर्थः । राजपुत्री क्षत्रियसुता द्रौपदी । अतः क्षात्रयुक्तमेव वक्ष्यतीति भावः । निरुद्धबाष्पोदयं संरुद्धरोदनं सन्नकण्ठं हीनस्वरम् ॥ अथ तयोरुभयोः कृतबहुव्रीह्योः क्रियाविशेषणयोर्विशेषणसमासः ॥ कृच्छ्रात्कथंचिदिति वक्ष्यमाणमुवाच ॥

अन्वयार्थः—(**वन्यद्विपेन**) जंगली हाथी से (**निदाघसिन्धुः इव**) ग्रीष्मकालीन नदी की भाँति, (**धैर्यावसादेन**) धैर्य्य-समाप्ति से (**हृतप्रसादा**) हर ली गई है प्रसन्नता जिसकी ऐसी (**राजपुत्री**) द्रौपदी (**निरुद्धबाष्पोदयसन्नकण्ठम्**) रुके हुए रोदन से रुँधे कण्ठ से (**कृच्छ्रात् इव उवाच**) कठिनाई से बोली—

ग्रीष्म कालीन नदी को [थोड़ा पानी होने से] जैसे जंगली हाथी मैला कर देता है उसी प्रकार धैर्य्य की कमी के कारण द्रौपदी की प्रसन्नता समाप्त हो गई थी। रुलाई को रोकने के कारण रुँधे हुए कण्ठ से बहुत कठिनाई से वह बोली :

38. With the peace of her mind destroyed (agitated at

heart) by the complete loss of fortitude, like a river in the sultry season, deprived its lucidity (muddled) by a wild elephant, the princess (Draupadī) spoke thus with difficulty, with her throat choked and the outburst of tears restrained.

Sl. 38. वन्य०—वने भव: वन्य: (this is added to indicate his a wilful play in the water); द्वाभ्यां शुण्डया मुखेन च पिबतीति द्विप: fr. द्वि+पा+आ (क:) वन्यश्चासौ द्विपश्च तेन । निदाघ०—नितरां दह्यते अत्र; निदह्+अ (घञ्;) तस्य सिन्धु: । The stream of a river is attenuated in summer and is easily rendered muddy. अव-साद:—fr. सद् with अव+अ (घञ्); destruction, loss. हृतप्र०— हृत: प्रसादो यस्या:; (1) dejected, agitated; (2) deprived of its lucidity; rendered turbid. निरुद्ध०—निरुद्ध: बास्पस्योदय: यथा स्यात्तथा; सन्न: (p. p. p. of सद्) choked कण्ठ: यस्मिन्कर्मणि तद्यथा तथा; now see com.

मग्नां द्विषच्छद्मनि पङ्कभूते संभावनां भूतिमिवोद्धरिष्यन् ।

आधिद्विषामा तपसां प्रसिद्धेरस्मद्विना मा भृशमुन्मनीभूः ॥ ३९ ॥

अन्वयः—पङ्कभूते द्विषच्छद्मनि मग्नां सम्भावनां भूतिम् इव उद्धरिष्यन् (त्वम्) आधिद्विषां तपसाम् आप्रसिद्धेः अस्मत् विना भृशं मा उन्मनीभूः ॥३९॥

मग्नामिति ॥ पङ्कभूते पङ्कोपमिते ॥ "भूतं क्ष्मादौ पिशाचादौ न्याय्ये सत्योपमानयोः ।" इति विश्वः ॥ द्विषच्छद्मनि शत्रुकपटे मग्नाम् । दुरुद्धरामित्यर्थः । संभावनां योग्यताम् । गौरवमिति यावत् । भूतिं संपदमिव ॥ "भूतिर्भस्मनि संपदि" इत्यमरः ॥ उद्धरिष्यन् । उद्धारकस्त्वमिति शेषः । आधिद्विषां दुःखच्छिदां तपसामाप्रसिद्धेः सम्यक्सिद्धिपर्यन्तमस्मद्विना । अस्माभिर्विनेत्यर्थः ॥ "पृथग्विना—" इत्यादिना विकल्पात्पञ्चमी ॥ भृशं मोन्मनीभूः । अस्मद्विरहाद् दुर्मना मा भूरित्यर्थः । दौर्मनस्यस्य तपःपरिपन्थित्वादिति भावः । "माङि—" इत्याशीरर्थे लुङ । "न माङ्योगे" इत्यडागमप्रतिषेधः ॥ अनुन्मना उन्मनाः संपद्यमान उन्मनी ॥ अभूततद्भावे च्विः । अरुर्मनश्चक्षुश्चेतोरहोरजसां लोपश्च" इति सकारलोपः । "अस्य च्वौ" इतीकारः ॥

अन्वयार्थः—(पङ्कभूते) कीचड़ के सदृश **(द्विषद्-छद्मनि)** शत्रु के कपट

में (**मग्नाम्**) डूबे हुए (**सम्भावनाम्**) गौरव का (**भूतिमिव**) ऐश्वर्य की तरह (**उद्धरिष्यन्**) उद्धार करते हुए [तुम] (**आधिद्विषाम्**) मनोव्यथा की विनाशक (**तपसाम्**) तपस्याओं की (**आप्रसिद्धेः**) सिद्धि-पर्यन्त (**अस्मत् विना**) हमारे बिना (**भृशम्**) अत्यन्त (**मा उन्मनी भूः**) दुःखित मन वाले मत होना।

शत्रु के कपट-रूपी कीचड़ में डूबे हुए ऐश्वर्य-रूपी गौरव का तुम उद्धार करो। हम सब की मानसिक व्यथाओं को समाप्त करने वाली तपस्या की सिद्धि-पर्यन्त, हमारे विरह से तुम व्यथित न होना।

39. Bent on preserving our glory (or greatness) like a precious treasure plunged into the mud of the deceit practised by our enemies, do you not be very uneasy at our separation, until your austerities, the removers of our mental affliction, attain fruition.

Sl. 39. **पङ्कभूते—पङ्कः भूतमुपमानं यस्य**; after Malli.; or **पङ्केन** **भूते** समे। द्विष॰—द्विषतां छद्म तस्मिन्। मग्नां pp. मस्ज्. आधि॰—आधिं द्विषन्तीति तेषाम्; द्विष् fr. द्विष् + क्विप् (०). प्रसिद्धेः—प्रकृष्टा सिद्धिः प्रसिद्धिः complete success. मा उन्मनी भूः—उन्मनी अभूः; The Aor. is used with the particle मा (माङ्) in the sense of आशिस् or benediction, gentle command &c. The augment अ of the Aor. is dropped after the prohibitive particle मा. उन्मनस्+च्विः; the स् of मनस् is dropped and the final अ is changed to ई before च्वि (०); see com.

अथानौत्सुक्यदार्ढ्यार्थं तस्य सर्वार्थसिद्धिनिदानत्वामाह—

यशोऽधिगन्तुं सुखलिप्सया वा मनुष्यसंख्यामतिवर्तितुं वा।
निरुत्सुकानामभियोगभाजां समुत्सुकेवाङ्कमुपैति सिद्धिः॥ ४० ॥

अन्वयः—यशः अधिगन्तुं सुखलिप्सया वा मनुष्यसंख्याम् अतिवर्तितुं वा अभियोगभाजां निरुत्सुकानां सिद्धिः समुत्सुकेव अङ्कम् उपैति॥ ४० ॥

यश इति॥ यशोऽधिगन्तुम। कीर्तिं लब्धुमित्यर्थः। सुखस्य लिप्सया लब्धुमिच्छया वा। मनुष्यसंख्यां मनुष्यगणनामतिवर्तितुमतिक्रमितुम्। अमानुषं कर्म कर्तुं वेत्यर्थः। अभियोगभाजामभिनिवेशवतां निरुत्सुकानाम्। अदुर्मनायमा-

नानामित्यर्थः। सिद्धिः पूर्वोक्तयशः सुखाद्यर्थसिद्धिः समुत्सुकेवानुरक्तकान्तेवाङ्कमन्तिकमुपैति । तस्मादस्मद्विरहदुःखमातपःसिद्धेः सोढव्यमिति भावः ।

अन्वयार्थः—(**यशः अधिगन्तुम्**) कीर्त्ति को पाने के लिए, (**सुखलिप्सया वा**) अथवा सुख की आकांक्षा से (**मनुष्यसंख्यामतिवर्तितुम् वा**) अथवा मनुष्य-गणना का अतिक्रमण करने के लिए (**अभियोगभाजाम्**) कार्य करने वाले (**निरुत्सुकानाम्**) उत्कण्ठा-रहितों की, (**सिद्धिः**) सफलता (**समुत्सुकेव**) अनुरक्त स्त्री की तरह, (**अङ्कम्**) गोद में (**उपैति**) प्राप्त होती है ।

"कीर्ति-लाभ के लिए, सुख के लिए अथवा मनुष्यों में सबसे बढ़कर कहे जाने के लिए कार्य करने वाले उत्कण्ठारहित व्यक्तियों की गोद में सफलता, अनुरक्त स्त्री की तरह आकर बैठती है ।"

40. Success (in the desired object) as if impelled by eagerness (or like a loving wife) comes to the lap of those who, without allowing their minds to be uneasy (or their energy to flag) work with strenuous efforts to gain fame or to attain happiness or far to excel (or tower high above) the generality of men (lit. to be above being counted among men).

Sl. 40. लिप्सा—Desid. *n.* in आ fr. लभ्. मनुष्य०—मनुष्येषु संख्या being counted among ताम्. अतिवर्तितुं—To transcend; *i. e.* to do something extraordinary. निरुत्सुकानामभि०—*i. e.* निरुत्सुकभूत्वाऽभि० who apply themselves to work without getting anxious or uneasy in mind (thinking of their relatives &c.), with an unagitated *i. e.* firm mind. This is added in support of उन्मनीभूः. अभियोग—close application, setting about a thing with a determined purpose. *Cf.* for another sense II. 46. समुत्सुका—eagerly longing for. उत्सुक fr. सु 1 cl. with उद्, उद् उद्योगं सवति; or सु 6 cl. उत्सुवति impels on, +क (कन्) irregularly formed.

Mammaṭa quotes this sl. in his K. p. VII as containing an instance of the fault called भग्नप्रक्रमत्व—here of the *infi.* termination. For instead of the Desi. gff. (स) in लिप्सया, the simple infinitive should have used, as the same has been used in the other two clauses. Thus there is the violation of the uniformity of affix. सुखमीहितुं वा is the reading suggested as keeping up symmetry.

Nāgojibhaṭṭa who reads लक्ष्मी: for सिद्ध:, connects the infinitive with निरुत्सुकानां which he takes in the sense of 'not anxious about.' Men as a general rule are seekers of money; one who does not care for money is rarely found and is, therefore, highly spoken of. Again sorrow falls to the lot of a man who seeks money but does not find it. A man who does not care for wealth is ever happy. He thus comes to be considered an extraordinary man. He says—**निरुत्सुकानां निरौत्सुक्यानामनुत्कण्ठानमाभियोगभाजां यत्नवताम् । तुमुनन्तानां निरुत्सुखानामित्यत्रान्वयः । लोके हि सर्वे लक्ष्म्युत्सुकास्तेष्वतिनिःस्पृहत्वरूपं यशो लब्धुमुत्कण्ठाविषयार्थासिद्धौ हि दुःखं भवति; लक्ष्म्यागमे हि न कोपि मनुष्यः स्वत आगच्छल्लक्ष्मीकस्तादृशश्चायं न मनुष्यगणनाविषय इति व्यवहारो भवति ।**

अथास्य मन्यूद्दीपनद्वारा तपःप्रवृत्तिं प्रथयितुमरिनिकारं तावच्चतुर्भिरुद्घाटयति—

लोकं विधात्रा विहितस्य गोप्तुं क्षत्रस्य मुष्णन्वसु जैत्रमोजः ।
तेजस्वितायाः विजयैकवृत्तेर्निघ्नन्प्रियं प्राणमिवाभिमानम् ॥ ४१ ॥

अन्वयः—विधात्रा लोकं गोप्तु विहितस्य क्षत्रस्य जैत्रम् ओजः (तदेव) वसु-मुष्णन्, विजयैकवृत्तेः तेजस्वितायाः प्रियं प्राणम् इव अभिमानं निघ्नन् ॥४१॥

लोकमिति ॥ विधात्रा ब्रह्मणा लोकं गोप्तुं विहितस्य सृष्टस्य क्षत्रस्य क्षत्रियजातेः संबन्धि । जयनशीलं जेतृ तदेव जैत्रम् ॥ जेतृशब्दात्तृजन्तात् "प्रज्ञादिभ्यश्च" इति स्वार्थेऽण्प्रत्ययः ॥ ओजो बलं दीप्तिर्वा ॥ "ओजो बले च दीप्तौ च" इति विश्वः ॥ तदेव वसु धनमिति रूपकालंकारः । मुष्णन्नपहरन् । अरिनिकृतस्य कुतः क्षात्रं तेज इति भावः । किंच विजयैकवृत्तेर्विजयैकजीवितायाः "क्षत्रियस्य विजितम्" इति स्मरणादिति भावः ॥ "वृत्तिर्वर्तनजीवने" इत्यमरः ॥ तेजस्वितायास्तेजस्विनामित्यर्थः । तेजःप्राधान्यद्योतनार्थं भावप्रधानो निर्देशः । प्रियं प्राणमिव । प्राणसममित्यर्थः । अभिमानमहंकारं निघ्नन्खण्डयन् । तेजस्विनां प्राणहानिप्राया मानहानिरिति भावः ॥

अन्वयार्थः—(**विधात्रा**) ब्रह्मा से (**लोकम्**) लोक की (**गोप्तुम्**) रक्षा करने के लिए (**विहितस्य**) बनाये गए, (**क्षत्रस्य**) क्षत्रिय जाति से सम्बन्धित

(जैत्रम्) जीतने का है स्वभाव जिसका ऐसे (ओजः) तेज [तदेव] वह ही है (वसुमुष्णन्) धन [उसको] चुराता हुआ, (विजयैकवृत्तेः) [और] विजय ही है एकमात्र आचरण जिसका ऐसी (तेजस्वितायाः) तेजस्विता के (प्रियं प्राणमिव) प्रिय प्राण की भांति (अभिमानम्) अभिमान को (निघ्नन्) समाप्त करता हुआ....

ब्रह्मा ने संसार की रक्षा के निमित्त जिस विजयशील क्षात्र तेज को बनाया है उस तेज-रूपी धन का अपहरण करता हुआ, तथा विजय मात्र स्वभाव वाली तेजस्विता के प्राण-सदृश प्रिय अभिमान को समाप्त करता हुआ...

41. [The indignity] which robbed (away) the victorious intrinsic valour (or majesty), the wealth of Kshatiyahood created by Brahmá for the protection of the world; which destroyed self-respect, dear as life to chivalrous spirits solely bent on gaining victory;

Sl. 41. Slokas 41-44 form a Kulaka (see notes on sl. 1). The epithets in slokas 41-43 qualify निकारः in sl. 44.

गोप्तु—the other forms are गोपायितुम्, गोपितु. क्षत्रस्य—see sl. 48. जैत्रं—Capable of conquering; fr. जि+तृ (added ताच्छील्ये) + अ (अण्) added स्वार्थे *i. e.* as a mere expletive, occasioning no change of meaning. It is added to words of the group headed by प्रज्ञ (as प्रज्ञ एव प्राज्ञः). Although जेतृ is not actually found in the group it may be included in it. वसु—is in apposition with ओजः विजयै°—विजय एव एकः or एका वृत्तिर्यस्याः तस्याः। तेजस्वितायाः—तेजः अस्यास्तीति तेजस्वी तस्य भावस्तत्ता तस्याः। abstract for the concrete (spirited men) to emphasise the prominence of martial spirit. प्राणमिव—Here प्राण is used in the sense of the principal vital air on which life depends, the soul, and hence the singular.

अधिक्षेपाद्यसहनं तेजः प्राणात्ययेष्वपि न त्याज्यमित्याह—

व्रीडानतैराप्तजनोपनीतः संशय्य कृच्छ्रेण नृपैः प्रपन्नः।
वितानभूतं विततं पृथिव्यां यशः समूहन्निव दिग्विकीर्णम्॥ ४२ ॥

अन्वयः—आप्तजनोपनीतः (तथापि) संशय्य व्रीडानतैः नृपैः कृच्छ्रेण प्रपन्नः पृथिव्यां वितानभूतं दिग्विकीर्णं विततं यशः समूहन् इव ॥ ४२ ॥

व्रीडेति ॥ पुनश्च । आप्तजनोपनीतः श्रावितः । प्रापित इत्यर्थः । तथापि संशय्य संदिह्य । असंभावितबुद्ध्येति भावः । व्रीडानतैः । जुगुप्सितवृत्तान्तश्रवणादिति भावः । नृपैर्देशान्तरस्थैः कृच्छ्रेण प्रपन्नः प्राप्तः । आप्तोक्तत्वात्कथंचिद्विश्वस्त इत्यर्थः । यः शृण्वतामपि दुःसहः किमुतानुभवतामिति भावः । इत्येषा पूर्वेषां व्याख्या ॥ अन्यथापि व्याख्यायते । आप्तजनोपनीतो ज्ञातिकृतः संशय्य कथमिदमन्याय्यमुपेक्ष्यमिति विचार्य व्रीडानतैः । जुगुप्सितकर्मदर्शनादिति भावः । नृपैः सभास्थैः कृच्छ्रेण प्रपन्नोऽङ्गीकृतः । गोत्रकलहेषु मध्यस्थैरुदासितव्यमिति बुद्ध्योपेक्षित इत्यर्थः । पक्षद्वयेऽपि प्रपन्न इत्यत्राप्तजनोपनीतत्वस्य पदार्थभूतस्य विशेषणगत्या हेतुत्वोक्त्या काव्यलिङ्गमलंकारः । पृथिव्यां वितानभूतमुल्लोचतुल्यम् ॥ "अस्त्री वितानमुल्लोचः" इत्यमरः ॥ दिग्विकीर्णं दिगन्तलग्नम् । वितानमपि दिगन्तलग्नमिति भावः । विततं प्रथितं यशः समूहन्निव संकोचयन्निवेत्युत्प्रेक्षा । अरातिपरिभूतस्य कुतः कीर्तिरिति भावः ॥

अन्वयार्थः—(**आप्तजनोपनीतः**) विश्वसनीय व्यक्तियों के द्वारा प्राप्त कराया गया [तो भी] (**संशय्य**) संदेह करके (**व्रीडानतैः नृपैः**) लज्जा से झुके हुए राजाओं से (**कृच्छ्रेण**) कठिनाई से (**प्रपन्नः**) स्वीकार किया हुआ (**पृथिव्याम्**) पृथ्वी पर (**वितानभूतम्**) शामियाना हुए २ (**दिग्विकीर्णम्**) दिशाओं में व्याप्त (**विततम्**) विस्तृत (**यशः**) यश को (**समूहन् इव**) संकुचित करता हुआ—

आप्त व्यक्तियों से कहे जाने पर भी पहले संदेह करके बाद में कठिनाई से लज्जावनत राजाओं से स्वीकार किया गया [दुःशासन द्वारा द्रौपदी का केशावकर्षण-अपमान] । पृथ्वी पर शामियाने की भांति फैले हुए दिशाओं में व्याप्त तुम्हारे विस्तृत यश को क्षीण करता हुआ...

42. Which was believed in (accepted as true) with great difficulty and after hesitation being communicated by trustworthy men, by kings bent low (hanging down their heads) through shame, [or, which, offered by relatives, was connived

at by the kings (seated in the assembly) bent low through shame, with considerable hesitation and uncertainty about their duty); which eclipsed (lit. narrowed the circle of) your glory spread in all quarters like a canopy extended over the world;

Sl. 42. The first line is capable of a double interpretation. Malli. first gives the view of the Commentators that preceded him and then his own. आप्त०—आप्तश्चासौ जनश्च तेन उपनीतः (1) communicated by trustworthy men; आप्तः यथार्थवक्ता one who always speaks the truth, (2) Brought on, offered by our relatives. नृपैः—(1) Kings abroad; (2) kings seated in the assembly. संशय्य—(1) doubting the veracity of the statement or report (2) doubtful as to their duty; not knowing what to do. प्रपन्नः—(1) accepted as true; (2) allowed to take place, connived at. वितान०—वितन्यते इति वितानः—नं *m*, *n*, fr. वितन्+अ (घञ्); तेन तस्य वा भूतं तुल्यं; Gen. or Inst. Tat. समूहन् Pres. p. of ऊह् with सम् 1. P. II. to collect what is dispersed, to bring within a narrower compass; hence to contract. Fig. see Malli; also alliteration.

वीर्यावदानेषु कृतावमर्षस्तन्वन्नभूतामिव संप्रतीतिम् ।
कुर्वन्प्रयामक्षयमायतीनामर्कत्विषामह्न इवावशेषः ॥ ४३ ॥

अन्वयः—वीर्यावदानेषु कृतावमर्षः (अत एव) संप्रतीतिम् अभूताम् इव तन्वन्, अह्नः अवशेषः अर्कत्विषामिव आयतीनां प्रयामक्षयं कुर्वन् ॥ ४३ ॥

वीर्येति ॥ पुनश्च वीर्याण्येवावदानानि तेषु कृतावमर्षः कृतास्कन्दनः । पुराकृतपराक्रमोद्भूतान्यपि प्रमृजन्नित्यर्थः ॥ "अवदानं कर्म वृत्तम्" इत्यमरः ॥ अतएव संप्रतीतिं ख्यातिम् ॥ "प्रतीते प्रथितख्यातवित्तविज्ञातविश्रुताः ।" इत्यमरः ॥ अभूतामविद्यमानामिवेत्युत्प्रेक्षा । सतोऽप्यसत्त्वमुत्प्रेक्ष्यते । तन्वन्कुर्वन् । पुनश्चाह्नोऽवशेषो दिनान्तोऽर्कत्विषामिवायतीनामुत्तरकालानां प्रयामक्षयं दैर्घ्यनाशं कुर्वन्निति श्रौती पूर्णेयमुपमा । अरिनिराकृतस्य कुतश्चिरावस्थानमिति भावः ॥

अन्वयार्थः—(**वीर्यावदानेषु**) पराक्रम के उज्ज्वल कार्यों पर (**कृतावमर्षः**) किया है आक्रमण जिसने ऐसा [अत एव] (**संप्रतीतिम्**) प्रसिद्धि को (**अभूता-**

मिव तन्वन्) मानो हुई ही न हो ऐसी करता हुआ, (**अह्नः**) दिन का (**अवशेषः**) अवसान (**अर्कत्विषामिव**) सूर्य-किरणों की भाँति (**आयतीनाम्**) उत्तर कालों के (**प्रयामक्षयम्**) सुदीर्घ विनाश को (**कुर्वन्**) करता हुआ...

आप द्वारा पूर्वकृत पराक्रम के कार्यों पर परदा डालता हुआ, अतएव पूर्व-अर्जित प्रसिद्धि को समाप्त करता हुआ, तथा दिन का अन्तिम भाग जिस प्रकार सूर्य-किरणों को समाप्त कर देता है इसी प्रकार, आपके उत्तर-काल के विस्तृत विनाश को करता हुआ. . . .

43. which making a sally on your glorious deeds of valour wiped away your reputation as if it did not exist; and which cut off all future prospects as evening cuts short; the length of the solar rays;

Sl. 43. वीर्याव०—अवदान fr. दै 1. P. with अव to brighten, to purify+अन (ल्युट् भावे); a bright or glorious deed; *cf.* प्रापदस्त्रमवदानतोषितात् &c. Rag. XI. 4. अवमर्षः—an attack. प्रयाम—(1) the continuity of; (2) length. अर्कत्विषां—of the rays of the sun. अर्कः—अर्च्यते इति fr. अर्च् to worship+अ (घञ्) च् being changed to क्; or by adding अ (क) by Uṇādi. III. 40.

प्रसह्य योऽस्मासु परैः प्रयुक्तः स्मर्तुं न शक्यः किमुताधिकर्तुम् ।
नवीकरिष्यत्युपशुष्यदार्द्रः स त्वद्विना मे हृदयं निकारः ॥ ४४ ॥

अन्वयः—परैः अस्मासु प्रसह्य प्रयुक्तः यः स्मर्तुं न शक्यः अधिकर्तुं किमुत, स (केशाकर्षणरूपः) निकारः त्वद्विना आर्द्रः (सन्) उपशुष्यत् मे हृदयं नवीकरिष्यति ॥ ४४ ॥

प्रसह्येति ॥ पुनश्च । परैः शत्रुभिरस्मासु प्रसह्य प्रयुक्त आचरितो यो निकारः परिभवः केशाकर्षणरूपः स्मर्तुं न शक्यः । अधिकर्तुमनुभवितु किमुत । यस्य स्मरणमपि दुःसहमनुभवस्तु सुतरां दुःसह इति किमु वक्तव्यमित्यर्थः । स निकारस्त्वद्विना त्वया विना ॥ "पृथग्विना—" इत्यादिना पञ्चमी ॥ आर्द्रः सन्कुतश्चिदभिभूतात्पुराणप्रहार इव । त्वद्विरहदुःखात्पुनर्नवीकरिष्यति । नवीभविष्यतीत्यर्थः । उपशुष्यत् त्वया विना शुष्कमिति भावः । दुःखस्तम्भनं शोषपदार्थो मे हृदयं नवी-

करिष्यत्यार्द्रीकरिष्यति । व्रणमिवेति भावः । दुःखितस्य पुनर्दुःखोपचयः प्रशान्त प्रायमपि दुःखहेतुं पुनरुद्घाटयतीत्यर्थः ।। अत्र शोषादिविशेषणसाम्याद्व्रणाद्यप्रस्तुतार्थप्रतीतेः समासोक्तिरलंकारः ।।

अन्वयार्थः—(**परैः**) शत्रुओं से (**अस्मासु**) हम पर (**प्रसह्य**) हठपूवक (**प्रयुक्तः**) प्रयुक्त किया गया (**यः**) जो, (**स्मर्तुं न शक्यः**) स्मरण [भी] नहीं किया जा सकता (**अधिकर्तुं किमुत**) सहन करने की तो बात ही क्या, (**सः**) वह [केशाकर्षण-रूप] (**निकारः**) तिरस्कार, (**त्वद्विना**) तुम्हारे बिना (**आर्द्रः** [सन्] गीले हुए-हुए (**उपशुष्यत् मे हृदयम्**) सूखते हुए मेरे हृदय को (**नवीकरिष्यति**) [फिर से] नया करेगा।

[उपर्युक्त कार्यों को करते हुए] शत्रु द्वारा जबरदस्ती किये गए केशावकर्षण-रूप तिरस्कार को स्मरण तक नहीं किया जा सकता, सहन करने की तो बात ही क्या ! यह तिरस्कार तुम्हारे अभाव में मेरे हृदय के सूखे [घाव] को, गीला करके फिर से हरा कर देगा।

44. That indignity, wrought upon us perforce by our enemies, which it is not possible even to think of (without pain) much less to experience (or forgive), being wet (revived) by (the pain of) your separation, will refresh (renew the pain of) my heart getting parched (somehow outwardly forgetting it).

Sl. 44. प्रसह्य—forcibly; absolutive of सह् with प्र (प्रकर्षेण सोढ्वा) used as an *adv.* अधिकर्तुं—*inf.* of कृ with अधि Atm. to bear or endure. अधेः प्रहसने । Pān. I. 3. 33. कृ with अधि is Atm. in the sense of bearing patiently or forgiving, overpowering. निकारः—Insult, humiliation; offence; fr. कृ with नि+अ (घञ्). आर्द्रः—(1) wet; (2) discharging pus. Bhāravi's style is often condensed and this is a good instance of it. The words आर्द्रः, परिशुष्यत् and नवीकरिष्यति suggest a parallelism between the condition of Draupadī's heart and a malignant ulcer. Draupadī's heart was deeply wounded by the flagrant insult offered to her and she appeared to have forgotten the pain caused by it for a time. It is compared to an ulcer with a crust formed over it which appears to be healed and dry for a time but which begins to discharge pus again when the crust is removed by some external injury as from an accidental blow. So the thought of separation from Arjuna acted as an incentive and revived the pain of the insult rankling in her mind. The fig Samāslokti is, there fore, implied in this śloka.

The next three ślokas form a Viśeshaka, being syntactically connected. See Malli.'s introduction to III. 1. They are to be taken in connection with the outrage on Draupadī when she was dragged into the assembly by Dusśāsana being violently pulled by the hair.

पुनः प्रकारान्तरेण मन्युमुद्दीपयति—"प्राप्तः"इत्यादिभिस्त्रिभिः । तत्र वक्ष्यमाणप्रत्यभिज्ञानहेतुभिर्धनंजयं विशिनष्टि—

प्राप्तोऽभिमानव्यसनादसह्यं दन्तीव दन्तव्यसनाद्विकारम् ।

द्विषत्प्रतापान्तरितोरुतेजाः शरद्घनाकीर्ण इवादिरह्नः ॥ ४५ ॥

अन्वयः—दन्तव्यसनात् दन्तीव अभिमानव्यसनात् असह्यं विकारं प्राप्तः, शरद्घनाकीर्णः अह्नः आदिः इव द्विषत्प्रतापान्तरितोरुतेजाः ॥ ४५ ॥

प्राप्त इति—अभिमानस्य व्यसनाद्भ्रंशात् । "व्यसनं विपदि भ्रंशे दोषे कामजकोपजे ।" इत्यमरः ॥ दन्तव्यसनाद्दन्तभङ्गाद्दन्तीवासह्यं विकारं वैरूप्यं प्राप्तः । अतो न प्रत्यभिज्ञायत इति भावः । एवमुत्तरत्रायनुसंधेयम् । पुनश्च । द्विषत्प्रतापेन शत्रुतेजसान्तरितं तिरस्कृतमुरुतेजः प्रतापो यस्य स तथोक्तः । अतएव शरद्घनाकीर्णः शरन्मेघच्छन्नोऽह्न आदिः प्रत्यूष इव स्थितः । तद्वदेवाप्रत्यभिज्ञायमान इत्यर्थः । मध्याह्नस्तु मेघावरणेऽपि कथंचित्प्रत्यभिज्ञायत एवेत्याशयेनोक्तमादिरिति ॥

अन्वयार्थः—(**दन्तव्यसनात्**) दाँत टूटने से (**दन्तीव**) हाथी की तरह (**अभिमानव्यसनात्**) अभिमान के नष्ट होने से (**असह्यम्**) असह्य (**विकारम्**) विकार को (**प्राप्तः**) प्राप्त हुए (**शरद्घनाकीर्णः**) शरद् ऋतु के वादलों से व्याप्त (अह्न) दिन के (**आदिः इव**) प्रारम्भ के समान (**द्विषत्प्रतापान्तरितोरुतेजाः**) शत्रु के प्रताप से तिरस्कृत है महान् प्रताप जिसका ऐसे,. . . .

दाँत टूटने से जिस प्रकार हाथी विरूप हो जाता है, उसी प्रकार अभिमान के नाश से [तुम] विरूप हो गये हो। शरद्-ऋतु के मेघों से व्याप्त प्रातःकाल की भाँति शत्रु-प्रताप से तुम्हारा प्रताप आच्छादित हो गया है।

45. Sadly (lit. unbearably) disfigured by the loss of self-respect, like an elephant by the breaking of his tusks; having your great brilliance eclipsed by the power of (or, the mental affliction caused by) the enemy like the beginning of day (with the sky) overcast with clouds;

Sl. 45. The Nominatives qualify त्वं in sl. 47. व्यसन—(1) the breaking of; (2) loss or destruction. विकार—change of form, deformity. द्विषत्प्रताप &c.—Malli. translates प्रताप by तेजस् and तेजस् by प्रताप or prowess. But then the simile becomes inappropriate. For प्रताप is compared to a cloud which has no tejas or brilliance but is rather a sign of gloominess. Draupadī in the next sl. also refers to the bodily appearance of Arjuna, So it seems better to take प्रताप in the sense of 'great affliction, or prowess' and उरुतेजस् in that of 'great brilliance of the body.'

शरद्घना०—शरदः शरत्सम्बन्धिनः घनाः तैः आकीर्णः The autumal cloud is taken because generally the mornings are delightful in autumn. *Cf.* दिवसं शारदमिव प्रारम्भसुखदर्शनम्। Rag. X. 9. It is only an occasional appearance of clouds that makes them gloomy-looking. Arjuna had the brilliance of the autumnal morning sun. But smarting under the insult offered by the enemy he looked gloomy all brilliance having faded away from his face, much so that he was not to be recognised as his own former self.

सव्रीडमन्दैरिव निष्क्रियत्वान्नात्यर्थमस्त्रैरवभासमानः ।
यशःक्षयक्षीणजलार्णवाभस्त्वमन्यमाकारमिवाभिपन्नः ॥ ४६ ॥

अन्वयः—निष्क्रियत्वात् सव्रीडमन्दैरिव (स्थितैः) अस्त्रैः अत्यर्थं न अवभासमानः यशःक्षयक्षीणजलार्णवाभः, त्वम् अन्यम् आकारम् अभिपन्न इव (स्थितः) ॥ ४६ ॥

सव्रीडेति ॥ पुनश्च । निष्क्रियत्वादर्थक्रियाशून्यत्वात्सव्रीडमन्दैरिव सव्रीडैरतएव मन्दैरपटुभिरिव स्थितैरित्युत्प्रेक्षा ॥ "मूढाल्पापटुनिर्भाग्या मन्दाः स्युः ।" इत्यमरः । अस्त्रैरत्यर्थं नावभासमानः न प्रकाशमानः । पूर्वं तु नैवमिति भावः । किंतु यशः-क्षयाद्धेतोः क्षीणजलो योऽर्णवस्तदाभस्तत्सदृशस्त्वमन्यमाकारमाभिपन्नः प्राप्त इव स्थित इवेत्युत्प्रेक्षा ॥ तस्य क्षीणजलार्णवाभ इत्युपमासंसृष्टिः ॥

अन्वयार्थः—(**निष्क्रियत्वात्**) निष्क्रिय होने के कारण (**सव्रीडमन्दैरिव**) लज्जायुक्त [अत एव] मन्द-से पड़े हुए (**अस्त्रैः**) आयुधों से (**अत्यर्थम्**) बहुत अधिकता से (**न अवभासमानः**) प्रकाशित न होता हुआ (**यशः क्षयक्षीणजलार्णवाभः**) यश के ह्रास के करण क्षीण जल वाले समुद्र के समान है आभा जिसकी ऐसे (**त्वम्**) तुम (**अन्यमाकारम्**) अन्य आकृति को (**अभिपन्नः इव**) प्राप्त हुए हुए से....

तुम्हारे अस्त्र निष्क्रिय होने के कारण लज्जित एवं कुण्ठित हुए पड़े हैं। इन आयुधों से तुम मन्द-तेज हो गये हो। तुम्हारा यश क्षीण हो गया है । बहुत कम पानी वाले समुद्र की भाँति तुम अपरिचित-सी शक्ल वाले प्रतीत होते हो।

46. not shining very much by your missiles, miserable-looking through shame as it were at their not being employed; and resembling an ocean with its (mass of) water reduced, owing to the loss of your wide fame, you who looked as if changed in form;

Sl. 46. निष्क्रियत्वात्—निर्गता क्रिया येषां तानि निष्क्रियाणि तेषां भावः निष्क्रियत्वं तस्मात् । सव्रीड &c.—व्रीडया व्रीडेन वा सहितानि सव्रीडानि; now see Malli., the whole is a Karm. Comp. अस्त्रैः—अस्यते इति अस्त्रं what is thrown; fr. अस् + त्र (Uṇādi aff. ष्ट्रन). It is a term applied to the class of weapons which are thrown or discharged at an enemy as distinguished from शस्त्रs which are taken in the hand and struck at an enemy, and includes the miraculous weapons presided over by deities such as fire, wind &c. अत्यर्थं—अर्थमतिक्रान्तं यथा तथा । यशः—means here world-wide reputation ; as it is compared to the water of an ocean. *Cf. supra* sl. 42. क्षीण &c.—क्षीणानि (p. p. p. of 1 p. to diminish or decay &c.) जलानि यस्य स क्षीणजलः स चासौ अर्णवश्च Karm.;

तेन सदृशः—अर्णभाव Nityasamāsa (which has no स्वपदविग्रह). अर्णवः—अर्णांसि अत्र सन्तीति; fr अर्णस् water+व, the स् being irregularly dropped. Fig. A fusion of *Utprekshā* and *Uapmā*)

दुःशासनामर्षरजोविकीर्णैरेभिर्विनाथैरिव भाग्यनाथैः ।
केशैः कदर्थीकृतवीर्यसारः कच्चित्स एवासि धनंजयस्त्वम् ॥ ४७ ॥

अन्वयः—दुःशासनामर्षरजोविकीर्णैः विनाथैरिव भाग्यनाथैः एभिः केशैः कदर्थीकृतवीर्यसारः त्वं स एव धनंजयोसि कच्चित् ॥ ४७ ॥

दुःशासनेति ॥ पुनश्च । दुःशासनस्य हर्तुरामर्ष आमर्षणं आकर्षणं स एव रजो धूलिः । मालिन्यहेतुत्वादिति भाव । तेन विकीर्णैर्विक्षिप्तैरतएव विनाथैरिव स्थितवतां युष्माकमसत्त्वप्रायत्वादनाथैरिव स्थितैरित्युत्प्रेक्षा । अन्यथा कथमियं दुर्दशेति भावः । किंतु भाग्यनाथैर्दैवमात्रशरणैः । अन्यथा स्वरूपमपि लुप्येतेति भावः । एभिः परिदृश्यमानैः । असंयमितैरिति भावः । केशैः शिरोरुहैः कुत्सितोऽर्थो वस्तु कदर्थः ॥ "अर्थोऽभिधेयैरवस्तुप्रयोजननिवृत्तिषु ।" इत्यमरः ॥ "कोः कत्तत्पुरुषेऽचि" इति कुशब्दस्य कदादेशः ॥ कदर्थीकृतौ गर्ह्यार्थीकृतौ वीर्यसारौ शौर्यबले यस्य स तथोक्तः । इत्थं पूर्वविलक्षणस्त्वं स एव धनंजयोऽसि कच्चित् ॥ "कच्चित्कामप्रवेदने" इत्यमरः ॥ स एव चेत्त्वं नैवमस्मानुपेक्षस इति भावः ॥

अन्वयार्थः—(**दुःशासनामर्षरजोविकीर्णैः**) दुःशासन के द्वारा खींचा जाना, तद्रूप धूल से विक्षिप्त [अत एव] (**विनाथैरिव**) अनाथ जैसे (**भाग्यनाथैः**) भाग्य ही है मालिक जिनका ऐसे (**एभिः केशैः**) इन बालों से (**कदर्थीकृतवीर्यसारः**) निन्दा के योग्य किया गया है शौर्य एवं बल जिस का ऐसे (**त्वम्**) तुम (**स एव धनञ्जयोसि कच्चित्**) भला वह ही अर्जुन हो ?

दुःशासन के खींचने से बिखरे हुए, अतएव असहाय भाग्य ही है स्वामी जिन का, ऐसे इन बालों के द्वारा जिस के शौर्य एवं बल को निन्दनीय बना दिया गया है—क्या तुम वही अर्जुन हो !

47. and whose valour and strength were shown to be shamefully worthless by these (my) tresses which scattered by the dust in the form of Dusśāsana's violent pullings, as if they had no protector, had to depend upon fate alone as a protector, —are you that same Arjuna (I should like to know)?

Sl. 47. आमर्षः—आमर्षणं fr. मृष् + अ (घञ्) added भावे; touching, handling violently. विनाथैः—विगतः नाथः येषां तैः। भाग्य०—भाग्यं नाथः protector येषां तैः०. कदर्थीकृत०— For कदर्थ see Malli.; कु is changed to कत् in a Tat. when the latter member begins with a vowel; as कदश्वः &c. न कदर्थः अकदर्थः; अकदर्थः कदर्थः सम्पद्यमानः कृतः कदर्थीकृतः; now see com. When Draupadī was openly insulted Arjuna with all his knowledge of the missiles and his physical strength could do nothing but had simply helplessly to look on.

स एव—*i. e.* who were reduced to a sad plight in that manner.

अथाप्युपेक्षण दोषमाहः—

स क्षत्रियस्त्राणसहः सतां यस्तत्कार्मुकं कर्मसु यस्य शक्तिः ।
वहन्द्वयीं यद्यफलेऽर्थजाते करोत्यसंस्कारहतामिवोक्तिम् ॥ ४८ ॥

अन्वयः—यः सतां त्राणसहः स क्षत्रियः; यस्य कर्मसु शक्तिः तत् कार्मुकं; द्वयीम् अपि उक्तिम् अफले अर्थजाते वहन् (तां) असंस्कारहताम् इव करोति ॥ ४८ ॥

स इति ॥ क्षतात् त्रायत इति क्षत्त्रं क्षत्रियकुलम् ॥ "सुपि" इति योगविभागात्कप्रत्ययः। पृषोदरादित्वात्पूर्वपदस्याकारलोपः। अथवा क्षदिति क्विबन्तोपपदात्कप्रत्ययः ॥ क्षत्रे जातः क्षत्रियः "क्षत्राद्धः" इति घप्रत्ययः ॥ कर्मणे प्रभवतीति कार्मुकम् ॥ "कर्मण उकञ्" इत्युकञ्प्रत्ययः ॥ एवं स्थिते वाक्यार्थः कथ्यते। यः सतां साधूनाम्। सहत इति सहः ॥ पचाद्यच् ॥ त्राणस्य सहस्त्राणसहो रक्षणक्षमः स एव क्षत्रियशब्दवाच्यः तथा यस्य कार्मुकस्य कर्मसु रणक्रियासु शक्तिः। अस्तीति शेषः। तदेव कार्मुकशब्दवाच्यम्। अत्रैवैतौ शब्दौ मुख्यौ। नान्यत्रेत्यर्थः। एवं स्थिते द्वयीं द्विविधामुक्तिम्। द्वाविमौ क्षत्रियकार्मुकशब्दावित्यर्थः। अफले। पूर्वोक्तावयवार्थशून्यावित्यर्थः। अर्थजाते। स्वाभिधेयसामान्यजातिमात्र इत्यर्थः ॥ "जातं जात्योघजन्मसु" इति विश्वः ॥ वहन्वर्तयन्। असंस्कारहतामव्युत्पत्तिदूषितामिव करोतीत्युत्प्रेक्षा ॥ तस्मात्त्वमस्मद्रक्षणेनोक्तदोषादात्मनं मोचयस्वेत्यर्थः ॥

अन्वयार्थः—(ये:) जो **(एताम्)** सज्जनों के **(त्राणसहः)** रक्षण में समर्थ है, **(सः)** वह **(क्षत्रियः)** क्षत्रिय है। **(यस्य)** जिस के **(कर्मसु)** [युद्ध] कार्यों में **(शक्तिः)** शक्ति है, **(तत् कार्मुकम्)** वह धनुष है। **(द्वयीम्)** दोनों प्रकार के **(अपि)** भी **(उक्तिम्)** कथन को **(अफले)** फल-रहित **(अर्थजाते)** शाब्दिक अर्थ सामान्य में **(वहन्)** धारण करता हुआ [व्यक्ति] [ताम्] उस उक्ति को **(असंस्कारहतामिव)** मानो व्युत्पत्ति के अभाव के दोष से दूषित **(करोति)** करता है।

जो सज्जनों का रक्षण कर सके वह क्षत्रिय है। जो युद्ध में सशक्त हो वही धनुष है। इन दोनों शब्दों को जो व्यक्ति उक्त फल-रहित, सामान्य अर्थ-मात्र में धारण करता है वह मानो इन शब्दों को व्युत्पत्यभाव-दोष से दूषित करता है।

48. He is (truly) a Kshatriya who is able to protect the righteous (or, good persons needing protection); that is a bow which has the capacity to accomplish its purposes (feats in a battle): if one wears these two (the title of a Kshatriya and a bow) not answering to their full significance, he makes the two terms as if vitiated by their being void of grammatical purity (not being true to their etymological sense).

Sl. 48. सतां—of righteous men (and not of evil doers). Generally the term सत् in connection with the term Kshatriya is used in the sense of 'those devoted to the performance of religious rites; 'and therefore needing protection. *Cf.* कुतो धर्म्यक्रियाविघ्नः सतां रक्षितरि त्वयि। Śak. V. 14.; रविमावसते सतां क्रियायै। Vik. III. 7.; and Mah. Bhār.— ब्राह्मणानां क्षतत्राणात्ततः क्षत्रिय उच्यते। Here सतां seems to be used in a wider sense, *viz.* in that of 'all good persons who deserve protection.' त्राणसहः—A Gen. Tat. क्षत्रियः—In deriving क्षत्रं as क्षतात् त्रायते (fr. क्षत+त्रै+क *i. e.* अ) Malli. follows Kālidāsa; *cf.* क्षतात्किलत्रायत इत्युदग्रः क्षत्रस्य शब्दो भुवनेषु रूढः। Rag. II. 53. He takes it as a comp. of the पृषोदरादि class, to account for the dropping of the final अ of क्षतः or it may be derived from क्षत् which he thus derives in his com. on the above passage from Rag.—क्षत् from the root क्षण् by the aff. क्विप (०) ण being dropped and substituted क्षणु हिंसाया-

मिति धातोः संपदादित्वात् क्विप् । गमादीनामिति वक्तव्यानुनासिक लोपे तुगागमे च क्षदिति रूपं सिद्धम् । क्षतः नाशात्त्रायते इति क्षत्त्रः । क्षत्रिय fr. क्षत्र+इय (घ). स क्षत्रियः; तत्कार्मुकं—The meaning is the two terms क्षत्रिय and Kārmuka principally express the senses of सतां त्राणसहत्व and कर्मणि शक्तिमत्त्व.

द्वयीं उक्ति—These two words. द्वय—द्वौ अवयवौ अस्य fr. द्वि+तय changed to अय optionally by द्वित्रिभ्यां तयस्यायज्वा । So द्वितय also; *fem.* द्वयी०. अफले—without their purpose *i. e.* not answering to. अर्थजात—their full literal sense. असंस्कारहितां—संस्कार is grammatical purity; here being true to the etymological sense न संस्कारः असंस्कारः तेन हता vitiated by.

अथ त्वद्गुणा अपि नोज्जीवयेयुरित्याह—

वीतौजसः संनिधिमात्रशेषा भवत्कृतां भूतिमपेक्षमाणाः ।
समानदुःखा इव नस्त्वदीयाः सरूपतां पार्थ गुणा भजन्ते ॥ ४९ ॥

अन्वयः—वीतौजसः सन्निधिमात्रशेषाः भवत्कृतां भूतिम् अपेक्षमाणाः त्वदीयाः गुणाः समानदुःखा इव (हे) पार्थ नः सरूपतां भजन्ते ॥ ४९ ॥

वीतेति ॥ हे पार्थ ! वीतौजसो निष्प्रभाः संनिधिमात्रशेषाः सत्तामात्रावशिष्टा भवत्कृतां भवता करिष्यमाणाम् ॥ "आशंसायां भूतवच्च" इति भूतवत्प्रत्ययः । भूतिमभ्युदयमपेक्षमाणास्त्वदीया गुणाः समानदुःखाः समदुःखभाज इव नोऽस्माकं सरूपतां वीतौजस्त्वादिसाधर्म्यं भजन्त इत्युपमा । सा च समानदुःखा इवेत्युत्प्रेक्षया वीतौजस्त्वादिसंभावितयानुप्राणितेत्यनुसंधेयम् ।

अन्वयार्थः—(**वीतौजसः**) निष्प्रभ (**संनिधिमात्रशेषाः**) समीपता मात्र है शेष जिनकी ऐसे, (**भवत्कृताम्**) आप द्वारा किए जाने वाले (**भूतिम्**) अभ्युदय की (**अपेक्षमाणाः**) अपेक्षा करते हुए (**त्वदीयाः गुणाः**) तुम्हारे गुण (**समानदुःखा इव**) समान है दुःख जिनका ऐसे (**पार्थ**) हे अर्जुन ! (**नः सरूपताम्**) हमारी समानता को (**भजन्ते**) भजते हैं।

जिस प्रकार आजकल हम निस्तेज हैं, एक-दूसरे की समीपता के अतिरिक्त और कुछ हमारे पास बचा नहीं है, तथा तुम्हारे द्वारा होने वाले अभ्युदय की प्रतीक्षा कर रहे हैं; उसी प्रकार तुम्हारे गुण भी हतप्रभ हैं, केवल मात्र अपनी

सत्ता बनाए हुए हैं तथा तुम से किए जाने वाले उत्कर्ष की प्रतीक्षा कर रहे हैं। इस प्रकार हम और तुम्हारे गुण समान रूप से दुःखी हैं।

49. With their lustre gone, having their mere existence left to them and expecting glory to be brought back to them by you, your qualities, O Son of Prthà, as if sympathising with us in our sorrow, experience a state similar to ours.

Sl. 49. वीतौजसः—वीतं ओजः येषां ते. संनिधि०—संनिधिरेव संनिधिमात्रं; संनिधिमात्रं शेषो येषां ते; संनिधि presence, existence, fr. धा with संनि and इ (किः). कृतां—here त is added in the sense of the future; see com. Draupadi was sure that Arjuna would do it and so treats it as an accomplished fact. भूति—prosperity in the form of their being raised up to their former magnificence or greatness. तव इमे त्वदीयाः fr. changed युष्मत् to त्वत् in the sing. +ईय (छ). सरूपतां—समानं रूपं येषां ते सरूपाः; तेषां भावः सरूपता, similarity, likeness, ताम्। Fig. *Upamā*, supported by *Utprekshā*.

तथापि ममैव कोऽयं भार इत्यत आह—

आक्षिप्यमाणं रिपुभिः प्रमादान्नागैरिवालूनसटं मृगेन्द्रम्।
त्वां धूरियं योग्यतयाधिरूढा दीप्त्या दिनश्रीरिव तिग्मरश्मिम्॥ ५०॥

अन्वयः—प्रमादात् रिपुभिः आक्षिप्यमाणम् (अत एव) प्रमादात् नागैः आलूनसटं मृगेन्द्रम् इव (स्थितं) त्वां तिग्मरश्मिं दीप्त्या दिनश्रीः इव इयं धूः योग्यतया अधिरूढा ॥ ५०॥

आक्षिप्येति॥ प्रमादात्प्रज्ञाहीनत्वात्। नतु दौर्बल्यादिति भावः। रिपुभिराक्षिप्यमाणमधिक्षिप्यमाणमतएव प्रमादात्। नागैर्गजैः। "ग्रहेभाहिगजा नागाः" इति वैजयन्ती॥ आलूनसटमाक्षिप्तकेसरम्॥ "सटा जटाकेसरयोः" इति विश्वः॥ मृगेन्द्रं सिंहमिव स्थितम्। त्वामियं धूः कार्यभारः। तिग्मरश्मि सूर्यं दीप्त्या दिनश्रीरिव। योग्यतया निर्वाहकतयाधिरूढारूढवती॥ कर्तरि क्तः॥ त्वदधीनेत्यर्थः॥

अन्वयार्थः—(**प्रमादात्**) असावधानी के कारण (**रिपुभिः**) शत्रुओं से (**आक्षिप्यमाणम्**) तिरस्कृत होते हुए [अत एव] (**प्रमादात्**) असावधानी

के कारण (नागैः) हाथियों से (आलूनसटम्) नोची गई हैं सटाएँ जिसकी ऐसे (मृगेन्द्रम् इव) सिंह की भाँति (स्थितम्) अवस्थित (त्वाम्) तुम को, (तिग्मरश्मिम्) सूर्य को (दीप्त्या) कान्ति के कारण (दिनश्रीः इव) दिन की शोभा की भाँति (इयं धूः) यह कार्य भार (योग्यतया) योग्य होने से (अधिरूढा) सौंपा है।

जिस प्रकार असावधानी के कारण हाथी सिंह की सटाओं को नोच लेता है उसी प्रकार तुम्हारे प्रमाद के कारण शत्रु तुम्हारा तिरस्कार कर सके हैं। जिस प्रकार कान्तिमान होने के कारण दिन की शोभा सूर्य पर आश्रित होती है, उसी प्रकार योग्य होने के कारण यह कार्य-भार तुम्हें सौंपा गया है।

50 This grave responsibility (*viz.* that mentioned in sl. 48) has devolved (rests), owing to your capacity, on you who are insulted by your enemies through heedlessness (to the consequences) (or after Malli—through your want of sense of duty) like a lion whose mane is plucked off by elephants, as the beauty of the day depends on the Sun by reason of his splendour.

Sl. 50. प्रमादात्—Through inattention to duty or negligence (and not through incamacity or want of power); (2) through (the lion's) carelessness. प्रमादात्—may be taken with enemies and elephants; through folly, not knowing the consequences. आक्षिप्यमाणं—having slights flung at you; Insulted. आलून०—आलूना (p. p. p. of लू with आ) plucked or pulled off, सटा यस्य. मृगेन्द्रं मृगेषु इन्द्र इव तम्. धूः—the Yoke *i. e.* responsibility of evenging the wrong done to us. योग्यतया—on account of your capability or fitness. Fig.—*Upamā.* By comparing Arjuna to a lion and the enemies to elephants Draupadi implies that he has the power to kill his enemies. Only he must have the will to use it.

पूर्वं निर्व्यवसायस्य "स क्षत्रियः" इत्यादिना दोष उक्तः। संप्रति व्यवसायिनो गुणमाह—

करोति योऽशेषजनातिरिक्तां संभावनामर्थवतीं क्रियाभिः।
संसत्सु जाते पुरुषाधिकारे न पूरणी तं समुपैति संख्या ॥ ५१ ॥

अन्वयः—यः अशषजनातिरिक्तां संभावनां क्रियाभिः अर्थवतीं करोति, तं संसत्सु पुरुषाधिकारे जाते पूरणी संख्या न समुपैति ॥ ५१ ॥

करोतीति ॥ यः पुमानशेषजनादितरजनादतिरिक्तामधिकाम् । सर्वादिशायिनीमित्यर्थः । संभावनां योग्यतां क्रियाभिश्चरितैरर्थवतीं सफलां करोति । त पुमांसं संसत्सु सभासु ॥ "सभासमितिसंसदः" इत्यमरः ॥ पुरुषाधिकारे योग्यपुरुषगणनाप्रस्तावे जाते सति । पूर्यतेऽनेनेति पूरणी संख्या द्वित्वादिसंख्या न समुपैति न गच्छति । अद्वितीयो भवतीत्यर्थः । तस्मादसाधारणलाभाय त्वयापि महानुत्साह आस्थेय इति भावः ॥

अन्वयार्थः—(**यः**) जो (**अशेषजनातिरिक्ताम्**) अन्य सब व्यक्तियों से अधिक (**संभावनाम्**) योग्यता को (**क्रियाभिः**) [अपने] आचरणों से (**अर्थवतीम्**) सफल (**करोति**) करता है (**तम्**) उस को, (**संसत्सु**) सभाओं में (**पुरुषाधिकारे जाते**) योग्य व्यक्तियों की गणना का प्रसङ्ग उपस्थित होने पर होने पर (**पूरणी संख्या**) [द्वितीय, तृतीय आदि] पूरक संख्या (**न समुपैति**) नहीं प्राप्त होती है ।

जो व्यक्ति सब का अतिक्रमण करने वाली योग्यता को अपने कार्यों से सार्थक करता है वह कभी भी सभा में योग्य व्यक्तियों की गणना शुरू किए जाने पर दूसरा या तीसरा आदि नहीं होता है—अर्थात् सदा ही सर्वश्रेष्ठ एवं प्रथम होता है ।

51. When the enumeration of (eminent) men is begun in assemblies no complimentary (second ordinal) number approaches him (he stands unapproachably high), who by his exploits gives significance to (proves) his worth surpassing that of all other men.

Sl. 51. अशेष०—नास्ति शेषः remainder यस्यासौ अशेषः; अशेषश्चासौ जनश्च तस्मात्, see Malli. संभावना lit. the estimation formed about one's capacity; hence fitness, ability. competency. अर्थवतीं—अर्थोऽस्या विद्यते तां full of significance, संसत्—संसीदन्त्यस्यां fr. संसद्+क्विप् (०) an assembly.

पुरुषाधिकारे—अधिकार beginning of the enumeration of, an occasion for counting men having a particular standard of excellence. **पूरणी**—making up a number fr. **पूर्** 4 Atm. to fill up;+**अन** (**ल्युट्**)+**ई**. **संख्या**—such as 2nd, 3rd &c. **न समुपैति**—*i. e.* no one comes up to his level; he stands unapproachingly high.

अथ द्वाभ्यां सुलभविपक्षस्य प्रोषितस्यार्जुनस्य कर्तव्यमुपदिशति—

प्रियेषु यैः पार्थ विनोपपत्तेर्विचिन्त्यमानैः क्लममेति चेतः ।

तव प्रयातस्य जयाय तेषां क्रियादघानां मघवा विघातम् ॥ ५२ ॥

अन्वयः—हे (पार्थ), प्रियेषु उपपत्तेः विना विचिन्त्यमानैः यैः (अघैः) चेतः क्लमम् एति, जयाय प्रयातस्य तव तेषाम् अघानां विघातं मघवा क्रियात् ॥ ५२ ॥

प्रियेष्विति ॥ हे पार्थ ! प्रियेष्वस्मासु विषय उपपत्तेः कारणाद्विनव विचिन्त्यमानैरकस्मादेवाशङ्क्यमानैर्यैरघैश्चेतः क्लमं खेदमेति । जयाय प्रयातस्य तव संबन्धिनां तेषामघानां व्यसनानाम् ॥ 'दुःखैनोव्यसनेष्वघम्" इत्यमरः ॥ मघवेन्द्रः य ऽस्माभिरुपास्यत इति भावः । विघातं निवारणं क्रियात्करोतु ॥ आशिषि लिङ ॥ तस्मादस्मच्चिन्तया न चेतः खेदयितव्यं जयार्थिना त्वया । अन्यथा तदसंभवादिति भावः ॥

अन्वयार्थः—(**पार्थ**) हे अर्जुन ! (**प्रियेषु**) प्रियजनों में (**उपपत्तेः विना**) कारण के बिना (**विचिन्त्यमानैः**) शङ्का किए जाते हुए (**यैः**) जिन (**अघैः**) कष्टों से (**चेतः क्लमम् एति**) चित्त खेद को प्राप्त होता है, (**जयाय**) विजय के लिए (**प्रयातस्य तव**) प्रयाण करते हुए तुम्हारे (**तेषाम्**) उन (**अघानाम्**) कष्टों का (**विघातम्**) निवारण (**मघवा**) इन्द्र (**क्रियात्**) करे ।

प्रिय जनों का मन बिना कारण के ही (अपने प्रिय के) कष्टों की शङ्का से दुःखित हुआ करता है । हे अर्जुन ! तुम विजय के लिए प्रस्थान कर रहे हो । तुम्हारे इन (बिना कारण शङ्का किए जाने वाले) कष्टों का इन्द्र निवारण करें ।

52. When you depart for the attainment of (means to get) victory (over your enemies) may Indra put an end to those evils, which being thought of (as likely to befall beloved persons)

without any reason, the mind experiences anguish (Malli.) [or may Indra remove those obstacles in your path when you depart &c. which being thought of &c.].

Sl. 52. प्रियेषु—With regard to persons held dear; वैषयिक-सप्तमी. Malli. प्रियेषु अस्मासु says in connecting with us. It may be taken in general प्रियेषु जनेषु विषये and then it may refer to Arjuna. उपपत्ति—What explains, a reason, cause. अघ—evils, dangers. मघवा—Indra; for derivation see *supra* Sl. 34. क्रियात्—Bened. 3rd sing.

मागाश्चिरायैकचरः प्रमादं वसन्नसंबाधशिवेऽपि देशे ।
मात्सर्यरागोपहतात्मनां हि स्खलन्ति साधुष्वपि मानसानि ॥ ५३ ॥

अन्वयः—असंबाधशिवे अपि देशे चिराय एकचरः वसन् प्रमादं मा गाः । मात्सर्यरागोपहतात्मनां मानसानि साधुषु अपि स्खलन्तिहि ॥ ५३ ॥

मागा इति ॥ असंबाधोऽसंकटः । विजन इत्यर्थः ॥ "संकटं ना तु संबाधः" इत्यमरः ॥ शिवो निर्बाधः ॥ द्वयोरन्यतरस्य विशेष्यत्वविवक्षायां विशेषणसमासः । अस्मिन्नसंबाधशिवेऽपि देशे चिराय चिरमेकचर एकाकी वसन्प्रमादं दौर्बल्यं मा गाः ॥ "इणो गा लुङि" इति गादेशः ॥ ननु निःस्पृहस्य ममाकिंचित्करः प्रमाद इति वाच्यमित्याशङ्क्याह—मात्सर्येति ॥ मत्सर एव मात्सर्यं द्वेषो रागः स्नेहस्ताभ्यामुपहतात्मनां रागद्वेषदूषितस्वभावानां मानसानि मनांसि साधुषु सज्जनेष्वपि विषये स्खलन्ति विकुर्वते हि ॥ अत्र प्रमादनिषेधलब्धाप्रमादरूपकारणेनार्थप्राप्तिरूपकार्यस्य व्यतिरेककारणसमर्थनाद्वैधर्म्येण कार्यकारणसमर्थनरूपोऽर्थान्तरन्यासः ॥

अन्वयार्थः—(**असम्बाधशिवे अपि**) निर्जन एवं बाधारहित भी (**देशे**) स्थान पर (**चिराय**) चिरकाल तक (**एकचरः**) एकाकी (**वसन्**) रहते हुए (**प्रमादं मा गाः**) दुर्बलता को प्राप्त मत होना । (**हि**) क्यों कि (**मात्सर्य-रागोपहतात्मानाम्**) द्वेष एवं राग से दूषित स्वभाव वालों के (**मानसानि**) मन (**साधुषु अपि**) सज्जनों में भी (**स्खलन्ति**) विकृत हो जाते हैं ।

यद्यपि तुम चिरकाल तक निर्जन एवं निर्बाध स्थान पर तपस्या करोगे, तो

भी अकेले रहते हुए कभी प्रमाद न करना, क्योंकि राग-द्वेष से दूषित लोगों के मन साधुओं के प्रति भी विकृत हो जाते हैं।

53. Do not be regardless (of personal safety) living alone for a long time in that place even though lonely and free from molestation : for the minds of those whose reasons are overpowered by hatred or love (of one's interest) go wrong (are evil-disposed) even towards good men.

Sl. 53. असम्बाध०—सम्यग् बाधते अत्र संबाधः; fr. बाध्+सं+अ (घञ्) by हलश्च crowded with (dangerous) men, or full of obstructions; न संबाधः असम्बाधः lonely sequestered; शिवः—free from dangers or molestation. Or असम्बाध free from dangers; शिव pleasant, auspicious (leading to blise); शिवं मङ्गलमस्यास्तीति by affixing अ (अर्शआदित्वाच्च) see note on विदित I. 1. एकचरः—चरतीति चरः. एकश्चासौ चरश्च moving alone. मा अगाः—Aor. of इ to go. राग—love of self-interest. मात्सर्यरागाभ्यामुपहतः overpowered आत्मा येषाम्. स्खलन्ति—fall from their proper nature; get affented. *Cf.* V. 49.

निगमयति—

तदाशु कुर्वन्वचनं महर्षेर्मनोरथान्नः सफलीकुरुष्व ।
प्रत्यागतं त्वास्मि कृतार्थमेव स्तनोपपीडं परिरब्धुकामा ॥ ५४ ॥

अन्वयः—तत् (तस्मात्) आशु महर्षेः वचनं कुर्वन् नः मनोरथान् सफलीकुरुष्व । कृतार्थं प्रत्यागतम् एव त्वां स्तनोपपीडं परिरब्धुकामा अस्मि ॥ ५४ ॥

तदिति ॥ तत्तस्मात्कारणात् । आशु शीघ्रं महर्षेर्वचनं कुर्वन् ॥ तपस्यन्नित्यर्थः । नोऽस्माकं मनोरथान्सफलीकुरुष्व । अरिनिर्यातनेनास्मान्प्रतिष्ठापयेत्यर्थः ॥ प्रार्थनायां लोट् ॥ किंच कृतार्थं कृतकृत्यं प्रत्यागतमेव त्वा त्वाम् ॥ "त्वामौ द्वितीयायाः" इति त्वादेशः ॥ स्तनयोरुपपीड्य स्तनोपपीडम् ॥ "सप्तम्यां चोपपीडरुधकर्षः" इति णमुल् ॥ परिरब्धुं कामो यस्याः सा परिरब्धुकामास्मि । आलिङ्गितुमिच्छामीत्यर्थः ॥ "तुंकाममनसोरपि" इति मकारलोपः ॥ प्रकृतकार्यसिद्धेः प्रमदालिङ्गनमपि न प्रीतिदमिति भावः ॥

अन्वयार्थः—(**तत्**) उस कारण से (**आशु**) शीघ्र (**महर्षेः**) महर्षि के (**वचनम्**) वचन को (**कुर्वन्**) करते हुए (**नः**) हमारे (**मनोरथान्**) मनोरथों को (**सफली कुरुष्व**) सफल करो। (**कृतार्थं प्रत्यागतम् एव**) कार्य करके लौटते ही (**त्वाम्**) तुम से (**स्तनोपपीडं परिरब्धुकामा अस्मि**) स्तनमर्दन पूर्वक आलिङ्गन की कामना वाली मैं हूँ।

अतः तुम शीघ्र जाकर महर्षि के कथनानुसार तपस्या करो और हमारे मनोरथों को पूरा करो। तुम्हारे लौटते ही तुम से गाढालिङ्गन करने के लिए मैं उत्सुक हूँ।

54. Acting up, therefore, to the direction of the great sage quickly fulfil our desires. I am anxious to embrace you pressing you closely to my bosom when you will return just with your object achieved.

Sl. 54. मनोरथ०—मन एव रथो यत्र; or मनसो रथ: the car of the mind; the desire carries the mind from one object to another as a car does a man. कृतार्थं—कृतः अर्थः येन तम्। स्तनो०—The gerund in अम् (Ṇamul) of रुध् and पीड preceded by उप is used with a word in the Inst. or Loc. used as an *Upapada*.

उदीरितां तामिति याज्ञसेन्या नवीकृतोद्ग्राहितविप्रकाराम्।
आसाद्य वाचं स भृशं दिदीपे काष्ठामुदीचीमिव तिग्मरश्मिः॥ ५५॥

अन्वयः—स याज्ञसेन्या इति उदीरितां नवीकृतोद्ग्राहितविप्रकारां वाचम् आसाद्य उदीचीं काष्ठाम् (आसाद्य) तिग्मरश्मिः इव भृशं दिदीपे॥ ५५॥

उदीरितामिति॥ सोऽर्जुन इतीत्थं यज्ञसेनस्यापत्येन स्त्रिया द्रौपद्योदीरितामुक्ताम्। नवीकृतः पुनरुद्घाटनेन तथा प्रत्यायितोऽतएवोद्ग्राहितो मनसि निधापितश्च विप्रकारः परिभवो यया सा तां वाचमासाद्य। आकर्ण्येत्यर्थः। उदीचीं काष्ठां दिशम्॥ "दिशस्तु ककुभः काष्ठा आशाश्च हरितश्च ताः" इत्यमरः॥ आसाद्य तिग्मरश्मिरिव। भृशं दिदीपे जज्वाल। चुक्रोधेत्यर्थः॥

अन्वयार्थः—(**सः**) वह (**अर्जुन**) (**याज्ञसेन्या**) यज्ञसेन की पुत्री (**द्रौपदी**) से (**इति**) इस प्रकार (**उदीरिताम्**) कही हुई, (**नवीकृतोद्ग्राहितविप्रकाराम्**) नया किया है (**मन में**) स्थित तिरस्कार को जिसने ऐसी, '(**वाचम्**) वाणी

को **आसाद्य**) प्राप्त करके (**उदीचीं काष्ठम्**) उत्तर दिशा को [प्राप्त करके] (**तिग्मरश्मिः इव**) सूर्य की भाँति (**भृशं**) अत्यधिक (**दिदीपे**) प्रज्वलित हुआ।

द्रौपदी की उपर्युक्त उक्ति से, अर्जुन के मन में स्थित शत्रु-कृत तिरस्कार पुनः नया हो गया। जिस प्रकार सूर्य अस्त होकर पुनः अत्यधिक तेज के साथ चमकता है उसी प्रकार अर्जुन भी इस भाषण को सुनकर अत्यधिक क्रोधित हुआ।

55. on hearing the words of Draupadî, thus uttered, which raked up the memory of past indignities, he shone very brightly (with the glow of anger enkindled) as does the sun on reaching the Northern direction.

Sl. 55. याज्ञसेन्या—यज्ञसेनस्य (a name of Draupadia) अपत्यं स्त्री याज्ञसेनी तया। See notes on I. 27. नवीकृता०—न नवः अनवः, अनवः नवः सम्पद्यमानः कृतः नवीकृतः; now ee Mails. उद्ग्राहित p. of ग्रह्, with उद् Cau. विप्रकारः—insult, contumely; injury, fr. विप्रकृ+घञ्, (अ) added भावे. निकारो विप्रकारः स्यात्। Amara. *Cf.* भर्तुविप्रकृतापि &c. Śāk. IV. 18. आसाद्य—having heard *i. e.* felt the force of it. उदीचीं—उदुत्तरमञ्चत्यर्कमिति उदीची fr. उदच् +ई;; the अ of अञ्च् is changed to after उद् when the nasal is dropped by उद ईत् Pān. VI. 4. 139. काष्ठा—काशते इति fr. काश +थ (क्थन्+अ Uṇādi. II. 2)

अथाभिपश्यन्निव विद्विषः पुरः पुरोधसारोपितहेतिसंहतिः।
बभार रम्योऽपि वपुः स भीषणं गतः क्रियां मन्त्र इवाभिचारिकीम्॥५६॥

अन्वयः—अथ विद्विषः पुरः अभिपश्यन् इव (स्थितः) पुरोधसा आरोपितहेतिसंहतिः स रम्योऽपि आभिचारिकीं क्रियां गतः मन्त्र इव भीषणं वपुः बभार॥ ५६॥

अथेति॥ अथ विद्विषः शत्रून्पुरोऽभिपश्यन्निव स्थितस्तथा पुरोधसा धौम्येनारोपिता समन्त्रं समाहिता हेतिसंहतिरायुधकलापो यस्य स तथोक्तः॥ "हेतिर्ज्वालाङ्कुरायुधे" इति वैजयन्ती॥ सोऽर्जुनो रम्यः सौम्यः सन्नपि। अभिचारः परहिंसा प्रयोजनं यस्याः साभिचारिकी॥ "तदस्य प्रयोजनम्" इति ठक्॥ तां क्रियां गतः। अभिचारकर्मणि नियुक्त इत्यर्थः। मन्त्र इव। रम्यः प्रकृत्या

रमणीयः। भीषयत इति भीषणम् ॥ नन्द्यादित्वाल्युप्रत्ययः ॥ वपुर्बभार। प्रशान्तो मन्त्रः प्रयोगभेदादिव सोऽप्यवस्थाभेदाद्भीषणो बभूवेत्यर्थः ॥

अन्वयार्थः—(**अथ**) इसके बाद (**विद्विषः**) शत्रुओं को (**पुरः**) सामने (**अभिपश्यन् इव**) देखता हुआ-सा, (**पुरोधसा**) पुरोहित (**धौम्य**) के द्वारा (**आरोपितहेतिसंहतिः**) स्थापित किया है अस्त्र-समूह जिसका ऐसा (**सः**) उस ने (**रम्यः अपि**) सौम्य होर हुए भी (**आभिचारिकीं क्रियां गतः**) परहिंसा है प्रयोजन जिसका ऐसी क्रिया को प्राप्त हुए (**मन्त्रः इव**) मन्त्र की भाँति (**भीषणम्**) भयंकर (**वपुः बभार**) शरीर को धारण किया।

तदनन्तर कुल-पुरोहित धौम्य ने अर्जुन के सभी अस्त्रों को वहाँ इकट्ठा कर दिया। उस समय अर्जुन, शत्रुओं को सामने देखता हुआ-सा स्वाभाविक रूप से सौम्य होते हुए भी भयङ्कर लग रहा था, जिस प्रकार अभिचार क्रिया में प्रवृत्त मन्त्र स्वाभाविक रूप से सौम्य होते हुए भी भयङ्कर लगता है।

56. Then equipped with weapons by the family priest and beholding, as it were, his inveterate foes before him, he (Arjuna), though (naturally) graceful, appeared fierce in form like a magical charm when employed on a dangerous mission.

Sl. 56. अभिपश्यन्निव &c. —The memory of the past being revived the whole scene stood vividly before his mental vision and he appeared to see nothing but his inveterate enemies before him and hence his fierce look. आरोपित—placed in the proper places with the repetition of holy *Mantras* to give additional power to them. *Cf.* for the power of Vedic *Mantras* Rag. V. 27; VIII. 4. हेति—a weapon; irregularly derived from हन् or हि; (हन्ति हिनोति वा, हन्यते अनया वा) + ति (क्तिन्); *cf.* ऊति यूति जूति साति हेति कीर्तयश्च। Pān. III. 3. 97. आभिचारिकी—अभिचार (fr. अभिचर+घञ् *i. e.* अ) the employment of magical spells or incantations for malevolent purposes such as bringing about the death of an enemy and the like. क्रियां गतः—made effective or ready to produce its intended effect. A Mantra is harmless by itself but to make it active and effective a certain process must be gone through such as repeating it a stated number of times, worshipping its presiding deity with particular things, offering oblations to fire and following a particular course of conduct, by the operator.

उक्तमायुधारोपणं विवृण्वन्प्रस्थानमाह त्रिभिः—

अविलङ्घ्यविकर्षणं परैः प्रथितज्यारवकर्म कार्मुकम् ।

अगतावरिदृष्टिगोचरं शितनिस्त्रिंशयुजौ महेषुधी ॥ ५७ ॥

अन्वयः—परैः अविलङ्घ्यविकर्षणं प्रथितज्यारवकर्म कार्मुकं (तथा) अरिदृष्टिगोचरम् अगतौ शितनिस्त्रिंशयुजौ महेषुधी ॥ ५७ ॥

अविलङ्घ्येति ॥ शत्रुभिरविलंघ्यमनतिक्रमणीयं विकर्षणं यस्य तत् अमोघाकर्षणमित्यर्थः । किंच प्रथितो ज्यारवो गुणध्वनिः कर्म बाणमोक्षणादिकं च यस्य तत्कार्मुकं चोद्वहन्नित्यन्वयः । तथारीणां दृष्टिगोचरं दृष्टिपथमगतौ । आहवेष्वनिर्वर्तित्वादस्येति भावः । निर्गतस्त्रिंशतोऽङ्गुलिभ्यो निस्त्रिंशः खड्गः ॥ डप्रत्यये संख्यायास्तत्पुरुषस्योपसंख्यानात्समासान्तः ॥ तेन शितेन तीक्ष्णेन युक्तं इति शितनिस्त्रिंशयुजौ ॥ "सत्सूद्विष—" इत्यादिना क्विप् ॥ महेषुधी महानिषङ्गौ । इषवो धीयन्तेऽनयोरिति विग्रहः ॥ "कर्मण्यधिकरणे च" इति किप्रत्ययः ॥ "तूणोपासङ्गतूणीरनिषङ्गा इषुधिर्द्वयोः । तूण्यां खड्गे तु निस्त्रिंशचन्द्रहासासिरिष्टयः ॥" इत्यमरः ॥

अन्वयार्थः—(**परैः**) शत्रुओं से (**अविलङ्घ्यविकर्षणम्**) नहीं है अतिक्रमणीय खींचा जाना जिसका ऐसे, (**प्रथितज्यारव कर्म**) विस्तृत—सर्वविदित —है प्रत्यञ्चा का शब्द एवं कार्य जिस का ऐसे, (**कार्मुकम्**) धनुष को [तथा] (**अरिदृष्टिगोचरम्**) शत्रुओं की आँख की पहुँच में (**अगतौ**) न गये हुए (**शितनिस्त्रिंशयुजौ**) तीक्ष्ण खड्ग-युक्त (**महेषुधी**) महान् दो तरकसों को, . . .

जिसका खींचा जाना अमोघ है, जिसकी प्रत्यञ्चा का घोष एवं कर्म सकल संसार-विदित है, उस धनुष को और शत्रुओं को कभी दिखाई न देने वाले तीक्ष्ण तलवार-युक्त दो तरकसों को, (धारण करता हुआ) . . .

57. Armed with his bow, the drawing of which was not to be withstood by the enemies and whose twang and the havoc made by which were well known, as also with his two large

quivers with a sharp sword attached to them and never exposed to the view of his foes (as he never turned back upon them);

Sl. 57. अविलङ्घ्य &c.—*i. e.* which when drawn was not to be faced by the enemies, so great was the havoc made by it. दृष्टिगोचरं— गावः इन्द्रियाणि चरन्त्यत्र इति गोचरः province,) scope or range of; गो + चर् + अ (घः) ; see Pān. III. 3. 119. दृष्टेः गोचरः दृष्टिगोचरस्तम्. The quivers were not seen by the enemies be cause Arjuna never turned his back towards them in a battle. शित—p. p. p. of शो 4 p. to whet. निस्त्रिंश—see com. Prādi Tat.; by the Vārtika संख्यायास्तत्पुरुषस्य वाच्यः such a compound also takes the Samāsanta अ (डच्). शितश्चासौ निस्त्रिंशश्च तेन युक्तः, युज् + क्विप् (०). Roots like सद्, सू, द्विष्, द्रुह्, युज &c. take क्विप् whether preceded by a preposition or not when a noun is used as an Upapada. इषुधि—fr. इषु + धा + इ (कि) added अधिकरणे

यशसेव तिरोदधन्मुहुर्महसा गोत्रभिदायुधक्षतीः ।
कवचं च सरत्नमुद्वहञ्ज्वलितज्योतिरिवान्तरं दिवः ॥ ५८ ॥

अन्वयः—(तथा गोत्रभिदायुधक्षतीः यशसेव महसा मुहुः तिरोदधद् सरत्नम् (अत एव) ज्वलितज्योतिः दिवः अन्तरमिव कवचं च उद्वहन् ॥ ५८ ॥

यशसेति ॥ किंच गोत्रभिद इन्द्रस्यायुधक्षतीर्वज्रप्रहाररन्ध्राणि । खाण्डवदाहसंभवा इति भावः । महसा स्वकान्त्या यशसेव मूर्तया कीर्त्येव मुहुस्तिरोदधदाच्छादयन् । सरत्नं रत्नसहितमतएव ज्वलितज्योतिर्दीप्ततारकम् ॥ "ज्योतिस्ताराग्निभा ज्वालादृक्पुत्रात्मधरात्मसु" इति वैजयन्ती ॥ दिवोऽन्तरं नभोमध्यमिवावस्थितम् ॥ "अन्तरं परिधानीये बाह्ये स्वीयेऽन्तरात्मनि । क्लीबे मध्ये प्रकाशे च" इति वैजयन्ती ॥ कवचं चोद्वहन् ।

अन्वयार्थः—[तथा] (**गोत्रभिदायुधक्षतीः**) इन्द्र के शस्त्र [वज्र] के प्रहार-चिह्नों को (**यशसा इव**) यश के सदृश (**महसा**) [अपनी] कान्ति से (**मुहुः**) पुनः-पुनः (**तिरोदधत्**) छिपाता हुआ (**च**) और (**सरत्नम्**) रत्नों सहित [अतएव] (**ज्वलितज्योतिः**) दीप्तिमान हैं तारे जिसमें ऐसे (**दिवः**)

अन्तरिक्ष के (**अन्तरमिव**) मध्य की भाँति (**कवचं उद्वहन्**) कवच को धारण करता हुआ।

. . . तथा खाण्डवदाह के समय इन्द्र के वज्र से हुए घाव-चिह्नों को यश-सदृश अपनी कान्ति से छिपाता हुआ, और जड़े हुए रत्नों के कारण दीप्तिमान तारों से युक्त अन्तरिक्ष के अन्तराल की भाँति कवच को धारण करता हुआ. . .

58. covering the wounds inflicted by the thunderbolt of Indra with his brilliance as though with his glory, (in a visible form), and wearing his armour which being set with jewels, resembled the region of the sky studded with golwing stars;

Sl. 58. गोत्रभिदः—See *supra* 29. आयुधानां क्षतयः आयुधक्षतदस्ताः। The reference here is to the burning of the Khaṇḍava forest in Kurukshetra by fire with the assistance of Kṛshṇa and Arjuna. The forest was sacred to India who had naturally to fight with Arjuna to prevent its destruction, which, however he was not able to do. Arjuna obtained at this time the bow Gāndiva from Agni along with two inexhaustible arrow-cases.

महसा—by his brilliance. Arjuna was white in complexion (and hence his name) and therefore his *Mahas* is compared to यशस् which is also represented by poets as white. *Cf.* शरदिन्दुकुन्दघनसारनीहारकाशनीकाशमूर्त्या कीर्त्या &c. Daś. Ch. I. 1. ज्वलित०—ज्वलितानि ज्योतींषि यस्मिन् with stars brightly shining in it. कवचं—The comparison of the steel-armour set with jewels to the star-fangled sky well indicates its largeness of size. It seems the Pǎṇḍavas were allowed to take with them their weapons and other equipments of war when they were exiled.

अलकाधिपभृत्यदर्शितं शिवमुर्वीधरवर्त्म संप्रयान् ।
हृदयानि समाविवेश स क्षणमुद्बाष्पदृशां तपोभृताम् ॥ ५९ ॥

अन्वयः—सः अलकाधिपभृत्यदर्शितं शिवम् उर्वीधरवर्त्म सम्प्रयान् क्षण उद्बाष्पदृशां तपोभृतां हृदयानि समाविवेश ॥ ५९ ॥

अलकेति ॥ सोऽर्जुनोऽलकाधिपभृत्येन यक्षेण दर्शितमतः शिवं निर्बाधमुर्वीधरवर्त्म हिमवन्मार्गं प्रति संप्रयान्प्रगच्छन् । क्षणमुद्बाष्पदृशां वियोगदुःखात्साश्रुनेत्राणां तपोभृतां द्वैतवननिवासिनां तपस्विनां हृदयानि समाविवेश । खेदयामासेत्यर्थः ॥ संपूर्वस्य विशतेः खेदार्थत्वमवसेयम् ॥

अन्वयार्थः—(**सः**) वह [अर्जुन] (**अलकाधिपभृत्यदर्शितम्**) अलकेश्वर के अनुचर [यक्ष] से दिखाये गये (**शिवम्**) निर्बाध (**उर्वीधरवर्त्म**) पृथ्वीधारी [हिमालय] के मार्ग पर (**संप्रयान्**) जाता हुआ (**क्षणम्**) क्षण भर के लिए (**उद्बाष्पदृशाम्**) उमड़ आये हैं आंसु जिन में हेसी आंखें हैं जिन की ऐसे (**तपोभृताम्**) तपस्वियों के (**हृदयानि**) हृदयों में (**समाविवेश**) प्रविष्ट हुआ।

यक्ष-प्रदर्शित निर्बाध हिमालय-मार्ग पर जाते हुए उस उपयुक्त अर्जुन ने क्षणभर के लिए अपने डबडबाई आँखों वाले तपस्वी भाइयों को दुःखित किया ।

59. he, proceeding by the safe path to the mountain shown by the servant of Kubera (Yaksha), entered (affected) the hearts of the ascetics (dwelling in Dvaitavana) whose eyes overflowed with tears for a moment.

Sl. 59. अलका—The capital of Kubera, the lord of wealth and regent of the North, is described in the Purāṇas as the land ofrgrandear and beauty.—तपसा निर्जिता राजन् स्वयं वैश्रवणेन सा। शशिप्रभा प्रावरणा कैलासशिखरोपमा ॥ दिव्या हेममयी ह्युच्चैः प्रासादैरुपशोभिता। महारत्नवती चित्रा दिव्यगन्धा मनोरमा ॥ &c. Bhāg. P. It is immortalised by Kālidāsa describing it in the Meg. Its other names are Vasudhāra, Vasusthali and Prabhā.— अधिप०—अधिपातीति अधिपः । आतश्चोपसर्गे इति कः (अ), अलकाया अधिपः तस्य भृत्यस्तेन दर्शितम् । उर्वीधर—उर्वी fr ऊर्णु॰. 2 P. A. to cover+उ. ऊर्णोति, उर्णुयते वा; irregularly formed ऊ being shortened and नु dropped before उ; fem. ऊर्वी. धरतीति धरः; उर्व्या धरः ऊर्वीधरस्तस्य वर्त्म उद्बाष्पदृशां—ऊद्गतानि बाष्पाणि यासां ता उद्बाष्पाः ऊद्बाष्पा दृशो येषां ते ऊद्बाष्पदशस्तेषाम् । तपो०—तपो बिभ्रतीति तपोभृतस्तेषाम् । This shows how much the ascetics in Dwaitavana loved the Pāṇḍavas. समाविवेश—entered so as to leave a mark there *i. e.* the ascetics felt pain at his separation.

अनुजगुरथ दिव्यं दुन्दुभिध्वानमाशाः
सुरकुसुमनिपातैर्व्योम्नि लक्ष्मीर्वितेने ।
प्रियमिव कथयिष्यन्नालिलिङ्ग स्फुरन्तीं
भुवमनिभृतवेलावीचिबाहुः पयोधिः ॥ ६० ॥

अन्वयः—अथ आशाः दिव्यं दुन्दुभिध्वान अनुजगुः, व्योम्नि सुरकुसुमनिपातैः लक्ष्मीः वितेने । अनिभृतवेलावीचिबाहुः पयोधिः स्फुरन्तीं भुवं प्रियं कथयिष्यन् इव आलिलिङ्ग ॥ ६० ॥

अनुजगुरिति ॥ अथाशा दिशाः । दिवि भवं दिव्यम् ॥ "दिवादिभ्यो यत्" । दुन्दुभिध्वानमनुजगुर्दध्वनुः ॥ अनुगायतेर्लिट् ॥ व्योम्नि सुरकुसुमनिपातैर्लक्ष्मीर्वितेने । पुष्पवृष्टिश्चाजनिष्टेत्यर्थः । किंच । अनिभृताश्चञ्चला वेलायां कूले या वीचयस्ता एव बाहवो यस्य स तथोक्तः । "वेला कूलविकारयोः" इति शाश्वतः ॥ पयोधिः स्फुरन्तीमुल्लसन्तीं हर्षात्स्पन्दमानां च भुवं प्रियमिष्टं भारावतारणरूपं कथयिष्यन्निव कथयितुमिवेत्यर्थः ॥ "लृट् शेषे च" इति चकारात्क्रियार्थायां क्रियायां लृट् ॥ आलिलिङ्ग । सर्वं चेदं शिवं दैवकार्यप्रवृत्तत्वादस्येति भावः ॥ अत्र विशेषणमात्रसाम्यादप्रस्तुतस्य गम्यत्वात्समासोक्तिरलंकारः । तत्र चाप्रस्तुतयोर्भूमिसमुद्रयोः प्रतिपन्नाभ्यां नायकाभ्यां भेदेऽभेदलक्षणातिशयोक्तिवशादालिङ्गनोक्तिरिति रहस्यम् । एवमतिशयोक्त्यनुप्राणिता समासोक्तिः । प्रियकथनात्स्नेहमुज्जीवयति तदङ्गभावं भजत इत्युभयोरङ्गाङ्गिभावेन संकर इति विवेचनीयम्॥

अन्वयार्थः—(**अथ**) तदुपरान्त (**आशाः**) दिशाओं ने (**दिव्यम्**) द्युलोक में होने वाले (**दुन्दुभिध्वानम्**) दुन्दुभि के शब्द को (**अनुजगुः**) प्रतिध्वनित किया (**व्योम्नि**) आकाश में (**सुरकुसुमनिपातैः**) देवताओं के पुष्पों की बखेर से (**लक्ष्मीः**) शोभा (**वितेने**) विस्तृत की गई। (**अनिभृतवेलावीचिबाहुः**) चञ्चल जो तट-लहरें वे ही हैं भुजाएँ जिसकी ऐसे (**पयोधिः**) समुद्र ने (**स्फुरन्तीम्**) उल्लास-युक्त (**भुवम्**) पृथ्वी को (**प्रियं कथयिष्यन् इव**) प्रिय (समाचार) को कहने के लिए मानो (**आलिलिङ्ग**) अलिङ्गित किया ।

अर्जुन के प्रस्थान के पश्चात् द्युलोक की दुन्दुभि-ध्वनि से दिशाएँ गूँज उठीं, आकाश देवपुष्पवृष्टि से सुशोभित हो उठा, समुद्र ने तटवर्ती चञ्चल लहरों-रूपी हाथों से उल्लास से भरी पृथ्वी का आलिङ्गन किया मानो उसे (तुम्हारा भार अब जल्दी ही समाप्त हो जायेगा—इस प्रिय को कहना चाहता हो।

60. Then (as he set out) the directions echoed with the sounds of the heavenly kettledrums; the sky looked beautiful all round by the showers of heavenly flowers; and the ocean, as if eager to communicate the gladsome tidings (that her burden would be soon removed) embraced the earth thrilling with joy, with his arms in the form of the waves rolling forward on (or dashing against) its shores.

Sl. 60. अथ—Just after the departure of Arjuna. दिव्यं—produced in the sky; fr. दिव् + यत् by द्युप्रागपागुदक्प्रतीचो यत्। Pān. IV... 2. 101. प्राच्यं ऊदीच्यं &c. दुंदुभि—दुं दु इति शब्देन भाति; fr. भा + इ (किः) or द्यामुं भति fills शब्देन (being taken as a comp. of the पृषोदरादि class). सुरकु॰— सुराणां कुसुमानि सुरकुसुमानि तेषां निपातैः। पयोधिः—पयाँसि धीयन्ते अस्मिन्, पयस्—धा—इ (किः) by कर्मण्यधिकरणे च। Pān. III. 3. 93. स्फुरन्ती—Here the earth is compared to an injured lady looking bright with joy at the thought of her grievance being removed. For figures of speech see com.

इति महामहोपाध्यायकोलाचलमल्लिनाथसूरिविरचितया घण्टापथसमाख्यया
व्याख्यया समेतः कविश्रीभारविकृतौ किरातार्जुनीये महाकाव्ये
धनंजयप्रस्थानो नाम तृतीयः सर्गः।

समाप्तिः।

Note on Metres.

CANTO I.

Sl.s 1—44 are written in the वंशस्थ or वंशस्थवली metre. The last but one sl. is in the पुष्पिताग्रा metre and the last one in the मालिनी.

CANTO II.

Sl.s 1—55 are composed in the वियोगिनी (also called सुन्दरी or वैतालीय). Sl. 57 is in the उपजाति metre; 58 in the पुष्पिताग्रा and the last in वसंततिलका metre.

CANTO III.

Sl.s 1—55 are generally composed in the उपजाति metre, there being a sl. in the इन्द्रवज्रा or उपेन्द्रवज्रा here and there. Sl. 56 is in the वंशस्थ metre; 57—60 in the वियोगिनी metre and sl. 60 in the मालिनी metre.

A short vowel is called लघु and is denoted by ल. A long vovel is called गुरु and is denoted by ग. A short vowel followed by a conjunct consonant or an Anuswāra or Visarga is considered as गुरु for the purpose of prosody.

A short syllable is marked as ; and a long one as—.

Three syllables form what is called गण or group.

The *Gaṇas* are—

य ◡ – –	ज ◡ – ◡
र – ◡ –	स ◡ ◡ –
त – – ◡	म – – –
भ – ◡ ◡	न ◡ ◡ ◡

आदिमध्यावसानेषु यरता यान्ति लाघवम् । भजसा गौरव यान्ति मनौ तु गुरुलाघवम् ।